British Political Theory in the
Twentieth Century

British Political Theory in the Twentieth Century

Edited by

Paul Kelly

A John Wiley & Sons, Ltd., Publication

This edition first published 2010
© 2010 Political Studies Association

Blackwell Publishing was acquired by John Wiley & Sons in February 2007. Blackwell's publishing program has been merged with Wiley's global Scientific, Technical, and Medical business to form Wiley-Blackwell.

Registered Office
John Wiley & Sons Ltd, The Atrium, Southern Gate, Chichester, West Sussex, PO19 8SQ, United Kingdom

Editorial Offices
350 Main Street, Malden, MA 02148-5020, USA
9600 Garsington Road, Oxford, OX4 2DQ, UK
The Atrium, Southern Gate, Chichester, West Sussex, PO19 8SQ, UK

For details of our global editorial offices, for customer services, and for information about how to apply for permission to reuse the copyright material in this book please see our website at www.wiley.com/wiley-blackwell.

The right of Paul kelly to be identified as the author of this work has been asserted in accordance with the Copyright, Designs and Patents Act 1988.

Library of Congress Cataloging-in-Publication Data

British political theory in the twentieth century / edited by Paul Kelly.
       p. cm.
   Includes bibliographical references and index.
   ISBN 978-1-4051-9999-5 (pbk. : alk. paper)   1. Political science–Great Britain–History.   2. Great Britain–Politics and government.   I. Kelly, P. J. (Paul Joseph)
   JN175.B74 2010
   320.01–dc22

                                                    2009051242

A catalogue record for this book is available from the British Library.

Set in 10.5/13Pt Minion by Toppan Best-set Premedia Limited
Printed and bound in Singapore
By Hó Printing Pte Ltd

1   2010

Contents

Introduction

Paul Kelly

Since the study of politics emerged as a distinct activity in Britain in the early twentieth century it has been clear that one aspect of it in particular, what has come to be known as political theory, has maintained a leading role. Many of the most influential figures in British political science have been political theorists, and chairs in political theory remain among the most prestigious for professors of politics or political science to hold. It is therefore appropriate that as part of the celebration of the Political Studies Association's 60th Anniversary a book on *British Political Theory in the Twentieth Century* should be published. What I offer here is a book composed of selections from some of the greatest figures in political theory, who both shape the development of the study of politics in the United Kingdom and engage with concerns that can be woven into a distinct British tradition, albeit that many have also gone on to hold significant international reputations.

By presenting such a collection I obviously court controversy and invite challenge. All such selections are in some sense arbitrary and all canons or traditions invite contest and subversion. I fully expect that my selection is both arbitrary and contestable, and most political theorists or students of British politics or British political history will have some favourite contributor that I have ignored or deliberately excluded. Taking all that as given, let me offer some justifications for the criteria of inclusion and identify some important areas that I have had consciously to exclude in order to produce a manageable volume.

My list of contributors is confined to a relatively new profession of academic political theorists. Many have held prestigious chairs, such as the Chichele Professorship of Social and Political Theory at Oxford (Cole, Berlin); the Chair of Political Science at Cambridge (Barker); or the Graham Wallas Chair of Political Science at the London School of Economics and Political Science (LSE) (Laski, Oakeshott and Barry). In making this choice I am conscious of excluding some of the most interesting political thinking produced in Britain in the twentieth century. Political activists and reflective politicians such as C. A. R. Crosland do indeed count as political thinkers. Others such as George Orwell or the main contributors of the great ideological traditions of British party politics might have been included and in many ways their contribution to politics and the interest of their ideas are certainly more important than the academic theorising of those included in this book. A book about political ideas in Britain in the twentieth century, or about British political ideologies or even the history of British political philosophy would be a very different book. A fascinating account of political thinking about Britain could have been assembled just by selecting poets such as Eliot, Yeats, Auden, MacNiece, Larkin and Heaney. For those who expect such a work, I can only counsel them either to look elsewhere or be patient with my own distinct enterprise.

In defence of my more narrow selection I have been guided by the important contribution that academic political theorists have made, not only to British political discourse, but also to the shaping of the discipline itself. Although somewhat drier and certainly further removed from the direct engagement with political power and influence, the story of the development and character of academic political theory in Britain is still important. Many thousands of students who have gone on to engage far more directly in British political life – as well as that of the wider world – have been shaped in part by the ideas that they will have encountered for the first time through their teachers or their teacher's teacher. Figures such as Bernard Bosanquet, Harold Laski, Ernest Barker, Isaiah Berlin and Michael Oakeshott have had a considerable impact on the real party and institutional politics of Britain and the wider world through the indirect impact they often still exert on subsequent students. It is very easy to underestimate just how influential the indirect impact of teaching and scholarship on institutional and professional politics can be; often it far exceeds the apparent impact of the more media-friendly academics who within a generation can disappear without trace. This book is intended to serve as a sourcebook for the study of the development of political theory in Britain, rather than a full survey of all the diverse strands of British political thinking.

Even within academic political theory I have had to be selective and am very conscious of having marginalised some extremely important scholarly debates. I have not, for example, included the responses to Peter Laslett's famous 1956 claim that political theory was dead. Nor have I included the hugely influential Cambridge School of the history of political thought associated with Quentin Skinner, John Dunn and J. G. A. Pocock, all of whom have shaped the study of political ideas for nearly half a century. A full defence of this exclusion would require a substantive essay, but one simple if crude reason is that they have been advocates of a reduction of political theory to history and therefore implicitly deny that there is a distinct activity of political theory. Feminist political thought gets no serious discussion and the inclusion of women is confined to Carole Pateman and Anne Phillips. Part of the reason for this exclusion is that for much of the twentieth century women played at best a limited role in British political studies of any form, although there were notable exceptions such as Phyllis Doyle, who wrote an important textbook on the history of political thought, and more recently Margaret Canovan, who has done much to introduce an Arendtian voice into British political theory. Pateman on the other hand is no token addition, as she is one of the most influential and widely cited political scientists in the world. Of contemporary thinkers, her claim to inclusion is perhaps the strongest of all, so perhaps political theory is leading the way in British political science in terms of opening access to the finest women scholars and proving to be one of the fields in which an increasing number of women are making international reputations. Anne Phillips, currently at the LSE, is another influential international voice in political theory, whose approach to issues of democracy, equality and inclusion has been shaped directly and indirectly by the British tradition of political theory. Other voices excluded include the Marxist left. As with the exclusion of the Cambridge School, an adequate explanation of the absence of Marxist scholars is a complex story that is not easy to summarise. In part this absence is attributable to the preoccupation of Marxists with the work of other Marxists, but also to the absence of the kind of leftist tradition that one finds in France, Germany or Italy where the most interesting variants of Marxist theory have thrived in the twentieth century. It might also be a result of what Perry Anderson described as an insular indifference to high theory and the absence of a British tradition of state theory. There is something in this claim, but I will challenge its central assumptions in the interpretative introductory essay that follows (Chapter 1).

Enough of excuses for exclusion. The task was to construct a coherent narrative about a distinctively British approach to political theory. My selection of thinkers does that in a number of ways. Firstly, all of the thinkers contribute to a distinctively British tradition that focuses on one of three distinct questions at the heart of the understanding of politics. The first question concerns the site of politics or the groups among whom political relationships hold. The second question concerns the appropriate institutions of politics and the third question concerns 'who gets what, where, when and how?' All of these questions are interconnected but they can be answered in different ways in different political traditions. Also, to follow Michael Oakeshott, the study of political science is always in part the pursuit of the intimations of a tradition and that manifests itself in the way these different questions assume different orderings of priority at different times. The story I wish to tell through my selection is about that ordering.

In the first instance the debates at the heart of British politics concern the nature and claims of the state – the British state. This is defended in Bernard Bosanquet's idealist defence of the state as the actualisation of the ethical idea. Yet the whole tenor of British political thought and experience has been deeply ambivalent about the state and its importance. L. T. Hobhouse's new liberalism shows a way in which the power of the state can be steered towards the liberal egalitarian task of positive freedom and welfare. This statist discourse came to final dominance during the decades following the success of wartime mobilisation and the development of a successful welfare state in the post-war period. However, the statist discourse found in Bosanquet and Hobhouse was the subject of serious political challenges from an alternative pluralist discourse which is represented in the work of J. N. Figgis, Harold Laski and G. D. H. Cole and which also partly informs Ernest Barker's writings on nationality and national identity. Political pluralism and its associated ideas

of corporate freedom, local democracy, subsidiarity and even devolution have had
a profound impact on British attitudes to the state and the nature and locus of state
power. The traditions of thinking about the state as the primary site of politics are
precisely what are being challenged by pluralism in the early twentieth century. The
collection concludes with a number of contemporary thinkers who indirectly resur-
rect some of those debates, as their own political theories engage with the political
currents of the British state. I have in mind especially Paul Hirst, David Miller, Anne
Phillips and Bhikhu Parekh. Parekh's Report of the Commission on the Future of
Multi-Ethnic Britain and his work as a theorist of multiculturalism has raised many
of the issues of group self-governance and the limited role of the centralised state
that were dominant in the early part of the century. Although the debate about
multiculturalism might itself be on the wane, the issues raised by Parekh remain of
fundamental significance for the future of British politics. Hirst used the idea of
political pluralism or associationalism as a way of thinking beyond the welfare state
in the 1980s and 1990s. He wished to recover a leftist pluralist discourse that could
be used to respond to the challenge to a centralised welfare state that grew up with
neoliberalism in the 1980s. Miller challenges the fragmentation of the polity that
he found in multiculturalism and asserts the need for a common national identity
to sustain the redistributive project of modern social democracy. Miller's work on
nationality has drawn fire from a number of his left liberal colleagues, but his impact
on the study of social justice and his concern with the preconditions of citizenship
echo similar concerns from idealists such as Bosanquet or idealist-influenced pro-
gressives such as Barker. The nature of the state and its relationship with other
candidate political communities or associations is a central part of the argument of
Chapter 1 of this book. Yet even by departing from the statist or communitarian
strands of British political theory, Miller's work is still related to this broad problem
about the identity of the political community.

The second broad theme that is related to the question of the nature and site of
political power is the idea of political liberty as it has developed in Britain. This
theme is illustrated in the work of a number of philosophical liberals, although
many would not identify themselves as liberals in politics. This theme is controver-
sially divided into what Berlin described as negative and positive liberty. The first
part of the book concerns positive libertarians such as Bosanquet and Hobhouse.
Alongside these we can include the pluralists such as Figgis, Laski and Cole, all of
whom drew on elements of a positive view of freedom and an account of political
liberty that depends on the relationship between different forms of association and
the dominant site of political power – usually the state. R. H. Tawney's defence of
equality as a constitutive part of the concept of freedom as a moral status also
forms part of this complex British tradition of positive liberty. Berlin's famous
lecture of 1958 marked a restatement of a negative libertarian tradition. I have not
chosen to include Berlin's lecture as it is widely reproduced, but the same themes
are found in the shorter defence of a negative libertarianism and liberal pluralism,
'The Pursuit of the Ideal'. Berlin is often accused of being a Cold War liberal, but
the debate he engages with is precisely the debate about the modern welfare state

as a centralised state and its impact upon the liberty of groups and individuals. This emphasis on the nature of freedom is also reflected in the philosophical liberalism of H. L. A. Hart and Brian Barry, who partly shape the agenda of modern political philosophy until John Rawls' *A Theory of Justice* in 1971. Hart and Barry are both in the intellectual tradition of J. S. Mill despite their lack of sympathy for his utilitarianism. Their critically supportive attitude to the Rawlsian revolution in political philosophy is based on a shared concern to save the liberal agenda from utilitarianism and retain an egalitarian strand in progressive political ideas which is sympathetic to individual liberty without being wholly sceptical about the state. Barry's early and influential paper on 'The Public Interest' provides an influential starting point for a tradition of liberal egalitarian thought with a distinctively British character which draws together the issues of democracy and social justice.

A final theme that runs through the selection concerns the nature of the activity of political theory itself. Almost all the thinkers covered have something important to contribute to the question of 'what is political theory?' and how it is to be conducted. Drawing on philosophy, history, economics, sociology, law or a combination of all of these, the contributors to this volume shape the study of the field. Great figures such as Laski and Oakeshott tried to shape the study of political theory in the image of their own work. The same can be said of earlier figures such as Barker, although his once-significant position in the profession is difficult fully to comprehend. Others such as Barry have done so less directly but, like Oakeshott, Barry was equally concerned with the relationship between political theory and political science and with fundamental questions about the nature and place of political theory on the intellectual map. Although two more different thinkers could hardly be imagined, the institutional experience of arriving at the LSE, a school of the social sciences (and a place where both Oakeshott and Barry had their greatest impacts as scholars and teachers), from the very different intellectual worlds of Cambridge and Oxford, respectively, encouraged both thinkers to engage with the interconnections between political philosophy and political science that mark the distinctiveness of political theory.

More recently, Pateman, Phillips and Parekh have challenged some of the presuppositions of this synthesis of political philosophy and political science, and in Phillips', Miller's and Parekh's cases have also exposed the importance of identity in political theory: an idea that we can see in Bosanquet and Barker at the beginning of the twentieth century.

That political theory should still be concerned with its own nature after a century of institutionalisation and professionalisation might for some indicate an activity that is either deeply flawed or an intellectual dead end. Perhaps the predominance of political theory within British political science is a sign that the process of professionalisation into a 'normal' social science is incomplete, and that returning to the history a hundred years hence might reveal a very different story. For what it is worth I would be highly sceptical about any such conclusion. The emergence of political science is an unfinished project, but whatever form it takes in the future there will remain a special role for political theory, because the latter continues to challenge our perceptions of the object of inquiry – the nature of the activity, institutions and values – that are manifested through political power and activity. However much methodological uniformity might be achieved, political theorists will continue to challenge the attempts at normalisation that follow from disciplinary specialisation. And just as there remain distinctive political communities, there will remain distinctive ways of theorising those political relationships. The subtly differing patterns of that activity will also remain of as much interest to students of politics as any of the other ways in which politics manifests itself.

Chapter 1

British Political Theory in the Twentieth Century

Paul Kelly

Throughout the twentieth century the study of politics in Britain has produced a long and distinguished list of theorists, from Bernard Bosanquet and Henry Sidgwick at the beginning of the century, followed by the likes of L. T. Hobhouse, R. H. Tawney, Harold Laski and G. D. H. Cole, until during the third quarter of the century we saw the remarkable efflorescence of liberal theory with the likes of Isaiah Berlin, H. L. A. Hart, Brian Barry and arguably Michael Oakeshott,[1] all of whom still shape the subject. The question that lies behind this essay is whether there is anything more distinctive to be said about British political theory in the twentieth century than could be found by producing a list of notable but perhaps disconnected figures who engage in a generic activity of political theory. The task of this essay is to explore the ways in which the diversity of British political theory can still be given an overall structure and to examine the ways in which it follows the contours of change and development in British politics.

This of courses raises a further question about why one might focus on a national tradition. If place of birth and first language is all that matters then we can identify national 'traditions' of political theory just as we can of chemistry or any other natural science where the question of national origin is purely a side issue of only biographical interest. Naturalistic political scientists are, perhaps rightly, suspicious of claims to national distinctiveness in their field of study precisely because such a claim in relation to any particular phenomenon is the outcome of an inquiry and not its presupposition. It may well be true that electorates or legislatures follow distinct patterns of behaviour in different political systems, but if they do and if national distinctiveness has anything to do with the explanation, then that is a conclusion and not a premise, and it is certainly not a matter that concerns the identity of the inquirer. Naturalistic political scientists also attempt to apply methods of inquiry that are generic across political systems: there are no national methods of inquiry. There is no reason, for instance, why the greatest or most qualified students of British or American politics should be British or American. Many contemporary philosophers adopt a similar attitude to their discipline. The point of view of philosophy is universal and non-contingent, and its methods, such as logico-linguistic analysis, are also generic and universal. If political theory is a philosophical activity, then again the place of Britishness appears at best biographical and ancillary to the real work of the discipline.

Yet there is an alternative view. Critics of a naturalistic science of politics assert the contingency and historical particularity of political experience. Only at the most abstract and therefore uninteresting level of experience can we speak about generic phenomena of politics. All that is interesting is located within political traditions and therefore the task of the student of politics is to comprehend the precise and distinctive contours of those political traditions. On this view the study of politics is a hermeneutic activity, concerned with understanding the internal coherence of such traditions rather than, as the naturalists claim, seeing these as merely manifestations of universal mechanisms. This hermeneutic approach to political inquiry reflects a similar approach to the activity of politics itself, as the 'pursuit of intimations' of a distinct political tradition.[2] Political theorists and philosophers have been particularly attracted to this hermeneutic or historicist approach, on the grounds that it reflects the historical contingency and fleetingness of much political and philosophical discourse. Ideas and concepts that once seemed dominant quickly fall from favour or disappear altogether. This fact makes political theorists equally cautious about making claims for their own methods and approaches, which are equally fleeting, as the history of philosophy shows (see Collingwood, 1993). It is precisely in this context of variety and contingency that the idea of national traditions of political theory flourishes, especially among those historians who focus on language and conceptual change.[3] This historicist and hermeneutic approach to political theory has yielded rich results, but raises an important problem that is central to my concern with the character of British political thought in the twentieth century. Most inquiries into traditions of political theory either make generalisations that are not peculiar to distinct national traditions (see Pocock, 2009) or else they collapse into the ideas of individual thinkers with the result that national traditions disappear into incoherence (Gray, 1993; 2000).

Mindful of the risk of providing an account of a tradition that is not distinctively British or reducing the idea of such a tradition to a mere collection of particular instances, I will focus on delineating an object of inquiry itself. This constructivist task[4] combines a number of different theorists' work and traces connections and discontinuities between them, but it does not claim that prior connections must already exist between these theorists, nor does it assume that only the narrative connection that I identify holds between these thinkers. In short, I do not claim that the conception of British political theory that I present and analyse is the only one possible, or that it is the only useful story that can be told. It is the task of the historian of political thought to sift between such constructed narratives, but it is one of the political theorist's tasks to construct them in the first place, as that involves sociological, ethical and philosophical considerations which fall outside the remit of history narrowly conceived but which do not fall outside the remit of a hybrid activity such as political theory. Indeed one of the main claims that I intend to exemplify in this essay is that the study of political ideas should not be subsumed into history, narrowly conceived, albeit that it might deploy the skills and techniques of the historian.[5]

One further point that distinguishes the approach in this essay from that of a historical approach to political theory is that I will also link the changing structure of political theory to changes in British politics; historians are generally cautious about making what appear to be causal claims. Yet in so doing the essay will not make any precise claims about the causal relationship between political forces and ideological or conceptual change or about the priority of ideas over events. The role of this essay is merely (though importantly) to suggest patterns and similarities between the structure of British politics and of British political theory which can then be fleshed out by more precise historical, empirical or philosophical studies.

Political Theory and Political Thought

Political thought takes many distinct forms and is a central component of politics under any possible understanding of that much contested term. Politicians argue in legislatures and cabinet rooms; they argue with each other in the public realm, on television and in the street. Ordinary citizens, rebels, marginalised groups and those denied citizenship or political rights, argue and complain about public matters, and defend and support their preferred political parties and agendas. Alongside this, serious commentators write histories, policy platforms and theoretical defences of principles and values. Novelists, playwrights and poets also have their say. Given the centrality of thought and discourse to the practice of politics, the study of political thought and political discourse must be an essential component of any conception of the study of politics. Indeed, political thought in all its diversity, including ballads and scripture, was the subject of the first recognisable history of political thought published in Britain in 1855.[6] The phenomenon of political thought considered in this most general sense can be categorised in a number of ways. Students of politics and political scientists have argued extensively over how that categorisation is made, and whether in making it one should attach priority or special weight to some forms of political thinking over others. Is the demotic thought and writings of participants in politics of lesser value and interest than the high theory of Plato, Hobbes and Hegel? This is sometimes presented as the distinction between political ideology and political philosophy: the subject of a debate that raged widely in British and American political science and theory in the 1950s and 1960s. However, as intellectual historians are quick to remind us, Hobbes and Locke were also engaged in practical, indeed in Locke's case, revolutionary politics (see Ashcraft, 1986). Others have warned about the need to distinguish philosophy and history from the practical mode of experience, as the latter is always a deliberately partial and engaged form of understanding (Oakeshott, 1962, *passim*). One can also argue about the distinctiveness of these categorisations. Is there a distinction between political theory and political philosophy?[7] Are both of these really only different manifestations of political ideology?

As this essay wishes to narrow its focus to British political theory as opposed to political thought more generally, it is perhaps useful to distinguish political theory from other forms of political thought.

The issue of the nature of political theory and its distinction from philosophy or ideology is a deeply contested matter, the roots of which are to be found in the emergence of the study of politics as an academic subject in the late nineteenth and early twentieth centuries. Political philosophy is an ancient subject that goes back at least to Plato and Aristotle; however if one considers the tradition of political philosophy from the Greeks to the nineteenth century one can see a complex narrative that combines many different activities, methods of inquiry and objects of study. It is clear that the 'great tradition' does not give anything remotely like a disciplinary identity or a single object of inquiry. The modern study of politics can be traced to the rise of new literatures within the broad subject of moral science, a field of inquiry that included what are now modern disciplines such as economics and law. It also has its roots in the political transformations of mass politics that developed throughout the nineteenth century, leading to political mobilisation, the rise of bureaucracies and a professional civil service, and the consequent reform of university curricula, away from a primary focus on clerical training and towards the cultivation of specialist scholarship and the education of governing elites. From this process of social transformation emerged a number of institutional changes that were to impact heavily on the activity of political theory and the debates that surround its nature and content. At Oxford, the university reforms of Benjamin Jowett and T. H. Green were reflected in the new subject of 'Greats' (philosophy and classical literature) that was to spawn both the British Idealist tradition in political philosophy, but also many of the key figures who were to transform the study of politics and the social sciences in the early twentieth century (see Wokler, 2001) including Idealist philosophers such as Bernard Bosanquet, as well as L.T. Hobhouse, the first professor of sociology in Britain, Graham Wallas, the first professor of political science in Britain and Sir Ernest Barker, the first holder of the Chair in Political Science at Cambridge. Cambridge's own contribution to the emergence of political science and political theory is equally important. Here the key figures are Sir John Seeley, Henry Sidgwick and Alfred Marshall: Seeley in particular, as he developed the History tripos within which political science and political theory is still taught.[8] This tradition produced figures such as J. N. Figgis, the historian of political thought and theorist of pluralism, and later still, Michael Oakeshott. The third institution of note was the establishment of the London School of Economics and Political Science (LSE) in 1895. This institution was deliberately intended to break away from the indigenous traditions of the ancient universities and to produce the future bureaucrats and governing class of the Fabian Utopia dreamed of by Sidney Webb and his associates.

The institutional factors at Oxford and Cambridge are particularly important in establishing the identity of political theory. The early products of the Oxford 'Greats' tradition tended to characterise their activity as political philosophy, given the importance of 'philosophy' as a formal part of their training. Cambridge students educated under the History tripos would have confronted the study of politics and political thought and ideas as a historical activity. Consequently, they would be less inclined to describe themselves as political philosophers, and in so far as they were political theorists or political scientists, these latter activities were seen as historical. For this reason, it is not wholly misleading to see the nomenclature of political theory or political philosophy as following institutional or even departmental histories. So we might say that political philosophy is theory conducted in philosophy departments whereas political theory is political philosophy conducted in government or political science departments. Those individuals such as Wallas, Barker, Laski and Cole who were responsible for developing the subject in the early twentieth century tended to allow their own institutional experience to characterise the way they described the activity that was passed down to their students. Thus a figure such as Wallas, who rejected the 'Greats' tradition of his youth, was more comfortable with the idea of political science, whereas Barker, who moved towards a greater sympathy with the Cambridge historical approach, became increasingly uncomfortable with the idea of political science, at least if this was to indicate a naturalistic mode of inquiry. For Barker and those influenced by him, political theory was a far more congenial term as it indicated an object of inquiry, namely systematic thought about politics that could be studied with the methods of the Cambridge historian.

A full institutional history of the growth and development of British political theory and political science should extend beyond these three important institutions as they influenced the development of other great departments for the study of politics in an expanding British university system. Yet those who were to develop departments at, for example, Manchester, or who were instrumental in the renewal of political science at Oxford with the establishment of Nuffield College, drew on traditions and training received at Oxford, Cambridge or the LSE.

These historical and institutional factors lend support to a practice-based account of political theory as the activity conducted by certain figures holding identifiable institutional roles, in this case within universities. In short, political theory is what is done by a series of important professors and by those who worked under them or who were influenced by them in their professional capacities. There is much to be said for this practice-based account as it enables us to identify who is a political theorist and who is not: George Orwell is not a political theorist whereas Harold Laski is. The practice-based account allows us to draw distinctions within the realm of political thought, between theorists and non-theorists, and for the purposes of this essay to delimit the object of inquiry.

However, while the practice-based account of political theory is useful it is not a sufficient account of political theory as it makes no substantive claims about what these practitioners do. Is everything written and said by a political theorist on this practice-based account political theory? One reason why we might be concerned not to concede this is illustrated by the figure of Harold Laski or that of his contemporary G. D. H. Cole. Both were enormously prolific authors and both were active Labour politicians, both serving on the executive of the Fabian Society, with Laski also serving on the National Executive Committee of the Labour party. Both wrote theoretical works but both also wrote works of political advocacy as politicians (Cole also wrote detective stories) (Barker, 1978, pp. 94–105; Laborde, 2000, pp. 69–100). But once we try to distinguish within their published outputs we are back with the problematic distinction between ideology and high theory.

Ideology, just as with theory and philosophy, is a controversial and deeply contested notion. The word was first coined in the early nineteenth century to cover the scientific study of political thought. It was adopted by Marx and Engels, and the modern usage develops from them. For Marx and Engels, all thought is a reflection of the relations of production and therefore relative to the conflict of material interests that underlies the thoughts, languages and cultural forms of society in a particular historical epoch. This understanding of the forces that shape and develop thought and argument encouraged sociologists of knowledge such as Karl Mannheim to treat political thought as a social fact to be examined sociologically, rather than in terms of its validity or truth content.[9] The identification of thought as ideology, or socially conditioned by more fundamental forces, had two important consequences. Among many mid-twentieth century historians, such as Sir Lewis Namier, there was a tendency to dismiss all political thought as a distraction, merely window dressing that disguised real conflicts of interest. Namier was no Marxist, but his reductionist approach to thought and ideas was similarly dismissive of the grand claims made by political philosophers or theorists. The second consequence was a tendency to regard political ideology as 'mere' practice and to question its claim to a place in the academy. This approach to 'ideological' thought was particularly prevalent from the late 1940s to the late 1960s and is partly a response to the wider context of the Cold War. If political thought and theory are partisan and practical in style, concerned with political advocacy of values and policies, then the question arises, why are they afforded authority in the academy? This worry underlies Michael Oakeshott's criticism of the attempt to pursue political theory in the practical mode. What might be acceptable in the press or in the street is not something that should hide behind the authority of a university chair or academic appointment. This argument is made particularly forcefully in Oakeshott's inaugural lecture, 'Political Education', which was partly directed at his predecessor at the LSE, Harold Laski (Oakeshott, 1962, pp. 115–23). One consequence of this anti-ideological perspective has been a deep suspicion of conceptions of political theory that appear to advocate substantive political agendas. These include the overtly partisan agendas of Laski and Cole in their role as Labour party supporters, and possibly also L. T. Hobhouse in his support of the new Liberal policy agenda of the Asquith administration. Also falling foul of the criticism of practical political theory is much contemporary 'normative' political theory which defends the priority of certain values such as rights, liberty and justice that we find in the work of thinkers such as Isaiah Berlin, H. L. A. Hart or Brian Barry. Yet if we reject such work as ideological advocacy, we are left with the question of what is left for political theory to do.

One response to the problem of ideology more generally is to see the task of political theory as the study of ideologies and the political theorist as a theorist of ideology: one who is interested in what ideologies are and how they change and transform. This approach can take two forms. Firstly, historians of political thought present themselves as theorists of ideology as historical languages or discourses. The most influential British example of this approach is the Cambridge School of historians associated with Quentin Skinner, J. G. A. Pocock and John Dunn. This group drew on ideas from philosophers of history such as R. G. Collingwood and linguistic philosophers such as J. L. Austin and John Searle, but they also continue an approach that can be found practised by earlier Cambridge historians such as J. N. Figgis in the early twentieth century (see Kelly, 1999). Skinner in particular uses the concept of ideology to cover the linguistic practices and discourses that his own approach to the history of political thought identifies as the appropriate object of inquiry. Here the concept of ideology is meant to signify no more than the contingent historically conditioned languages of the past, and to suggest that all contemporary thought is equally historically contingent. There cannot be any perennial problems that are illuminated by philosophical inquiry. As such the writings of contemporary normative political philosophers have no special epistemic or moral authority. This historical approach concentrates on the particular thinkers and their individual texts or utterances and tends to be sceptical about constructions or 'isms' such as conservatism, socialism and liberalism that other theorists see as central to the study of ideology. It also denies any intellectual space for normative deliberations and it reduces the method of political theory to that of history. One reason why the Cambridge School does not play a larger role in my argument is because it has tended to deny the possibility of political theory as a distinct activity.

Contemporary theorists of ideology such as Michael Freeden are sceptical of this historical approach precisely because of its tendency to overlook ideological forms such as liberalism and conservatism, which he takes to be important objects of the political world and to be structures through which high theory and practical engagement are connected.[10] Ideologies are distinct phenomena that need to be analysed with appropriate theoretical methods, just as with any other phenomena of political life. For Freeden ideologies include both the high theory and the engaged practical discourse that usually frame the ideology versus philosophy debate. Ideological discourse is presented in its most general form as the process of de-contesting essentially contested concepts as part of a political process of deploying these de-contested concepts to advance a particular political agenda. The contemporary political philosopher's task of presenting a correct or true theory of justice is just as much an ideological activity of de-contestation as that of a political party trying to claim the mantel of liberty for its policies and deny it to those of its opponents. On Freeden's account of ideology we cannot draw a distinction between the theoretical and the practical work of political theorists as the two will always overlap and therefore the distinction will be one of degree. That leaves only one distinct role for the political theorist to adopt if he or she is going to be free of the charge of ideology, and that is to see the role of political theory as a second-order activity concerned with explaining the nature and forms of first-order political thought. Freeden's own theory of ideology is one such second-order approach, as indeed would be the methodological writings of the Cambridge School historians of political thought. This sort of second-order understanding of the task of political theory is akin to that of positive theory or methodology in political science. It is also similar to the dominant strands of British philosophy in the mid-twentieth century, namely logical positivism and linguistic philosophy, which encouraged a rejection of substantive philosophical defences of values and principles, and which encouraged for a brief period the idea that political philosophy might be dead.[11] Among a generation of philosophers influenced by developments in philosophical logic and the philosophy of language the tasks and activity of philosophy were radically transformed from the speculative metaphysics of Bosanquet's Idealism at the turn of the twentieth century. This new philosophical approach at its most sceptical (Ayer's Logical Positivism) considered moral and political philosophy a non-subject, literally nonsense (see Ayer, 1936; Weldon, 1953). The more circumspect ordinary language philosophy of the 1950s and early 1960s conceived of the philosopher's task as one of unravelling conceptual incoherence within the terms of political and ethical debate rather than defending values or principles. Out of this philosophical climate emerged W. B. Gallie's thesis about essentially contested concepts[12] that was later taken up in Freeden's analysis of political ideology. It also encouraged a style of writing such as Berlin's famous inaugural lecture, 'Two Concepts of Liberty', which on one level appeared to be offering a conceptual analysis, whereas in fact it was offering a defence of a particular ideal of freedom and a substantive claim about value pluralism (Berlin, 1998, pp. 191–242). Although this form of philosophical analysis was to have an important impact on British political theory, none of the holders of the main political theory chairs (Laski, Cole, Barker, Brogan, Oakeshott) during the high point of logical positivism or ordinary language analytical philosophy showed any interest in it. Oakeshott's conception of philosophy, though very different from analytic philosophy, comes closest to the type of disengaged and non-substantive activity that flourished in Britain in the mid-twentieth century. Ordinary language philosophy also chimed with the Cold War climate that was suspicious of ideology and the possibility of substantive arguments about fundamental values and principles. Such values and principles were merely preferences or wants, which could be stated but not rationally defended in argument. They were therefore an object of the dispassionate study of the historian or theorist of ideology, or merely one element that needed to be factored into economic calculations of welfare maximisation of theories of social choice. Although British political theory never suffered the same level of threat from positive and behavioural political science that faced American political theory and philosophy in the 1950s and 1960s, it was still thought possible that a more naturalistic political science might displace the idea of political theory altogether as a mere residue of a more primitive study of politics.[13] It was no doubt in part as a response to this perceived threat that the Cambridge School attracted such attention, although in retrospect the turn to history as a distinct discipline advocated by some of the Cambridge School's more combative followers has contributed to weakening the role of political theory as a distinct activity within the British political science profession.

The retreat from normative recommendation into a form of political philosophy as narrow conceptual analysis was already being challenged by philosophers and political theorists such as Hart and Berlin in the late 1950s, both of whom had been part of the first generation of Oxford linguistic philosophy. Yet the most striking illustration of the return to normative argument in political theory was illustrated by the publication of Brian Barry's *Political Argument* in 1965. Barry's first book and all his subsequent writings combined a commitment to liberal social-democratic values, the philosophical precision of the Oxford analytic tradition and a profound interest in the development of political science methods such as rational choice theory and the study of voting behaviour as it developed in American political science. Although Barry's clear starting point is a form of pluralist liberalism, i.e. that there is an irreducible plurality of valuable ways of living, he did not draw a conclusion similar to Berlin's, which is that there is consequently little for political theory to do other than describe and explain those values. Barry is concerned with the way in which values and principles interact with one another and inform institutions and practices, and on these matters he defends the view that there can indeed be rational arguments and therefore normative work for the political theorist. It is also worth noting that in contrast to Berlin, who argued that political theory is a branch of ethics,[14] Barry saw ethics or moral philosophy as only one component of political theory. Indeed one can argue that his conception of political theory is closely linked to the social sciences and informed by them.[15] In this way Barry's approach is a more technically sophisticated version of the early modern conceptions of 'moral science' from which the modern disciplines of the social sciences emerged. One certainly should not draw the conclusion that Barry's model of political theory is a definitive account of political theory as an activity. Yet this mixed-mode activity is a more accurate representation of the practice of most political theorists than the more prescriptive versions of the activity presented by ideologists and philosophers.

In consequence we can conclude that political theory is not identical with philosophy or ethics, although philosophy provides some methods used by political theorists and ethics provides some (though not all) of the problems that occupy political theorists. It is most appropriate to see philosophy offering a set of tools to political theorists, which can be deployed alongside tools derived from social sciences such as economics or anthropology as well as history. When these tools are deployed instead of other rhetorical or literary tools we can make a general distinction between theoretical and practical concerns and thus provide a loose distinction between political theory and ideological activity, when this is conceived of in narrow terms as practical political advocacy. In practice such distinctions will not be categorical, but they can still do useful work. Although Barry's approach has by no means been adopted by all contemporary political theorists, even those who criticise him tend to deploy some version of this mixed-mode form of inquiry. Indeed the criticism of Barry's own work is that it is too narrow in its conception of the appropriate tools and problems facing political theory rather than that he is too expansive in his conception of the components of political theory. The distinctions between contemporary political theorists such as Miller, Parekh, Pateman and Phillips tend to be differences of detail rather than rejections of this mixed-mode conception of the activity.

Of course this still leaves open the question raised by sociologists of knowledge, namely that this activity is still a form of ideological discourse broadly conceived, in that it is a historically contingent activity thrown up by the structure of modernity and reflecting the structures and distribution of power that underlie it. But we do not need to concede this meta-theoretical claim as it is a controversial claim contested by different theorists depending upon how radical and wide-ranging the claim is meant to be. Indeed we can conclude this section by pointing out that it is one further distinguishing feature of political theory and ideological political thought that the former is concerned with the question of the nature and status of its own claims and the character of its own activity. Political theorists tend to challenge Marx's claim that 'The philosophers have only interpreted the world, in various ways; the point is to change it' (Marx, 1977, p. 158). Political theorists are still very much concerned with interpreting the world and understanding the presuppositions of the ways in which they do so, as well as with changing the world. In this way political theory might seem much closer to what Andrew Vincent has described as the traditional metaphysical conception of political philosophy (Vincent, 2004, pp. 324–6). The problem with his choice of the term metaphysics is that it is either a subdivision of philosophy and therefore entails a substantive subject matter that is far removed from the concerns of actual political theorists, or else it suggests an *a priori* mode of inquiry that begs the questions about the most appropriate way of studying political ideas and arguments. Debate over what is the appropriate method for systematic thought about politics and its study remains one of the primary concerns of political theory in the twenty-first century. To claim the priority of a particular philosophical approach in this activity is either to beg the question or to prescribe rather than describe and explain the character of the activity itself.

British Political Theory and the Nature of the Political

The previous account of the activity of political theory as a mixed mode that uses tools drawn from across the humanities and social sciences to apply to a variety of issues is sufficiently general to capture the way the activity has been carried out by British political theorists across the twentieth century. Those who might have described themselves as philosophers still deployed methods other than logico-linguistic analysis and engaged with the social sciences and humanities in their work. Idealist philosophers such as Bosanquet were open to the methods and lessons of history and were concerned with challenging the presuppositions of economics. Other philosophers from the mid-twentieth century were also open to the lessons of the social sciences. Although this mixed-mode activity is sufficiently general to accommodate all the main strands of British political theory in the twentieth century, there is still one important substantive matter that is not covered in this analysis. This is the issue that is infelicitously described as the nature of the 'political', or the question we might better pose as what distinguishes political theory from ethics or sociology?

The simple answer is that political theory is concerned with the 'political', but what do we mean by that? This is an important issue as we have already seen that some political theorists who have a philosophical training, such as Berlin, tend to see political theory as a branch of ethics. In other words there is nothing distinct about the 'political'; it is merely a matter of ethics scaled up to large communities and sets of institutions.[16] Yet the idea of the 'political' remains deeply contested, and the way in which it is understood goes to the very heart of debates about the nature of political theory. Late twentieth- and early twenty-first-century English-speaking political theorists who are most exercised by the question tend to look to continental thinkers such as Carl Schmitt or Hannah Arendt for inspiration rather than to the domestic traditions of the United States or Britain (Arendt, 1958; Connolly, 1991; Honig, 1993; Schmitt, 1976). The domestic traditions of both countries are accused of reducing all questions of political theory to questions about the 'social' or to essentially ethical questions of distribution and of rights, liberties and resources. The sources and nature of political power are taken as given and the issues for political theory are about how one turns political power towards achieving moral ends or goods. The nature and extent of political power and the institutions through which it is constituted and exercised are supposedly taken as problematic in a way in which the nature of moral authority or the institutions and rules through which it is exercised are not. The frustration of many contemporary political theorists with the hegemonic role of questions of social justice in their subject reflects this concern with the absence of a serious engagement with the nature of the 'political'. At its most simple, this is because morality and ethics presuppose that there is only one appropriate form of human association, namely individuals pursuing ethical relationships. This neglects the fact that there are other forms of human association such as politics, the economy or social forms that can be characterised as civil society. Each of the forms of human association has its own distinctive logics and goals and it is the challenge of thinkers such as Schmitt and Arendt to force us to distinguish these forms of association and explain their relationships. With the exception of Oakeshott, most contemporary British political theorists of the last 50 years appear indifferent to these questions. Critics of the moralism of contemporary British political theory argue that it fails to be political in two important senses. First, it fails to recognise that there are different modes of association that come into conflict with one another. This is not only an abstract problem of categorisation: it goes to the heart of real political life in terms of the relationship between state power, the economy and the claims of other forms of association that can be seen to underlie much of twentieth-century British politics such as the rise of the welfare state in the 1930s and 1940s, its relative dominance throughout the 1960s and 1970s and its subsequent challenge from the New Right in the 1970s and 1980s.[17] The claims of politics emerge through the relationships and conflicts between these distinct forms of association. The second way in which political moralism is un-political is that it fails to acknowledge that within this fact of plural forms of association there is also a question of who should arbitrate and on what terms. This is a higher form of pluralism which raises questions about the priority of modes of association and the arbitration of their claims. What principles, values and forces should arbitrate such conflicts is also a contested question, yet this is precisely what the moralist's approach seems to presume.

In light of this discussion about the nature of the 'political', an important question arises about the character of British political theory, namely whether it is really 'political' theory at all. The response of critics of the 'moralism' of contemporary political theory suggest that the political thought of key figures such as Berlin, Hart, Barry and their students is not really political at all. But it is not only the critics of contemporary political theory who make this claim. Versions of it can be found among New Left thinkers such as Perry Anderson, in his criticism of the parochialism of British leftist theory and its hostility to the grand theory of continental Marxism and its successors (Anderson, 1966), or in the more familiar view that British political theory has always lacked a 'state theory' despite the existence of figures such as Thomas Hobbes, because of its common law tradition as opposed to the Roman law tradition of many European countries where issues of the site and nature of political power and the idea of the state are much more familiar parts of the intellectual landscape (Dyson, 1980, p. 8). The absence of a state tradition in the form that it is found in French or German political theory would certainly suggest that there is an important distinction between British and other continental traditions of political theorising (American political theory is closer to the British view than the European continental traditions, in this regard). This curious attitude of British political theory towards the state also lends support to the claim that it subordinates political theory to 'moralism' or ethics. This tendency is not however a peculiarity of twentieth-century British theory, but goes back as far as John Locke in the seventeenth century, who challenged the Hobbesian argument for the autonomy of politics by subordinating political power to ethical or moral principles.[18]

All that said, the absence of a state theory and the emergence of a 'moralist' tendency in the 1960s and 1970s does not show that British political theory lacks any sense of the problem of politics that underlies these criticisms. Indeed it is clear that British political theory is deeply engaged in trying to make sense of the claims of politics and its relationship to other modes of human association. The rise of political moralism as the default mode of political theory in the third quarter of the twentieth century should not be seen as an abandonment of political theory as some critics claim (see especially Geuss, 2008, *passim*); instead it should be understood as a response to the question of the nature and claims of the 'political'. The question that is more interesting than 'is political "moralism" an abandonment of the "political"?' is 'why was "moralism" taken to be an appropriate response to the claims of politics for much of late twentieth-century political theory?' British political theory does not answer this question in quite the same way as the political theory of other national traditions. That it does not do so is part of what distinguishes British political theory. But more importantly, British political theory can be seen as a series of different and interconnected debates about the nature and scope of the 'political' which is every bit as rich as that of other national traditions. Indeed, as the next sections will show, British political theory in its main institutional guises is an attempt to wrestle with the nature and claims of the state and the boundaries and scope of the 'political'. This can be more or less explicit at different stages of the century, but that this is so merely reflects the more fundamental transformations in British politics in the twentieth century.

Ethical State: The Ambiguous Legacy of the Nineteenth Century

At the close of the nineteenth century there were two dominant strands of British political theory, the empiricist utilitarianism of Henry Sidgwick exemplified in his *The Elements of Politics* (1891), and the Idealist tradition inherited from T. H. Green and F. H. Bradley and best exemplified in Bosanquet's *The Philosophical Theory of the State* (1899). Sidgwick's book, which remained a standard textbook until the 1930s, continued the tradition of utilitarian empiricism that had its roots in the philosophical radicalism of Jeremy Bentham. The Idealist tradition of Bosanquet originated among diverse sources such as the writings of Coleridge, mid-nineteenth-century intuitionism and German Idealism. In many ways the pairing of Sidgwick and Bosanquet continues and updates the pairing of Bentham and Coleridge in J. S. Mill's famous essays of 1839–40 (reprinted in Mill, 1875). Just as Bentham and Coleridge offered to Mill's generation two distinct ways of understanding political and social developments during the early nineteenth century, so Sidgwick and Bosanquet continue that into the early twentieth. Sidgwick represented the rationalist tradition of Bentham and the philosophical radicals who saw the tasks of political theory as serving the reform and rationalisation of the institutions of government and the state. Within this tradition the state or institutions of government are a given fact of history and the task of political theory is to ensure that they are achieving their goal of the general welfare: unlike social contract theory, utilitarianism has no theory of the origin of the state or a single *a priori* model of the ideal state. Where utilitarianism does engage in theorising about the state, it tends to instrumentalism and reformism by offering new mechanisms for delivering common goals. The characteristic feature of this tradition is its rationalism, lack of sentimentality and its hostility towards intuition, or unarticulated beliefs and values. The growth of this rationalist approach to politics throughout the nineteenth century had led later Victorians such as A. V. Dicey to describe the nineteenth century as an age of Benthamism (Dicey, 1905). Yet Benthamism had always faced challenges. In the early nineteenth century writers such as the Romantic poet S. T. Coleridge had sought to explain political relationships in an anti-instrumental fashion, drawing on the idea of a political community as a more encompassing form of society pursuing higher ends and directed by an intellectual and moral elite or clerisy (Coleridge, 1839). Coleridge's conception of a more expansive and hierarchically ordered political society with a commitment to the perfection of the people was no mere affectation. The British state in the nineteenth century was close to the encompassing model of the anti-rationalists, given the role and influence of the national church and the privileged position of the ancient universities and the continuity of state and social sites of power and authority. This vision of the polity as intimately intertwined with the national church was widely shared. W. E. Gladstone, who was to do so much to disentangle church and state in the late nineteenth century, was an ardent supporter of this integralist view, as a young man.

What held this integralist view together was the widespread acceptance of Anglican Christianity as the common bond of political society. However this was already being challenged by the accommodation of dissenters in institutions such as the new University of London, which did not require submission to religious tests in order to take a degree, and to the re-emergence of Roman Catholicism as a public force, through Catholic Emancipation, immigration and cultural forces such as the Oxford Movement. Yet the greatest challenge to the integralist view of the British polity from the mid-to-late nineteenth century was the growth of secularism and the impact of Darwin on religious attitudes of the intellectual elites.

The late nineteenth-century crisis of faith provided further support of the rationalist utilitarian view of the state and ethical relations as illustrated by Sidgwick's own crisis of faith. Yet the social and cultural forces that challenged the nature and understanding of the Victorian state, as it emerged through a succession of Reform Acts as a nascent liberal democracy, were not exclusively empiricist, liberal and utilitarian. The Idealist tradition that began with the work of T. H. Green and his influence on a generation of students who passed through Balliol College, Oxford managed to combine a robust liberal politics with a rejection of the utilitarian legacy of Bentham and philosophical radicalism. Green's philosophical project inspired many who were left cold by the narrow individualism and egoistic hedonism of the utilitarian tradition, yet experienced the collapse of traditional religious faith in light of Darwinian evolution as a crisis. Green and F. H. Bradley[19] drew on the philosophies of Kant and Hegel in constructing a philosophical position that chimed with a moral and ethical culture that had begun to lose confidence in its Christian foundations. For many of those who experienced as a loss the demise of the integrating effect of shared faith as a basis of a public philosophy that combined personal ethics and public political action, Idealism offered a way of reinterpreting both political action and the institutional context in which that took place. Idealism comprised an ethical politics of public engagement which coincided with and supported the Oxford settlement movement in the slums of London, which in turn had a major impact on the growth of social work as a profession and the study of social policy as a distinct branch of the social sciences. Jose Harris shows that philosophical Idealism remained a major current in departments of social policy, such as that at the LSE well into the 1940s, long after it had ceased to be a major voice in philosophy departments (Harris, 1992; 1996). The political consequences of British Idealism are therefore complex and diverse in that the tradition explicitly rejects the narrow instrumentalist view of the state that utilitarianism had contributed to classical liberal theory. However, that opposition to utilitarian liberalism was largely manifested through a perfectionist liberal ethic that is still taken to be the main insight of Green's political philosophy (see Brink, 2004). Bosanquet's contribution to Idealist political philosophy was to develop a conception of the state as an ethical community. Drawing on Rousseau's conception of the general will and the philosophy of Hegel, Bosanquet explained and gave content to the idea of the state, not merely as a set of bureaucratic and coercive institutions, but as an ethical community in which individuals could realise their personality. This is an ambiguous and controversial idea that has been contested by subsequent scholars. Bosanquet's idea of the state as an ethical idea was certainly taken by some as an alternative foundation for a conception of the state as the culmination and completion of the economy and civil society, not unlike that hoped for by the nineteenth-century integralists who challenged the selfish and godless utilitarianism of the reform movements. This is most clearly illustrated in the case of writers discussed by Harris who saw Idealism as an underpinning for a new welfare state which fulfilled its ethical role by completing and complementing the institutions of the economy and of civil society. In this way the idea of the state as an ethical ideal justified the early twentieth-century British state in taking a more active role in public life and drawing many more functions into its remit. If we follow W. H. Greenleaf's view of the essential dynamic of British politics as a struggle between collectivism and individualism, it would seem that the Idealist position firmly supported the collectivists. Yet as already mentioned, Bosanquet's idea of the state as an ethical idea is ambiguous in that he was distinctly hostile to the idea of the welfare state through his role in the Charity Organisation Society, which campaigned against state welfare provision and the expansion of the state's role into many areas that in the later twentieth century were taken for granted. What Bosanquet was certainly concerned with was the integration of ethical and political life in a single overarching conception of community. His philosophy rejected the privatisation of ethical and moral judgement and action that has its roots in utilitarianism and the conception of the state as a mechanism for achieving essentially private ends. To this extent, Bosanquet's contribution to political philosophy is to deal with the problem of the 'political' as something that cannot be reduced merely to a question of individual ends and interests, and to see the role of the state as the political vehicle through which this is achieved. Bosanquet therefore sets the agenda for British political theory in the twentieth century by raising the question of the nature and claims of political life and their connection to institutional questions – precisely the sort of state theory that British political theory is supposed to lack.

The forces behind the expansion of the late nineteenth- and early twentieth-century British state were complex, drawing as they did on theories of imperialism and national political economy which led to debates over free trade and imperial preference. Yet while these forces developed independently of the philosophical conditions of British Idealism, the two certainly came together, with Idealism offering a rich discourse in terms of which the modern British state and its reform and transformation could be articulated and defended. In this way it contributed to the intellectual climate from which the new liberalism of L. T. Hobhouse and J. A. Hobson emerged, although it was by no means the only or most significant factor (see Freeden, 1978). Hobhouse was educated in the Oxford 'Greats' tradition and was influenced by the prevalent Idealist philosophy of the time. He was an influential figure in the growth of sociology as an academic subject in Britain, being the first holder of a chair in sociology (see Collini, 1979): his interest in sociology as a subject distinct from economics and wider than political theory understood as the study of government reflects the more encompassing ideal of the state that underlay Bosanquet's view of the state as an ethical community. Yet Hobhouse was not a follower of Bosanquet, and his new liberalism, expounded in his 1911 book *Liberalism*, provides a case for a more interventionist view of the state that is similar to that of the Asquith administration as opposed to the robust non-interventionism of the Charity Organisation Society. Indeed, while Idealism provides one of the intellectual sources deployed by early advocates of the welfare state, the new liberalism of the likes of Hobhouse developed in a more empirical and instrumental direction despite retaining a scepticism and realism about empiricist utilitarianism. For Hobhouse the state as a set of institutions could contribute to the task of achieving liberal ends, but as with the followers of Sidgwick the state remained an instrumental good and not constitutive of an ethical life. Hobhouse became increasingly sceptical of the idea of the state as an ethical good or community to the extent that in the preface to his *The Metaphysical Theory of the State*, published in 1918, he refers to witnessing a Zeppelin bombing raid on London as follows: 'I had just witnessed the visible and tangible outcome of a false and wicked doctrine, the foundations of which lay, as I believe in the book before me' (Hobhouse, 1918, p. 6). The volume he had before him was by Hegel, the principle source of Idealist philosophy, but the target of Hobhouse's book was clearly Bosanquet, in view of the similarity of title between Hobhouse's and Bosanquet's books. Bosanquet and other philosophical Idealists had been taken in by the un-British ideology of the 'god state' that had led to 'Prussianism' and the Great War that Hobhouse was witnessing from his garden in Highgate. This criticism is obviously an *ad hominem* that fails to address the argument of either Hegel or Bosanquet, but it was not to be an unfamiliar move in British political theory. Karl Popper (an Austrian by birth but honorary British political theorist) was to make the same criticism of Hegel, this time a source of totalitarianism in his *The Open Society and its Enemies* (Popper, 1945) during the Second World War. Taken together, the 'realist' new liberalism of Hobhouse and the Idealism of Bosanquet offer a number of themes that shape the emergence and development of British political theory in the early twentieth century, although both predate the emergence of chairs in political science and the distinctive activity of political theory within it.

Both Bosanquet and Hobhouse abstract from and theorise about issues of the emerging twentieth-century British state and its roles and functions. Bosanquet's focus is more closely connected to theorising the state as a distinct form of association. In that way his philosophical interests turn to the nature of political activity, political power and the nature of the state. Yet his attempts to conceptualise the state as an ethical community devoted to perfectionist ends raises the important issue of the relationship between political and ethical forms of association. The Idealist vision tried to combine both perspectives in a new synthesis that would avoid a simplistic choice between realism and moralism. This opposition was to have a major impact on the subsequent development of British political theory throughout the century. The opposition to the ethical conception of the state is exemplified by Hobhouse's realism. Although he shares with Bosanquet an anti-utilitarian view of the state as nothing more than a mechanism for arbitrating between individual interests, he rejects the idea of the state as an ethical community and acknowledges a discontinuity between ethical life and politics. For Hobhouse the fatal flaw of Idealism was the attempt to elide moral and political obligation: that path led to state worship and 'Prussianism'. Hobhouse is more of a collectivist than a communitarian. This element of realism and wariness of politics is a further feature of British political thinking that informs the development of political theory throughout the middle of the twentieth century, and is one of the themes that is particularly current in contemporary British politics. Hobhouse's assault on the 'alien' sources of Bosanquet's thought also contributes to the development of scepticism in British political theory regarding foreign theories and philosophies. Although British political theory retains complex interconnections with continental and American developments in philosophy and political science, there remains a strong undercurrent of scepticism about what is done elsewhere, whether this be an incomprehension of the contemporary post-Marxism of thinkers such as Slavoj Žižek, or the rejection by John Gray and Bernard Williams of US ivory tower liberal theories of justice.

Pluralism and Statism

Taking Bosanquet and Hobhouse as representative figures from the early part of the twentieth century shows how thinking about the nature and scope of the state and political society was always central to British political theory. Yet it would be wrong to think that the statism of both Idealists and new liberals exhausted the terrain of political theory in the first four decades of the twentieth century. With the expansion of state power and responsibility throughout the early twentieth century, particularly following the impact of the Great War, it would be easy to see the idea of the state as exhausting the sphere of the political. Yet in the work of an extraordinary group of British political theorists, two of whom were to be among the most influential professors in the early twentieth century, we can see the question of the nature and authority of political society developing in a different direction to that of Bosanquet or Hobhouse.

The English pluralists, John Figgis, Harold Laski and G. D. H. Cole, were to dominate British political theory until the late 1930s, after which they were eclipsed by the rise of liberal moralism in political theory, only to be rediscovered from the 1980s as some of their concerns were seen to persist in thinking about the nature of political life in Britain.

Whereas the works of Bosanquet and Hobhouse can be represented as two theoretical responses to the slow steady expansion of the modern state, the pluralists challenged the idea of the state as the sole site of political power, authority and action. Figgis, Laski, Cole and other pluralists such as Ernest Barker or A. D. Lindsey drew on a wide variety of intellectual sources including the Philosophical Idealism that sustained the conception of statism that they all rejected. Yet they all acknowledge the fact of pluralism and sectional conflict within British politics in the early twentieth century. The late nineteenth and early twentieth centuries were marked by a period of major challenges to the idea of the state as a settled and homogeneous expression of the British political society. Indeed the very idea of Britishness was being challenged by Irish nationalism, including a violent insurgency leading to secession and civil war in Ireland, as well as a counter-secessionist struggle among unionists in what became Northern Ireland. The very idea of the identity and territorial continuity of the state was subject to challenge at this time. But national identity was not the only issue. Trade unionism was growing as a distinct site of political as well as economic power, as also were claims for labour representation which posed questions about parliamentary versus more radical versions of the struggle between labour and capital. Both Laski's and Cole's contributions to British political theory were based on an awareness of the way in which traditional models of the sovereign state were historical constructions that masked the real distribution and organisation of political power in Britain. Barker, who was similarly associated with both Idealism and pluralism, was more concerned with the idea of British, or more properly English, national identity in the face of plural challenges to the state and its tendency to assert unanimity against the fact of diversity.[20] Figgis, the Cambridge historian of ideas, is another good example of a pluralist theorist whose historical work on medieval political theory in part contributed to contesting the dominance of the modern idea of state sovereignty.

Where the Idealism of Bosanquet can be seen in the context of a restatement of the idea of the British polity as a single ethical community or a philosophical version of the idea of the unity of church and state, Figgis set out to show how the idea of the modern absolutist idea of state sovereignty grew up in late medieval church politics and was used against churches to subordinate them to a unified form of secular rule. Churches, for Figgis, are distinct legal entities in their own right and do not require the existence of the state to confer authority on them or to give them legitimacy. The true fact of the matter was not the existence of a unified community of church and state of the kind celebrated by Coleridgeans or as reformulated by later Idealists. But nor was it the idea of an association of individuals pooling their power in order to overcome the inconveniences of a state of nature or to maximise overall utility as either contractarians or utilitarians claimed. The facts of history showed a plurality of corporations and associations which conferred identity on individuals and which existed prior to and independently of the modern state

(Figgis, 1913). Modern politics as the rise of the state embodied an attempt to capture state power and use it as a vehicle for challenging alternative sources of authority and power in society. Rather than seeing the state as an ethical community that combined moral and political agency, or as a mere mechanism for arbitrating between individual claims, Figgis and the pluralists saw the state as one vehicle through which factions and interests could seek to gain dominance and power.

Figgis' concern was to analyse the origins of absolute sovereignty and, as a churchman, to defend the idea of church authority from the incursions of political power, but other pluralists such as Laski and Cole were more concerned with the ways in which state power could be co-opted by narrow class interests to exercise domination over the majority. Cole's important early contribution to socialist theory rejected the idea of the state or welfarism as a way of achieving socialist objectives. Instead he contributed to the development of guild socialism, which drew as much on British trade unionism and the ideas of William Morris as it did on syndicalism and Georges Sorel (see Laborde, 2000, pp. 69–100). In place of the unitary and absolutist state, Cole envisaged a collection of self-governing functional associations within a federalist structure. These functional associations were not narrowly economic, but they did include whole industries which would organise themselves along democratic lines: for Cole the question was as much democratic legitimacy as it was economic and managerial efficiency (Cole, 1921). Cole's guild socialism was less concerned with the parliamentary franchise or labour representation than with the form that representation would take. He was committed to the idea that guild representation was a more effective way of delivering democratic empowerment than merely relying on the territorial franchise that arose out of nineteenth- and early twentieth-century Reform Acts. Like R. H. Tawney, Cole saw fundamental goals of socialism in terms of social action and the self-government of equals as opposed merely to extending an acquisitive society and the distribution of material goods. This form of industrial democracy was to live on into the 1970s in various attempts at workers' control and industrial democracy. In the intervening years Cole's version of democratic and local socialism had been displaced by the administrative socialism of the welfare state.

Laski's contribution to the pluralist tradition is more complex than that of Figgis and Cole, as he moved from a suspicion of the absolutist state towards recognition of the unitary state as a model for political authority in the face of industrial and social change. As the successor to Graham Wallas at the LSE, Laski wrote extensively on the emergence of the modern state from the seventeenth century onwards and took seriously the problem of sovereignty and the source and nature of political authority. The subsequent development of Laski's thought involves reconciliation with the coercive character of state sovereignty, illustrated in his *A Grammar of Politics* (Laski, 1925), and owes much to his own experiences of the Labour government of 1931 and to the subsequent Attlee government of 1945–51.

The pluralist tradition is an important strand of political thought that had an impact on the practical politics of the British left in the early to mid-twentieth century. But it also had an important impact on the development of political theory as an academic discipline through the work of Laski at the LSE and Cole as the first Chichele Professor of Social and Political Theory at Oxford. Both saw the primary object of political theory as the nature and site of political power and authority. Neither showed much interest in what would be called political 'moralism' and neither saw the task of political theory as an extension of ethics. Indeed it is arguable that both Laski and Cole saw the subject matter of political theory as coextensive with political science, and that either would have been uncomfortable with a distinction that suggested that political theory and political science were two separate activities.[21] Although influenced by the climate of Philosophical Idealism, the pluralists took a far more realist view of politics as an object of inquiry. Both Laski and Cole also drew heavily on history in their style of theoretical writing despite being schooled in the Oxford 'Greats' tradition: this is clearly illustrated in many of Laski's writings which would now often be classed as the history of political thought. Figgis, whose life and teaching career were much shorter, was schooled in the Cambridge tradition of historical scholarship, yet unlike the feigned indifference of some contemporary Cambridge historians he saw the history of political ideas as an important contribution to political theory.

Although Laski and Cole had begun to modify their political commitment to pluralism earlier in their careers, both continued to hold significant roles in the academy in the middle of the twentieth century and to shape the nature and study of political theory in light of the interest in the nature and study of British politics. The nature and object of that activity remained the analysis, explanation and critique of political authority and the state, thus contradicting the view that British political theory had no conception of the state or failed to take seriously the autonomy of politics. Yet given this fact we are left with the question of why political theory appears to have been displaced by political 'moralism' for much of the remainder of the twentieth century.

Triumph of the State and Turn to Morality

Cole's successor as Chichele Professor of Social and Political Theory was Isaiah Berlin. This change of personnel was to mark a substantial change in the character of British political theory for the remainder of the twentieth century. Berlin was one of a group of Oxford philosophers, which included Gilbert Ryle and J. L. Austin, who created an approach known as ordinary language philosophy. This approach had grown out of the logical realism of the early twentieth-century reaction against Philosophical Idealism that was associated with Bertrand Russell and G. E. Moore and subsequently the logical positivism popularised by Berlin's contemporary A. J. Ayer. Also involved in this group was a philosopher turned chancery barrister and sometime intelligence officer, H. L. A. Hart, who was subsequently to transform English jurisprudence and contribute significantly to the growth and development of English-speaking political philosophy.[22] What is extraordinary about the accession of Berlin and Hart to such prominent positions in British political theory is that the style of philosophy in which both were trained was unsympathetic to sub-stantive moral theorising or normative political philosophy. Indeed the approach gave rise to figures such as T. D. Weldon in whose influential book *The Vocabulary of Politics* the task of political theory was handed to empirical political science on the grounds that there was little for philosophy or theory to contribute beyond the clarification of conceptual confusion (Weldon, 1953). Weldon applied the same sort of scepticism to traditional political theory that the logical positivists had applied to metaphysics and morality. Such questions were either verifiable (and thus quasi-scientific questions) or they were meaningless and therefore not subject to rational deliberation and inquiry. If they were verifiable they could be the subject of a naturalistic political science. This legacy of mid-twentieth-century British phi-losophy coincided with the growth of the American science of politics and its impact on British political studies. Yet the curious feature of this philosophical tradition is that it produced influential figures such as Berlin and Hart as well as their students, who were to transform British political theory and reassert its connection to ethics. Berlin's inaugural lecture 'Two Concepts of Liberty' and Hart's paper on the concept of natural rights (Hart, 1955) took the form of careful logical analysis but both also opened the door for the form of normative political theory that was to dominate political theory and philosophy from the 1960s to the present. This form of political theory is concerned with defending values such as liberty and equality, and distribu-tive principles such as those of justice. Although both Hart and Berlin remained cautious about advancing their own 'theories' of freedom, equality and justice, their successors such as Brian Barry have made contributions to theorising about justice that parallel the systematic normative theories developed by American contempo-raries such as John Rawls or Ronald Dworkin. Berlin and Hart employed different styles of theoretical writing. Berlin's works are complex syntheses of the ideas of past political thinkers, designed to frame and suggest political principles and values, most especially the plurality of ultimate values. He is often seen as a historian of political ideas, but his use of past political thinkers is much more flexible than the precise scholarship employed by most professional historians. Instead Berlin offers a series of reflections and conversations with past philosophers and traditions. Hart, on the other hand, deployed a forensic style of conceptual analysis which drew on both his legal and philosophical training, but which also recovered the tradition of English analytical jurisprudence that goes back to Jeremy Bentham, who was the subject of a number of Hart's major writings (Hart, 1982). Taken together both Hart and Berlin show the importance of historical engagement and philosophical analysis to the rational appraisal and defence of normative values and principles. Initially, this project was conducted as a second-order activity, very similar to the way in which ordinary language philosophy related to the natural sciences in clarify-ing terms and cutting away false problems that arise from conceptual confusion and imprecise use of language. Yet this second-order task soon gave way to a more direct engagement with substantive principles and values as the analysis and critique of some positions lent support to others. Berlin's contrast between positive and negative liberty functions in this way. Instead of simply defending a negative or classical liberal conception of freedom, Berlin contrasts it with an alternative view derived loosely from Rousseau and Hegel and uses this to support the negative case. This approach is further refined and defended in Barry's *Political Argument*, and in his subsequent works, where a substantive argument is built from the critical engagement with other candidate theories and positions. This form of political theory as an inward-looking debate among political theories is still the dominant style of contemporary political theory at the beginning of the twenty-first century.

Yet what is most striking about this form of theory is not its style or the way in which it has come to dominate the field, but its abandonment of a concern with the nature and location of political authority in favour of what is characterised as 'moralism'. The replacement of political with ethical or moral questions takes a number of forms. First, it is exemplified in the preoccupation of political theorists with questions about the nature of ethical values such as justice, rights, freedom and equality. Second, the 'moralist' uses these values to determine the legitimacy of political actions and institutions, thus assuming that ethical matters are both of a higher order or priority and are less contestable than political decisions or actions. Third, political 'moralism' analyses all political goods as essentially goods for individuals and components of individual welfare. In this final respect the perspective of political 'moralism' continues to approach politics through an individualist vision of utilitarian rationalism and has nothing to say about the nature of things 'political'. This indifference to the claims of the 'political' is taken to be definitive of British political theory, but as we have seen it is clearly a departure from the style of theorising that predominated in the first half of the twentieth century. The question remains: why was there this transition?

One answer to this question is that the intellectual division of labour within the study of politics changed with the linguistic turn within philosophy and the growth of empirical and naturalistic political science. But this does not fully explain the matter, as it could just as well explain the demise of normative theory and not the replacement of a focus on political matters with a concern for ethics. Indeed, the parallel development of historicist approaches to the history of ideas, which culminates in Britain in the rise of the Cambridge School of Skinner, Dunn and Pocock, is often explained in terms of the threat of the rise of behaviouralism in American political science. Their response was to reassert the claims of history in the face of scepticism about naturalistic social science, but in so doing they also inadvertently mounted a parallel assault on political theory.

A more suitable place to explain the change of focus from politics to 'moralism' is to locate it within the wider political forces that provide the context for political theory in the late twentieth century. The most important of these changes is the triumph of the welfare state over other ways of organising political power and authority. The triumph of the state begins with the response to the Great Depression and comes to fruition with the triumph of the modern state system during the Second World War. The state had proved itself to be the superior mechanism for achieving progressive ends, whether in terms of organising the economy or promoting individual welfare.[23] Trends that began in the 1930s came to fruition in the war years and were applied to social reform in the Attlee government and the post-war settlement until the 1970s. Pluralists such as Laski and Cole had reconciled themselves to the idea of state sovereignty, and under the leadership of a popularly elected Labour government they saw the possibility of state power being harnessed to their progressive purposes. Fabians, who had always trusted in the mobilisation of the state for progressive ends, found their faith vindicated. The conservative accommodation to the Attlee government reforms also created an ideological common ground that lent empirical support to the 'end of ideology' thesis being proposed by American political scientists such as Daniel Bell. A further context for the apparent triumph of the state was the Cold War struggle against totalitarianism. This intellectual debate and political struggle was between two models of the state, the Western liberal democratic state and the Soviet state and command economy which was characterised by many as totalitarian. British political theory did not give rise to theories of totalitarianism such as those of Freidrich or Arendt in the United States, but the Cold War context did impact on British political theory through Isaiah Berlin[24] and Karl Popper.

The triumph of the welfare state and the challenge to totalitarianism shifted attention from the question of the nature and site of political agency and power to the terms under which that power was deployed. In the wider context of British politics, the debate focused on who best managed the state and economy and how far it should extend taxation or public ownership of particular industries: arguments that were largely made in technical terms of efficiency rather than in terms of democracy or freedom. In the same way in the field of political theory, debate shifted from what Popper described as utopian to piecemeal social engineering (Popper, 1963). This involves small-to-medium-scale problem solving within a settled structure of political institutions rather than challenges to those institutions. Popper's impact on twentieth-century political theory is as considerable as his contribution to the philosophy of science; however he had much less of a personal impact on reshaping the personnel and agenda of political theory than did Berlin or Hart and their respective students. All that said, the Popperian view of piecemeal social engineering fitted the conception of normative political theory that emanated from Berlin, Hart and Barry.[25] For all of these thinkers, the urgent questions of political theory were not about the nature of the state but rather what it should and should not do. In this context the questions of justice and freedom have a particular salience which has continued into contemporary political theory. One should not underestimate the importance of some of the questions that fall under Popper's designation of piecemeal social engineering. The agenda of normative political theory that Berlin and Hart initiated paralleled and supported significant moves to liberalise British political life, in ways that have transformed the lives of many people.[26] A similar plea for the political significance of this form of political theory is found in Barry's final book, *Why Social Justice Matters* (2005). Nor should it be assumed that thinkers as sophisticated as Berlin, Hart and Barry just ignored the problem of the state or politics in the way that some critics of political 'moralism' claim. The charge of 'moralism' suggests an easy dismissal of modern political theory as non-political. Yet the position defended by these thinkers in subtle ways involves a positive endorsement of the state as the settled background condition of ethical questions that are also political. So rather than failing to take seriously the autonomy of the 'political', the political theorists of the mid-to-late twentieth century were denying a categorical separation between the political and ethical matters and were also advancing a form of methodological individualism as the only defensible way of analysing political phenomena.

It would be wrong to suggest that this liberal conception of political theory was the only form of theorising around; that would certainly be a mistake and would deny the significance of other voices that were to surface later in opposition to it. The point is merely that it came to assert a dominant position in terms of how the subject developed over the subsequent generations and the reasons for that. There were indeed major sceptical voices of equal significance to those of Hart and Berlin. That of Michael Oakeshott at the LSE was perhaps the most influential in political theory and the British study of politics more generally. Oakeshott took a robustly historicist view of political theory and denied the possibility of a naturalistic political science; consequently his critique of political rationalism and ideological politics included the kind of normative political theory practised by Berlin (of whom he was somewhat contemptuous) and Hart (whom he respected). Oakeshott's philosophical politics left no room for the kind of issue-driven normative theorising that has preoccupied contemporary liberal political theory. Much of his published work during his period at the LSE was more closely focused on theorising the development of the study of British politics and the general study of politics within the British university system.[27] That said, his post-retirement writings show an engagement with political theory and the state that supports and develops the perspective that underlies the liberal theory of Berlin and Hart. Oakeshott's last major work, *On Human Conduct* (1975), offers a theoretical reflection on the modern state through the dialectical opposition between the idea of an enterprise or a civil association. Both perspectives are categorically distinct but are also ideal types never fully instantiated in history. Yet the tensions between seeing the state as either an enterprise or a civil association does capture the debate between the more activist political moralists and those who remain sceptical about the claims of normative theory. One way of interpreting Oakeshott's concerns in *On Human Conduct* is as the development of a vocabulary for politics that does not reduce politics to ethics, but which still acknowledges the claims of the state and seeks to avoid utopian radicalism as an alternative to liberal 'moralism'.

The dominant strand of British political theory during the post-war period was not only suited to the times in orienting students to the structure of the political world in which they found themselves, but it was also realistically utopian in challenging the limits of our political and ethical self-understandings.[28] By combining both concerns it also avoided the charge of theoretical conservatism that Hobhouse had levelled at Bosanquet's Idealist theory of the ethical state. This model of political theory was and still is criticised for its narrow dependence on a settled view of the state and a model of judicial politics that is derived from the United States (Gray,

2000, *passim*). But it has been able to withstand these challenges as long as it fits political experience and orientates students and scholars within a settled set of political institutions. The question that has unsettled British political theory at the end of the twentieth century is whether this is in fact still the case.

Pluralism and Statism Revisited: Political Theory at the End of the Twentieth Century

The rise to dominance of the liberal 'moralist' style of political theory makes sense against the backdrop of a settled view of the liberal democratic welfare state and its powers and it was in this context that the style, questions and methods of liberal political theory came to exercise a dominant position in British universities. But it is certainly not being claimed that this was the only style and approach to political theory in the mid-to-late twentieth century. Throughout that period there were dissident voices and alternative models of political theory being practised in British universities. We have already seen the case of Michael Oakeshott and his followers. Other notable figures such as Ralph Miliband applied Marxist ideas to the analysis of the state and politics and indirectly challenged the 'cosy' liberalism then shaping British political thought. New Left thinkers challenged the style of Marxism defended by Miliband, and the second New Left of the 1960s challenged the under-theorised approach of historian activists such as E. P. Thompson. Feminism also continued to offer a significant critique of the dominant liberal paradigm. Although it has been a slow struggle for feminist theorists to enter the dominant departments of political theory and they are still some way from capturing the main established chairs in the subject, feminist theory has nevertheless provided a number of the most internationally significant British political theorists, who were anything but underlabourers in the liberal moralist paradigm. Yet all this diversity cannot disguise the fact that the liberal 'moralist' paradigm continued (and continues) to exercise a dominant position in British political theory. That said, the last three decades of the twentieth century have seen an increasingly successful challenge to the dominant paradigm, and one that can be measured by the elevation of a number of these critics to significant positions in the discipline such as Fellowships of the British Academy and in one case elevation to the House of Lords.[29]

Why these critiques gained in saliency in the late twentieth century when other equally forceful challenges earlier in the century were less successful requires us to look outside the terms of debate to the public political context. Signs that the settled nature of the state could not be taken for granted have been forcing themselves to the surface of British politics for the last four decades of the century. Not only has there been an assault on the post-war welfare state from the 1970s under Thatcherite conservatism and New Labour, but echoing the experience of the young Laski and Cole, the unsettled and fundamentally plural character of the state reasserted itself through the growth of nationalist movements for self-government throughout the Union, culminating in the constitutional reforms of the last years of the twentieth century. The rise of nationalism, identity and culture as the basis of challenges to the unified statist model of liberal 'moralism' has its roots in complex changes in British society. The claims of nationalism had been forced off the agenda of British politics and British political theory because of external events for much of the century. The nature of national identity was a respectable question for someone such as Sir Ernest Barker in the 1920s and 1930s, yet by the 1980s it was hardly considered respectable to address questions of identity and nationality among political theorists except by way of criticising the analytic usefulness of the concept. It was either a concept tainted by European experience or one deployed by political demagogues such as Enoch Powell. Yet in the mid-1990s the ideas of nationality and national identity were back at the centre of debates about social and political justice, with the publication of important books by David Miller (1995) and Margaret Canovan (1996). Miller is particularly interesting in this instance as his early work on social justice appeared squarely within the liberal 'moralist' paradigm. Yet Miller's work on social justice has developed to encompass questions about the nature of political community in terms of the scope and limits of legitimate claims about justice and about the status of principles of justice and their relationship to the shared values of actual political communities. One consequence of this has been that where some liberal 'moralists' have adopted a simple cosmopolitanism when thinking about the limits of their principles, Miller has defended a particularistic view that limits the full range of issues of social justice to political societies, with a more limited set of obligations holding in the international and inter-state realm (Miller, 2007). His defence of nationality as a presupposition of distributive communities developed in response to a familiar dissatisfaction with the procedural conception of liberal theories of justice, but it is also a response to another theoretical and practical challenge to the idea of the state as the main focus of distributive and political questions. This challenge arose from the emergence of multicultural political theory in the 1980s and 1990s.

Multiculturalism as a phenomenon of modern British politics developed in response to the politics of race and immigration. In the early post-war period, immigration from the British Commonwealth had been encouraged by successive governments as a way of managing labour shortages. However, as large communities of immigrants first from the Caribbean and subsequently the Indian subcontinent settled in and transformed many of the major cities in Britain, they confronted a domestic population which, while happy to exploit their labour, was often deeply suspicious and unwelcoming. Racial politics became an important if depressing feature of British political life. But race was only one factor of this legacy of Britain's post-imperial and post-colonial legacy. As group difference and self-identity were not solely marked by skin colour but often by beliefs and social norms, these waves of immigration and the subsequent generations of hyphenated Britons created a new discourse of multiculturalism to articulate the ways in which discrimination manifested itself. Many of the most prominent theorists of this new multiculturalism had experienced the pressures of integration and assimilation at first hand, both in wider British society and in the peculiar microcosm of British academic life. Yet, as in the case of Bhikhu Parekh, their theory was no mere generalisation from personal experience, but was informed by a thorough grounding in the political ideas and theories of the Western tradition being reapplied to the circumstances of a more obviously plural and diverse society than traditional liberal thought, from Mill or the Idealists through to Hart and Barry, tended to acknowledge. The underlying problem for Parekh was the way in which the norms or conditions of group integration and accommodation, deployed in both public life and in egalitarian liberalism, contained presuppositions that reinforced the discrimination and disadvantage of ethnic and cultural groups. By cultural groups he meant communities with settled patterns of belief with an institutional manifestation such as legal authority. The accommodation of such groups could not be achieved by the imposition of universal general laws and sets of rights, as the nature and authority of these laws and rights was often challenged. Parekh's work (see Parekh, 2000a; 2000b) draws on ideas that were familiar to early pluralists such as Cole and Laski, while his critique of monistic universalism draws on familiar lines of criticism advanced by the British Idealists and by Michael Oakeshott. The multicultural challenge to the unity of the British state and to the ideal of universal rights and provision was forcefully criticised by liberal egalitarians such as Brian Barry (2001) who saw it as a confused and dangerous retreat from the progressive values of the liberal state, but it was also seen by less universalistic theorists like Miller as a challenge to the conception of common political identity that was necessary to sustain the idea of social democracy in Britain. While the multicultural challenge is not unique to Britain, the way in which it has been absorbed into British political theory is significantly different from the way in which Canadian or Australian theorists have addressed the same issue (see Kukathas, 2002; Kymlicka, 1995; Tully, 1995). What it has done is raise a number of important issues about the role and accommodation of identity in British political theory: not least the question of what it is to be British. This question, along with the rise of nationalist aspirations in the territorial politics of Britain, has reminded theorists and their audience of the tendency to collapse Britishness into Englishness, and to have a narrow conception of Englishness that is located somewhere between Oxford, Cambridge and London.

The multiculturalists were not the only theorists to rediscover the legacy of pluralism. Many on the democratic left within academic political theory also rediscovered the idea of pluralism and associationalism as paths to democracy. There are many sources for this rediscovery of pluralism as an alternative path for theorising political relationships, some of which have their roots in ideas of 'workers' control' and industrial democracy that resurfaced in the 1970s. An important manifestation of this trend is exemplified in the work of the political sociologist and radical political theorist Paul Hirst. Hirst had been a radical left thinker in the late 1960s and early 1970s and was influenced by the distinctly un-British ideas of Louis Althusser and Nicos Poulantzas: both French[30] Marxist political philosophers who were precisely the sort of thinkers that Perry Anderson thought that the British left lacked interest in. Yet Hirst distanced himself from this tradition and from Marxism and in the process rediscovered the ideas of pluralists such as Laski. Yet in a curious way, Hirst's intellectual trajectory was the reverse of Laski's. By the time of his *A Grammar of Politics* in 1925, Laski had already accommodated himself to the idea of state sovereignty and subsequently he became influenced by Marxist theory. Following the defeat of 1931 and the subsequent Labour victory of 1945 he also became an unequivocal supporter of unlimited majoritarianism, rejecting ideas such as proportional representation of mechanisms within parliament, such as select committees, which might hinder the exercise of unlimited executive power. This strategy might well have looked attractive to Laski in the 1940s, but following a period of unbroken Conservative rule with large parliamentary majorities based on minority shares of the vote, it looked far less attractive to many theorists on the left such as Hirst. As Laski moved from pluralism to democratic collectivism, so Hirst moved in the opposite direction, advocating a return to a more pluralist form of political organisation that could accommodate not only the claims of multi-culturalists but also those for regional government under the guise of British nationalism, and most importantly industrial democracy. Hirst's ideas and those of other pluralist thinkers enjoyed a brief period of public interest before falling foul of Labour majoritarianism following the Blair landslide of 1997. Yet they remain important as they illustrate the way in which the saliency of ideas and concepts follows developments in the wider culture of British politics, but also because they demonstrate the extent to which thinking about the nature and sites of political authority and agency had become a central concern within British political theory in ways that had not been true since the pre-war period.

Conceptions of identity and the non-neutral nature of liberal egalitarian models of the state and social justice had been a long-standing target of feminist political theorists. But in the last decades of the twentieth century these concerns were given a new impetus by the work of feminist political theorists such as Carole Pateman and Anne Phillips. Where the liberal discourse of social justice had come to treat all significant political questions as ones of distribution or 'who gets what, where, when and why', feminist theories asked the question of who decides what is to be distributed and by whom. This marked a shift from questions of justice to democracy or from ethics back to politics. Pateman's work on democratic participation and equality came together in her hugely influential book, *The Sexual Contract* (Pateman, 1974; 1979; 1988; 1990)' where she provides a sustained critique of the patriarchal nature of social contract theory. Contract theories provide a powerful image for understanding social relations and the idea was often invoked in the political discourse of the 1970s, but it was also the dominant model of social justice since the publication of Rawls' *A Theory of Justice* in 1971. Pateman's work is essentially a powerful critique of the dominant discourse of politics which rejects the individualistic and voluntaristic conceptions of political relationships that underpin liberal democracy and its inability to address structures of domination and exclusion. The exclusive focus of contractarian conceptions of politics is on the distribution of rights, but this for Pateman ignores the more important issue of structures of power that form the backdrop against which rights are exercised. Without addressing the question of power, social contract theories, and by implication liberal theories of justice, simply reinforce the existing structural inequalities of society. In this way, Pateman's work converges with similar arguments made by multiculturalist and pluralist critics of liberal 'moralism'. Anne Phillips' work is similarly focused on questions of representation and political equality and most recently the question of the relationship between feminism and multiculturalism (Phillips, 1991; 1995; 1999; 2007). For Phillips questions of identity are at the heart of an adequate political conception of equality and her recent work has involved challenging the liberal paradigm's reliance on pre-theorised values and concepts, thus divorcing them from the need for political contestation and legitimation. This has not involved a wholesale rejection of debates about justice and equality but rather a transformation of their terms from essentially ethical debates which are addressed philosophically to political debates that can only be addressed in relation to democracy. The feminist contribution to late twentieth-century British political theory is not the exclusive source of a return to political questions such as democracy, but it has been one of the most significant sites of the theoretical inter-connection between debates about justice, identity and democracy.

Conclusion: Exceptionalism in British Political Theory

The outline narrative of twentieth-century British political theory provides an account of a practice that has changed over the course of the century in both the methodology and style of arguments deployed and in terms of the subjects studied. We have seen that the outline of these changes can be traced to the broad patterns of British politics and in particular questions relating to the nature and scope of the British state. This context is certainly more visible in the ideological forms of British political thought and many commentators will probably still think that is the best place to concentrate one's attention. Others will see this interconnection between theory and practice best illustrated in the academic study of British politics, which after all was not distinct from political theory or the general study of politics until the mid-twentieth century. Yet the fortunes of the study of British politics have waxed and waned in recent years as the sub-discipline of political science has 'pro-fessionalised' and the distinctiveness of British politics has itself been absorbed into the study of European politics, or fragmented into specialisms that lose the 'excep-tionalism' that once made British politics the core of the curriculum rather than merely one option among many facing the student of political science. Political theory has suffered less at the hands of the 'professionalisers', some of whom were political theorists (see Barry, 1999; Goodin, 2009), than have other fields of the sub-discipline where the distinctiveness of a national approach has been receding over the last four decades. This is no doubt a curious conclusion given that political theory aspires to study politics in its most general forms and uses methods and approaches that if at all valid are universally so. Yet, as we have seen, the selection and balance of dominant methods and principal questions goes hand in hand, and the broad pattern of the rise and dominance of approaches in the field of political theory acquires its salience against the backdrop of what is happening in the wider institutional political context.

One benefit that political theory has and continues to enjoy in Britain, which is not the case everywhere, is the absence of a tradition of subsuming fundamental political theory into other disciplines such as law. Where Laski's European audience and interlocutors were constitutional and public lawyers, in Britain his academic audience remained political scientists and philosophers. Even at the LSE where the idea of the study of law as a social science was most strongly entrenched, legal scholars failed to displace the authority and institutional position of the distinctive activity of political science and political theory. Curiously, in the field of political theory a number of prominent jurists such as Hart have tended to downplay the significance of law as a superior discipline for political theorising in contrast to the United States, where many prominent political philosophers are also academic jurists, such as Ronald Dworkin, Bruce Ackerman and Cass Sunstein.

There are a number of factors that distinguish British political theory from that of other countries or traditions, a fact that is often obscured by the tendency to lump English-language political theory together. But that still leaves a final question of what is to be learned by focusing on the patterns of British political theory. Here the answer is simple and complex. At the level of the nature, style and method of theory the idea of Britishness gives at best some contingent insights into how the subject has developed. The sources of the dominant method and style are to be found in the complex histories of other academic disciplines such as history, philosophy and the social sciences. At this level British political theory, just like British political identity, is mongrelised, drawing as it does on thinkers, theories and approaches from wherever they are developed. In the early twentieth century the sources were primarily European, during the mid-century Vienna exercised a very particular impact and most recently the United States has loomed most large in political theory and political science. British scholars have noted and often lamented this fact but it remains as central to British theory as does our eclectic ethnic and linguistic history to our national identity or identities. This is not to say that all that is of interest is from somewhere else, although it is part of the genius of the British to take from others and claim it as our own: many British scholars have shaped these more cosmopolitan traditions. Indeed, a similar history of twentieth-century American political theory would have to give a significant place to the impact of British influences on the likes of John Rawls or Ronald Dworkin. In this respect tracing the lineaments of British political theory will involve acknowledging much that is not British and thus apparently weakening the point of concentrating on 'British' political theory. If we turn attention from style and method to the subject matter of political theory such as political principles and values or the source and extent of political authority, we find that the contours of British politics have much greater significance in determining the salience of some issues and approaches over others. This also explains how the nature and form of political theory change over time. It is a truism about political theory that it is a peculiarly self-reflexive activity that spends much of its time challenging its own presuppositions. For some this can seem like a dog chasing its tail: something of limited value as a spectator sport. Yet these apparently inward-looking concerns have a bearing on how we understand politics and how we make sense of claims of importance and priority among values, principles, institutional arrangements and sites of power and authority. How those questions are addressed by practitioners of the study of political theory and why some approaches and questions achieve dominance over others can best be explained by relating these trends to patterns in the structure of British politics, which remains, for the time being, the most urgent site of politics despite the work and hopes of globalisation theorists and cosmopolitans.

Notes

1   Arguably only in the sense that Michael Oakeshott is a unique and complex figure in twentieth-century political theory. He is claimed by many as a conservative and therefore hostile to the dominant liberal rationalism that is exemplified in the works of Barry and many contemporary political theorists. Such a view is not incorrect, but it obscures his complex and subtle connection with liberalism and with contemporaries such as Hart. See Nardin, 2001; Franco, 2004.

2   See Oakeshott, 'Political Education', in *Rationalism in Politics* (1962, pp. 133–6). For the most forceful statements of the hermeneutic approach to the study of human experience see Gadamer (1975); Ricoeur (2004).

3   Skinner, 1974. See also Koselleck, 1985; Freeden, 1996. A particularly useful study of these issues is provided by the contributions to Castiglioni and Hampsher-Monk (2001).

4   There are philosophers of history such as Michael Oakeshott who imply that this form of constructivism is precisely what distinguishes the historical mode of understanding from other forms of explanation. However, the sceptical anti-foundationalism that is implicit in this approach to history is one that most historians would be comfortable with. See Oakeshott, 'The Activity of Being an Historian', in *Rationalism in Politics* (1962, pp. 137–67).

5   Many historians of political thought claim that the study of political ideas is either history or it is nothing. This is a view that has been most closely associated with Cambridge historians such as John Dunn and Quentin Skinner. For a recent corrective and defence of the subordination of history to political theory, see Philp (2008).

6   Blakey, 1855; see also the discussion in Boucher (1989); Farr (2006).

7   I have argued elsewhere that the distinction between political theory and philosophy is largely institutional, in that those in philosophy departments who study political thought tend to describe themselves as philosophers, whereas those in political science departments tend to describe themselves as political theorists; see Kelly (2006). That judgement is perhaps a little crude, although I will continue to defend an essentially institutional or practice-based account of political theory in this essay.

8   Collini, 1983. I exclude F. W. Maitland from the list as although he casts a long shadow over the development of political studies at Cambridge, his view that political science is 'either history or humbug' puts him outside the development of political theory as a distinct activity.

9   Mannheim, 1966. Mannheim was an émigré sociologist who settled in Britain and had a significant impact on British social and political theory.

10   Freeden, 1996. Freeden's work and his establishment of the *Journal of Political Ideologies*, although not yet as influential as the Cambridge School, has done much to rehabilitate the concept of ideology and the study of ideologies as a respectable activity in political theory and one that is not simply reducible to the history of political thought.

11   A good account of the so-called death of political philosophy can be found in Andrew Vincent's excellent study *The Nature of Political Theory* (2004, pp. 91–3). An equally sceptical view of the death

of political philosophy can be found in Brian Barry's 'Political Argument after Twenty Five Years', in *Political Argument* (1990).

12   Gallie, 1955–6. Gallie was to be the third holder of the Cambridge Chair of Political Science.

13   This worry was reflected in the choice of Political Studies as opposed to Political Science in the title of the main professional association of students and scholars of politics in the United Kingdom, the Political Studies Association. See Chester, 1975.

14   Berlin, 'The Pursuit of the Ideal', in *The Proper Study of Mankind* (1998, p. 1).

15   Particularly as he identifies both an *a priori* and an empirical approach as two parts of an adequate political theory. See Barry, 1995, pp. 200–13.

16   This issue has recently returned to the forefront of political theory in the works of those who criticise the 'moralism' of contemporary political theory; see Mouffe, 1993; Newey, 2001; Geuss, 2008.

17   For a recent illustration of this see Marquand (2008).

18   Mindful of the extensive literature on Locke following Laslett's famous introduction to his edition of the *Two Treatises of Government* (1960), I am not suggesting that Locke was intentionally responding to Hobbes' argument or ignoring the importance of Locke's rebuttal of Sir Robert Filmer in the *First Treatise*.

19   Bradley was perhaps the most philosophically sophisticated and penetrating of the Idealists; however his limited contribution to political philosophy was overshadowed by that of Green and especially Bosanquet. See Nicholson, 1990.

20   For a comprehensive discussion of Barker's thought see Stapleton (1994).

21   For a recent account of the origins of British political studies that illustrates and emphasises the connection between Laski's and Cole's contributions both as students of British politics and as political theorists see Kavanagh (2009).

22   For Hart's full and complex life see Lacey (2004). Hart was to have a profound influence on the ideas of the young American political philosopher John Rawls, whose subsequent book *A Theory of Justice* published in 1971 was to transform English-speaking political theory and philosophy.

23   It was precisely the fear that the wartime state would be mobilised to the problems of peace and reconstruction that underpinned F. A. Hayek's *Road to Serfdom* (1944). Hayek warned of the dangers of the state at precisely the time that many former pluralists were making their peace with the state.

24   On his involvement with organisations such as the Congress for Cultural Freedom and the magazine *Encounter* which actively challenged Soviet totalitarianism and propaganda, see Stoner-Saunders (2000).

25   A fact that is illustrated by the quotation from Popper that serves as an epigraph to Barry's 1995 book *Justice as Impartiality*.

26   Of particular interest is H. L. A. Hart's *Law, Liberty and Morality* (1963) which provides a defence and justification of the 1959 Wolfenden Committee's report on Homosexual Offences and Prostitution. See Mendus (2008).

27   A particularly Procrustean version of an Oakeshottian approach to the study of politics can be found in Johnson (1989). My own view is that Oakeshott's rejection of naturalism is much more subtle than Johnson's polemic. See Kelly (2009).

28   These are two of the four main tasks of an adequate political philosophy as set out in Rawls (2001).

29   For examples of the first see Carole Pateman, Anne Phillips and Bhikhu Parekh; for the latter see Parekh again.

30   Poulantzas counts as an honorary Frenchman as Isaiah Berlin or Karl Popper count as honorary Englishmen.

References

Anderson, P. (1966) 'Socialism and Pseudo-Empiricism', *New Left Review*, I/35, 2–42.

Arendt, H. (1958) *The Human Condition*. Chicago IL: University of Chicago Press.

Ashcraft, R. (1986) *Revolutionary Politics and Locke's Two Treatises of Government*. Princeton, NJ: Princeton University Press.

Ayer, A. J. (1936) *Language, Truth and Logic*. London: Gollancz.

Barker, R. (1978) *Political Ideas in Modern Britain*. London: Methuen.

Barry, B. (1990) 'Political Argument after Twenty Five Years', in *Political Argument*. Hemel Hempstead: Harvester Wheatsheaf, pp. xix–lxxii.

Barry, B. (1995) *Justice as Impartiality*. Oxford: Clarendon Press.

Barry, B. (1999) 'The Study of Politics as a Vocation', in J. Hayward, B. Barry and A. Brown (eds), *The British Study of Politics in the Twentieth Century*. Oxford: British Academy, pp. 423–67.

Barry, B. (2001) *Culture and Equality*. Cambridge: Polity Press.

Barry, B. (2005) *Why Social Justice Matters*. Cambridge: Polity Press.

Berlin, I. (1998) *The Proper Study of Mankind*. London: Pimlico.

Blakey, R. (1855) *The History of Political Literature from the Earliest Times*. London: Richard Bentley.

Bosanquet, B. (1899) *The Philosophical Theory of the State*. London: Macmillan.

Boucher, D. (1989) 'Philosophy, History and Practical Life: The Emergence of the History of Political Thought in England', *The Australian Journal of Politics and History*, 35 (2), 220–38.

Brink, D. O. (2004) *Perfectionism and the Common Good: Themes in the Philosophy of T. H. Green*. Oxford: Clarendon Press.

Canovan, M. (1996) *Nationhood and Political Theory*. Cheltenham: Edward Elgar.

Castiglioni, D. and Hampsher-Monk, I. (eds) (2001) *The History of Political Thought in National Context*. Cambridge: Cambridge University Press.

Chester, N. (1975) 'Political Studies in Britain: Recollections and Comments', *Political Studies*, 23 (2–3), 151–64.

Cole, G. D. H. (1921) *Guild Socialism Re-stated*. London: Leonard Parsons.

Coleridge, S. T. (1839) *On the Constitution of the Church and State According to the Idea of Each*. London: William Pickering.

Collingwood, R. G. (1993) *The Idea of History, revised edition*. Oxford: Clarendon Press.

Collini, S. (1979) *Liberalism and Sociology: L. T. Hobhouse and Political Argument in England, 1880–1914*. Cambridge: Cambridge University Press.

Collini, S. (1983) 'A Place in the Syllabus: Political Science at Cambridge', in S. Collini, D. Winch and J. Burrow, *That Noble Science of Politics*. Cambridge: Cambridge University Press, pp. 339–64.

Connolly, W. (1991) *Identity/Difference: Democratic Negotiations of the Political Paradox*. Ithaca NY: Cornell University Press.

Dicey, A.V. (1905) *Lectures on the Relation of Law and Public Opinion in England during the Nineteenth-Century*. London: Macmillan.

Dyson, K. H. F. (1980) *The State Tradition in Western Europe*. Oxford: Oxford University Press.

Farr, J. (2006) 'The History of Political Thought as a Disciplinary Genre', in J. Dryzek, B. Honig and A. Phillips (eds), *The Oxford Handbook of Political Theory*. Oxford: Oxford University Press, pp. 225–42.

Figgis, J. N. (1913) *Churches and the Modern State*. London: Longmans, Green and Co.

Franco, P. (2004) *Michael Oakeshott*. New Haven CT: Yale University Press.

Freeden, M. (1978) *The New Liberalism*. Oxford: Clarendon Press.

Freeden, M. (1996) *Ideologies and Political Theory: A Conceptual Approach*. Oxford: Clarendon Press.

Gadamer, H. G. (1975) *Truth and Method*. London: Sheed and Ward.

Gallie, W. B. (1955–6) 'Essentially Contested Concepts', *Proceedings of the Aristotelian Society*, 56, 167–98.

Geuss, R. (2008) *Philosophy and Real Politics*. Princeton NJ: Princeton University Press.

Goodin, R. E. (2009) 'The British Study of Politics', in M. Flinders, A. Gamble, C. Hay and M. Kenny (eds), *The Oxford Handbook of British Politics*. Oxford: Oxford University Press, pp. 42–55.

Gray, J. (1993) 'Oakeshott as a Liberal', in *Post-Liberalism: Studies in Political Thought*. London: Routledge, pp. 32–40.

Gray, J. (2000) *Two Faces of Liberalism*. Cambridge: Polity Press.

Harris, J. (1992) 'Political Thought and the Welfare State 1870–1940: An Intellectual Framework for British Social Policy', *Past and Present*, 135 (May), pp. 116–41.

Harris, J. (1996) 'Political Thought and the State', in S. J. D. Green and R. C. Whiting (eds), *The Boundaries of the State in Modern Britain*. Cambridge: Cambridge University Press, pp. 15–28.

Hart, H. L. A. (1955) 'Are There Any Natural Rights?' *Philosophical Review*, 64, pp. 175–91.

Hart, H. L. A. (1963) *Law, Liberty and Morality*. Oxford: Oxford University Press.

Hart, H. L. A. (1982) *Essays on Bentham*. Oxford: Clarendon Press.

Hayek, F. A. (1944) *Road to Serfdom*. London: Routledge.

Hobhouse, L. T. (1918) *The Metaphysical Theory of the State*. London: George Allen & Unwin.

Honig, B. (1993) *Political Theory and the Displacement of Politics*. Ithaca NY: Cornell University Press.

Johnson, N. (1989) *The Limits of Political Science*. Oxford: Clarendon Press.

Kavanagh, D. (2009) 'Antecedents', in M. Flinders, A. Gamble, C. Hay and M. Kenny (eds), *The Oxford Handbook of British Politics*. Oxford: Oxford University Press, pp. 29–32.

Kelly, P. (1999) 'Contextual and Non-contextual Histories of Political Thought', in J. Hayward, B. Barry and A. Brown (eds), *The British Study of Politics in the Twentieth Century*. Oxford: British Academy, pp. 37–62.

Kelly, P. (2006) 'Political Theory: The State of the Art', *Politics*, 26 (1), 47–53.

Kelly, P. (2009) 'The Oakeshottians', in M. Flinders, A. Gamble, C. Hay and M. Kenny (eds), *The Oxford Handbook of British Politics*. Oxford: Oxford University Press, pp. 154–71.

Koselleck R. (1985) *Futures Past*. Cambridge MA: MIT Press.

Kukathas, C. (2002) *The Liberal Archipelago*. Oxford: Clarendon Press.

Kymlicka, W. (1995) *Multicultural Citizenship*. Oxford: Clarendon Press.

Laborde, C. (2000) *Pluralist Thought and the State in Britain and France, 1900–25*. Basingstoke: Macmillan.

Lacey, N. (2004) *A Life of H. L. A. Hart: The Nightmare and the Noble Dream*. Oxford: Clarendon Press.

Laski, H. J. (1925) *A Grammar of Politics*. London: Allen & Unwin.

Laslett, P. (1960) 'Introduction', in *Locke: Two Treatises of Government*, ed. P. Laslett. Cambridge: Cambridge University Press, 1960, pp. 3–120.

Mannheim, K. (1966) *Ideology and Utopia: An Introduction to the Sociology of Knowledge*. London: Routledge.

Marquand, D. (2008) *Britain since 1918: The Strange Career of British Democracy*. London: Weidenfeld and Nicholson.

Marx, K. (1977) 'Theses on Feuerbach', in D. McLellan (ed.), *Karl Marx: Selected Writings*. Oxford: Oxford University Press, pp. 156–8.

Mendus, S. (2008) 'Private Faces in Public Places', in M. Kramer, C. Grant, B. Colburn and A. Hatzistuvrou (eds), *The Legacy of H. L. A. Hart: Legal, Political and Moral Philosophy*. Oxford: Clarendon Press, pp. 299–313.

Mill, J. S. (1875) *Dissertations and Discussions* (4 vols). London: Longmans, Green, Reader and Dyer.

Miller, D. (1995) *On Nationality*. Oxford: Oxford University Press.

Miller, D. (2007) *National Responsibility and Global Justice*. Oxford: Oxford University Press.

Mouffe, C. (1993) *The Return of the Political*. London: Verso.

Nardin, T. (2001) *The Philosophy of Michael Oakeshott*. University Park PA: Pennsylvania State University Press.

Newey, G. (2001) *After Politics*. Basingstoke: Palgrave.

Nicholson, P. P. (1990) *The Political Philosophy of the British Idealists: Selected Essays*. Cambridge: Cambridge University Press.

Oakeshott, M. (1962) *Rationalism in Politics*. London: Methuen.

Oakeshott, M. (1975) *On Human Conduct*. Oxford: Clarendon Press.

Parekh, B. (2000a) *The Future of a Multi-Ethnic Britain*. London: Profile Books.

Parekh, B. (2000b) *Rethinking Multiculturalism*. Basingstoke: Palgrave.

Pateman, C. (1974) *Participation and Democratic Theory*. Cambridge: Cambridge University Press.

Pateman, C. (1979) *The Problem of Political Obligation*. Chichester: John Wiley.

Pateman, C. (1988) *The Sexual Contract*. Cambridge: Polity Press.

Pateman, C. (1990) *The Disorder of Women*. Cambridge: Polity Press.

Phillips, A. (1991) *Engendering Democracy*. Cambridge: Polity Press.

Phillips, A. (1995) *The Politics of Presence*. Oxford: Oxford University Press.

Phillips, A. (1999) *Which Inequalities Matter*. Cambridge: Polity Press.

Phillips, A. (2007) *Multiculturalism without Culture*. Princeton NJ: Princeton University Press.

Philp, M. (2008) 'Political Theory and History', in D. Leopold and M. Stears (eds), *Political Theory: Methods and Approaches*. Oxford: Oxford University Press, pp. 128–49.

Pocock, J. G. A. (2009) *Political Thought and History*. Cambridge: Cambridge University Press.

Popper, K. (1945) *The Open Society and Its Enemies, Vol. 2: Hegel and Marx*. London: Routledge and Kegan Paul.

Popper, K. (1963) *Conjectures and Refutations*. London: Routledge.

Rawls, J. (2001) *Justice as Fairness: A Restatement*, Cambridge MA: Harvard University Press.

Ricoeur, P. (2004) *Memory, History and Forgetting*. Chicago IL: University of Chicago Press.

Schmitt, C. (1976) *The Concept of the Political*, ed. G. Schwab. New Brunswick NJ: Rutgers University Press.

Sidgwick, H. (1891) *The Elements of Politics*. London: Macmillan.

Skinner, Q. (1974) 'Some Problems in the Analysis of Political Thought and Action', *Political Theory*, 2 (3), 277–303.

Stapleton, J. (1994) *Englishness and the Study of Politics*. Cambridge: Cambridge University Press.

Stoner-Saunders, F. (2000) *Who Paid the Piper*. London: Granta.

Tully, J. (1995) *Strange Multiplicity*. Cambridge: Cambridge University Press.

Vincent, A. (2004) *The Nature of Political Theory*. Oxford: Clarendon Press.

Weldon, T. D. (1953) *The Vocabulary of Politics*. Harmondsworth: Penguin.

Wokler, R. (2001) 'The Professoriate of Political Thought in England since 1914: A Tale of Three Chairs', in D. Castiglioni and I. Hampsher-Monk (eds), *The History of Political Thought in National Context*. Cambridge: Cambridge University Press, pp. 134–58.

Chapter 2

Nature of the End of the State and Consequent Limit of State Action

Bernard Bosanquet

1

According to the course of thought which we have been pursuing, the distinction between the individual on the one hand, and the social or political whole on the other, is not relevant to the question where the "end" of man in Society is to be sought. For the conceptions of Society and the individual are correlative conceptions through and through; at whatever level, therefore, we take the one, we are bound to construe the other as at the same level; so that, to distinguish the one element from the other as superior from inferior, or as means from end, becomes a contradiction in terms. If we begin by drawing boundaries round the individual, the boundaries which we draw reproduce themselves in society conceived as a total of such individuals, and the question of means and end, as we saw in Bentham's case,[1] takes the form whether "each" is the means to the welfare of "all," or "all" to the welfare of "each"; the distinction thus becoming purely verbal. While, if we set no limit to individuality, accepting it as an end which may involve any degree of self-completeness and therefore of comprehensiveness, we find it to be actually one with, to consist in, a realisation of the stuff and content of which social unity is made. Such apparent exceptions as art and religion, which may be taken to be independent of the social medium, are really, as we shall see, its quintessence,[2] though at a stage where plurality of persons becomes unimportant. They are therefore not truly to be considered as ends pertaining to the individual, in any sense in which the individual is held to have an essence separable from that of society. This antithesis is really, however, absurd. There are not two opposable sets of contents concerned in the matter at all; but a single web of content which in its totality is society and in its differentiations the individuals. To make the totality the means to the differentiations or vice versa is like making a drama the means to the characters, or the characters to the drama. But the poet or the religious genius may be like a character that concentrates in itself the significance of the entire drama, and so in some degree transcends the dramatic form. Only, this is done by including the essence of the whole plurality, not by being independent of it.[3]

The only way, then, in which the idea of means and end can be applied to the social whole and its parts, is to take Society when at its lower level, being dealt with under the aspect of mere plurality, as a means to what it is at its higher level, when realised as a communion of individualities at their best. But from this point of view we get no distinction of means and end as between Individuals and Society. What we get is Individuals and Society alike, as understood and partly existing at one level (that of commonplace Individualism and Collectivism), taken as a means to both Individuals and Society at a higher level. As we have seen, the only true explanation of self-government is to throw the reality of the self outside what passes for its average nature, and in this sense the average nature may be treated as a means to the truer or fuller self – as something, that is to say, which is instrumental to the latter, and has no rights against it.[4]

2

For us, then, the ultimate end of Society and the State as of the individual is the realisation of the best life. The difficulty of defining the best life does not trouble us, because we rely throughout on the fundamental logic of human nature qua rational. We think ourselves no more called upon to specify in advance what will be the details of the life which satisfies an intelligent being as such, than we are called upon to specify in advance what will be the details of the knowledge which satisfies an intelligent being as such. Wherever a human being touches practice, as wherever he touches theory, we find him driven on by his intolerance of contradictions towards shaping his life as a whole. What we mean by "good" and "truth" is practical and theoretical experience in so far as the logic which underlies man's whole nature permits him to repose in it. And the best life is the life which has most of this general character – the character which, so far as realised, satisfies the fundamental logic of man's capacities.

Now, it is plain that this best life can only be realised in consciousness, that being the medium of all satisfaction and the only true type of a whole in experience. And all consciousness, as experienced by man, is on one side particular, attached to bodies, and exclusive of consciousnesses attached to other bodies. In a sense, it is true that no one consciousness can partake of or actually enter into another. Thus, it is apt to be held, as we have amply seen, that the essential danger of State interference lies in the intrusion of something originated by "others" upon a distinct particular consciousness, whose distinction and particularity – its freedom – are thus impaired. It is all-important to our point of view that this prejudice should be dispelled. Force or automatic custom or authoritative tradition or "suggestion" are not hostile to one individuality because they come from "others," but because their nature is contradictory to the nature of the highest self-assertion of mind, because they are, so to speak, in a medium incompatible with its medium. They are just as hostile to this self-assertion, just as alien, if they emanate, as they constantly do, from conflicting elements in our complex private experience, as if they come to us, as we say, "from without." The question is of their "nature" and tendency, not of their centre of origin. Individuals are limited and isolated in many ways. But their true individuality does not lie in their isolation but in that distinctive act or service by which they pass into unique contributions to the universal. True individuality, as we have said, is not in the minimisation which forbids further subdivision, but in the maximisation which includes the greatest possible being in an inviolable unity. It is not, therefore, the intrusion upon isolation, as such, that interferes with individuality, it is the intrusion, upon a growing unity of consciousness, of a medium hostile to its growth.

But we have seen that force, automatism, and suggestion are in some ways neces-sary to the support and maintenance of the human consciousness, owing to its animal limitations. They are, indeed, as is well known, the condition of its progress. Therefore, in promoting the best life, these aids must be employed by society as exercising absolute power – viz., by the State. And the problem presented by their employment is *not* a question of the "interference of the State with the Individual" – an antithesis which is meaningless so far as it implies that society can be interfer-ing with the individual, and not interfering with itself; but it is a question how far and in what way the use of force and the like by the State is a hindrance to the end for which the State, the social power, itself exists. In other words, it is to be ascer-tained how far the fullest self-assertion of the social universal in its differences – the best life – can be promoted or is likely to be endangered by means which are of a different order, and so in some circumstances opposed to it. The point is not that I and some thousands more break in by force upon *you* in particular and violate *your* isolation; but that such breaking in by force, whoever does it and whoever suffers by it, and even if through passion or obsession *you* do it to *yourself* and *I* to *my* self, is hostile prima facie to the living logic of the will, which alone can create a unity and realise a best. How then, and under what reservations, in the complicated conflict of the fuller and narrower self, can this dangerous drug of violence be administered, so to speak, as a counter-poison to tendencies which would otherwise give no chance to the logical will? With this difficulty in our minds, we will endeavour to determine the general principle on which force and menace should be used by the State, and a routine be mechanically maintained by it.

3

We have hitherto spoken of the State and Society as almost convertible terms.[5] And in fact it is part of our argument that the influences of Society differ only in degree from the powers of the State, and that the explanation of both is ultimately the same. But on the other hand, it is also part of our argument that the State as such is a necessary factor in civilised life; and that no true ideal lies in the direction of minimising its individuality or restricting its absolute power. By the State, then, we mean Society as a unit, recognised as rightly exercising control over its members through absolute physical power. The limits of the unit are, of course, determined by what looks like historical accident; but there is logic underneath the apparent accident, and the most tremendous political questions turn upon the delimitation of political units. A principle, so to speak, of political parsimony – *entia non sunt multiplicanda praeter necessitatem*, "two organisations will not survive when one can do the work" – is always tending to expand the political unit. The limits of the common experience necessary for effective self-government are always operating to control this expansion. We might therefore suggest, as a principle determining the area of states, "the widest territorial area compatible with the unity of experience which is demanded by effective self-government." But the State de facto (which is also *de jure*) is the Society which is recognised as exercising compulsory power over its members, and as presenting itself qua a single independent corporation among other independent corporations. Without such power, or where, if anywhere, it does not exist, there can be no ultimate and effective adjustment of the claims of individuals, and of the various social groups in which individuals are involved. It is the need for this ultimate effective adjustment which constitutes the need that every individual in civilised life should belong to one state, and to one only. Otherwise conflicting adjustments might be imposed upon him by diverse authorities having equal power and right to enforce his obedience. That Society, then, is a State, which is habitually recognised as a unit lawfully exercising force. We saw that the characteristics of Society pass gradually into those of the State. It would not be true that Society is a State only as actually exercising force; but it would perhaps be true to say that State action as such, though far from being limited to the downright exercise of force, yet consists of all that side of social action which depends on the character of ultimate arbiter and regulator, maintainer of mechanical routine, and source of authoritative suggestion, a character which is one with the right to exercise force in the last resort.

The end of the State, then, is the end of Society and of the Individual – the best life, as determined by the fundamental logic of the will. The means at its disposal, qua State, always partake of the nature of force, though this does not exclude their having other aspects as well. Taxation may have the most reasonable and even the most popular purpose, yet the generality and justice of its incidence, and the certainty of its productiveness, can only be secured by compulsion. No State could undertake its work on the basis of voluntary contributions. A universal end, we might say, is indeed not a mere general rule; but you cannot carry out a universal end in a plurality of units – and a set of human individuals is always in one aspect a plurality of units – without enforcing general rules.

4

Here, then, we have our problem more closely determined than in previous chapters [of PTS]. There we saw, in general, that self-government can have no meaning unless we can "really" will something which we do not always "actually" will. And we were led to look for a clue to our real or implied will in the social spirit as incorporated in laws and institutions, that is to say in Society as a working whole reflected in the full system of the consciousness which composed it.

We supposed ourselves prepared, then, it would seem, to do and suffer anything which would promote the best life of the whole – that maximisation of our being which, from the nature of our real will, we saw to be imperative upon us – a demand implied in every volition and from which we could never escape.

But now we are face to face with the question what we *are* called upon to do or to suffer as members of a State, in promotion of the best life. We have here to renew, from another standpoint, the discussions of chapter iii [PTS]. The governing fact of the situation is that the means of action at our disposal as members of a State are not, on their distinctive side, *in pari materia*[6] with the end. It is true that the State, as an intelligent system, can appeal by reasoning and persuasion to the logical will as such. It constantly does so in various forms, and a State which did nothing of the kind either directly or indirectly would not possess the recognition which is necessary to its very existence. So far its work is *in pari materia* with the end, being a direct element in the expansion of mind and character in their own spiritual medium of thought and will. But this side of its work is not distinctive of the State, and, therefore, is not that for which more particularly it exists. Its distinctive attribute is to be ultimate arbiter and regulator of claims, the guarantor of life as *at least* a workable system in the bodily world. It is in its ultimateness de facto that the differentia lies which separates it from the innumerable other groupings and associations which go to make up our complex life. This is shown in the fact that each of us, as we have said, must belong to a State, and can belong to one only. It is because the authority is ultimate that it must be single. Now, authority which is to be ultimate in a sphere including the world of bodily action, must be an authority which can use force. And it is for this reason that, as we said, force is involved in the distinctive attributes of the State.

But force is not *in pari materia* with the expansion of mind and character in their spiritual medium. And, thus, there at once appears an inadequacy of means to end as between the distinctive *modus operandi*[7] of the State and the end in virtue of which it claims to represent the "real" will.

What is the bearing of this inadequacy? What is the most that the State, in its distinctive capacity, can do towards promoting a form of life which it recognises as desirable? Its direct power is limited to securing the performance of external[8] actions. This does not mean merely the performance of outward bodily movements, such as might be brought to pass by actual physical force. It is remarkable that actual physical force plays a very small part in the work of any decently ordered State. When we say that the State can do no more than secure the performance of external actions, we do not exclude from the action the intention to act in a certain way. Without such an intention there is no action in the sense of human action at all, but merely a muscular movement. It is necessary for the State to attach importance to intention, which is involved in the idea of human action, and is the only medium through which the muscular movements of human beings can be determined with any degree of certainty. The State, then, through its authority, backed ultimately by physical force, can produce, with a fair degree of certainty, the intention to act in a certain way, and therefore the actions themselves. Why do we call intentional actions, so produced, external actions only?

It is because the State is unable to determine that the action shall be done from the ground or motive which alone would give it immediate value or durable certainty as an element in the best life. On the contrary, in so far as the doing of the action is due to the distinctive mode of operation which belongs to the State, due, that is to say, to the hope of reward or the fear of punishment, its value as an element in the best life is *ipso facto* destroyed, except in so far as its ulterior effects are concerned. An action performed in this sense under compulsion is not a true part of the will.[9] It is an intention adopted from submissiveness or selfishness, and lacks not only the moral value, but what is partly the same thing, the reliable constancy of principle, displayed in an action which arises out of the permanent purposes of a life.

The State, then, as such, can only secure the performance of external actions. That is to say, it can only enforce as much intention[10] as is necessary to ensure, on the whole, compliance with requirements stated in terms of movements affecting the outer world. So far from promoting the performance of actions which enter into the best life, its operations, where effective, must directly narrow the area of such actions by stimulating lower motives as regards some portion of it.

5

The State, then, in its distinctive capacity, has no agency at its command for influencing conduct, but such as may be used to produce an external course of behaviour by the injunction or prohibition of external acts, in enforcing which acts the State will take note of intentions, so far as it can infer them, because it is only through them that its influence can be exerted.

The relation of such a means to the imperative end, on which we have seen that political obligation depends, must be in a certain sense negative. The means is one which cannot directly promote the end, and which even tends to narrow its sphere. What it can effect is to remove obstacles, to destroy conditions hostile to the realisation of the end. This brings us back to a principle laid down by Kant,[11] and in its bare statement strongly resembling Mill's contention. When force is opposed to freedom, a force that repels that force is *right*. Here, of course, all depends upon what we mean by freedom, and in what sense we think that force can hinder hindrances to it. If freedom meant for us the empty hexagon[12] round each individual, the principle would take us back to Mill's Liberty. If, on the other hand, we failed to grasp the discrepancy between force of any kind and the positive nature of the common good which we take to be freedom, the principle would lead us straight to a machine-made Utopia. For its negative character cannot restrain it from some degree of positive action. It is only through positive operation that a negation or opposition can find reality in the world. And the limits of its positive action must depend on the precise bearings of the negation which it puts in force.

Now, for us, after the explanations which have been given, the negative nature of our principle is to be seriously pressed, although its action has to take positive form. The State is in its right when it forcibly hinders a hindrance to the best life or common good. In hindering such hindrances it will indeed do positive acts. It may try to hinder illiteracy and intemperance by compelling education and by municipalising the liquor traffic. Why not, it will be asked, hinder also unemployment by universal employment, overcrowding by universal house building, and immorality by punishing immoral and rewarding moral actions? Here comes the value of remembering that, according to our principle State action is negative in its immediate bearing, though positive both in its actual doings and its ultimate purpose. On every problem the question must recur, "Is the proposed measure *bona fide* confined to hindering a hindrance, or is it attempting direct promotion of the common good by force?" For it is to be borne in mind throughout that whatever acts are enforced are, so far as the force operates, withdrawn from the higher life. The promotion of morality by force, for instance, is an absolute self-contradiction.[13] No general principle will tell us how in particular to solve this subtle question, apart from common sense and special experience. But there is perhaps more to be learned from this principle, if approached with *bona fides*,[14] than from most generalities of philosophy on social or ethical topics. It is well, I think, constantly to apply the idea of removing hindrances, in criticism of our efforts to promote the best life by means involving compulsion. We ought, as a rule, when we propose action involving compulsion, to be able to show a definite tendency to growth, or a definite reserve of capacity, which is frustrated by a known impediment, the removal of which is a small matter compared to the capacities to be set free.[15] For it should be remarked that every act done by the public power has one aspect of encroachment, however slight, on the sphere of character and intelligence, if only by using funds raised by taxation, or by introducing an automatic arrangement into life. It can, therefore, only be justified if it liberates resources of character and intelligence greater beyond all question than the encroachment which it involves. This relation is altogether perversely presented, as we saw above, if it is treated as an encroachment of society upon individuals. All this is beside the mark. The serious point is, that it is an interference, *so far as compulsion operates in it*, of one type of action with another and higher type of action; of automatism, so to speak, with intelligent volition. The higher type of action, the embodiment of the common good in logical growth, is so far from being merely individual as opposed to social, that it is the whole end and purpose in the name of which allegiance to society can be demanded from any individual. As in the private so in the general life, every encroachment of automatism must be justified by opening new possibilities to self-conscious development, if it is not to mean degeneration and senility.

It is the same principle in other words which Green lays down when he says in effect[16] that only such acts (or omissions) should be enforced by the public power as it is better should take place from any motive whatever than not take place at all. When, that is, we enforce an act (or omission) by law, we should be prepared to say, "Granting that this act, which might conceivably have come to be done from a sense of duty, now may come to be done for the most part from a fear of punishment, or from a mechanical tendency to submit to external rules (attended by the practical inconveniences of insensibility, half-heartedness, and evasion which attach to acts so enforced), still so much depends, for the higher life of the people, upon the external conditions at stake, that we think it worth while to enforce the act (or omission) though our eyes are fully open to the risk of extended automatism."

Here we may have to meet our own arguments against Mill. "You said it was a contradiction," we shall be told, "to admit coercion as a means to liberty. But here you are advocating coercion as a means to something as incompatible with it, in so far as it is operative, as our 'liberty,' viz., a certain state of mind and will. If the area of coercion is necessarily subtracted from the area of liberty, as you argued above, is not the area of coercion necessarily subtracted from that to be occupied by the desired growth of will and character?"

The answer depends, as we indicated in chapter iii [PTS], on the difference between bare liberty and a determinate growth. If your liberty is wholly indeterminate, then every restraint is a reduction of it. You cannot increase a quantity which is all of one kind by taking away a part of it. And, in fact, the idea that there was or could have been a previous general liberty, of which a part was given up in exchange for more, is a mere illusion. Liberty has grown up within the positive determinations of life, as they have expanded and come to fit mankind better.

But if the quantity to be increased is a determinate growth, of a type whose general character is known, the problem is transformed. It is the commonest of experiences that hindrances can be removed and favourable conditions maintained, if this has to be done, not with a view to every conceivable and inconceivable development, but for a growth the general line of which is known. In this case, as the whole expands, the restraints and the liberty, the room for action, may even increase together.[17] This is not only true in universal theory, but much more important than is always remembered in special theory or practice. The possibility of promoting freedom or well-being by compulsion depends very greatly indeed on the unity of habit and experience which binds together a single community. The more the life has in common, the more definite and automatic arrangements you may safely make in promotion of it. The rules of my household, which inconvenience its members no more than their clothes do, would produce a rebellion if they were enforced by law even throughout our village.

Thus, then, we may maintain our principle of the limits of distinctive State action. The peculiarity of it is that it allows of positive acts and interferences motived by an ultimate positive purpose, but with a bearing on that purpose which is primarily negative or indirect. However positive, as actual facts, are the conditions which it may become advisable to maintain, they may always, on the side which is distinctively due to State compulsion, be regarded as the hindrance of hindrances. And the *bona-fide* application of this principle will really be, when aided by special experience, in some degree a valuable clue to what ought to be done. It is only putting in other words the rule of action followed by all practical men in matters of which they have genuine experience. We may think, for instance, of the problem involved in State maintenance of universities. It is easy to vote money, to build buildings, and to pass statutes. But none of these things will secure the objects of a university. Money and buildings and statutes may throw open an arena, so to speak, for the work of willing minds in learning and education. But the work itself is in a different medium from anything which can be produced by compulsion, and is so far less vital as it is conditioned by the operation of force upon minds which demand no work of the kind.

But here we meet a difficulty of principle.[18] Do we say that no external conditions are more than hindrances of hindrances to the best life? Do we deny that the best life can be positively promoted by external conditions; or if we admit this, do we still deny that it can be positively promoted by the work of the State? The answer has already been implied, but may be explicitly restated. We refused[19] to separate mind from its embodiment in material things, and so to be drawn into a purely inward theory of morality. It would be exaggeration to call such external conditions as, e.g., first-rate educational apparatus,[20] mere negative conditions of the best life. But then, we are now asked, cannot the State supply such external conditions by expenditure compulsorily provided for, and if so, is not our principle destroyed, viz., the limitation of State action to the hindrance of hindrances?

The difficulty springs from the fact, that the State, as using compulsion, is only one side of Society, and its action is only one side of social action. If first-rate educational apparatus is called into existence by a State endowment, the first-rateness of the apparatus is not due to the compulsion applied to taxpayers, which rather, so far, negatives the action of intelligent will as such. But it must be due, in one way or another, to the fact that first-rate ability in the way of devising apparatus was somewhere pressing for an outlet, which, by a stroke of the pickaxe, so to speak, the public power was able to provide for it. We must not confuse the element of compulsion, which is the side of social action distinctly belonging to State interference, with the whole of the material results which liberated intelligence produces. When we say, then, that the State as such can do nothing for the best life but hinder hindrances to it, the principle applies in the strictest sense only to the compulsory or automatic side of State action, which must, so to speak, be reckoned against it[21] in comparing its products with those which are spontaneous social growths throughout.

But it is further true that material conditions which come close to life, such as houses, wages, educational apparatus, do not wholly escape our principle. They occupy a very interesting middle region between mere hindrances of hindrances and the actual stimulation of mind and will. On the one side they are charged with mind and character, and so far are actual elements in the best life. On the other side they depend on external actions, and therefore seem accessible to State compulsion, which extends to all external doings and omissions. But what we have to observe is, and it is in practice most important, that, *as charged with mind and will,* these material facts may not be accessible to State compulsion while, *as accessible to State compulsion* pure and simple they may forfeit their character of being charged with mind and will. This shows itself in two ways. First, just because they are facts of a kind which come so close to life (in other words depend so greatly upon being charged with mind and will), state compulsion cannot with certainty secure even their apparent existence. They fail bodily, like human beings, if there is no spirit to keep them alive. The relation of wages to the standard of life illustrates this point. Secondly, supposing that for a time, by Herculean efforts of compulsion, which must call active intelligence to its aid, such facts are made to present a satisfactory appearance of existence, none the less, so far as they are characterised by compulsion, they may lose their character as elements in the best life. That is to say, they may fail to benefit those whom they are meant to benefit. The fact may fail to be absorbed in the life.

The principle of the hindrance of hindrances is most valuable and luminous when rightly grasped, just in these middle cases. A pretty and healthy house, which its inhabitant is fond of, is an element in the best life. Who could doubt it who knows what home life is? But in order that putting a family out of a bad house into a good one should give rise to such an element of the best life, it is strictly and precisely necessary that the case or policy should come under our principle. That is to say, unless there was a better life struggling to utter itself, and the deadlift of interference[22] just removed an obstacle which bound it down, the good house will not be an element in a better life, and the encroachment on the ground of volition will have been made without compensation – a fact which may show itself in many fatal ways. If, on the other hand, the struggling tendency to a better life has power[23] to effect the change without the deadlift from outside, then the result is certain and wholly to the good.

Thus we may say that every law and institution, every external fact maintained by the public power, must be judged by the degree in which it sets at liberty a growth of mind and spirit. It is a problem partly of removing obstacles to growth, and partly of the division of labour between consciousness and automatism.

It ought to occur to the reader that the ground here assigned for the limitation of State action – that is, of social action through the public power – is not prima facie in harmony with the account of political obligation, according to which laws and institutions represented a real self or general will, recognised by individuals as implied in the common good which was imperative upon them. We spoke, for example, of being forced to be free, and of the system of law and order as representing the higher self.[24] And yet we are now saying that in as far as force is operative through compulsion and authoritative suggestion, it is a means which can only reach its end through a negation.

But this prima facie contradiction is really a proof of the vitality of our principle. It follows from the fact that we accept self-government in the full strength of both its factors and can deal with it on this basis. The social system under which we live, taking it as one which does not demand immediate revolution, represents the general will and higher self as a whole to the community as a whole and can only stand by virtue of that representation being recognised. Our loyalty to it makes us men and citizens, and is the main spiritualising force of our lives. But something in all of us, and much in some of us, is recalcitrant through rebellion, indolence, incompetence, or ignorance. And it is only on these elements that the public power operates as power through compulsion or authoritative suggestion. Thus, the general will when it meets us as force, and authority resting on force, and not as a social suggestion which we spontaneously rise to accept, comes to us *ex hypothesi* as something which claims to be ourself, but which, for the moment, we more or less fail to recognise. And, according to the adjustment between it and our complex and largely unintelligent self, it may abandon us to automatism, or stir us in rebellion or recognition, and so may hinder the fuller life in us or remove hindrances to it. It seems worth while to distinguish two main cases of the relation between the ordinary self and the general will. One of these cases covers the whole of our everyday law-abiding life, in its grades of active loyalty, acceptance of suggestion, and automatic acquiescence; and consists of the relation of our ordinary self to the general system of rights maintained by the State as ultimate regulator and arbiter. The other is confined to more exceptional situations, and has to do with collision between the particular and the general will, as treated in the theory of punishment. The subject of reward may be mentioned at the same time, if only to show why it is almost an empty heading in political theory. We will end this chapter, therefore, with a general account of the system of rights and of reward and punishment.

6

The idea of individual rights comes down to us from the doctrine of natural right, and has generally been discussed with reference to it. We need not now go back upon the illusions connected with the notion of natural right. It is enough if we bear in mind that we inherit from it the important idea of a positive law which is what it ought to be. A right,[25] then, has both a legal and a moral reference. It is a claim which can be enforced at law, which no moral imperative can be; but it is also recognised to be a claim which ought to be capable of enforcement at law, and thus it has a moral aspect. The case in which positive enactment and the moral "ought" appear to diverge will be considered below. But a typical "right" unites the two sides. It both is, and ought to be, capable of being enforced at law.

Its peculiar position follows from what we have seen to be the end of the State, and the means at its disposal. The end of the State is moral purpose, imperative on its members. But its distinctive action is restricted to removing hindrances to the end, that is, to lending its force to overcome – both in mind and in externals essential to mind – obstacles which otherwise would obstruct the realisation of the end. The whole of the conditions thus enforced is the whole of "rights" attaching to the selves, who, standing in definite relations, constitute the community. For it is in these selves that the end of the State is real, and it is by maintaining and regulating their claims to the removal of obstructions that the State is able to promote the end for which it exists. Rights then are claims recognised by the State, i.e., by Society acting as ultimate authority, to the maintenance of conditions favourable to the best life. And if we ask in general for a definition and limitation of State action as such, the answer is, in a simple phrase, that State action is coincident with the maintenance of rights.

The system of rights which the State maintains may be regarded from different points of view.

First, (α) from the point of view of the whole community, that is, as the general result in the promotion of good life obtained by the working of a free Society, as a statesman or outside critic might regard it. Thus looked at, the system of rights may be described as "the organic whole of the outward conditions necessary to the rational life," or "that which is really necessary to the maintenance of material conditions essential to the existence and perfection of human personality."[26] This point of view is essential as a full contradiction of that uncritical conception by which rights are regarded as something with which the individual is invested in his aspect of isolation, and independently of his relation to the end. It forces us away from this false particularisation, and compels us to consider the whole State-maintained order in its connectedness as a single expression of a common good or will, in so far as such a good can find utterance in a system of external acts and habits. And it enables us to weigh the value which belongs to the maintenance of any tolerable social order, simply because it is an order, and so far enables life to be lived, and a determinate, if limited, common good to be realised. From other points of view we are apt to neglect this characteristic, and to forget how great is the effect, for the possibilities of life throughout, of the mere fact that a social order exists. Hegel observes that a man thinks it a matter of course that he goes back to his house after nightfall in security. He does not reflect to what he owes it. Yet this very naturalness, so to speak, of living in a social order is perhaps the most important foundation which the State can furnish to the better life. "*Si monumentum quaeris, circumspice.*"[27] If we ask how it affects our will, the answer is that it forms our world. Speaking broadly, the members of a civilised community have seen nothing but order in their lives, and could not accommodate their action to anything else.

It should be mentioned as a danger of this point of view that, fascinated by the spectacle of the social fabric as a whole, we may fail to distinguish what in it is the mere maintenance of rights, and what is the growth which such maintenance can promote but cannot constitute. Thus we may lose all idea of the true limits of State action.

(β) We may regard this complex of rights from the standpoint of the selves or persons who compose the community. It is in these selves, as we have seen, that the social good is actual, and it is to their differentiated functions,[28] which constitute their life and the end of the community, that the sub-groupings of rights, or conditions of good life, have to be adjusted each to each like suits of clothes. The rights are, from this point of view, primarily the external incidents, so far as maintained by law – the authoritative vesture as it were – of a person's position in the world of his community. And we shall do well to regard the nature of rights, as attaching to selves or persons, from this point of view of a place or position in the order determined by law. It has been argued, I do not know with what justice, that, in considering the relations of particles in space, the proper course would be to regard their positions or distances from each other as the primary fact, and to treat attributions of attractive and repulsive forces as modes of expressing the maintenance of the necessary positions rather than as descriptive of real causes which bring it about. At least, it appears to me, such a conception may well be applied to the relative ideas of right and obligation. What comes first, we may say, is the position, the place or places, function or functions, determined by the nature of the best life as displayed in a certain community, and the capacity of the individual self for a unique contribution to that best life. Such places and functions are imperative; they are the fuller self in the particular person, and make up the particular person as he passes into the fuller self. His hold on this *is* his true will, in other words, his apprehension of the general will. Such a way of speaking may seem unreally simplified when we look at the myriad relations of modern life and the sort of abstraction by which the individual is apt to become a rolling stone with no assignable place – indeed "gathering no moss" – and to pass through his positions and relations as if they were stations on a railway journey. But in truth it is only simplified and not falsified. If we look with care we shall see that it, or nothing, is true of all lives.

The Position, then, is the real fact – the vocation, place or function, which is simply one reading of the person's actual self and relations in the world in which he lives. Having thoroughly grasped this primary fact, we can readily deal with the points of view which present the position or its incidents in the partial aspects of rights or obligations.

(i) A right, we said, is a *claim* recognised by society and enforced by the State. My place or position, then, and its incidents, so far as sanctioned by the State, constitute my rights, when thought of as something which I claim, or regard as powers instrumental to my purposes. A right thus regarded is not anything primary. It is a way of looking at certain conditions, which, by reason of their relation to the end of the whole as manifested in me, are imperative alike for me and for others. It is, further, the particular way of looking at these conditions which is in question when I claim them or am presumed to claim them, as powers secured to me with a view to an end which I accept as mine. I *have* the rights no less in virtue of my presumed capacity for the end, if I am in fact indifferent to the end. But, in this case, though attributed *ab extra*[29] as rights, they tend to pass into obligations.

(ii) If rights are an imperative "position" or function, when looked at as a group of State-secured powers claimed by a person for a certain end, obligations are the opposite aspect of such a position or group of powers. That is to say, the conditions of a "position" are regarded as obligations in as far as they are thought of as requiring enforcement, and therefore, primarily, from the point of view of persons not directly identified with the "position" or end to which they are instrumental. Rights are claimed, obligations are owed. And prima facie rights are claimed *by* a person, and obligations are owed *to* a person, being his rights as regarded by those against whom they are enforceable.

Thus, the distinction of self and others, which we refused to take as the basis of society, makes itself prominent in the region of compulsion. The reason is that compulsion is confined to hindering or producing external acts, and is excluded from producing an act in its relation to a moral end, that is, the exercise of a right in its true sense; though it can enforce an act which in fact favours the possibility of acting towards a moral end – that is, an obligation. This is the same thing as saying that normally a right is what *I* claim, and the obligation relative to it is what *you* owe; as an obligation is that which can be enforced, and that is an act or omission apart from the willing of an end; and a right involves what cannot be enforced, viz., the relation of an act to an end in a person's will. But even here the distinction of self and others is hardly ultimate. The obligation on me to maintain my parents becomes almost a right[30] if I claim the task as a privilege. And many rights of my position may actually be erected into, or more commonly may give rise to, obligations incumbent on me for the sake of my position or function. If the exercise of the franchise were made compulsory that would be a right treated also as an obligation; but it might be urged that qua obligation it was held due to the position of others, and only qua right to my own "position." But if the law interferes with my poisoning myself[31] either by drains or with alcohol, that, I presume, is the enforcement of an obligation arising out of my own position and function as a man and a citizen, which makes reasonable care for my life imperative upon me.

(γ) It is commonly said that every right implies a duty. This has two meanings, which should be distinguished.

In the one case, (i) for "duty" should be read "obligation," i.e., a demand enforceable by law. This simply means that every "position" may be regarded as involving either powers secured or conditions enforced, which are one and the same thing differently looked at. Roughly speaking, they are the same thing as differently looked at by one person and by other persons. My right to walk along the high-road involves an obligation upon all other persons not to obstruct me, and in the last resort the State will send horse, foot and artillery rather than let me be causelessly obstructed in walking along the high-road.

It is also true that every position which can be the source of obligations enforceable in favour of my rights is likewise a link with obligations enforceable on me in favour of the rights of others. By claiming a right in virtue of my position I recognise and testify to the general system of law according to which I am reciprocally under obligation to respect the rights, or rather the function and position, of others. My rights then imply obligations both in others, and perhaps in myself, correlative to these rights, and in me correlative to the rights of others. But it cannot strictly be said that the obligations are the source of the rights, or the rights of the obligations. Both are the varied external conditions of "positions" as regarded from different points of view.

But (ii) there is a different sense in which every right implies a duty. And this, the true meaning of the phrase, is involved in what we have said of the nature of a "position." All rights, as claims which both are and ought to be enforceable by law, derive their imperative authority from their relation to an end which enters into the better life. All rights, then, are powers instrumental to making the best of human capacities, and can only be recognised or exercised upon this ground.

In this sense, the duty is the purpose with a view to which the right is secured, and not merely a corresponding obligation equally derived from a common ground; and the right and duty are not distinguished as something claimed by self and something owed to others, but the duty as an imperative purpose, and the right as a power secured because instrumental to it.

(δ) We have treated rights throughout as claims, the enforcement of which by the State is merely the climax of their recognition by society. Why do we thus demand recognition for rights? If we deny that there can be unrecognised rights, do we not surrender human freedom to despotism or to popular caprice?

(i) In dealing with the general question why recognition is demanded as an essential of rights, we must remember what we took to be the nature of society and the source of obligation. We conceived a society to be a structure of intelligences so related as to co-operate with and to imply one another. We took the source of obligation to lie in the fact that the logic of the whole is operative in every part, and consequently that every part has a reality which goes beyond its average self and identifies it with the whole, making demands upon it in doing so.

Now, we are said to "recognise" anything when it comes to us with a consciousness of familiarity, as something in which we feel at home. And this is our general attitude to the demands which the logic of the whole, implied in our every act, is continuously making upon us. It is involved in the interdependence of minds which has been explained to constitute *the mind* of which the visible community is the body. A teacher's behaviour towards his pupils, for example, implies a certain special kind of interdependence between their minds. What he can do for them is conditioned by what they expect of him and are ready to do for him and vice versa. The relation of each to the other is a special form of "recognition." That is to say, the mind of each has a definite and positive attitude towards that of the other, which is based on, or rather, so far as it goes, simply *is*, the relation of their "positions" to each other. Thus, social positions or vocations actually have their being in the medium of recognition. They *are* the attitudes of minds towards one another, through which their several distinct characteristics are instrumental to a common good.

Thus, then, a right, being a power secured in order to fill a position, is simply a part of the fact that such a position is recognised as instrumental to the common good. It is impossible to argue that the position may exist, and not be recognised. For we are speaking of a relation of minds, and, in so far as minds are united into a single system by their attitudes towards each other, their "positions" and the recognition of them are one and the same thing. Their attitude, receptive, co-operative, tolerant, and the like, is so far a recognition, though not necessarily a reflective recognition. Probably this is what is intended by those who speak of imitation or other analogous principles as the ultimate social fact. They do not mean the repetition of another person's conduct, though that may enter in part into the relation of interdependence. They mean the conscious adoption[32] of an attitude towards

others, embodying the relations between the "positions" which social logic assigns
to each.

(ii) But then the question presses upon us – "If we deny that there can be unrecognised rights, do we not surrender human freedom to despotism or to popular
caprice?"

The sting of this suggestion is taken out when we thoroughly grasp the idea that
recognition is a matter of logic, working on and through experience, and not of
choice or fancy. If my mind has *no* attitude to yours, there is no interdependence
and I cannot be a party to securing you rights. You are not, for me, a sharer in a
capacity for a common good, which each of us inevitably respects. A dog or a tree
may be an instrument to the good life, and it may therefore be right to treat it in a
certain way, but it cannot be a subject of rights. If my mind *has* an attitude to yours,
then there is certainly a recognition between us, and the nature of that recognition
and what it involves are matters for reasoning and for the appeal to experience. It
is idle for me, for instance, to communicate with you by language or to buy and
sell with you, perhaps even idle to go to war with you,[33] and still to say that I recognise no capacity in you for a common good. My behaviour is then inconsistent
with itself, and the question takes the form what rights are involved in the recognition of you which experience demonstrates. No person and no society is consistent
with itself, and the proof and amendment of their inconsistency is always possible.
And, one inconsistency being amended, the path is opened to progress by the
emergence of another. If slaves come to be recognised as free but not as citizens,
this of itself opens a road by which the new freeman may make good his claim that
it is an inconsistency not to recognise him as a citizen.

But no right can be founded on my mere desire to do what I like.[34] The wish for
this is the sting of the claim to unrecognised rights, and this wish is to be met, as
the fear that our view might lead to despotism was met. The matter is one of fact
and logic, not of fancies and wishes. If I desire to assert an unrecognised right, I
must show what "position" involves it, and how that position asserts itself in the
system of recognitions which is the social mind, and my point can only be established universally with regard to a certain type of position, and not merely for myself
as a particular A or B. In other words, I must show that the alleged right is a requirement of the realisation of capacities for good and, further, that it does not demand
a sacrifice of capacities now being realised, out of proportion to the capacities which
it would enable to assert themselves. I must show, in short, that in so far as the
claim in question is not secured by the State, Society is inconsistent with itself, and
falls short of being what it professes to be, an organ of good life. And all my showing
gives no *right*, till it has modified the law. To maintain a right against the State by
force or disobedience is rebellion, and, in considering the duty of rebellion, we have
to set the whole value of the existence of social order against the importance of the
matter in which we think Society defective. There can hardly be a duty to rebellion
in a State in which law can be altered by constitutional process.

The State-maintained system of rights, then, in its relation to the normal self and
will of ordinary citizens with their varying moods of enthusiasm and indolence,

may be compared to the automatic action of a human body. Automatic actions are such as we perform in walking, eating, dressing, playing the piano or riding the bicycle. They have been formed by consciousness, and are of a character subservient to its purposes, and obedient to its signals. As a rule, they demand no effort of attention, and in this way attention is economised and enabled to devote itself to problems which demand its intenser efforts. They are relegated to automatism because they are uniform, necessary, and external – "external" in the sense explained above, that the way in which they are required makes it enough if they are done, whatever their motives, or with no motives at all.

By far the greater bulk of the system of rights is related in this way to normal consciousness. We may pay taxes, abstain from fraud and assault, use the roads and the post-office, and enjoy our general security, without knowing that we are doing or enjoying anything that demands special attention. Partly, of course, attention is being given by other consciousnesses to maintaining the securities and facilities of our life. Even so, the arrangement is automatic in so far as there is no reason for arousing the general attention in respect to it; but to a varying extent it is automatic throughout, and engrained in the system and habits of the whole people. We are all supposed to know the whole law. Not even a judge has it all in his knowledge at any one time; but the meaning is that it roughly expresses our habits, and we live according to it without great difficulty, and expect each other to do so. This automatism is not harmful, but absolutely right and necessary, so long as we relegate to it only "external" matters; i.e. such as are necessary to be done, motive or no motive, in some way which can be generally laid down. Thus used, it is an indispensable condition of progress. It represents the ground won and settled by our civilisation, and leaves us free to think and will such matters as have their value in and through being thought and willed rightly. If we try to relegate these to automatism, then moral and intellectual death has set in.

But if the system of rights is automatic, how can it rest on recognition? Automatic actions, we must remember, are still of a texture, so to speak, continuous with consciousness. "Recognition" expresses very fairly our habitual attitude towards them in ourselves and others. We might think, for example, of the system of habits and expectations which forms our household routine. We go through it for the most part automatically, while "recognising" the "position" of those who share it with us, and respecting the life which is its end. At points here and there in which it affects the deeper possibilities of our being, our attention becomes active, and we assert our position with enthusiasm and conscientiousness. Our attitude to the social system of rights is something like this. The whole order has our habitual recognition; we are aware of and respect more or less the imperative end on which it rests – the claim of a common good upon us all. Within the framework of this order there is room for all degrees of laxity and conscientiousness; but, in any case, it is only at certain points, which either concern our special capacity or demand readjustment in the general interest, that intense active attention is possible or desirable.

The view here taken of automatism and attention in the social whole impairs neither the unity of intelligence throughout society nor the individual's recognition of this unity as a self liable to be opposed to his usual self. As to the former point, every individual mind shows exactly the same phenomena, of a *continuum* largely automatic, and thoroughly alive only in certain regions, connected, but not thoroughly coherent. As to the latter point, permeation of the individual by the habits of social automatism does not prevent, but rather gives material for, his tendency to abstract himself from the whole, and to frame an attitude for himself inconsistent with his true "position," against which tendency the imperative recognition of his true self has constantly to be exerted.

7

We have finally to deal with the actual application by the State of its ultimate resource for the maintenance of rights, viz., force. Superior force may be exercised upon human nature both by rewards and by punishments. In both respects its exercise by the State would fall generally within the lines of automatism; that is to say, it would be a case of the promotion of an end by means other than the influence of an idea of that end upon the will. But, owing to the subtle continuity of human nature throughout all its phases, we shall find that there is something more than this to be said, and that the idea of the end is operative in a peculiar way just where the agencies that promote it appear to be most alien and mechanical. In so far as this is the case, the general theory of the negative character of State action has to be modified, as we foresaw,[35] by the theory of punishment. Prima facie, however, it is true that reward and punishment belong to the automatic element of social life. They arise in no direct relation of the will to the end. They are a reaction of the automatic system, instrumental to the end, against a friction or obstacle which intrudes upon it, or (in the case of rewards) upon the opposite of a friction or obstacle. There is no object in pressing a comparison into every detail; but perhaps, as social and individual automatism do really bear the same kind of relation to consciousness, it may be pointed out that reward and punishment correspond in some degree to the pleasures and pains of a high-class secondary automatism, say of riding or of reading, i.e. of something specially conducive to enhanced life. Such activities bring pleasure when unimpeded, and pain when sharply interrupted by a start or blunder which jars upon us. Putting this latter case in language which carries out the analogy to punishment, we might say that the formed habit of action, unconsciously or semi-consciously relevant to the end or fuller life, is obstructed by some partial state of mind, and their conflict is accompanied with recognition, pain, and vexation. "What a fool I was," we exclaim, "to ride carelessly at that corner," or "to let that plan for a holiday interrupt me in my morning's reading."

It may seem remarkable that reward plays a small and apparently decreasing part in the self-management of society by the public power. To the naive Athenian,[36] it seemed a natural instrument for the encouragement of public spirit, probably rather by a want of discrimination between motives than by a real belief in political selfishness. In European countries honours still appear to play a considerable part, but on analysis it would be found less than it seems. Partly they are recognitions of important functions, and thus conditions rather than rewards. To a great extent, again, they recognise existing facts, and are rather consequences of the respect which society feels for certain types of life (with very curious results in regions where the general mind is inexperienced, e.g. in fine art) than means employed to regulate the conduct of citizens. We should think a soldier mean whose aim was a peerage, still more a poet or an artist. I hardly know that rewards adjudged by the State, as distinct from compensations, exist in the United States of America.[37] Rewards then fill no place correlative to that of punishments, and the reason seems plain. Punishment corresponds much better to the negative method which alone is open to the State for the maintenance of rights. For Punishment proclaims its negative character, and no one can suppose it laudable simply to be deterred from wrong-doing by fear of punishment. But though precisely the same principle applies to meritorious actions done with a view to reward, an illusion is almost certain to arise which will hide the principle in this case. For, if reward is largely used as an induce-ment to actions conducive to the best life, it is almost certain that it will be used as an inducement to actions the value and certainty of which depend on the state of will to which they are due. And then the distinction between getting them done, motive or no motive, which is the true region of State action, and their being done with a certain motive, which is necessary to give them either the highest practical or any moral value, is pretty sure to be obliterated, and the range of the moral will trenched upon in its higher portion and with a constant tendency to self-decep-tion.[38] It is the same truth in other words when we point out that taking reward and punishment, as interferences, only to deal with exceptional cases, reward would deal with the exceptionally good. Therefore, again, reward must either make an impossible attempt to deal with all the normal as good which involves the danger of *de*-moralising the whole of normal life, or must take the line of specially promot-ing what is exceptionally conducive to good life; in which case confusion is certain to arise from interference with the delicate middle class of external actions analysed above.[39] And thus it is only what we should expect when we find that States having no *damnosa hereditas*[40] of a craving for personal honours are hardly acquainted with the bestowal of rewards by the public power.

It will be sufficient, then, to complete the account of State action in maintenance of rights by some account of the nature and principles of punishment.

And we may profitably begin by recalling M. Durkheim's suggestion, which was mentioned in a former chapter [PTS].[41] Punishment, he observes, from the simplest and most actual point of view, includes in itself all those sides which theory has tended to regard as incompatible. It is, in essence, simply the reaction of a strong and determinate collective sentiment against an act which offends it. It is idle to include such a reaction entirely under the head either of reformation, or of retali-ation, or of prevention. An aggression is *ipso facto* a sign of character, an injury, and a menace; and the reaction against it is equally *ipso facto* an attempt to affect character, a retaliation against an injury, and a deterrent or preventive against a menace. When we fire up at aggression it is pretty much a chance whether we say

"I am going to teach him better manners," or "I am going to serve him out," or "I am going to see that he doesn't do that again." A consideration of each of these aspects is necessary to do justice both to the theories and to the facts.

(i) An obvious point of view, and the first perhaps to appear in philosophy, though strongly opposed to early law, is that the aim of punishment is to make the offender good. As test of the adequacy of this doctrine by itself, the question may be put, "If pleasures would cure the offender, ought he to be given pleasures?" The doctrine, however, does not, by any means, altogether incline to leniency. For it carries as a corollary the extirpation of the incurable, which Plato proposes in a passage of singularly modern quality, when he suggests the co-operation of judges and physicians in maintaining the moral and physical health of society.[42]

The first comment that occurs to us is, that by a mere medical treatment of the offender, including or consisting of pleasant conditions, if helpful to his cure, the interest of society seems to be disregarded. What is to become of the maintenance of rights, if aggressors have to anticipate a pleasant or lenient "cure"? It may be true that brutal punishments stimulate a criminal temper in the people rather than check it; but it is a long way from this to laying down that there is no need for terror to be associated with crime. To suppose that pleasures may simply act throughout as pains, is playing with words and throws no light on the question. If we leave words their meaning, we must say that punishment must be deterrent for others as well as reformatory for the offender, and therefore in some degree painful. It is true, however, that the offender, as a human being, and presumably capable of a common good, has, as Green puts it, "reversionary rights" of humanity, and these punishment must so far as possible respect.

But there is a deeper difficulty. If the reformation theory is to be seriously distinguished from the other theories of punishment, it has a meaning which is unjust to the offender himself. It implies that his offence is a merely natural evil, like disease, and can be cured by therapeutic treatment directed to removing its causes. But this is to treat him not as a human being; to treat him as a "patient," not as an agent; to exclude him from the general recognition that makes us men. (If the therapeutic treatment includes a recognition and chastisement of the offender's bad will[43] – the form of which chastisement may, of course, be very variously modified – then there is no longer anything to distinguish the reformatory theory from other theories of punishment.) It has been lately pointed out[44] what a confusion is involved in the claim that beings, who are irresponsible and so incapable of guilt, are therefore in the strict sense innocent. Here are the true objects for a pure reformatory theory. Here that may freely be done, as to creatures incapable of rights, which is kindest for them and safest for society, from quasi-medical treatment to extirpation. There is no guilt in them to demand punishment, but there is no human will in them to have the rights of innocence.

But, applied to responsible human beings, such a theory, if really kept to its distinctive contention, is an insult. It leads to the notion that the State may take hold of any man, whose life or ideas are thought capable of improvement, and set to work to ameliorate them by forcible treatment. There is no true punishment except where one is an offender against a system of rights which he shares, and therefore against himself. And such an offender has a right to the recognition of his hostile will; it is inhuman to treat him as a wild animal or a child, whom we simply mould to our aims, Without such a recognition, to be punished is not, according to the old Scotch phrase, to be "justified."

(ii) The idea of retaliation or retribution, though in history the oldest conception of punishment,[45] may be taken in theory as a protest against the conception that punishment is only a means for making a man better. Its strong point is its definite idea of the offender. The offender is a responsible person, belonging to a certain order which he recognises as entering into him and as entered into by him, and he has made actual an intention hostile to this order. He has, as Plato's Socrates insists in the *Crito*, destroyed the order so far as in him lies.[46] In other words, he has violated the system of rights which the State exists to maintain, and by which alone he and others are secured in the exercise of any capacity for good, this security consisting in their reciprocal respect for the system. His hostile will stands up and defies the right, in so far as his personality is asserted through a tangible deed which embodies the wrong. It is necessary, then, that the power which maintains the system of rights should not merely, if possible, undo the external harm which has been done, but should strike down the hostile will which has defied the right by doing that harm. The end or true self is in the medium of mind and will, and is contradicted and nullified so far as a hostile will is permitted to triumph.

It is obvious, however, that the means by which the hostile will can be negatived fall prima facie within the region of automatism. The recalcitrant element of consciousness is not susceptible to the end as an idea or it would not be recalcitrant. The end can here assert itself, agreeably to the general principle of State action, only through external action the mental effects of which cannot be precisely estimated. It might, therefore, seem that the pain produced by the reaction of the automatic system on the aberrant consciousness – the punishment – was simply a natural pain, which might act as a deterrent from aberration, but had no visible connection with the true whole or end for the mind of the offender. We shall speak below of the sense in which punishment is deterrent or preventive. But it is to be noted at this point that a high-class secondary automatism, with which all along we have compared the system of rights as engrained in the habits of a people, retains a very close connection with consciousness. We do not indeed will every step that we walk, but we only walk while we will to walk, and so with the whole system of routine automatism which is the method and organ of our daily life. At any interruption, any hindrance or failure, consciousness starts up, and the end of the whole routine comes sharply back upon us through our aberration.

So it is with punishment. Primarily, no doubt, chastisement by pain, and the appeal to fear and to submissiveness, is effective through our lower nature, and, in as far as operative, substitutes selfish motives for the will that wills the good, and so narrows its sphere. But there is more behind. The automatic system is pulsing with the vitality of the end to which it is instrumental; and when we kick against the pricks, and it reacts upon us in pain, this pain has subtle connections throughout the whole of our being. It brings us to our senses, as we say; that is, it suggests, more or less, a consciousness of what the habitual system means, and of what we have committed in offending against it. When one stumbles and hurts his foot, he may look up and see that he is off the path. If a man is told that the way he works his factory or keeps his tenement houses is rendering him liable to fine or imprisonment, then, if he is an ordinary, careless, but respectable citizen, he will feel something of a shock, and recognise that he was getting too neglectful of the rights of other, and that, in being pulled up, he is brought back to himself. His citizen honour will be touched. He will not like to be below the average which the common conscience had embodied in law.

When we come to the actual criminal consciousness, the form which the recognition may take in fact may vary greatly; and as an extreme there may be a furious hostility against the whole recognised system of law, either involving self-outlawry through a despair of reconciliation, or arising through some sort of habitual conspiracy in which the man finds his chosen law and order as against that recognised by the State.[47] But after all, we are dealing with a question of social logic and not of empirical psychology. And it must be laid down that, in as far as any sane man fails altogether to recognise in any form the assertion of something which he normally respects in the law which punishes him (putting aside what he takes to be miscarriage of justice), he is outlawed by himself and the essentials of citizenship are not in him. Doubtless, if an uneducated man were told, in theoretical language, that in being punished for an assault he was realising his own will, he would think it cruel nonsense. But this is a mere question of language, and has really nothing to do with the essential state of his consciousness. He would understand perfectly well that he was being served as he would say anyone should be served, whom he saw acting as he had done, in a case where his own passions were not engaged. And this recognition, in whatever form it is admitted, carries the consequence which we affirm.

In short, then, compulsion through punishment and the fear of it, though primarily acting on the lower self, does tend, when the conditions of true punishment exist (i.e. the reaction of a system of rights violated by one who shares in it), to a recognition of the end by the person punished, and may so far be regarded as his own will, implied in the maintenance of a system to which he is a party, returning upon himself in the form of pain. And this is the theory of punishment as retributive. The test doctrine of the theory may be found in Kant's saying that, even though a society were about to be dissolved by agreement, the last murderer in prison must be executed before it breaks up.[48] The punishment is, so to speak, his right, of which he must not be defrauded.

There are two natural perversions of this theory.

The first is to confuse the necessary retribution or reaction of the general self, through the State, with personal vengeance.[49] Even in the vulgar form, when a brutal murder evokes a general desire to have the offender served out,[50] the general or social indignation is not the same as the selfish desire for revenge. It is the offspring of a rough notion of law and humanity, and of the feeling that a striking aggression upon them demands to be strikingly put down. Such a sentiment is a part of the consciousness which maintains the system of rights, and can hardly be absent where that consciousness is strong.

The second perversion consists in the superstition that punishment should be "equivalent" to offence. In a sense, we have seen, it is *identical*; i.e. it is a return of the offender's act upon himself by a connection inevitable in a moral organism. But as for *equivalence* of pain inflicted, either with the pain caused by the offence or with its guilt, the state knows nothing of it and has no means of securing it. It cannot estimate either pain or moral guilt. Punishment cannot be adapted to factors which cannot be known. And further, the attempt to punish for immorality has evils of its own.[51] The graduation of punishments must depend on wholly different principles, which we will consider in speaking of punishment as preventive or deterrent.

(iii) The graduation of punishments must be almost entirely determined by experience of their operation as deterrents. It is to be borne in mind, indeed, (a) that the "reversionary rights" of humanity in the offender are not to be needlessly sacrificed, and (b) that the true essence of punishment, as punishment, the negation of the offender's anti-social will, is in some way to be secured. But these conditions are included in the preventive or deterrent theory of punishment, if completely understood; if, that is to say, it is made clear precisely what it is that is to be prevented.

If we speak of punishment, then, as having for its aim to be deterrent or preventive, we must not understand this to mean that a majority, or any persons in power, may rightly prevent, by the threat of penalties, any acts that seem to them to be inconvenient.

That which is to be prevented by punishment is a violation of the State-maintained system of rights by a person who is a party to that system, and therefore the above-mentioned conditions, implied in a true understanding of the reformatory and retributive aspects of punishment, are also involved in it as deterrent. But, this being admitted, we may add to them the distinctive principle on which a deterrent theory insists. If a lighter punishment deter as effectively as a heavier, it is wrong to impose the heavier. For the precise aim of State action is the maintenance of rights; and if rights are effectively maintained without the heavier punishment, the aim of the State does not justify its imposition. It is well known that success in the maintenance of rights depends not only on the severity of punishments, but also on the true adjustment of the rights themselves to human ends, and on that certainty of detecting crime which is a result of efficient government. And it must always be considered, in dealing with a relative failure of the deterrent power of punishment in regard to certain offences, whether a better adjustment of rights or a greater certainty of detection will not meet the end more effectively than increased severity of punishment. We have seen that the equivalence of punishment and offence is really a meaningless superstition. And there is no principle on which punishment can be rationally graduated, except its deterrent power as learned by experience. This view corresponds to the true limits of State action as determined by the means at its disposal compared with the end which is its justification, and is therefore, when grasped in its full meaning as not denying the nature of punishment, the true theory of it.

We saw, in speaking of punishment as retributive, in what sense it can and cannot rest upon a judgment imputing moral guilt. Of degrees of moral guilt as manifested in the particular acts of individuals, the State, like all of us, is necessarily ignorant. But this is not to say that punishment is wholly divorced from a just moral sentiment. Undoubtedly it implies and rests upon a disapproval of that hostile attitude to the system of rights which is implied in the realised intention constituting the violation of right. Though in practice the distinction between civil and criminal law in England carries out no thoroughly logical demarcation, yet it is true on the whole to say with Hegel that, in the matter of a civil action, there is no violation of right as such, but only a question in whom a certain right resides; while in a matter of criminal law there is involved an infraction of right as such, which by implication is a denial of the whole sphere of law and order.[52] This infraction the general conscience disapproves, and its disapproval is embodied in a forcible dealing with the offender, however that dealing may be graduated by other considerations.

I may touch here on an interesting point of detail, following Green. If punishment is essentially graduated according to its deterrent power, and not according to moral guilt, how does it come to pass that "extenuating circumstances" are allowed to influence sentences? That they do so really, if not nominally, even in England, there can be no doubt. Is it not that they indicate a less degree of wickedness in the offender than the offence in question would normally presuppose? It would seem that judges themselves are sometimes under this impression. But it may well be that they act under a right instinct and assign a wrong reason. For it is impossible to get over the fact that moral iniquity is something which cannot be really estimated. The true reason for allowing circumstances which change the character of the act to influence the sentence is that in changing its character, they may take it out of the class of offences to which it prima facie belongs, and from which men need to be deterred by a recognised amount of severity. If a man is starving and steals a turnip, his offence, being so exceptionally conditioned, does not threaten the general right of property, and does not need to be associated with any high degree of terror in order to protect that right. A man who steals under no extraordinary pressure of need does what might become a common practice if not associated with as much terror as is found by experience to deter men from theft.

It may be said, in some exceptional emergency, "But many men are now starving; ought not the theft of food, on the principle of prevention, to be now punished with extreme severity, as otherwise it is likely to become common?" Or in general, ought not severity to increase with temptation or provocation, as a greater deterrent is needed to counterbalance this? The case in which the temptation or provocation is exceptional has just been dealt with. But if abnormal temptation or provocation becomes common, as in a famine, or in some excited condition of public feeling, then it must be remembered that not one right only, but the system of rights as such, is what the State has to maintain. If starvation is common, some readjustment of rights, or at least some temporary protection of the right to live, is the remedy indicated, and not, or not solely, increased severity in dealing with theft.[53] If provocation becomes common, then the rights of those provoked must be remembered, and the provocation itself perhaps made punishable, like the singing of faction songs in Ireland. Punishment is to protect rights, not to encourage wrongs.

Thus, we have seen the true nature and aims of punishment as following from the aim of the State in maintaining the system of rights instrumental to the fullest life. The three main aspects of punishment which we have considered are really inseparable, and each, if properly explained, expands so as to include the others.[54]

We may, in conclusion, sum up the whole theory of State action in the formula which we inherit from Rousseau – that Sovereignty is the exercise of the General Will.

First. All State action is General in its bearing and justification, even if particular, or rather concrete, in its details. It is embodied in a *system* of rights, and there is no element of it which is not determined by a bearing upon a public interest. The verification of this truth, throughout, for example, our English system of public and private Acts of Parliament, would run parallel to the logical theory of the Universal Judgment as it passes into Judgments whose subjects are proper names. But the immediate point is that no rights are absolute, or detached from the whole, but all have their warrant in the aim of the whole, which at the same time implies their adjustment and regulation according to general principles. This generality of law is practically an immense protection to individuals against arbitrary interference. It makes every regulation strike a class and not a single person.

And, secondly. All State action is at bottom the exercise of a Will; the real Will, or the Will as logically implied in intelligences as such, and more or less recognised as imperative upon them. And therefore, though in the form of force it acts through automatism, that is, not directly as conscious Will, but through a system which gives rise to acts by influences apparently alien, yet the root and source of the whole structure is of the nature of Will, and its end, like that of organic automatism, is to clear the road for true volition; it is "forcing men to be free." And in so far as by misdirection of the automatic[55] process it encroaches on the region of living Will – the region where the good realises itself directly by its own force as a motive – it is "sawing off the branch on which it sits," and superseding the aim by the instrument.

Notes

1 Chapter iii [*The Philosophical Theory of the State* (hereafter PTS)].
2 This is well put, if slightly exaggerated, by Mr [R.R.] Marett, *Threshold of Religion*, [London: Methuen, 1909, 1914], pp. 159–60: "Primarily and directly the subject, the owner, as it were, of religious experience, is the religious society not the individual."
3 See Introd. to 2nd edn, p. 23 [above] [PTS].
4 [Compare here T.H. Green's remark that "a right against society, as such, is an impossibility." *Lectures on the Principles of Political Obligation*, with preface by Bernard Bosanquet (London: Longmans, Green, 1895), p. 145 (sect. 141).]

5   See, however, pp. 156ff., and Introd. to 2nd edn, p. 22 [PTS]. [On the distinction between state and society, see "Letters on 'Society and State,'" below, pp. 312–23.] [PTS]

6   [See Introd. to 2nd edn, note 10.] [PTS]

7   [*modus operandi*: a plan of working]

8   Green, *Principles of Political Obligation*, [loc. cit., note 4] pp. 34, 35 [sect. 11].

9   The theory of punishment will modify this proposition in some degree.

10   On this question *vide* [see] Green's very thorough discussion. [*Principles of Political Obligation*, loc. cit., note 4, sects 11ff.] It is true, of course, that the law takes account of intention, and does not, e.g., treat accidental homicide as murder, the difference between them being a difference of intention. But it is obvious that, in attempting to influence human action at all, so much account as this must be taken of intention; for intention is necessary to constitute a human action. An unintentional movement of the muscles cannot be guarded against by laws and penalties; it is only through the intention that deterrent or other motives can get at the action, and a constant law-abiding disposition is the best security for law-abiding action. On the importance of intention and disposition as affording a certainty of action, Bentham, who wholly rejects judgment according to moral motive, is as emphatic as possible. [See Jeremy Bentham, *An Introduction to the Principles of Morals and Legislation*, ed. J.H. Burns and H.L.A. Hart (Oxford: Clarendon Press, 1996), chs viii, x, xi.]

11   W., [ch.] ix, [p.] 34. [See *Immanuel Kant's Sämmtliche Werke*, ed. Karl Rosenkranz and Wilhelm Friedrich Schubert (Leipzig: L. Voss, 1838–42), 14 v. Kant argues that "Any opposition that counteracts the hindrance of an effect promotes that effect and is consistent with it. Now, everything that is unjust is a hindrance to freedom according to universal laws. Coercion, however, is a hindrance or opposition to freedom. Consequently, if a certain use of freedom is itself a hindrance to freedom according to universal laws (that is, unjust), then the use of coercion to counteract it, in as much as it is the prevention of a hindrance to freedom, is consistent with freedom according to universal laws; in other words, this use of coercion is just." See Kant, *The Metaphysical Elements of Justice*, trans. John Ladd (Indianapolis: Bobbs-Merrill, 1965), pp. 35–6, (Introduction, sect. E), vol, VI, p. 231 of the Königliche Preussische Akademie der Wissenschaft edn (Berlin, 1902–38)]. Fichte remarked on the pregnancy of this principle. [Gottlieb Fichte (1762–1814) was a disciple of Kant, and an important idealist philosopher in his own right. See his *The Science of Ethics as Based on the Science of Knowledge*, trans. A.E. Kroger (London: K. Paul, Trench, Trubner, 1897).] See further on this question, Introd. to 2nd edn, pp. 20ff.

12   See above p. 99 [PTS].

13   "You will admit," it was once said, "that compulsory religion is better than no religion." "I fail to see the distinction," was the reply.

14   Among true students *bona fides* [good faith, honest intention] is presupposed. The range opened to sophistry by a principle of this kind, which commends positive action with a negative bearing for a positive end, is, of course, immeasurable. Practically, I believe that *bona fides* is about the first and last necessity for the application of political ideas.

15   Perhaps I may adduce an instance of real interest. It has been argued that ship-masters should be induced by a premium to ship boys as apprentices to the trade of seamanship, and that training for this trade should be fostered by local authorities like any other form of technical education. The argument which really told in the discussion consisted of statistics which seemed to prove a widespread eagerness on the part of boys and their parents that they should enter a maritime life, and the existence of a hindrance simply in the absence of adequate training for a few years during boyhood.

16   *Principles of Political Obligation*, [loc. cit., note 4] p. 38 [sect. 15].

17   See the author's essay "Liberty and Legislation" in [his] *Civilisation of Christendom* [(London: Swan Sonnenschein, 1899), pp. 358–83.]

18   See further Introd. to 2nd edn, pp. 25ff. [PTS]

19   See above, pp. 66ff. [PTS]

20   See Thring on the importance of this, in Parkin's Life of him. [Sir George Robert Parkin, *Edward Thring* (London: Macmillan, 1898).] Note, however, also the modification of his view by the adventure of Uppingham-on-the-Sea. [Edward Thring (1821–1887) was a school master and reformer; his reforms at the Uppingham School influenced English public schools.]

21 Subject to what will be said on the theory of rights and punishment.

22 The policy of a deadlift in the housing of the people is justified by the arrears incurred during the war, and by the public demand that has been awakened. But it is quite plain that if a recurrence of the deficit is to be avoided, a quite new and thoroughly popular interest in the work must be sustained. [Note added in] 1919.

23 Many forms of *social* co-operation, it must be remembered, need no deadlift from the *State* as such. We are not setting self-help against co-operation, but will against automatism.

24 [See above, pp. 101ff., 116, 153ff.]. [PTS]

25 This is a right in the fullest sense. The nature of a merely legal or merely moral right will be illustrated below.

26 Kraus and Henrici, cited by Green, *Principles of Political Obligation*, [loc. cit., note 4], p. 35 [sect. 11]. Cp, "The system of right is the realm of realised freedom, the world of mind produced by the mind as a second nature." (Hegel, *Philosophie d. Rechts*, sect. 4). [In his note Green actually cites Herman Ulrici's discussion of Kraus' and Henrici's two definitions of "Recht" or "jus naturæ." Ulrici, *Gott und der Mensch*, vol. II, *Grundzüge der Praktischen Philosophie, Naturrecht, Ethik und Aesthetik* (Leipzig: Y. O. Weigel, 1873–4), p. 219. See also Hegel, *The Philosophy of Right*, trans. T.M. Knox (Oxford: Clarendon Press, 1942), p. 30 (sect. 4). Knox translates the passage: "the system of right is the realm of freedom made actual, the world of mind brought out of itself like a second nature."]

27 [*Si monumentum quaeris, circumspice*: If you seek his monument, look around.]

28 I do not say merely social functions, i.e., functions dealing directly with "others" as such.

29 [*ab extra*: from without].

30 I do not know that I can compel my parents to be maintained by me, and therefore it is not my legal right to maintain them; but at least the obligation, if I claim it, ceases to depend on force. An East-End Londoner will say, "He had a right to maintain his father," meaning that he was bound to do so; and Jeannie Deans says, "I have no right to have stories told about my family without my consent," representing her own claim as a negative obligation on herself as well as on others. She represents the thought, "I have a right that you should not tell stories," etc., in a form which puts it as a case of the thought, "You have no right to tell stories," disregarding the distinction between herself and others as accidental. [Jeannie Deans is the heroine of Sir Walter Scott's *The Heart of Midlothian* (London: J.M. Dent, 1988). Jeannie Deans goes to London to obtain a pardon for her half-sister, who has been convicted of the murder of her illegitimate child.]

31 The law used to interfere with bad sanitation only as a "nuisance," i.e. as an annoyance to "others." It now interferes with any state of things dangerous to life as such, which probably means that a change of theory has unconsciously set in. Legislation for dangerous trades almost proves the point, though here it is possible to urge that the employer is put under obligation for the sake of his workers, and not the workers for their own sake. But the distinction is hardly real.

32 To call this imitation is something like calling fine art imitation. Really, in both cases, we find a re-arrangement and modification of material, incident to a new expression. The process, if we must name it, is "relative suggestion" rather than imitation.

33 As distinct from hunting. We do not go to war with lions and tigers.

34 Green, *Principles of Political Obligation*, [loc. cit., note 4] p. 149 [sect. 144].

35 See pp. 190ff [PTS].

36 "Speech of Pericles," Thucydides, ii. 46: "Where there are the greatest rewards of merit, there will be the best men to do the work of the State." [Rex Warner translates the passage thus: "Where the rewards of valour are the greatest, there you will find also the best and the bravest spirits among the people." "Pericles' Funeral Oration," in Thucydides, *The Peloponnesian War* (Harmondsworth: Penguin, 1978), p. 151 (Book II, 46).] Contrast Plato's principle that there can be no sound government while public service is done with a view to reward. ["And for this reason, I said, money and honour have no attraction for them; good men do not wish to be openly demanding payment for governing and so to get the name of hirelings, nor by secretly helping themselves out of the public revenues to get the name of thieves. And not being ambitious they do not care about honour." Jowett translation of Plato's *Republic* (New York: Vintage Books [1894] 1991), Book I, 347.]

37   The precise theory of the grants in money made to soldiers or sailors, for distinguished service, is not easy to state. But it seems clear that they are not intended to act as motives. They are essentially a recognition after the act, not an inducement held out before it.

38   It is perhaps permissible to observe in general, what is very well known to all who have much experience of what is called philanthropy, that the tendency to distinguish it by public honours is exceedingly dangerous to its quality, which depends entirely on that energy and purity of intelligence which can only accompany the deepest and highest motives. Mere vulgar self-seeking is not the danger (though it does occur) so much as obfuscation of intelligence through a mixture of aims and ideas. [Bosanquet was deeply involved in the work of Charity Organisation Society. See the editors' Introduction and the essay on "Idealism in Social Work," (pp. 358ff.) in this volume [PTS].]

39   See p. 190 [PTS].

40   [*damnosa hereditas*: a damaging inheritance, an inheritance that involves a loss.]

41   [Chapter ii.] See p. 73 [PTS].

42   *Republic*, 409, 410. ["Why, I said, you join physicians and judges. Now the most skilful physicians are those who, from their youth upwards, have combined with the knowledge of their art the greatest experience of disease; they had better not be robust in health, and should have had all manner of diseases in their own persons. For the body, as I conceive, is not the instrument with which they cure the body; in that case we could not allow them ever to be or to have been sickly; but they cure the body with the mind, and the mind which has become and is sick can cure nothing. ... This is the sort of medicine, and this is the sort of law, which you sanction in your State. They will minister to better natures, giving health both of soul and of body; but those who are diseased in their bodies they will leave to die, and the corrupt and incurable souls they will put an end to themselves. That is clearly the best thing both for the patients and for the State." Jowett translation of *The Republic*, loc. cit., note 36, Book III, 408–9.]

43   Plato's reformatory theory seems to involve this. And the author of *Erewhon*, to the best of my recollection, only half adheres to his principle that disease is to be punished, and wickedness medically treated. For his "treatment" of wickedness is plainly punitive, and thus he altogether abandons the idea of medical cure which his antithesis suggests. [Samuel Butler (1835–1902), was the author of the utopian *Erewhon; or, Over the Range* (London: Trübner, 1872).]

44   Mr [F.H.] Bradley ["Some Remarks on Punishment"] in the *International Journal of Ethics*, [vol. 4] April, 1894 [pp. 269–84].

45   We saw that, even in its earliest forms, it cannot really be taken to exclude the other aspects.

46   [In this Platonic dialogue Crito, while visiting Socrates in prison, is trying to convince him to escape. Socrates imagines himself in a discussion with the Laws (about whether he should escape), and they say to him: "Now Socrates, what are you proposing to do? Can you deny that by this act you are contemplating you intend, so far as you have the power, to destroy us, the Laws, and the whole State as well?" *Crito*, 50b, trans. Hugh Tredennick (Harmondsworth: Penguin, 1954), pp. 89–90.]

47   See the account of the Mafia in Marion Crawford's *Corleone* [, *a tale of Sicily* (London: Macmillan, 1896)]. Accepting this as described, it simply is the social will in which the population of a certain region find their substitute for the State.

48   [Kant, *The Metaphysical Elements of Justice*, loc. cit., note 11, p. 102. Vol. VI, p. 333 of the Preussische Akademie edition.]

49   It may be noted that Durkheim, relying chiefly on early religious sentiment, denies Maine's view that criminal law arises out of private feud. [Sir Henry Maine (1822–1888) is best known for his *Ancient Law: its Connection with the Early History of Society and its Relation to Modern Society* (London: Murray, 1885). Maine was an exponent of historical legal scholarship, seeking to trace the evolution of human society and its forms of social organisation.]

50   Green, *Principles of Political Obligation*, [loc. cit., note 4] p. 184 [sect. 183].

51   See above, p. 94 [PTS].

52   [See Hegel, *The Philosophy of Right*, loc. cit., note 26, pp. 64–73 (sects. 82–103).]

53   Though for the sake of all parties, and to avoid temptation, a strong policing of threatened districts may be desirable in such circumstances.

54   See further the essay "On the Growing Repugnance to Punishment" in *Some Suggestions in Ethics* (London: Macmillan, 1918) [ch. viii].

55   It must not be forgotten that the State is, by its nature, under a constant temptation to throw its weight on the side of the automatic process. A most striking example is its adoption of the automatic water-carriage system in drainage, with far-reaching economic consequences. See [George Vivian] Poore's [*Essays on*] *Rural Hygiene* [(London: Longmans, Green, 1893)] and *The Dwelling House* [(London: Longmans, Green, 1897)].

Chapter 3

The State and the Individual

L. T. Hobhouse

We have seen something of the principle underlying the Liberal idea and of its various applications. We have now to put the test question. Are these different applications compatible? Will they work together to make that harmonious whole of which it is easy enough to talk in abstract terms? Are they themselves really harmonious in theory and in practice? Does scope for individual development, for example, consort with the idea of equality? Is popular sovereignty a practicable basis of personal freedom, or does it open an avenue to the tyranny of the mob? Will the sentiment of nationality dwell in unison with the ideal of peace? Is the love of liberty compatible with the full realization of the common will? If reconcilable in theory, may not these ideals collide in practice? Are there not clearly occasions demonstrable in history when development in one direction involves retrogression in another? If so, how are we to strike the balance of gain and loss? Does political progress offer us nothing but a choice of evils, or may we have some confidence that, in solving the most pressing problem of the moment, we shall in the end be in a better position for grappling with the obstacles that come next in turn?

I shall deal with these questions as far as limits of space allow, and I will take first the question of liberty and the common will upon which everything turns. Enough has already been said on this topic to enable us to shorten the discussion. We have seen that social liberty rests on restraint. A man can be free to direct his own life only in so far as others are prevented from molesting and interfering with him. So far there is no real departure from the strictest tenets of individualism. We have, indeed, had occasion to examine the application of the doctrine to freedom of contract on the one hand, and to the action of combinations on the other, and have seen reason to think that in either case nominal freedom, that is to say, the absence of legal restraint, might have the effect of impairing real freedom, that is to say, would allow the stronger party to coerce the weaker. We have also seen that the effect of combination may be double edged, that it may restrict freedom on one side and enlarge it on the other. In all these cases our contention has been simply that we should be guided by real and not by verbal considerations, – that we should ask in every case what policy will yield effective freedom – and we have found a close connection in each instance between freedom and equality. In these cases, however, we were dealing with the relations of one man with another, or of one body of men with another, and we could regard the community as an arbiter between them whose business it was to see justice done and prevent the abuse of coercive power. Hence we could treat a very large part of the modern development of social control as motived by the desire for a more effective liberty. The case is not so clear when we find the will of the individual in conflict with the will of the community as a whole. When such conflict occurs, it would seem that we must be prepared for one of two things. Either we must admit the legitimacy of coercion, avowedly not in the interests of freedom but in furtherance, without regard to freedom, of other ends which the community deems good. Or we must admit limitations which may cramp the development of the general will, and perchance prove a serious obstacle to collective progress. Is there any means of avoiding this conflict? Must we leave the question to be fought out in each case by a balance of advantages and disadvantages, or are there any general considerations which help us to determine the true sphere of collective and of private action?

Let us first observe that, as Mill pointed out long ago, there are many forms of collective action which do not involve coercion. The State may provide for certain objects which it deems good without compelling any one to make use of them. Thus it may maintain hospitals, though any one who can pay for them remains free to employ his own doctors and nurses. It may and does maintain a great educational system, while leaving every one free to maintain or to attend a private school. It maintains parks and picture galleries without driving any one into them. There is a municipal tramway service, which does not prevent private people from running motor 'buses along the same streets, and so on. It is true that for the support of these objects rates and taxes are compulsorily levied, but this form of compulsion raises a set of questions of which we shall have to speak in another connection, and does not concern us here. For the moment we have to deal only with those actions of State which compel all citizens, or all whom they concern, to fall in with them and allow of no divergence. This kind of coercion tends to increase. Is its extension necessarily an encroachment upon liberty, or are the elements of value secured by collective control distinct from the elements of value secured by individual choice, so that within due limits each may develop side by side?

We have already declined to solve the problem by applying Mill's distinction between self-regarding and other-regarding actions, first because there are no actions which may not directly or indirectly affect others, secondly because even if there were they would not cease to be matter of concern to others. The common good includes the good of every member of the community, and the injury which a man inflicts upon himself is matter of common concern, even apart from any ulterior effect upon others. If we refrain from coercing a man for his own good, it is not because his good is indifferent to us, but because it cannot be furthered by coercion. The difficulty is founded on the nature of the good itself, which on its personal side depends on the spontaneous flow of feeling checked and guided not by external restraint but by rational self-control. To try to form character by coercion is to destroy it in the making. Personality is not built up from without but grows from within, and the function of the outer order is not to create it, but to provide for it the most suitable conditions of growth. Thus, to the common question whether it is possible to make men good by Act of Parliament, the reply is that it is not possible to compel morality because morality is the act or character of a free agent, but that it is possible to create the conditions under which morality can develop, and among these not the least important is freedom from compulsion by others.

The argument suggests that compulsion is limited not by indifference – how could the character of its members be matter of indifference to the community? – but by its own incapacity to achieve its ends. The spirit cannot be forced. Nor, conversely, can it prevail by force. It may require social expression. It may build up an association, a church for example, to carry out the common objects and maintain the common life of all who are like-minded. But the association must be free, because spiritually everything depends not on what is done but on the will with which it is done. The limit to the value of coercion thus lies not in the restriction of social purpose, but in the conditions of personal life. No force can compel growth. Whatever elements of social value depend on the accord of feeling, on comprehension of meaning, on the assent of will, must come through liberty. Here is the sphere and function of liberty in the social harmony.

Where, then, is the sphere of compulsion, and what is its value? The reply is that compulsion is of value where outward conformity is of value, and this may be in any case where the nonconformity of one wrecks the purpose of others. We have already remarked that liberty itself only rests upon restraint. Thus a religious body is not, properly speaking, free to march in procession through the streets unless people of a different religion are restrained from pelting the procession with stones and pursuing it with insolence. We restrain them from disorder not to teach them the genuine spirit of religion, which they will not learn in the police court, but to secure to the other party the right of worship unmolested. The enforced restraint has its value in the action that it sets free. But we may not only restrain one man from obstructing another – and the extent to which we do this is the measure of the freedom that we maintain – but we may also restrain him from obstructing the general will; and this we have to do whenever uniformity is necessary to the end which the general will has in view. The majority of employers in a trade we may suppose would be willing to adopt certain precautions for the health or safety of their workers, to lower hours or to raise the rate of wages. They are unable to do so, however, as long as a minority, perhaps as long as a single employer, stands out. He would beat them in competition if they were voluntarily to undertake expenses from which he is free. In this case, the will of a minority, possibly the will of one man, thwarts that of the remainder. It coerces them, indirectly, but quite as effectively as if he were their master. If they, by combination, can coerce him no principle of liberty is violated. It is coercion against coercion, differing possibly in form and method, but not in principle or in spirit. Further, if the community as a whole sympathizes with the one side rather than the other, it can reasonably bring the law into play. Its object is not the moral education of the recusant individuals. Its object is to secure certain conditions which it believes necessary for the welfare of its members, and which can only be secured by an enforced uniformity.

It appears, then, that the true distinction is not between self-regarding and other-regarding actions, but between coercive and non-coercive actions. The function of State coercion is to override individual coercion, and, of course, coercion exercised by any association of individuals within the State. It is by this means that it maintains liberty of expression, security of person and property, genuine freedom of contract, the rights of public meeting and association, and finally its own power to carry out common objects undefeated by the recalcitrance of individual members. Undoubtedly it endows both individuals and associations with powers as well as with rights. But over these powers it must exercise supervision in the interests of equal justice. Just as compulsion failed in the sphere of liberty, the sphere of spiritual growth, so liberty fails in the external order wherever, by the mere absence of supervisory restriction, men are able directly or indirectly to put constraint on one another. This is why there is no intrinsic and inevitable conflict between liberty and compulsion, but at bottom a mutual need. The object of compulsion is to secure the most favourable external conditions of inward growth and happiness so far as these conditions depend on combined action and uniform observance. The sphere of liberty is the sphere of growth itself. There is no true opposition between liberty as such and control as such, for every liberty rests on a corresponding act of control. The true opposition is between the control that cramps the personal life and the spiritual order, and the control that is aimed at securing the external and material conditions of their free and unimpeded development.

I do not pretend that this delimitation solves all problems. The "inward" life will seek to express itself in outward acts. A religious ordinance may bid the devout refuse military service, or withhold the payment of a tax, or decline to submit a building to inspection. Here are external matters where conscience and the State come into direct conflict, and where is the court of appeal that is to decide between them? In any given case the right, as judged by the ultimate effect on human welfare, may, of course, be on the one side, or on the other, or between the two. But is there anything to guide the two parties as long as each believes itself to be in the right and sees no ground for waiving its opinion? To begin with, clearly the State does well to avoid such conflicts by substituting alternatives. Other duties than that of military service may be found for a follower of Tolstoy, and as long as he is willing to take his full share of burdens the difficulty is fairly met. Again, the mere convenience of the majority cannot be fairly weighed against the religious convictions of the few. It might be convenient that certain public work should be done on Saturday, but mere convenience would be an insufficient ground for compelling Jews to participate in it. Religious and ethical conviction must be weighed against religious and ethical conviction. It is not number that counts morally, but the belief that is reasoned out according to the best of one's lights as to the necessities of the common good. But the conscience of the community has its rights just as much as the conscience of the individual. If we are convinced that the inspection of a convent laundry is required in the interest, not of mere official routine, but of justice and humanity, we can do nothing but insist upon it, and when all has been done that can be done to save the individual conscience the common conviction of the common good must have its way. In the end the external order belongs to the community, and the right of protest to the individual.

On the other side, the individual owes more to the community than is always recognized. Under modern conditions he is too much inclined to take for granted what the State does for him and to use the personal security and liberty of speech which it affords him as a vantage ground from which he can in safety denounce its works and repudiate its authority. He assumes the right to be in or out of the social system as he chooses. He relies on the general law which protects him, and emancipates himself from some particular law which he finds oppressive to his conscience. He forgets or does not take the trouble to reflect that, if every one were to act as he does, the social machine would come to a stop. He certainly fails to make it clear how a society would subsist in which every man should claim the right of unrestricted disobedience to a law which he happens to think wrong. In fact, it is possible for an over-tender conscience to consort with an insufficient sense of social responsibility. The combination is unfortunate; and we may fairly say that, if the State owes the utmost consideration to the conscience, its owner owes a corresponding debt to the State. With such mutual consideration, and with the development of the civic sense, conflicts between law and conscience are capable of being brought within very narrow limits, though their complete reconciliation will always remain a problem until men are generally agreed as to the fundamental conditions of the social harmony.

It may be asked, on the other hand, whether in insisting on the free development of personality we have not understated the duty of society to its members. We all admit a collective responsibility for children. Are there not grown-up people who stand just as much in need of care? What of the idiot, the imbecile, the feeble-minded or the drunkard? What does rational self-determination mean for these classes? They may injure no one but themselves except by the contagion of bad example. But have we no duty towards them, having in view their own good alone and leaving every other consideration aside? Have we not the right to take the feeble-minded under our care and to keep the drunkard from drink, purely for their own good and apart from every ulterior consideration? And, if so, must we not extend the whole sphere of permissible coercion, and admit that a man may for his own sake and with no ulterior object, be compelled to do what we think right and avoid what we think wrong?

The reply is that the argument is weak just where it seeks to generalize. We are compelled to put the insane under restraint for social reasons apart from their own benefit. But their own benefit would be a fully sufficient reason if no other existed. To them, by their misfortune, liberty, as we understand the term, has no application, because they are incapable of rational choice and therefore of the kind of growth for the sake of which freedom is valuable. The same thing is true of the feeble-minded, and if they are not yet treated on the same principle it is merely because the recognition of their type as a type is relatively modern. But the same thing is also in its degree true of the drunkard, so far as he is the victim of an impulse which he has allowed to grow beyond his own control; and the question whether he should be regarded as a fit object for tutelage or not is to be decided in each case by asking whether such capacity of self-control as he retains would be impaired or repaired by a period of tutelar restraint. There is nothing in all this to touch the essential of liberty which is the value of the power of self-governance where it exists. All that is proved is that where it does not exist it is right to save men from suffer-ing, and if the case admits to put them under conditions in which the normal balance of impulse is most likely to be restored. It may be added that, in the case of the drunkard – and I think the argument applies to all cases where overwhelming impulse is apt to master the will – it is a still more obvious and elementary duty to remove the sources of temptation, and to treat as anti-social in the highest degree every attempt to make profit out of human weakness, misery, and wrong-doing. The case is not unlike that of a very unequal contract. The tempter is coolly seeking his profit, and the sufferer is beset with a fiend within. There is a form of coercion here which the genuine spirit of liberty will not fail to recognize as its enemy, and a form of injury to another which is not the less real because its weapon is an impulse which forces that other to the consent which he yields.

I conclude that there is nothing in the doctrine of liberty to hinder the movement of general will in the sphere in which it is really efficient, and nothing in a just conception of the objects and methods of the general will to curtail liberty in the performance of the functions, social and personal, in which its value lies. Liberty and compulsion have complementary functions, and the self-governing State is at once the product and the condition of the self-governing individual.

Thus there is no difficulty in understanding why the extension of State control on one side goes along with determined resistance to encroachments on another. It is a question not of increasing or diminishing, but of reorganizing, restraints. The period which has witnessed a rapid extension of industrial legislation has seen as determined a resistance to anything like the establishment of doctrinal religious teaching by a State authority,[1] and the distinction is perfectly just. At bottom it is the same conception of liberty and the same conception of the common will that prompts the regulation of industry and the severence of religious worship and doctrinal teaching from the mechanism of State control.

So far we have been considering what the State compels the individual to do. If we pass to the question what the State is to do for the individual, a different but parallel question arises, and we have to note a corresponding movement of opinion. If the State does for the individual what he ought to do for himself what will be the effect on character, initiative, enterprise? It is a question now not of freedom, but of responsibility, and it is one that has caused many searchings of heart, and in respect of which opinion has undergone a remarkable change. Thus, in relation to poverty the older view was that the first thing needful was self-help. It was the business of every man to provide for himself and his family. If, indeed, he utterly failed, neither he nor they could be left to starve, and there was the Poor Law machinery to deal with his case. But the aim of every sincere friend of the poor must be to keep them away from the Poor Law machine. Experience of the forty years before 1834 had taught us what came of free resort to public funds by way of subvention to inadequate wages. It meant simply that the standard of remuneration was lowered in proportion as men could rely on public aid to make good the deficiency, while at the same time the incentives to independent labour were weakened when the pauper stood on an equal footing with the hard-working man. In general, if the attempt was made to substitute for personal effort the help of others, the result would only sap individual initiative and in the end bring down the rate of industrial remuneration. It was thought, for example – and this very point was urged against proposals for Old Age Pensions – that if any of the objects for which a man will, if possible, provide were removed from the scope of his own activity, he would in consequence be content with proportionally lower wages; if the employer was to compensate him for accident, he would fail to make provision for accidents on his own account; if his children were fed by the ratepayers, he would not earn the money wherewith to feed them. Hence, on the one hand, it was urged that the rate of wages would tend to adapt itself to the necessities of the wage earner, that in proportion as his necessities were met from other sources his wages would fall, that accordingly the apparent relief would be in large measure illusory, while finally, in view of the diminished stimulus to individual exertion, the productivity of labour would fall off, the incentives to industry would be diminished, and the community as a whole would be poorer. Upon the other hand, it was conceived that, however deplorable the condition of the working classes might be, the right way of raising them was to trust to individual enterprise and possibly, according to some thinkers, to voluntary combination. By these means the efficiency of labour might be enhanced and its regular remuneration raised. By sternly withholding all external supports we should teach the working classes to stand alone, and if there were pain in the disciplinary process there was yet hope in the future. They would come by degrees to a position of economic independence in which they would be able to face the risks of life, not in reliance upon the State, but by the force of their own brains and the strength of their own right arms.

These views no longer command the same measure of assent. On all sides we find the State making active provision for the poorer classes and not by any means for the destitute alone. We find it educating the children, providing medical inspection, authorizing the feeding of the necessitous at the expense of the ratepayers, helping them to obtain employment through free Labour Exchanges, seeking to organize the labour market with a view to the mitigation of unemployment, and providing old age pensions for all whose incomes fall below thirteen shillings a week, without exacting any contribution. Now, in all this, we may well ask, is the State going forward blindly on the paths of broad and generous but unconsidered charity? Is it and can it remain indifferent to the effect on individual initiative and personal or parental responsibility? Or may we suppose that the wiser heads are well aware of what they are about, have looked at the matter on all sides, and are guided by a reasonable conception of the duty of the State and the responsibilities of the individual? Are we, in fact – for this is really the question – seeking charity or justice?

We said above that it was the function of the State to secure the conditions upon which mind and character may develop themselves. Similarly we may say now that the function of the State is to secure conditions upon which its citizens are able to win by their own efforts all that is necessary to a full civic efficiency. It is not for the State to feed, house, or clothe them. It is for the State to take care that the economic conditions are such that the normal man who is not defective in mind or body or will can by useful labour feed, house, and clothe himself and his family. The "right to work" and the right to a "living wage" are just as valid as the rights of person or property. That is to say, they are integral conditions of a good social order. A society in which a single honest man of normal capacity is definitely unable to find the means of maintaining himself by useful work is to that extent suffering from malorganization. There is somewhere a defect in the social system, a hitch in the economic machine. Now, the individual workman cannot put the machine straight. He is the last person to have any say in the control of the market. It is not his fault if there is over-production in his industry, or if a new and cheaper process has been introduced which makes his particular skill, perhaps the product of years of application, a drug in the market. He does not direct or regulate industry. He is not responsible for its ups and downs, but he has to pay for them. That is why it is not charity but justice for which he is asking. Now, it may be infinitely difficult to meet his demand. To do so may involve a far-reaching economic reconstruction. The industrial questions involved may be so little understood that we may easily make matters worse in the attempt to make them better. All this shows the difficulty in finding means of meeting this particular claim of justice, but it does not shake its position as a claim of justice. A right is a right none the less though the means of securing it be imperfectly known; and the workman who is unemployed or underpaid through economic malorganization will remain a reproach not to the charity but to the justice of society as long as he is to be seen in the land.

If this view of the duty of the State and the right of the workman is coming to prevail, it is owing partly to an enhanced sense of common responsibility, and partly to the teaching of experience. In the earlier days of the Free Trade era, it was permissible to hope that self-help would be an adequate solvent, and that with cheap food and expanding commerce the average workman would be able by the exercise of prudence and thrift not only to maintain himself in good times, but to lay by for sickness, unemployment, and old age. The actual course of events has in large measure disappointed these hopes. It is true that the standard of living in England has progressively advanced throughout the nineteenth century. It is true, in particular, that, since the disastrous period that preceded the Repeal of the Corn Laws and the passing of the Ten Hours' Act, social improvement has been real and marked. Trade Unionism and co-operation have grown, wages upon the whole have increased, the cost of living has diminished, housing and sanitation have improved, the death rate has fallen from about twenty-two to less than fifteen per thousand. But with all this improvement the prospect of a complete and lifelong economic independence for the average workman upon the lines of individual competition, even when supplemented and guarded by the collective bargaining of the Trade Union, appears exceedingly remote. The increase of wages does not appear to be by any means proportionate to the general growth of wealth. The whole standard of living has risen; the very provision of education has brought with it new needs and has almost compelled a higher standard of life in order to satisfy them. As a whole, the working classes of England, though less thrifty than those of some Continental countries, cannot be accused of undue negligence with regard to the future. The accumulation of savings in Friendly Societies, Trade Unions, Co-operative Societies, and Savings Banks shows an increase which has more than kept pace with the rise in the level of wages; yet there appears no likelihood that the average manual worker will attain the goal of that full independence, covering all the risks of life for self and family, which can alone render the competitive system really adequate to the demands of a civilized conscience. The careful researches of Mr Booth in London and Mr Rowntree in York, and of others in country districts, have revealed that a considerable percentage of the working classes are actually unable to earn a sum of money representing the full cost of the barest physical necessities for an average family; and, though the bulk of the working classes are undoubtedly in a better position than this, these researches go to show that even the relatively well-to-do gravitate towards this line of primary poverty in seasons of stress, at the time when the children are still at school, for example, or from the moment when the principal wage-earner begins to fail, in the decline of middle life. If only some ten per cent of the population are actually living upon the poverty line at any given time,[2] twice or three times that number, it is reasonable to suppose, must approach the line in one period or other of their lives. But when we ascend from the conception of a bare physical maintenance for an average family to such a wage as would provide the real minimum requirements of a civilized life and meet all its contingencies without having to lean on any external prop, we should have to make additions to Mr Rowntree's figure which have not yet been computed, but as to which it is probably well within the mark to say that none but the most highly skilled artisans are able to earn a remuneration meeting the requirements of the case. But, if that is so, it is clear that the system of industrial competition fails to meet the ethical demand embodied in the conception of the "living wage." That system holds out no hope of an improvement which shall bring the means of such a healthy and independent existence as should be the birthright of every citizen of a free state within the grasp of the mass of the people of the United Kingdom. It is this belief slowly penetrating the public mind which has turned it to new thoughts of social regeneration. The sum and substance of the changes that I have mentioned may be expressed in the principle that the individual cannot stand alone, but that between him and the State there is a reciprocal obligation. He owes the State the duty of industriously working for himself and his family. He is not to exploit the labour of his young children, but to submit to the public requirements for their education, health, cleanliness and general well-being. On the other side society owes to him the means of maintaining a civilized standard of life, and this debt is not adequately discharged by leaving him to secure such wages as he can in the higgling of the market.

This view of social obligation lays increased stress on public but by no means ignores private responsibility. It is a simple principle of applied ethics that responsibility should be commensurate with power. Now, given the opportunity of adequately remunerated work, a man has the power to earn his living. It is his right and his duty to make the best use of his opportunity, and if he fails he may fairly suffer the penalty of being treated as a pauper or even, in an extreme case, as a criminal. But the opportunity itself he cannot command with the same freedom. It is only within narrow limits that it comes within the sphere of his control. The opportunities of work and the remuneration for work are determined by a complex mass of social forces which no individual, certainly no individual workman, can shape. They can be controlled, if at all, by the organized action of the community, and therefore, by a just apportionment of responsibility, it is for the community to deal with them.

But this, it will be said, is not Liberalism but Socialism. Pursuing the economic rights of the individual we have been led to contemplate a Socialistic organization of industry. But a word like Socialism has many meanings, and it is possible that there should be a Liberal Socialism, as well as a Socialism that is illiberal. Let us, then, without sticking at a word, seek to follow out the Liberal view of the State in the sphere of economics. Let us try to determine in very general terms what is involved in realizing those primary conditions of industrial well-being which have been laid down, and how they consort with the rights of property and the claims of free industrial enterprise.

Notes

1   The objection most often taken to "undenominationalism" itself is that it is in reality a form of doctrinal teaching seeking State endowment.
2   I do not include those living in "secondary poverty," as defined by Mr Rowntree, as the responsibility in this case is partly personal. It must, however, be remembered that great poverty increases the difficulty of efficient management.

Chapter 4

The Great Leviathan

J. N. Figgis

We have seen that the refusal of many lawyers to recognise in Churches, as such, any real rights of life and development is widespread and inveterate; that it cannot be attributed merely to anti-clerical prejudice, strong though that has always been in the profession, for it is based on principles which must also deny the similar right to other non-religious societies. We have seen also that it is not specially English, but European, and that it is of the nature rather of an unconscious presupposition than a mere theory. For those holding the current view seem almost unable to conceive what Churchmen mean by claiming any freedom for religious bodies. Thus it would appear that the causes of this antipathy are not new, and that we must seek for the historical origin of this prejudice far back in history. It will be the purpose of this lecture to try and show how it arose, and to urge that it relates originally to a condition long since passed away, and that we ought to demand a view of politics which has more vital relation to the facts, instead of what is little more than an abstract theory deduced from the notion of unity. In this lecture, and indeed in the whole course, I cannot overestimate my debt to that great monument, both of erudition and profound thought, the *Das Deutsche Genossenschaftsrecht of* Dr Otto Gierke. A very small portion, by no means the most valuable, was translated by Maitland, and his Introduction forms an almost indispensable preliminary to this study. But it is greatly to be wished that sombody would translate the whole of Gierke's three volumes, or at least the last. Another work of Dr Gierke, *Die Genossenschafts Theorie*, is less well known in England, but it is worth studying. There it is attempted to show how under the facts of modern life the civilian theory of corporations is breaking down on all hands, and that even in Germany, in spite of the deliberate adoption of the Romanist doctrine, the courts and sometimes even the laws are being constantly driven to treat corporate societies as though they were real and not fictitious persons, and to regard such personality as the natural consequence of permanent association, not a mere mark to be imposed or withheld by the sovereign power. The value of all these books is the greater for our purpose that they are in no sense ecclesiastical in tone, and that the English introduction was the work of one who described himself as a "dissenter from all the Churches." More directly concerned with ecclesiastical liberty, but at the same time universal in application, are some of the essays by Acton in the volume on "Freedom."

That the problem is really concerned with the liberty alike of the individual and of the corporate society, is best proved by such words as those of M. Emile Combes: "There are, there can be no rights except the right of the State, and there are, and there can be no other authority than the authority of the Republic."[1] Nowhere, perhaps, has the creed of materialist politics been expressed with such naked cynicism. Such a doctrine, if accepted, lies at the roots of all higher morality and all religious freedom. It is the denial at once of the fact of conscience, the institutions of religion and the reality of the family. That this is the direction in which the forces represented by M. Combes would wish to drive Europe is clear from many circumstances. And though for the nonce this orgy of State absolutism may be restrained by certain surviving institutions of freedom and by the facts of human life, the words here quoted show the danger those are in who surrender themselves blindly to those forces, which from Machiavelli through Hobbes and Bodin have come to be dominant in politics, and are at this moment dangerously ascendant owing to the horror of that very economic and industrial oppression which is the distinctive gift of modern capitalism to history. In this country, however, few are likely to go quite so far as M. Combes. Owing partly to the continuance of ideas that have come down from the Middle Ages, partly to the struggles of the seventeenth century, the notion of individual liberty is very strong. Individual rights of conscience are recognised – even in such matters as public health. And though there are not wanting indications that this sentiment is very much on the wane, it is still the case, that so far as principle goes, few English statesmen could deny the authority of the individual conscience. At the same time, utterances like those of M. Combes and certain movements violent at this moment in England should prevent our being too certain in this matter. Entire capitulation to this prevailing tendency to deify the State, if only in the matter of corporate institutions, will in the long run be no more favourable to individual liberty than the so-called "free-labour" movement organised by capitalists is likely to be to the economic freedom of the artisan classes. Yet our concern, as I showed last time, is not with individual, but rather with corporate liberty.

And here I have no doubt that objections will be raised. How, it will be asked, can you say that we need to do battle for the rights of corporations when already the country is groaning under their tyranny, and the law of limited companies is the cover under which is carried every form of that exploitation which, if conducted by millionaires, is known as "high finance," and if practised by their clerks is called by a different name? I am not denying that corporate societies exist, or that they exist in large numbers; no complex state of civilisation can exist without this phenomenon appearing; and if it appears, the law must somehow or other take account of it. What is wrong is not the fact but the nature of existence allowed to these bodies in legal theory. Any corporate body, in the ordinary and not the technical sense, of a society of men bound together for a permanent interest inevitably acts with that unity and sense of direction which we attribute to personality. The question is, how is this personality to be conceived? Is it a natural fact, the expression of the social union; or is it merely something artificial imposed upon the body for its own convenience by the State? Is it real or fictitious, this legal personality? Under the dominant theory the corporate person is a fiction, a *nomen juris*; in order that societies of men may be able to act, to hold property, to sue and be sued, it is necessary to treat them as what they are not, *i.e.* as persons; therefore the sovereign power by its own act grants to such bodies as it pleases the name of corporation, and with it endows them with a "fictitious" personality; since, however, it is a mere matter of convenient imagination on the part of the law, and corresponds to no reality in the collective body, its entire genesis and right are merely a delegation of the sovereign authority. All corporations owe their existence to a grant or concession of the State, tacit if not express, which may be given or withheld. Other societies, if they exist at all, are purely contractual, and have no such power of suing or being sued. They are *collegia* or *societates*, not "universities." The Romans approached, though they did not entirely reach, this position.[2] The final word was really said by the great canonist Sinibaldo Fieschi, afterwards Pope Innocent IV. With the large number of cathedral chapters and religious orders in the Church, it became very necessary to arrive at clear views on the matter, and Innocent IV, starting from the doctrine of the civil law as to the nature of sovereign power and the rights of individuals, came quite definitely to the view that it was necessary to call such bodies persons; but that their personality was purely fictitious, *nomen juris*, and therefore entirely within the power of the prince.[3] Under the influences which led to the reception of the Roman Civil Law in Germany and its dominance throughout Western Europe, this view developed into the full doctrine of the concession theory of corporate life. Although Roman Law, as such, was never accepted in England, yet through the influence of chancellors trained partly as canonists, and through the general development of absolutism in the sixteenth century, a view substantially the same became prevalent in this country, and is still the official doctrine, although more and more influences are tending in the opposite direction. The present state of affairs can be seen from the perusal of the inaugural lecture at Oxford of Dr Geldart on *Legal Personality*. An instance of the way in which facts are proving too strong for it, was the judgment in the *Taff Vale Case* confirmed by the House of Lords. In order to save their funds from certain dangers, the Acts which enfranchised the *Trades Unions* in 1875, and relieved them from the law of conspiracy, had expressly denied to them the character of corporations. Thus the common chest of the union could not be raided for any illegal acts of its agents. In the *Taff Vale Case*, however, it was decided, that though they were not corporate bodies legally, yet since their acts were of a nature so closely akin to those of persons, so far as the question of damages was concerned they were to be treated as such, and made responsible for the acts of agents. Outcries were raised against this judgment, which was certainly contrary to what had for nearly a generation been supposed to be the law; and eventually the *Trades Disputes Act* was passed to relieve the unions in regard to picketing. This, however, is irrelevant. Whatever other influences may have assisted in forming the minds of the judges, the truth is that the judgment bears witness to the fact that corporate personality, this unity of life and action, is a thing which grows up naturally and inevitably in bodies of men united for a permanent end, and that it cannot in the long run be denied merely by the process of saying that it is not there. In other words, this personality is inherent in the nature of the society as such, and is not a mere name to be granted or denied at the pleasure of the sovereign authority. That so much was actually declared by the House of Lords, I do not say; but that this was the inner meaning of their decision seems undoubted. On the other hand, in the Osborne judgment the old prejudice must have been largely at the bottom of the decision, which forbad to the unions the power to use their funds as a whole to pay Members of Parliament. In other words, the members of the union are a mere collection of individuals, who are unchanged by their membership of the society, and cannot therefore have the funds subscribed turned to a purpose to which, though even in a minority, they object. A similar view is at the bottom of a recent decision about the power of a club to raise its subscription. A well-known London club attempted to do this; one of the members refused to pay the additional amount, and was expelled in consequence. He brought an action, and the courts decided in his favour, *i.e.* that it was all a matter of contract, and that the club had no authority, no real inherent life, which could enable it to pass beyond the arrangements made with the individual member at his election, who might thus enjoy every kind of new improvement or addition to the club without paying his share in the extra cost.

So long as this doctrine or anything like it be dominant, it would probably be an evil rather than a benefit if the Church of England were to become, what it now is not, a corporation recognised as such by the law. For that would under existing conditions mean that it was subject to all sorts of restrictions, while at the same time it would still be denied inherent rights of self-development. True, facts are always stronger than abstract theories, and the fact of corporate life might not improbably be too strong for any legal theories which denied it. This was the case in the Scotch instance. But at present this could hardly be guaranteed. On the other hand, it was shown in a very interesting essay of Maitland,[4] that part of the practical difficulty has been solved in this country by the institution of trusts. Under cover of trusteeship, a great deal of action has taken place which is really that of corporate personality, without the society being subject to the disabilities incident to the "concession theory." He points out in regard to the Inns of Court, which, being bodies of lawyers, may be supposed to know what is their interest, that they have always refused incorporation, finding that they can under the doctrine of trusteeship do what they want and have most of the safeguards without the disabilities of corporate life. At the same time, it was probably through the lack of a proper corporate recognition that a scandal was possible, like that by which the property of Serjeant's Inn could be treated as the individual possession of its existing members and divided up between them. The essay is very interesting and valuable, for it shows how the practical good sense of Englishmen has enabled them to accept an abstract doctrine of the nature of the corporation, not germane to the realities of life, while denuding it of many of its most grievous consequences.

It may seem that these considerations are matters merely of legal theory, and that they do not concern us in the practical problem of securing reasonable liberty for the Church as a self-developing body. I think that this is not the case. For let us consider what is at the back of it all. Since the corporate society is only a *persona ficta*, with the name given it by the law, but no real inward life, we have on this view but two social entities, the State on the one hand and the individual on the other. The rights or actions of the one are private, those of the other are public. The State may be of any kind of structure, monarchic, aristocratic, or purely collectivist; but in all cases there are recognised by the law, no real social entities, no true powers, except the sovereign on the one hand with irresistible authority, and the mass of individuals on the other. Societies, so far as they exist, are mere collections of individuals who remain unchanged by their membership, and whose unity of action is narrowly circumscribed by the State, and where allowed is allowed on grounds quite arbitrary. Under such a view there can be no possible place for the religious body, in the sense of a Church living a supernatural life, and the claim is quite just that no Church should have any standard of morals different from those of the State.

But is not this woefully to misconceive the actual facts of social life, as they present themselves to our eyes, and to get a wrong notion of the State? Let me give an instance. Throughout the education controversy much has been heard against the iniquity of privately managed schools receiving public money, at least in the form of rates (for the income-tax is not concerned with conscience). Now surely (except in the case of the one-man manager) this is a total misconception. As opposed to State management, perhaps the word private may be admitted, but when it implies, as it ought, purely individual management, a false view is suggested. These social bodies other than the State are not only not private, but in their working they are more akin to the State than they are to the individual. I mean that both of them are cases of a society acting as one, to which the individual members are subject. The relations between the member and his society are more akin to those of a citizen to a State than to anything in the individual. It is very easy to say that universities, colleges, trade unions, inns of court, &c. &c., are purely private, and in one sense it is true; they are not delegates of the State or parts of its machinery; but they are in a very real sense public, *i.e.* they are collective, not individual, in their constitution. The popular use of the word "Public School" to denote a school under collective management is a far more reasonable and realistic habit, though I suppose that it is not technically justified. The point is that it is the public communal character of all such institutions that is the salient fact; and that we do wrong to adopt a rigid division into public and private, if we mean by the latter any and every institution that is not a delegation from the State. What we actually see in the world is not on the one hand the State, and on the other a mass of unrelated individuals; but a vast complex of gathered unions, in which alone we find individuals, families, clubs, trades unions, colleges, professions, and so forth; and further, that there are exercised functions within these groups which are of the nature of government, including its three aspects, legislative, executive, and judicial; though, of course, only with reference to their own members. So far as the people who actually belong to it are concerned, such a body is every whit as communal in its character as a municipal corporation or a provincial parliament.

Not only, however, is this view false to the true character of the State; it is entirely wrong in its view of the individual citizen. As a matter of fact, personality is a social fact; no individual could ever come to himself except as a member of a society, and the membership of any society does not leave even the adult individual where he was. There is an interpenetration of his life with that of the society, and his personality is constantly being changed by this fellowship. Too often on the part of those who strongly believe in human personality, the necessities of controversy against doctrines which virtually deny it has led to an insistence on the individual to the neglect of the social side. Correction of this error will be found in a very valuable book by Mr Wilfrid Richmond, *Personality as a Philosophical Principle*. We cannot, however, too often emphasize in regard to politics, that not the individual but the family is the real social unit, and that personality as a fact never grows up except within one or more social unions. That, however, will be met by the claim that this is just what citizenship means; that "the State is prior" to the individual, and that true personality is to grow up in the great collective union of national life. This seems to me to lie at the root of the difficulty.

When Aristotle uttered his famous dictum, the State meant, as all know, a small body of persons, not more than could be gathered in one place; and although we may hold that the antique State was too all-embracing, at least it was not unreasonable to maintain that the compact City-State of ancient Greece was the social home of all the individuals comprising it, and no more was needed. In the modern world, however, no such assertion is possible. Whatever the State may attempt, she cannot be the mother of all her citizens in the same sense as the City-State of old; and, as a fact, men will grow to maturity and be moulded in their prejudices, their tastes, their capacities, and their moral ideals not merely by the great main stream of national life, but also, and perhaps more deeply, by their own family connections, their local communal life in village or town, their educational society (for it is of the essence of education to be in a society), and countless other collective organisms. It is these that make up the life of the modern world, and to deny them all real existence or power, whether it be in the interests of legal theory or of an abstract economic collectivism, seems to me to be in principle false to the facts, and in practice to be steering straight for the rocks. It must not be forgotten that on the ideal system which arose out of the Greek City-State the fact of the family as a real entity disappears; and Plato would allow a community in wives.

What has really happened is that a conception of sovereignty which more or less expressed the facts in the ancient City-State was extended to the vast world-empire of the Romans, developed and concentrated in the autocrat at its head. The doctrine of the unity of the sovereign power and the complete non-existence of all other real authorities became the settled presupposition of the lawyers, and crystallised into maxims which are familiar to all, such as *quod principi placuit legis habet vigorem*, that the Emperor was *legibus solutus*, and so forth. Moreover, the fact that there remained in the account of the *lex regia* a tradition of the popular origin of the Imperial authority has rendered it more easy to apply the same doctrine to a modern State. Whether or no, as the *lex regia* implies, all power was originally in the people, who transferred it by irrevocable act to the prince, it is equally clear that the essential doctrine of a single irresistible authority "inalienable, indivisible, and incapable of legal limitation" is ready to hand in the Roman system, and may be applied with equal facility to a modern democracy like France or an ancient empire like Rome. In either case it is equally destructive of any real recognition of the rights of social unions other than the State. Except as its own delegations, the Imperial Government was extremely suspicious of all such societies; and, as I have said, it treated corporations in a way which differed from the more developed "concession theory" only in that it had not reached so far even as the notion that they were fictitious persons. But the point is that of all real life in such bodies the Government was most suspicious, and Sir William Ramsay in his *Church and the Roman Empire* has shown that it was just in this fact, that the Church claimed a different sanction, a separate life, and a new non-Roman unity, that lay the whole ground of the long persecution. Unfortunately, when the Church triumphed, she for the time virtually abandoned the claim to freedom within the State which had deluged the Coliseum with blood. There was no change in the antique Græco-Roman conception of a single all-absorbing omnicompetent power, the source of every right, and facing with no intermediates the vast masses of individual citizens. The only difference made was that this State from being Pagan became Christian, and after the proscription of Paganism by Theodosius the Great there was no need for men to worry themselves with forming a totally new doctrine of the structure of civil society. The *De Civitate Dei of* St Augustine provided the framework in which all the political thinking of men was done for more than a thousand years, nor is its influence even yet extinct. The mediæval doctrine of the *Holy Roman Empire* crystallised this ideal in a form which, if not very practicable, was at least an object to work for, and did as a fact direct the life and work of many of its greatest leaders. An ideal which Charles the Great, Otho the Great, Pope Sylvester II, Henry of Luxemburg were content even to try to realise cannot be dismissed as of no influence on the lives of men. If it was not realised, it at least caused people to do what they would otherwise have left undone and ruled their imaginations, a fact which is plain from Dante's *De Monarchia* and from many of the most striking passages in the *Divina Commedia*.

On the other hand, the Teutonic polity and habit of mind, if it did not quite produce, approached a view of the relation of the individual to the society and of the smaller societies to the whole, which is that to which we are being driven. The enormous development of corporate life in the Middle Ages, guilds of every kind, and the whole notion of the system of estates in the body politic all testified to the same fact. There was a very definite sense of the individual, not as something separate, but as moulded and interpenetrated by the life of the society. There was, further, the very definite sense that the societies all were organic, that they lived by an inherent spontaneity of life, and that as communal societies they had their own rights and liberty, which did not originate in the grant of the sovereign. As Gierke, however, points out, this was instinctive rather than theoretical; they had not reached the difficult and developed conception of corporate personality. And this, among many other causes, is the explanation of the ease with which the ancient ideas of corporate liberty and real social life went down before the logically developed and erudite system which ruled the minds of the lawyers from the Renaissance onwards.[5]

Nor must it be supposed that the Church was an exception. The theory of the Church came from the Roman Empire. Neither Churchmen nor statesmen believed in two separate social entities, the Church and the State, each composed of the same persons. Nor indeed was that necessary in the mediæval idea of a Christian State. Rather, when conflict is spoken of between Church and State, it is conflict between two bodies of officials, the civil and the ecclesiastical. When Henry IV resisted Hildebrand, he admitted that for the case of heresy he might be deposed; and the whole atmosphere of the mediæval mind was such that we cannot picture them as treating the two as really separate societies. When the liberty of the Church is claimed, it almost always denotes the liberty of the hierarchy, not that of the whole body. Alike on the Imperial and the Papal side, the claims raised would have been inconceivable, had it not been admitted that both Popes and Emperors were rulers in one society. I do not say that there was no approximation to the idea of a "free Church in a free State"; but so long as persecution was taken for granted, and a coercive Church-State was the ideal, the claims which we put forward were not seriously entertained. That was the root of the difficulty.

With the then existing presuppositions and the argument from abstract unity so strong – strong partly because of the universal lawlessness – the claim to freedom, whether put forward by the civil or the ecclesiastical power, became inevitably a claim to supremacy, and was therefore never really admitted by the others. The Popes could never allow that matters of religion and conscience were to be at the mercy of politicians; the Emperors could never allow that the State merely existed on sufferance of the spiritual power. This conflict could never be solved so long as both parties maintained the right and duty of persecution, *i.e.* the necessary connection of membership of the Church with citizenship in the State. Furthermore, inside the polity of the Church, the other system had triumphed and the development of the Papal system meant the transference to the Pope of all the notions of illimitable authority claimed by the Emperor in truth. The great *Leviathan* of Hobbes, the *plenitudo potestatis* of the canonists, the *arcana imperii*, the sovereignty of Austin, are all names of the same thing – the unlimited and illimitable power of the law-giver in the State, deduced from the notion of its unity. It makes no difference whether it is the State or the Church that is being considered.

Towards the close of the Middle Ages it might seem as though the way was being paved for a more natural system. So far as the European monarchs were concerned, the Imperial claim remained no more than honorific, and after the conflict between Philippe le Bel and Boniface VIII there seemed no possibility of asserting claims of the Papacy against the rising national powers. Within those national powers, institutions had arisen all over Europe, which expressed the fact that the State was a *communitas communitatum*. This is the true meaning of our word Commons; not the mass of the common people, but the community of the communities. However imperfect in theory, there was a practical recognition of merchant and craft guilds, with borough charters, guild liberties, the baronial honours, with courts Christian, courts royal, and courts manor, all functioning, with special laws and customs recognised even for fairs and markets and universities. These facts, together with the traditions of fellowship life coming down from a long past, might well make it seem that a system of universal liberties and balanced powers would result, that at last the lion of the throne would lie down with the lamb of spiritual freedom in a semi-federalist polity.

But it was not to be. The lion got outside of the lamb. Roman Law became more and more the norm; 1495 is the date of its reception in Germany; national and local customs were decried by the civilians, learned, classical, Romanist to the core. The dangers of anarchy under feudalism made the mass of men blind to the dangers of autocracy. All the learning of the Renaissance was in favour of the power of the prince, save for a few dreamers who looked to a republic. Clerical immunities had been abused; the religious orders were too much of an *imperium in imperio*. With the Lutheran movement, there went on the one hand the destruction of the ancient conception of Christendom as a single polity, under the leadership of Pope and Emperor and the Lordship of Christ; and on the other, the transference to the prince as head of a compact territorial unity of the bulk of the prerogatives of both spiritual and secular power. The doctrine of *cujus regio ejus religio* of the religious peace of Augsburg was the natural expression of this fact; so that one elector could say quite readily that his people's conscience belonged to him. That was, of course, the notion of Henry VIII. It was formulated into a complete theory of the State by Jean Bodin in France, and afterwards by Thomas Hobbes in England. Hobbes denied every kind of right not derived from the sovereign; and devotes one book of his *Leviathan* to "the kingdom of darkness," in other words the Roman Church, which he thus denominates because its claims would break up the unity of the sovereign power. In the seventeenth century, both in England and on the Continent, this notion of a compact omnicompetent sovereign, by whose permission alone existed the right to breathe, was mixed up with the theory of the divine right of kings. But it is not really tied thereto. The eighteenth century saw it asserted of Parliament; and the claim to parliamentary omnipotence was the real cause of the American Revolution. In the other hemisphere was set up a State which, as being federal, was largely a denial of this claim; but the civil war seems to have proved the contrary. Even now, however, the doctrine of State rights is still strong, is said to be gaining rather than losing adherents, and we may learn much from the attitude of the American courts to such problems as those of the free development of religious bodies.

In France, unlike England, the theory of sovereignty had been crystallised in the person of the monarch; but it was not overthrown by the Revolution. What was overthrown was the surviving remnant of feudalism and the last relics of local and partial liberty. The doctrine of a single uniform all-absorbing power has been carried to a height further than even Louis XIV could have dreamed; and, as we have seen, even religious toleration exists only in name. This doctrine has found in England classical expression in the writings of John Austin, which do little more than formulate the Roman theory of sovereignty, and is imbued with the same notion of the entire distinction between public and private, which forbids any right classification of social institutions. Austin has been subjected to much criticism, but with certain slight qualifications his notions still rule the legal mind – except, of course, those who are definitely working towards a new doctrine of corporate life. And in regard to the Church, to morals alike, it is taken as an axiom that the law is morally binding, and by many that what is legally right cannot be morally wrong.

This doctrine is, however, becoming more and more difficult to reconcile with the facts. As a mere verbal theory I do not know that this view of sovereign power is assailable; and by means of the proviso that whatever the sovereign permits he commands, we cannot positively say that any measure of freedom is inconsistent with it. Practically, however, it is clear that we need something different and more profound. We have seen one salient instance of the pitfalls it is apt to lead to. We must bear in mind that Parliament is nominally sovereign, not only in England but in every portion of the Empire, and that no local liberty exists in theory but as a delegated authority for the will of the Imperial Parliament. Yet in regard to the immigration law in South Africa, it was admitted that the Imperial Parliament dare not override the will of the local bodies even though they were doing a manifest injustice to their fellow-subjects. In other words, the local body had a real independent life, and could not be touched.

The theory of government which is at the root of all the trouble is briefly this. All and every right is the creation of the one and indivisible sovereign; whether the sovereign be a monarch or an assembly is not material. No prescription, no conscience, no corporate life can be pleaded against its authority, which is without legal limitation. In every State there must be some power entirely above the law, because it can alter the law. To talk of rights as against it is to talk nonsense. In so far as every State is a State, this view is held to be not only true but self-evident. In so far as it is not true, it is because the State is in a condition of incipient dissolution and anarchy is already setting in. The doctrine of sovereignty is, in fact, a deduction partly from the universality of law in a stable commonwealth, and partly from the abstract notion of unity. That this latter has much to do with it will be evident to all who are acquainted with the controversialist literature of either the Middle Ages or the seventeenth century. Filmer's *Anarchy of a Mixed Monarchy* is a brief statement of this standpoint.

But the truth is, that this State in a sense of absolute superhuman unity has never really existed, and that it cannot exist. In theory it represents a despot ruling over slaves; in practice even a despot is limited by the fact that slaves are, after all, human; deny their personality as you like, there comes a point at which it asserts itself, and they will kill either the despot or themselves. At bottom the doctrine represents a State, which is a super-man ruling individuals who are below men. It is like the absolute of the Bradleyan philosophy which absorbs and ultimately annihilates all individual distinction. It is partly symbolised by the title-page of the *Leviathan* of Hobbes. Attempts are made to get out of the difficulty by saying that the sovereign power, though theoretically illimitable, is limited in practice very materially; psychologically by its own nature, and externally by the fact that there are certain things which no government can do without provoking resistance, *e.g.* Louis XIV could not have established Mohammedanism, even if he had wished. In this way custom on the one hand, local liberties or individual rights on the other, would acquire a place. We are, I admit, brought nearer to the facts.[6] But it seems a weakness in a doctrine that you can only fit the facts into its framework by making such serious qualifications, and it would appear a more reasonable maxim to get a theory of law and government not by laying down an abstract doctrine of unity, but by observing the facts of life as it is lived, and trying to set down the actual features of civil society. What do we find as a fact? Not, surely, a sand-heap of individuals, all equal and undifferentiated, unrelated except to the State, but an ascending hierarchy of groups, family, school, town, county, union, Church, &c. &c. All these groups (or many of them) live with a real life; they act towards one another with a unity of will and mind as though they were single persons; they all need to be allowed reasonable freedom, but must be restrained from acts of injustice towards one another or the individual; they are all means by which the individual comes to himself. For in truth the notion of isolated individuality is the shadow of a dream, and would never have come into being but for the vast social structure which allows a few individuals to make play, as though they were independent, when their whole economic position of freedom is symbolic of a long history and complex social organisation. In the real world, the isolated individual does not exist; he begins always as a member of something, and, as I said earlier, his personality can develop only in society, and in some way or other he always embodies some social institution. I do not mean to deny the distinctness of individual life, but this distinction can function only inside a society. Membership in a social union means a direction of personality, which interpenetrates it, and, according to your predilection, you may call either an extension or a narrowing; it is in truth both. You cannot be a member of any society and be the same as though you were not a member; it affects your rights and duties, limits at once and increases your opportunities, and makes you a different being, although in many different degrees, according to the nature of the society and the individual member. You are not merely John Doe or Richard Roe, but as John may probably be a member of the Christian Church by baptism, a Doe by family, an Englishman by race; all three are social institutions, which have grown into you. In addition to this you are a member of a school, an alumnus of a college, a sharer in this club, a president of that, and so forth. All these groups and unions have their effect, and limit and develop your life, make you do, or refrain from doing, what otherwise you would not, and in so far prevent you being a free and untrammelled citizen of the State. More than that, they penetrate your imagination and your thought and alter not only what you do but what you want to do. Between all these groups there will be relations, and not merely between the individuals composing them. To prevent injustice between them and to secure their rights, a strong power above them is needed. It is largely to regulate such groups and to ensure that they do not outstep the bounds of justice that the coercive force of the State exists. It does not create them; nor is it in many matters in direct and immediate contact with the individual. The claim of the Church in matters of education is the claim that she shall be recognised as a group, in which the natural authority over its members extends to the provision of a social atmosphere; and this ought to be admitted, provided the requirements of citizenship in secular culture be provided and controlled.

All this, it will be said, lessens the hold of the State over the individual. But this is needful the moment you reach any large and complex society. In a developed state of civilisation many interests must be allowed social expression, which in one sense are a separating influence. Even a member of a musical club is so far separated from those who are excluded; and he is changed by the fact of this club-life, which enters into him. In the Middle Ages there was an appropriate dress for every calling; under the modern notion we have all been trying to dress alike, and most of us doing it very badly. The old custom survives in clergy and in butcher boys, and we are seeing revivals in the costumes of boy scouts. Instead of an iron uniformity, we need more and more a reasonable distinction of groups, all of which should be honourable. There is a whole philosophy in school colours.

Recent discussions are making men ask once more in matters other than religion, what are the limits of the authority of Parliament. The idolatry of the State is receiving shrewd blows. It is said, however, especially in regard to the Church, that to recognise its rights is dangerous. But if it is a fact, it must be more dangerous not to recognise its real life. The same is true of individuals. However you may proclaim with M. Combes that "there are no rights but the rights of the State," you find individuals who habitually act as if they had them; and even when you go on to say that "there is no authority but the authority of the republic," you do not in practice prevent all kinds of societies from behaving in a way that implies authority over their members. Nor can you. It is impossible. Society is inherent in human nature, and that means inevitably the growth of a communal life and social ties; nor is it possible to confine this to the single society we call the State, unless it be on a very small scale, and even then there is the family to reckon with. Of course such societies may come into collision with the State; so may individuals. Always there is a possibility of civil war. But you will not escape the possibility by ignoring the facts. The only way to be sure an individual will never become a criminal is to execute him; the only way to secure a State from all danger on the part of its members is to have none. Every State is a synthesis of living wills. Harmony must ever be a matter of balance and adjustment, and this at any moment might be upset, owing to the fact that man is a spiritual being and not a mere automaton. It would seem to be wiser to treat all these great and small corporate entities which make up our national life as real, as living beings, i.e. practically as persons, and then when this is once realised, limit them in their action, than it is to try and treat them as what they are not, i.e. as dead bodies, dry bones, into which nothing but an arbitrary fiat gives a simulacrum of life, which may at any moment be withdrawn. After all, the Roman Government did not destroy the living unity of the Church by denying its claim to exist; but it nearly destroyed itself in the attempt.

Notes

1   This was stated in an article in *The Independent Review*, September 1905.

2   So wurde schliesslich die römische Jurisprudenz unabweislich zu der Annahme gedrängt, dass die Persönlichkeit der *Universitas* – eine Fiktion sei. Zwar haben die Römer diesen Gedanken weder mit Einem Schlage noch überhaupt im voller Schärfe formulirt, geschweige denn über Natur und Inhalt dieses Fiktion theoretische Erwägungen angestellt. Allein der gesammte Aufbau ihres Korporationsrechts gipfelte in dem Satz, dass hier von positiven Recht eine Nichtperson personificirt sei. (Gierke, *op. cit.*, iii.103.)

Cf. also the following:

Als publicistisches war die *Universitas* – eine reale Einheit aber keine Person. Als Privatrechtssubject war sie eine Person, aber keine reale Einheit. Eine wirkliche Person war nur der Mensch, weil nur er ein Individuum und nur das Individuum Person war. Wenn eine *Universitas* obwohl sie ihren realen Substrat nach kein Individuum war, als Person und somit als Individuum gesetzt wurde, so lag darin die vom Recht vollzogene Behandlung einer in Wirklichkeit nicht existenten Thatsache, als sei sie existent. (Gierke, iii. 103.)

Der Verbandsbegriff der römischen Jurisprudenz.

3   Derselbe Papst (Innocent III) verbot zugleich wegen der gesteigerten Mannichfaltigkeit der Kongregationen die Begründung neuer Orden, ein Verbot, von dem freilich bald darauf zu Gunsten der Bettelmönche wieder abgegangen wurden musste, das aber doch deutlich zeigt *wie auch dem gewaltigen Aufschwung der religiösen Association* gegenüber die Kirche an dem Standpunkt festhielt, dass die Existenz einer geistlichen Genossenschaft von der päpstlichen Sanktion abhängig sei. In der That setzte jetzt wie später die Kirche es durch, das alle neu entstehenden geistlichen Gesellschaften von einiger Bedeutung ihrer Regel und Verfassung sich – formell wenigstens – vom päpstlichen Stuhle ertheilen liessen und von ihm die Gesammtheit ihrer Rechte herleiteten, so dass auch die sponstansten Ordensvereinigungen ebenso wie die einzelnen Ordensgemeinden nie unter den Begriff völlig freier Gesellschaften fielen, sondern als kirchliche Anstalten mit gesellschaftlicher Verfassung betrachtet wurden. (Gierke, i. 293.)

4   *Collected Papers*, vol. iii. pp. 321–404.

5   An interesting account of the contrast between the learned, gentlemanly Roman system and the ancient Teutonic communal law will be found in the essay of the Germanist, Georg Beseler, *Volksrecht und Juristenrecht.*

6   This view is most lucidly stated by Professor Dicey in *The Law of the Constitution*, pp. 72–81.

Chapter 5

Nationality

Ernest Barker

Three writers[1] – all, as it chances, known to the writer of this article – have addressed themselves of late to the solution of a riddle which the Sphinx of history is propounding to our generation. "What is a nation," the impassive Sphinx inquires, "and what are the rights that belong to a nation?"

"What is a nation?" "The product of various concurrent forces" – Lord Bryce cautiously replies, adducing as examples of such forces race, language, religion, a common literature and common memories – "which have given to a section or group of men a sense of their unity, as the conscious possessors of common qualities and tendencies which are in some way distinctive, marking off the group from others, and creating in it the feeling of a corporate life." In this answer we may note the last two phrases, which imply, or seem to imply, that a nation is something exclusive, something "marked off" from other similar things, and again that it has the "feeling" (if not, perhaps, the fact) of a "corporate life," which demands (so one may guess) some measure of autonomy for its expression. The implications of Lord Bryce's definition seem to become explicit in that of Professor Muir. A nation is "a body of people who feel themselves to be naturally linked together by certain affinities which are so strong and real for them that they can live happily together, are dissatisfied when disunited, and cannot tolerate subjection to peoples who do not share these ties." It is obvious from the concluding words of this definition that Professor Muir assumes – apparently without doubt or examination – that a nation is, or should be, a State, and that it has a right (a sort of "natural right") to political independence. This is a large assumption, and in fact a *petitio principii*. It is a grave question, needing much deliberation, whether nations, as such, ought also to be States; and to demand an affirmative answer in a preliminary definition of terms is to evade the core and gist of the riddle that stands in debate. Mr Zimmern's definition makes no such demand. On the contrary – so far as political rights are concerned – it contains a piece of significant reticence. A nation – so runs Mr Zimmern's definition, thrice repeated in three different chapters – is "a body of people united by a corporate sentiment of peculiar intensity, intimacy, and dignity, related to a definite home-country." In this definition it is the silence that is really suggestive. As Mr Zimmern develops his argument, this silence, already suggestive, becomes very definite. A nation, he believes, has no necessary right to a separate and independent political existence. There is no divine right of the nation to govern itself. The rights of a nation are *social* rights. They belong to the sphere of education and literature, but not to the sphere of politics. The members of a nation should be free to be educated in their own schools, by their own Press, in their own way, according to their own culture; but politically they may be members of a State too broad and too wide in its membership to be limited to a single nation.

In many ways, and for many reasons, it is impossible not to sympathise with Mr Zimmern. History does not prove that a nation should be a State, or a State a nation. On the contrary, it shows that a single nation may be divided, and live its best life while it is divided, in a number of States; and, conversely, that a State may embrace, and embrace in contentment and prosperity, a number of nations. Ancient Greece is an example of the first possibility; the Roman Empire in its best days, and the British Empire of to-day (or at any rate, one hopes, of tomorrow) are examples of the second. The example of ancient Greece is peculiarly interesting. The Greeks were, and knew that they were, a nation. They were, as Herodotus remarks in a famous passage, of one blood, one tongue, one religion ("with common shrines and sacrifices to the Gods"), and one culture ("with ways of life after the same fashion"). Plato, in a passage of the *Laws*, almost repeats Herodotus: he speaks of one stock, one speech, one religion, one law. We may roughly paraphrase Herodotus and Plato by saying that the Greeks had a common stock of ideas, both about the other world and about the right way of behaviour in this world, and a common language (in spite of varieties of dialect) for communicating their ideas, and that, on the strength of these common elements, they regarded themselves as constituting a single society. But if they were one society, they were not, and they were resolved not to be, one State. The State in which they believed, and in which they lived, was a city; and they had many cities, and therefore many States. These Greek City-States gave their members the good life they sought, and gave it fully and abundantly. A national Greek State would have been pitched on a lower key, and would have made a poorer music. A prophet of nationality in Greece who identified the nation with the State would hardly have been a prophet of progress. The national State would have been a bigger thing; but is the Big necessarily the Good?

The Greeks, then, did not identify the national society with the political State. Mr Zimmern, who, if any man, understands "the Greek Commonwealth," has good precedent for the distinction which he seeks to draw between the nation and the State. To Professor Muir, a modernist, the Greeks are perhaps old-fashioned. His interest is in the nineteenth century; and his reading of the nineteenth century leads him to believe that "every nation has a *right* to freedom and unity" – in other words, that nationality is a political principle, and that nations either are or ought to be States. He accepts as "the culmination of modern history" this principle, which has been at work – not without rivals – for about one hundred, or at the most for four hundred, years (the recorded history of our race is now about seven thousand years old); and he thinks that its out-and-out acceptance might bring "good hope of a cessation of strife." The same principle of a "divine right of nationality" to an independent political expression would also appear to commend itself to Lord Bryce. He sees, indeed, the practical difficulties in the way of its application; and he occupies himself in examining those difficulties in the different areas of Europe and Asia in which they present themselves. Against Lord Bryce and Professor Muir Mr Zimmern takes his stand with a totally different principle. He denies their major premiss. Nationality, he asserts, is a social fact – and therefore (if we may father upon him a paradox which he may himself reject) it is a matter for the individual. It is a social fact in the sense that it belongs to the area of education and social intercourse; it is a matter of wearing kilts, or talkie dialect, or keeping Saturday instead of Sunday, or educating your children in a traditional way. Now these things are all things that touch the individual in his daily life; and that is the sense in which this "social" nationality is really individual. It is not a matter of a corporate life finding corporate expression in a political structure controlled by the common action of all the corporators; it is a matter of individual tastes and fancies – which happen, it is true, to agree with those of many other individuals – finding free play within a State which eschews all interference with these manifestations of the individual's liberty.

One's heart warms to a brave heretic – particularly if one is inclined to a little gentle heresy on one's own account. Some, indeed, of Mr Zimmern's heresies are perhaps really exaggerated orthodoxies; and his adoration of the State and its "Statehood" (to use the vocabulary of the *Round Table*) – an adoration which is the other side of his doubts about the nation and its "nationhood," and leads him, incidentally, to throw as much doubt on internationalism as upon nationalism – excites heretical feelings in the writer of these lines. Not all of us would agree that the State (as Mr Zimmern makes Aristotle say; but where did he say it?) is "a sovereign association, embracing *and superseding* all other associations." But we may dismiss, in spite of all temptations to controversy, this reverse side of Mr Zimmern's views on nationality, and we may turn at once to some appreciation of their obverse and obvious side. Roughly, he desires a moderate and non-political nationalism, manifested in the realm of social life and social intercourse and education, as an antidote to the vapid and *banal* cosmopolitanism which the agglomeration of all types in the great industrial machinery of our times is tending to produce. He sees two extremes and a golden mean. One extreme is that of denationalised, delocalised, deracinated cosmopolitanism; it is represented by the Argive greengrocer, at home on holiday from the USA in ancient Argos, who, being asked by Mr Zimmern if he thought of marrying in his old country, replied: "Not on your life. I mean to marry an American girl. Think of the custom I shall get from my wife's relations." The other extreme is that of fervent, exclusive political nationalism: it is represented by the Balkan prince, who, being promised in a dream any boon he craved, with the proviso that a double portion of that boon should descend on the people of a neighbouring nation, prayed that all his people might be smitten blind of one eye. Between the Argive greengrocer and the Balkan prince Mr Zimmern erects a figure of animated moderation, which (as it were) wears trews and speaks Gaelic, but does not and will not care about nationalist politics, though it is willing to pay homage (apparently) to the Statehood of a great multi-national State or Commonwealth. Nationality thus appears "not as a political creed for oppressed peoples, but rather as an educational creed for the diverse national groups of which the industrialised and largely migratory democracies in our large modern States must be increasingly composed." As Mr Zimmern says in another place, it is "not a political, but an educational conception."

There are thus three factors in Mr Zimmern's thought. The first is a belief in the great State or Commonwealth, such as the British Empire, which "embraces *and supersedes* all other associations." This belief in the great political society, not resting on any one nationalist basis, or on anything peculiar or particular, but ordered to universal ends of liberty and law – this belief, in spite of its elements of truth and in spite of its nobler aspects, seems almost to run to an adoration or *proskynesis* of political organisation that is Hellenistic rather than British. And this first factor is also the dominant factor; the two others are secondary and consequential. These two other factors are a grading and a classification of nationality as something in the sphere not of the State, but of society (belonging, as Hegel would say, not to *der Staat*, but to *der bürgerliche Gesellschaft*), and a doubt and fear – at any rate in the earlier essays in Mr Zimmern's book; there is a modification in the later essays – a doubt and a fear of international organisation that interferes untimely or too rudely with the sovereign State. These, then, are the factors of Mr Zimmern's philosophy; what are the causes and reasons of his embracing that philosophy? In the first place, he belongs himself to the Jewish nationality; and that nationality (perhaps in this respect unlike other nationalities, and perhaps, therefore, not a safe basis for generalisation) has been content to exist in the social sphere, being a nationality of the dispersion, and has not claimed political expression or independence. In the second place, he belongs to the *étatistes* of the Round Table; and the Round Table, dealing in terms of mechanics rather than of biology, thinks rather of political structures and systems than of national groups and their growth. It is perhaps for this latter reason that Mr Zimmern appears to think that Nationalism is a peculiar product of Europe, and that elsewhere, "if left to itself, it would slowly die of inanition" – an implication which hardly seems just or true when one thinks of the growth of Nationalism in Australia or Canada or South Africa, or, again – most striking of all instances – in the United States, where the war appears to have produced a degree of Nationalism before unknown.

To Mr Zimmern the State which is based on Nationalism is based on the particular, and not on the universal – on a particular national temperament and point of view, and not on the universal principles of law and justice, of liberty and equality. There is much propriety in this accusation, especially as it affects the German State, and the German theory of the State, of the last fifty years; and there is much truth in Mr Zimmern's paradox that it was the Germans and their allies, and not

Great Britain and her allies, who were the protagonists of Nationalism during the war. The Germans identified the "folk" with the State, and grounded the State on "folk-will" and "folk-right" to so dire an extent, and to such sad confusion of universal principles of right and wrong, that they were ultimately ready to condone their violation of the neutrality of Belgium on the plea of what one may call "folk-necessity." It is not good that a State should be based peculiarly or primarily on Nationalism. But if Nationalism is a poor foundation, perhaps it is a necessary, or at any rate a very useful, mortar. It supplies a cohesion, or unity of sentiment, to the various members living in the shelter of a political structure, which goes a long way to keep that structure together. In the old days loyalty to a common monarch kept the State at unity; in these days – more equalitarian and more republican – the sentiment of a common national brotherhood seems to take the place of filial devotion to a patriarchal king. At any rate one thing is sure – and that is that you cannot at present confine Nationalism, as Mr Zimmern is eager to do, to the social side of life. It is easy to make dichotomies and divisions; but the penetrating and percolating waters of life ooze through the dams and banks of logic. "The State for politics; Nationalism only permitted in social intercourse" – one may erect the warning; but will it be obeyed? Will it be obeyed on *either* side? Will the State refrain from interfering with social manifestations of Nationalism, or social manifestations of Nationalism refrain themselves from spilling over (or – perhaps it is better to say – blazing up) into political issues? Experience – the actual record and digest of facts – gives a negative answer. The State does actually interfere with the social manifestations of Nationalism, such as the use of a vernacular speech in the Press or in schools. It has done so in Germany; it does so, according to the testimony of French Canadians, in the Dominion of Canada; and the reason for what it does is its sense of the increased cohesion due to the use of a single common speech in daily intercourse. Perhaps the State is foolish in what it does – you only encourage a vernacular literature when you try to discourage it by the use of force – but the point of importance for our argument is simply the fact that it actually makes the attempt. *Vice versa*, social manifestations of Nationalism cannot but tend to issue in political aspirations and propaganda. Mr Zimmern seems to expect that you may have a Gaelic League for the use of Erse, and never proceed to think of an Irish Republic. Actually you do proceed to think of an Irish Republic. Mr Zimmern argues that this result only follows "when arbitrary government, by repressing the spontaneous manifestations of nationality, lures it into political channels." But the British Government has not repressed the "spontaneous manifestation" of the desire to speak Erse. This instance of Ireland, it would seem, is somewhat adverse to Mr Zimmern's philosophy. Indeed, that philosophy becomes somewhat inconsistent with itself when Mr Zimmern applies it to Ireland. He writes in one passage of the soul of the true Irish Nationalist as satisfied, when he knows that "somewhere Irish life is being lived under true Irish conditions" – the "somewhere" being "in the definite home-country" which, it will be remembered, is part of his definition of nationality. But "the living of an Irish life in Ireland under true Irish conditions" surely means something political; and to nine Irishmen out of ten (outside Ulster) it would mean an Irish Republic. *Ergo*, Irish Nationalism, even in Mr Zimmern's sense of the word, ultimately issues "somewhere" into politics.

The theory of an exclusively "social" Nationalism is one which has long been familiar in that mosaic of nationalities – Austria-Hungary. Msr Eisenmann, in *Le Compromis*, has discussed the various theories of the "rights of nationality" which a State so rich in nationalities has produced. Some writers (he explains) have taken pride in the multi-national character of their State. These writers would tell Mr Zimmern, who sets his hope "not in the Nation-State, which is only a stage, and in the West an outworn stage … but in States which find room for all sorts and conditions of communities and nations" – they would tell him (or they would have told him, before the war shattered Austria-Hungary into fragments) that his hopes were already realised in Austria-Hungary. He is not likely to be comforted by receiving any such news. He has, as it were, an assignation with the British Empire in his hopes of a multi-national State; and when Austria-Hungary turns up instead to keep the assignation, he is likely to look ruefully upon her. But Austria-Hungary remains worthy of study. Many of her thinkers had come upon Mr Zimmern's philosophy – that nationality belongs to social life, and is a matter for each individual in his daily intercourse with other individuals; and they had pitted their philosophy against the counter-philosophy of those who held that nationality belonged to political life, and was a matter for the corporate nation seeking to find political emancipation and embodiment. The school to which Mr Zimmern inclines has not been victorious. Nationality has proved in Austria-Hungary that it is a political fact. Mr Zimmern, like the Austro-Hungarian thinkers to whom he is akin, wrote before the collapse of the multi-national Austrian State in November, 1918.

Yet on the whole it may be said that Mr Zimmern administers shrewd thrusts to the easy-going Victorian cult of nationality (as embodied in Kossuth and Garibaldi) which survives in an eloquent simplicity in the pages of Professor Muir. He presents a point of view new to many of us, and presents it freshly, new smelted, as it were, from the ore of his own experience. He can understand the artificial and factitious character which Nationalism can assume in the Balkans, where journalists can fan (and indeed create) nationalist passions by articles composed over the midnight oil (how much literary propaganda may go to the making of a nation!), and where bishops may distribute rifles to guerilla bands for purposes which one may gently call by the name of national (here synonymous with that of religious) proselytisation. He realises the difficulties of the whole question; but his solution can hardly stand. It is really impossible to draw a firm line and to say "Thus far and no further" to Nationalism. Nationalism may never reach that line, or it may overflow it; but it will not be greatly affected by the line in any case. Nationalism is one of the fundamental human sentiments, like religion. Like other human sentiments (just because it is human) it may make for good, and it may make for evil. It may make for good, in developing a new aspect or facet of humanity – a new way of looking at life, peculiar to some single nation; it may make for evil, in narrowing the mind and its outlook, in intensifying oppositions, in dividing peoples and countries. Sometimes the fullness of the good it can do will only come if it attains political expression; sometimes the unbinding of political Nationalism may only be the unbinding of Satan. Exclusive introspective Nationalism of the German type has been a worse scourge to Europe than any nomadic incursion from Central Asia. A broad inclusive Nationalism after the heart of Mazzini – a Nationalism which makes a nation ask itself, "What can I do for the world?" and then go and do it – this may well be a light to lighten humanity.

The writer has dwelled long on Mr Zimmern, and has left himself little space for dealing with Lord Bryce or Professor Muir. Lord Bryce, writing a year ago, is chiefly concerned with the application of the principle of nationality to the coming nego-tiations for peace; Professor Muir, who has written three volumes round the theme of nationality during the war, is concerned to prove that, of four developments which a review of modern history suggests, the growth of the idea of nationality is the first, and the foundation of all the rest. Lord Bryce can see spots in the sun of Nationalism, and can admit that it has led to quasi-religious wars as terrible as the religious wars of the sixteenth century; Professor Muir appears to be too much blinded by the sun to maintain any critical poise. He can defend Nationalism by saying that the German interpretation of it is not Nationalism, but racialism – an assertion which involves a curious twisting of the sense of the word "race." He can lay down the proposition (it is true with the qualification that it is "loosely" asserted) that "every nation has a right to freedom," but he never explains what this freedom is, or why every nation has a right to it. He can write that "the principle of national-ity … asserts that the unity of sentiment which we call the national spirit constitutes the only sound basis for the organisation of the State"; but he does not tell us why this should be the case, and he never examines Lord Acton's contention (which Mr Zimmern more than once quotes) that the principle of nationality ruins the true universal character of the State. But nationality in Professor Muir's hands is a Protean thing; and it is difficult to grip his terminology firmly. In one sentence Britain is a "super-nationality," which incorporates, without weakening, four nationalities; in the next we are confronted with the "nationhood" of the British Empire.

As the connotation of Nationalism seems to vary in Professor Muir's view, so do its connections. It is connected with war, in the sense that (in spite of its right to freedom) "nationhood must mainly determine itself by conflict"; it is connected with peace, in the sense that "if the whole of Europe could once be … divided on national lines, there might be good hope of a cessation of strife." In the volume on the *Expansion of Europe* it is connected with imperialism; it is no accident, we are told, that "all the great colonising Powers have been unified Nation-States, and that imperial activities have been most vigorous when national sentiment has been strongest." In the volume on *National Self-Government* Nationalism is connected with democracy: "the national spirit has alone made modern self-government pos-sible"; "the era of national unification was also the era of constitutional settlement – the triumph of Nationalism was the decay of revolutionism." But this Protean and elusive spirit, though it seems inconsistent in its manifestations, appears in the pages of Professor Muir to be uniformly beneficent. Of the Satanic aspect which it can assume – of its dividingness; of its exclusiveness; of the atmosphere of a forcing-house which it can generate for rancours and animosities – we hear little or nothing. Yet surely the historian – sweeping on broad pinions over the past, and remembering the days of City-States, of Hellenistic monarchies, of the Roman Empire, of the mediæval polity – must recognise that Nationalism is a fairly recent, perhaps a temporary, and at any rate a mixed force. Nationalism is not all; and patriotism – so far as it is based on Nationalism – is not enough.

For Nationalism, after all, is only one of the bases on which men can organise their group-life. There are other and rival bases. There is the basis of even-handed law and equal liberty, which gives us the State. There is the basis of contiguity, which gives us the geographical region within whose bounds men buy and sell and meet in many other ways. There is the basis of common occupation, which gives us the organised guild or *syndicat*. All these bases, and all the structures built on these bases, are rivals with one another to-day. There is the nation, and there is also the State; there is the region, and there is also the occupation. Some men are Nationalists, and some are *Étatistes*; some men are Regionalists, and some are Occupationalists – or, as the name generally goes, Syndicalists. The interest of the hour in which we live is the struggle of these different conceptions. Two of them are in high fashion – two which are not very compatible with one another – Nationalism with one set of thinkers, Syndicalism with another. Nationalism can make its peace with the State, and, in the form of Collectivism, it can come to terms with Socialism. Syndicalism is the enemy of the nation, and no friend of the State. While Nationalism and Syndicalism fight, there may be a chance for the State – a State, one may hope, based on contiguity and brotherly neighbourliness – to come by its own. After all, it is in some ways better – better and easier – to love one's neighbour than to love one's kinsman or fellow-national. Neighbourliness is a quiet virtue – quiet but deep and permeating. It is a virtue that pays. To get on well with one's neighbours across the water, or across the ridges, means business ties and common economic interests. That is why the economist is enamoured of contiguity as a basis of political grouping; but the political theorist may well share his affection. There is one great thing about neighbourliness: it can grow to include more and more, while Nationalism is limited to the given number of its nationals. For the extent of a neighbourhood, and the number of persons included in a neighbourhood, depend on the communications that make the neighbourhood. Steam has made neighbourhoods of vastly greater scope. The internal combustion engine, working in motor car and aeroplane, is making neighbourhoods greater still. It is along these lines that some of us can confidently and quietly look forward to a time when the whole of our planet will be one connected neighbourhood, and, one hopes, a single connected commonwealth. In that day Mr Zimmern's vision may be realised; and Nationalism may become an undisturbed and undisturbing factor of social life, while over its head, based on the fundamental neighbourliness of humanity, and ordered to the common human ends of law and liberty, the universal State moves on its solemn task.

Note

1   Viscount Bryce, *Essays and Addresses in War-time*, Macmillan and Co., 1918 (chapter vii); A. E. Zimmern, *Nationality and Government*, Chatto and Windus, 1918 (chapters ii–iv); Ramsay Muir, *Nationalism and Internationalism*, Constable, 1916 (chapter ii); *The Expansion of Europe*, 1917; *National Self-Government*, 1918.

Chapter 6

The Pluralistic State

Harold Laski

Every student of politics must begin his researches with humble obeisance to the work of Aristotle; and therein, I take it, he makes confession of the inspiration and assistance he has had from the effort of philosophers. Indeed, if one took only the last century of intellectual history, names like Hegel, Green, and Bosanquet must induce in him a certain sense of humility. For the direction of his analysis has been given its perspective by their thought. The end his effort must achieve has been by no other thinkers so clearly or so wisely defined.

Yet the philosophic interpretation of politics has suffered from one serious weakness. It is rather with *staatslehre* than with *politik* that it has concerned itself. Ideals and forms have provided the main substance of its debates. So that even if, as with Hegel and Green, it has had the battles of the market-place most clearly in mind, it has somehow, at least ultimately, withdrawn itself from the arena of hard facts to those remoter heights where what a good Platonist has called[1] the 'pure instance' of the state may be dissected. Nor has it seen political philosophy sufficiently outside the area of its own problems. Aristotle apart, its weakness has lain exactly in those minutiæ of psychology which, collectively, are all-important to the student of administration. Philosophy seems, in politics at least, to take too little thought for the categories of space and time.

The legal attitude has been impaired by a somewhat similar limitation. The lawyer, perhaps of necessity, has concerned himself not with right but with rights, and his consequent preoccupation with the problem of origins, the place of ultimate reference, has made him, at least to the interested outsider, unduly eager to confound the legally ancient with the politically justifiable. One might even make out a case for the assertion that the lawyer is the head and centre of our modern trouble; for the monistic theory of the state goes back, in its scientific statement, to Jean Bodin. The latter became the spiritual parent of Hobbes, and thence, through Bentham, the ancestor of Austin. On Austin I will make no comment here; though a reference to an ingenious equation of Maitland's may perhaps be pardoned.[2]

It is with the lawyers that the problem of the modern state originates as an actual theory; for the lawyer's formulæ have been rather amplified than denied by the philosophers. Upon the historic events which surround their effort I would say one word, since it is germane to the argument I have presently to make. We must ceaselessly remember that the monistic theory of the state was born in an age of crisis and that each period of its revivification has synchronised with some momentous event which has signalised a change in the distribution of political power. Bodin, as is well known, was of that party which, in an age of religious warfare, asserted, lest it perish in an alien battle, the supremacy of the state.[3] Hobbes sought the means of order in a period when King and Parliament battled for the balance of power. Bentham published his *Fragment* on the eve of the Declaration of Independence; and Adam Smith, in the same year, was outlining the programme of another and profounder revolution. Hegel's philosophy was the outcome of a vision of German multiplicity destroyed by the unity of France. Austin's book was conceived when the middle classes of France and England had, in their various ways, achieved the conquest of a state hitherto but partly open to their ambition.

It seems of peculiar significance that each assertion of the monistic theory should have this background. I cannot stay here to disentangle the motives through which men so different in character should have embraced a theory as similar in substance. The result, with all of them, is to assert the supremacy of the state over all other institutions. Its primary organs have the first claim upon the allegiance of men; and Hobbes's insistence[4] that corporations other than the state are but the manifestations of disease is perhaps the best example of its ruthless logic. Hobbes and Hegel apart, the men I have noted were lawyers; and they were seeking a means whereby the source of power may have some adequate justification. Bentham, of course, at no point beatified the state; though zeal for it is not wanting in the earlier thinkers or in Hegel. What, I would urge, the lawyers did was to provide a foundation for the moral superstructure of the philosophers. It was by the latter that the monistic state was elevated from the plane of logic to the plane of ethics. Its rights then became matter of right. Its sovereignty became spiritualised into moral preëminence.

The transition is simple enough. The state is today the one compulsory form of association;[5] and for more than two thousand years we have been taught that its purpose is the perfect life. It thus seems to acquire a flavor of generality which is absent from all other institutions. It becomes instinct with an universal interest to which, as it appears, no other association may without inaccuracy lay claim. Its sovereignty thus seems to represent the protection of the universal aspect of men – what Rousseau called the common good – against the intrusion of more private aspects at the hands of which it might otherwise suffer humiliation. The state is an absorptive animal; and there are few more amazing tracts of history than that which records its triumphs over the challenge of competing groups. There seems, at least today, no certain method of escape from its demands. Its conscience is supreme over any private conception of good the individual may hold. It sets the terms upon which the lives of trade-unions may be lived. It dictates their doctrine to churches;

and, in England at least, it was a state tribunal which, as Lord Westbury said, dismissed hell with costs.[6] The area of its enterprise has consistently grown until today there is no field of human activity over which, in some degree, its pervading influence may not be detected.

But it is at this point pertinent to inquire what exact meaning is to be attached to an institution so vital as this. With one definition only I shall trouble you. "A state," writes Mr Zimmern,[7] "can be defined, in legal language, as a territory over which there is a government claiming unlimited authority." The definition, indeed, is not quite correct; for no government in the United States could claim, though it might usurp, unlimited power. But it is a foible of the lawyers to insist upon the absence of legal limit to the authority of the state; and it is, I think, ultimately clear that the monistic theory is bound up with some such assumption. But it is exactly here that our main difficulty begins to emerge. The state, as Mr Zimmern here points out, must act through organs; and, in the analysis of its significance, it is upon government that we must concentrate our main attention.[8]

Legally, no one can deny that there exists in every state some organ whose authority is unlimited. But that legality is no more than a fiction of logic. No man has stated more clearly than Professor Dicey[9] the sovereign character of the King in Parliament; no man has been also so quick to point out the practical limits to this supremacy. And if logic is thus out of accord with the facts of life the obvious question to be asked is why unlimited authority may be claimed. The answer, I take it, is reducible to the belief that government expresses the largest aspect of man and is thus entitled to institutional expression of the area covered by its interests. A history, of course, lies back of that attitude, the main part of which would be concerned with the early struggle of the modern state to be born. Nor do I think the logical character of the doctrine has all the sanction claimed for it. It is only with the decline of theories of natural law that Parliament becomes the complete master of its destinies. And the internal limits which the jurist is driven to admit prove, on examination, to be the main problem for consideration.

There are many different angles from which this claim to unlimited authority may be proved inadequate. That government is the most important of institutions few, except theocrats, could be found to deny; but that its importance warrants the monistic assumption herein implied raises far wider questions. The test, I would urge, is not an *a priori* statement of claim. Nothing has led us farther on the wrong path than the simple teleological terms in which Aristotle stated his conclusions. For when we say that political institutions aim at the good life, we need to know not only the meaning of good, but also those who are to achieve it, and the methods by which it is to be attained. What, in fact, we have to do is to study the way in which this monistic theory has worked; for our judgment upon it must depend upon its consequences to the mass of men and women. I would not trouble you unduly with history. But it is worth while to bear in mind that this worship of state-unity is almost entirely the offspring of the Reformation and therein, most largely, an adaptation of the practice of the medieval church. The fear of variety was not, in its early days, an altogether unnatural thing. Challenged from within and from without, uniformity seemed the key to self-preservation.[10] But when the internal history of the state is examined, its supposed unity of purpose and of effort sinks, with acquaintance, into nothingness. What in fact confronts us is a complex of interests; and between not few of them ultimate reconciliation is impossible. We cannot, for example, harmonise the modern secular state with a Roman Church based upon the principles of the Encyclical of 1864; nor can we find the basis of enduring collaboration between trade-unions aiming at the control of industry through the destruction of capitalistic organization and the upholders of capitalism. Historically, we always find that any system of government is dominated by those who at the time wield economic power; and what they mean by 'good' is, for the most part, the preservation of their own interests. Perhaps I put it too crudely; refined analysis would, maybe, suggest that they are limited by the circle of the ideas to which their interests would at the first instance give rise. The history of England in the period of the Industrial Revolution is perhaps the most striking example of this truth. To suggest, for instance, that the government of the younger Pitt was, in its agricultural policy, actuated by some conception of public welfare which was equal as between squire and laborer, is, in the light of the evidence so superbly discussed by Mr and Mrs Hammond, utterly impossible.[11] There is nowhere and at no time assurance of that consistent generality of motive in the practice of government which theory would suppose it to possess.

We cannot, that is to say, at any point, take for granted the motives of governmental policy, with the natural implication that we must erect safeguards against their abuse. These, I venture to think, the monistic theory of the state at no point, in actual practice, supplies. For its insistence on unlimited authority in the governmental organ makes over to it the immense power that comes from the possession of legality. What, in the stress of conflict, this comes to mean is the attribution of inherent rightness to acts of government. These are somehow taken, and that with but feeble regard to their actual substance, to be acts of the community. Something that, for want of a better term, we call the communal conscience, is supposed to want certain things. We rarely inquire either how it comes to want them or to need them. We simply know that the government enforces the demand so made and that the individual or group is expected to give way before them. Yet it may well happen, as we have sufficiently seen in our experience, that the individual or the group may be right. And it is difficult to see how a policy which thus penalizes all dissent, at least in active form, from government, can claim affinity with freedom. For freedom, as Mr Graham Wallas has finely said,[12] implies the chance of continuous initiative. But the ultimate implication of the monistic state in a society so complex as our own is the transference of that freedom from ordinary men to their rulers.

I cannot here dwell upon the more technical results of this doctrine, more particularly on the absence of liability for the faults of government that it has involved.[13] But it is in some such background as this that the pluralistic theory of the state takes its origin. It agrees with Mr Zimmern that a state is a territorial society divided into government and subjects, but it differs, as you will observe, from his definition in that it makes no assumptions as to the authority a government should possess.

And the reason for this fact is simply that it is consistently experimentalist in temper. It realizes that the state has a history and it is unwilling to assume that we have today given to it any permanence of form. There is an admirable remark of Tocqueville's on this point which we too little bear in mind.[14] And if it be deemed necessary to dignify this outlook by antiquity we can, I think, produce great names as its sponsors. At least it could be shown that the germs of our protest are in men like Nicholas of Cusa, like Althusius, Locke, and Royer-Collard.

It thus seems that we have a twofold problem. The monistic state is an hierarchical structure in which power is, for ultimate purposes, collected at a single centre. The advocates of pluralism are convinced that this is both administratively incomplete and ethically inadequate. You will observe that I have made no reference here to the lawyer's problem. Nor do I deem it necessary; for when we are dealing, as the lawyer deals, with sources of ultimate reference, the questions are no more difficult, perhaps I should also add, no easier, than those arising under the conflict of jurisdictions in a federal state.

It is with other questions that we are concerned. Let us note, in the first place, the tendency in the modern state for men to become the mere subjects of administration. It is perhaps as yet too early to insist, reversing a famous generalisation of Sir Henry Maine, that the movement of our society is from contract to status; but there is at least one sense in which that remark is significant. Amid much vague enthusiasm for the thing itself, every observer must note a decline in freedom. What we most greatly need is to beware lest we lose that sense of spontaneity which enabled Aristotle to define citizenship as the capacity to rule not less than to be ruled in turn.[15] We believe that this can best be achieved in a state of which the structure is not hierarchical but coördinate, in which, that is to say, sovereignty is partitioned upon some basis of function. For the division of power makes men more apt to responsibility than its accumulation. A man, or even a legislature that is overburdened with a multiplicity of business, will not merely neglect that which he ought to do; he will, in actual experience, surrender his powers into the hands of forceful interests which know the way to compel his attention. He will treat the unseen as non-existent and the inarticulate as contented. The result may, indeed, be revolution; but experience suggests that it is more likely to be the parent of a despotism.

Nor is this all. Such a system must needs result in a futile attempt to apply equal and uniform methods to varied and unequal things. Every administrator has told us of the effort to arrive at an intellectual routine; and where the problems of government are as manifold as at present that leads to an assumption of similarity which is rarely borne out by the facts. The person who wishes to govern America must know that he cannot assume identity of conditions in North and South, East and West. He must, that is to say, assume that his first duty is not to assert a greatest common measure of equality but to prove it. That will, I suggest, lead most critical observers to perceive that the unit with which we are trying to deal is too large for effective administration. The curiosities, say of the experiment in North Dakota, are largely due to this attempt on the part of predominating interests to neglect vital differences of outlook. Such differences, moreover, require a sovereignty of their own to express the needs they imply. Nor must we neglect the important fact that in an area like the United States the individual will too often get lost in its very vastness. He gets a sense of impotence as a political factor of which the result is a failure properly to estimate the worth of citizenship. I cannot stay to analyse the result of that mistaken estimate. I can only say here that I am convinced that it is the nurse of social corruption.

Administratively, therefore, we need decentralisation; or, if you like, we need to revivify the conception of federalism which is the great contribution of America to political science. But we must not think of federalism today merely in the old spatial terms. It applies not less to functions than to territories. It applies not less to the government of the cotton industry, or of the civil service, than it does to the government of Kansas and Rhode Island. Indeed, the greatest lesson the student of government has to learn is the need for him to understand the significance for politics of industrial structure and, above all, the structure of the trade-union movement.[16] The main factor in political organization that we have to recover is the factor of consent, and here trade-union federalism has much to teach us. It has found, whether the unit be a territorial one like the average local, or an industrial like that envisaged by the shop-steward movement in England, units sufficiently small to make the individual feel significant in them. What, moreover, this development of industrial organization has done is to separate the processes of production and consumption in such fashion as to destroy, for practical purposes, the unique sovereignty of a territorial parliament. It is a nice question for the upholders of the monistic theory to debate as to where the effective sovereignty of America lay in the controversy over the Adamson law; or to consider what is meant by the vision of that consultative industrial body which recent English experience seems likely, in the not distant future, to bring into being.[17]

The facts, I suggest, are driving us towards an effort at the partition of power. The evidence for that conclusion you can find on all sides. The civil services of England and France are pressing for such a reorganization.[18] It is towards such a conclusion that what we call too vaguely the labor movement has directed its main energies.[19] We are in the midst of a new movement for the conquest of self-government. It finds its main impulse in the attempt to disperse the sovereign power because it is realised that where administrative organization is made responsive to the actual associations of men, there is a greater chance not merely of efficiency but of freedom also. That is why, in France, there has been for some time a vigorous renewal of that earlier effort of the sixties in which the great Odillon-Barrot did his noblest work;[20] and it does not seem unlikely that some reconstruction of the ancient provinces will at last compensate for the dangerous absorptiveness of Paris. The British House of Commons has debated federalism as the remedy for its manifold ills;[21] and the unused potentialities of German decentralisation may lead to the results so long expected now that the deadening pressure of Prussian domination has been withdrawn. We are learning, as John Stuart Mill pointed out in an admirable passage,[22] that "all the facilities which a government enjoys of access to information, all the means which it possesses of remunerating, and therefore of commanding, the best available talent in the market, are not an equivalent for the one great disadvantage of an inferior interest in the result." For we now know that the consequent of that inferior interest is the consistent degradation of freedom.[23]

I have spoken of the desire for genuine responsibility and the direction in which it may be found for administrative purposes. To this aspect the ethical side of political pluralism stands in the closest relation. Fundamentally, it is a denial that a law can be explained merely as a command of the sovereign for the simple reason that it denies, ultimately, the sovereignty of anything save right conduct. The philosophers since, particularly, the time of T. H. Green, have told us insistently that the state is based upon will; though they have too little examined the problem of what will is most likely to receive obedience. With history behind us, we are compelled to conclude that no such will can by definition be a good will; and the individual must therefore, whether by himself or in concert with others, pass judgment upon its validity by examining its substance. That, it is clear enough, makes an end of the sovereignty of the state in its classical conception. It puts the state's acts – practically, as I have pointed out, the acts of its primary organ, government – on a moral parity with the acts of any other association. It gives to the judgments of the State exactly the power they inherently possess by virtue of their moral content, and no other. If the English state should wish, as in 1776, to refuse colonial freedom; if Prussia should choose to embark upon a Kulturkampf; if any state, to take the decisive instance, should choose to embark upon war; in each case there is no *a priori* rightness about its policy. You and I are part of the leverage by which that policy is ultimately enacted. It therefore becomes a moral duty on our part to examine the foundations of state-action. The last sin in politics is unthinking acquiescence in important decisions.

I have elsewhere dealt with the criticism that this view results in anarchy.[24] What it is more profitable here to examine is its results in our scheme of political organization. It is, in the first place, clear that there are no demands upon our allegiance except the demands of what we deem right conduct. Clearly, in such an aspect, we need the means of ensuring that we shall know right when we see it. Here, I would urge, the problem of rights becomes significant. For the duties of citizenship cannot be fulfilled, save under certain conditions; and it is necessary to ensure the attainment of those conditions against the encroachments of authority. I cannot here attempt any sort of detail; but it is obvious enough that freedom of speech,[25] a living wage, an adequate education, a proper amount of leisure, the power to combine for social effort, are all of them integral to citizenship. They are natural rights in the sense that without them the purpose of the state cannot be fulfilled. They are natural also in the sense that they do not depend upon the state for their validity. They are inherent in the eminent worth of human personality. Where they are denied, the state clearly destroys whatever claims it has upon the loyalty of men.

Rights such as these are necessary to freedom because without them man is lost in a world almost beyond the reach of his understanding. We have put them outside the power of the state to traverse; and this again must mean a limit upon its sovereignty. If you ask what guarantee exists against their destruction in a state where power is distributed, the answer, I think, is that only in such a state have the masses of men the opportunity to understand what is meant by their denial. It is surely, for example, significant that the movement for the revival of what we broadly term natural law should derive its main strength from organized trade-unionism. It is hardly less important that among those who have perceived the real significance of the attitude of labor in the Taff Vale and Osborne cases should have been a high churchman most deeply concerned with the restoration of the church.[26] That is what coördinate organization will above all imply, and its main value is the fact that what, otherwise, must strike us most in the modern state is the inert receptiveness of the multitude. Every student of politics knows well enough what this means. Most would, on analysis, admit that its dissipation is mainly dependent upon an understanding of social mechanisms now largely hidden from the multitude. The only hopeful way of breaking down this inertia is by the multiplication of centres of authority. When a man is trained to service in a trade-union, he cannot avoid seeing how that activity is related to the world outside. When he gets on a school-committee, the general problems of education begin to unfold themselves before him. Paradoxically, indeed, we may say that a consistent decentralisation is the only effective cure for an undue localism. That is because institutions with genuine power become ethical ideas and thus organs of genuine citizenship. But if the Local Government Board, or the Prefect, sit outside, the result is a balked disposition of which the results are psychologically well known. A man may obtain some compensation for his practical exclusion from the inwardness of politics by devotion to golf. But I doubt whether the compensation is what is technically termed sublimation, and it almost always results in social loss.

Here, indeed, is where the main superiority of the pluralistic state is manifest. For the more profoundly we analyse the psychological characteristics of its opposite, the less adequate does it seem relative to the basic impulses of men. And this, after all, is the primary need to satisfy. It was easy enough for Aristotle to make a fundamental division between masters and men and adapt his technique to the demands of the former; but it was a state less ample than a moderate-sized city that he had in mind. It was simple for Hobbes to assume the inherent badness of men and the consequent need of making government strong, lest their evil nature bring it to ruin; yet even he must have seen, what our own generation has emphasized, that the strength of governments consists only in the ideas of which they dispose. It was even simple for Bentham to insist on the ruling motive of self-interest; but he wrote before it had become clear that altruism was an instinct implied in the existence of the herd. We know at least that the data are more complex. Our main business has become the adaptation of our institutions to a variety of impulses with the knowledge that we must at all costs prevent their inversion. In the absence of such transmutation what must mainly impress us is the wastage upon which our present system is builded. The executioner, as Maistre said, is the corner-stone of our society. But it is because we refuse to release the creative energies of men.

After all, our political systems must be judged not merely by the ends they serve, but also by the way in which they serve those ends. The modern state provides a path whereby a younger Pitt may control the destinies of a people; it even gives men of leisure a field of passionate interest to cultivate. But the humbler man is less fortunate in the avenues we afford; and if we have record of notable achievement after difficult struggle, we are too impressed by the achievement to take due note of the anguish upon which it is too often founded. This, it may be remarked, is the touchstone by which the major portion of our institutions will be tested in the future; and I do not think we can be unduly certain that they will stand the test. The modern state, at bottom, is too much an historic category not to change its nature with the advent of new needs.

Those new needs, it may be added, are upon us, and the future of our civilization most largely depends upon the temper in which we confront them. Those who take refuge in the irrefutable logic of the sovereign state may sometimes take thought that for many centuries of medieval history the very notion of sovereignty was unknown. I would not seek unduly to magnify those far-off times; but it is worth while to remember that no thoughts were dearer to the heart of medieval thinkers than ideals of right and justice. Shrunken and narrow, it may be, their fulfillment often was; but that was not because they did not know how to dream. Our finely articulated structure is being tested by men who do not know what labor and thought have gone into its building. It is a cruder test they will apply. Yet it is only by seeking to understand their desires that we shall be able worthily to meet it.

Notes

1   Barker, *Political Thought in England from Herbert Spencer to Today*, p. 68 f.
2   Cf. *The Life of F. W. Maitland*, by H. A. L. Fisher, p. 117.
3   The background of his book has recently been exhaustively outlined by Roger Chauviré in his *Jean Bodin* (Paris, 1916), esp. pp. 312 f.
4   *Leviathan*, Chap. XLIV.
5   I say today; for it is important to remember that, for the Western World, this was true of the Church until the Reformation.
6   A. W. Benn, *History of English Rationalism in the Nineteenth Century*, Vol. II, p. 133.
7   *Nationality and Government*, p. 56.
8   Cf. my *Authority in the Modern State*, pp. 26 ff.
9   Cf. *The Law of the Constitution* (8th edn), pp. 37 ff.
10   Cf. Professor McIlwain's introduction to his edition of the *Political Works of James I*, and my comment thereon, *Pol. Sci. Quarterly*, Vol. 34, p. 290.
11   See their brilliant volume, *The Village Laborer* (1911).
12   Cf. his article in the *New Statesman*, Sept. 25, 1915. I owe my knowledge of this winning definition to Mr A. E. Zimmern's *Nationality and Government*, p. 57.
13   Cf. my paper on the Responsibility of the State in England. 32 *Harv. L. Rev.*, p. 447.
14   *Souvenirs*, p. 102.
15   *Politics*, Bk. III, C. I, 1275a.
16   A book that would do for the English-speaking world what M. Paul-Boncour did twenty years ago for France in his *Fédéralisme Économique* would be of great service.
17   See the *Report of the Provisional Joint Committee of the Industrial Conference*. London, 1919.
18   See my *Authority in the Modern State*, Chap. V.

19   Cf. Cole, *Self-Government in Industry*, passim., esp. Chap. III.

20   Odillon-Barrot, *De la centralization*.

21   *Parliamentary Debates*, June 4th and 5th, 1919.

22   *Principles of Political Economy* (2d edn), Vol. II, p. 181.

23   On all this, cf. my *Problem of Administrative Areas* (Smith College Studies, Vol. IV, No. I).

24   *Authority in the Modern State*, pp. 93–4.

25   Cf. the brilliant article of my colleague, Professor Z. Chafee, Jr, in 32 *Harv. L. Rev.*, 932 f.

26   J. Neville Figgis, *Churches in the Modern State*. The recent death of Dr Figgis is an irreparable blow to English scholarship.

Chapter 7

A Guild in Being

G. D. H. Cole

The name "Guild" is taken from the Middle Ages. Throughout the mediæval period the predominant form of industrial organisation throughout the civilisation of Christendom was the Gild or Guild, an association of independent producers or merchants for the regulation of production or sale. The mediæval Gild was not indeed confined to industry: it was the common form of popular association in the mediæval town. There were Gilds for social and charitable, and for educational, as well as for industrial purposes; and every Gild, whatever its specific function, had a strong religious basis and an essentially religious form. This is not the place to enter into a discussion of the rise, organisation and decline of the mediæval system; but it is necessary to show, both what are the fundamental differences between mediæval Gilds and modern Guilds,[1] and what is the essential unity of idea between them.

The mediæval Gild was essentially local, and the Gilds in a single town formed a separate system. This applies less to the merchant than to the craft bodies, but it is true as a generalisation, and especially true of the British Gilds. This fact, which corresponds to the comparative localisation of markets owing to the scanty facilities for transit, of course largely accounts for the break-up of the Gilds at the close of the Middle Ages. The mediæval Gild again was an association of independent producers, each of whom worked on his own with a small number of journeymen and apprentices. It was an organisation based on small-scale handicraft production, and it broke down before the accumulation of wealth which made large-scale enterprise possible. The Gild was a regulative rather than a directly controlling or managing body. It did not itself manage the industry, though it sometimes acted as a purchasing agent for materials: it left actual management in the hands of its members, the master-craftsmen; but it laid down elaborate regulations governing the actions and professional code of the members. These regulations, which are the essence of the mediæval Gild system, had as their basis the double object of maintaining both the liberties and rights of the craft and its tradition of good workmanship and faithful communal service, as expressed in the "Just Price." They declared war on shoddy work, on extortion and usury, and on unregulated production. They afforded to their members a considerable security, and an assured communal status. They held, in mediæval Society, a recognised position as economic organs of the body social, possessing a tradition of free service, and, on the strength of that tradition, filling an honourable place in the public life of the mediæval City.

I am far from contending that the Gilds were perfect, or that they always, even in their best days, lived up to the full demands of their principles. Certainly, in the days of their decline, when they were fighting a losing battle in a hostile environment, they departed very far from their tradition. But we are concerned less with their actual achievement – which was, for a period of centuries, very great indeed – than with the spirit which animated them, and the principles upon which their power was based. We want to see what in these principles is of value to us in confronting the problems of our own time, and, if their spirit is one that we would gladly recapture, what lessons we can learn from them concerning the foundation on which this spirit rested. For a fundamental difference between mediæval industry and industry to-day is that the former was imbued through and through with the spirit of free communal service, whereas this motive is almost wholly lacking in modern industrialism, and the attempt to replace it by the motives of greed on one side and fear on the other is manifestly breaking down. It is undoubtedly the case that, though there were sharp practices and profiteering in the Middle Ages, the Gildsman or the Gild that committed or sanctioned them did so in flat violation of moral principles which he or it had explicitly accepted as the basis of the industrial order, whereas to-day moral principles are regarded almost as intruders in the industrial sphere, and many forms of sharp practice and profiteering rank as the highest manifestations of commercial sagacity. In the Middle Ages, there were industrial sinners, but they were conscious of sin; for commercial morality and communal morality were the same. To-day, commercial morality has made a code of its own, and most of its clauses are flat denials of the principles of communal morality. In the Middle Ages, the motives to which the industrial system made its appeal were motives of free communal service: to-day, they are motives of greed and fear.

Clearly, we cannot seek to restore the mediæval – that is, the communal – spirit in industry by restoring the material conditions of the Middle Ages. We cannot go back to "town economy," a general régime of handicraft and master-craftsmanship, tiny-scale production. We can neither pull up our railways, fill in our mines, and dismantle our factories, nor conduct our large-scale enterprises under a system developed to fit the needs of a local market and a narrowly-restricted production. If the mediæval system has lessons for us, they are not parrot-lessons of slavish imitation, but lessons of the spirit, by which we may learn how to build up, on the basis of large-scale production and the world-market, a system of industrial organisation that appeals to the finest human motives and is capable of developing the tradition of free communal service. I fully believe that, when we have established these free conditions, there will come, from producer and consumer alike, a widespread demand for goods of finer quality than the shoddy which we turn out in such quantity to-day, and that this will bring about a new standard of craftsmanship and a return, over a considerable sphere, to small-scale production. But this, if it comes, will come only as the deliberate choice of free men in a free Society. Our present problem is, taking the conditions of production substantially as we find them, to reintroduce into industry the communal spirit, by re-fashioning industrialism in such a way as to set the communal motives free to operate.

The element of identity between the mediæval Gilds and the National Guilds proposed by the Guild Socialists to-day is thus far more of spirit than of organisation. A National Guild would be an association of all the workers by hand and brain concerned in the carrying on of a particular industry or service, and its function would be actually to carry on that industry or service on behalf of the whole community. Thus, the Railway Guild would include all the workers of every type – from general managers and technicians to porters and engine cleaners required for the conduct of the railways as a public service. This association would be entrusted by the community with the duty and responsibility of administering the railways efficiently for the public benefit, and would be left itself to make the internal arrangements for the running of trains and to choose its own officers, administrators, and methods of organisation.

I do not pretend to know or prophesy exactly how many Guilds there would be, or what would be the lines of demarcation between them. For example, railways and road transport might be organised by separate Guilds, or by a single Guild with internal subdivisions. So might engineering and shipbuilding, and a host of other closely-related industries. This is a matter, not of principle, but of convenience; for there is no reason why the various Guilds should be of anything like uniform size. The general basis of the proposed Guild organisation is clear enough: it is industrial, and each National Guild will represent a distinct and coherent service or group of services.

It must not, however, be imagined that Guildsmen are advocating a highly centralised system, in which the whole of each industry will be placed under a rigid central control. The degree of centralisation will largely depend on the character of the service. Thus, the railway industry obviously demands a much higher degree of centralisation than the building industry, which serves mainly a local market. But, apart from this, Guildsmen are keen advocates of the greatest possible extension of local initiative and of autonomy for the small group, in which they see the best chance of keeping the whole organisation keen, fresh and adaptable, and of avoiding the tendency to rigidity and conservatism in the wrong things, so characteristic of large-scale organisation, and especially of trusts and combines under capitalism to-day. The National Guilds would be, indeed, for the most part co-ordinating rather than directly controlling bodies, and would be concerned more with the adjustment of supply and demand than with the direct control or management of their several industries. This will appear more plainly when we have studied the internal organisation of the Guilds.

The members of the Guild will be scattered over the country, in accordance with the local distribution of their particular industry, and will be at work in the various factories, mines, or other productive units belonging to their form of service. The factory, or place of work, will be the natural unit of Guild life. It will be, to a great extent, internally self-governing, and it will be the unit and basis of the wider local and national government of the Guild. The freedom of the particular factory as a unit is of fundamental importance, because the object of the whole Guild system is to call out the spirit of free service by establishing really democratic conditions in industry. This democracy, if it is to be real, must come home to, and be exercisable directly by, every individual member of the Guild. He must feel that he is enjoying real self-government and freedom *at his work*; or he will not work well and under the impulse of the communal spirit. Moreover, the essential basis of the Guild being associative service, the spirit of association must be given free play in the sphere in which it is best able to find expression. This is manifestly the factory, in which men have the habit and tradition of working together. The factory is the natural and fundamental unit of industrial democracy. This involves, not only that the factory must be free, as far as possible, to manage its own affairs, but also that the democratic unit of the factory must be made the basis of the larger democracy of the Guild, and that the larger organs of Guild administration and government must be based largely on the principle of factory[2] representation. This raises, of course, important financial considerations, which will be dealt with in their place, when we discuss the financial basis of the Guild Socialist community.

Before, however, we attempt to consider in detail how either a Guild factory or the larger administrative machinery of a Guild would be organised, it is necessary to discuss certain general questions which affect the whole character of the organisation. I have spoken of the Guilds as examples of "industrial democracy" and "democratic association," and we must understand clearly wherein this Guild democracy consists, and especially how it bears on the relations between the different classes of workers included in a single Guild. For since a Guild includes *all* the workers by hand and brain engaged in a common service, it is clear that there will be among its members very wide divergences of function, of technical skill, and of administrative authority. Neither the Guild as a whole nor the Guild factory can determine all issues by the expedient of the mass vote, nor can Guild democracy mean that, on all questions, each member is to count as one and none as more than one. A mass vote on a matter of technique understood only by a few experts would be a manifest absurdity, and, even if the element of technique is left out of account, a factory administered by constant mass votes would be neither efficient nor at all a pleasant place to work in. There will be in the Guilds technicians occupying special positions by virtue of their knowledge, and there will be administrators possessing special authority by virtue both of skill and ability and of personal qualifications. What are to be the methods of choosing these officers and administrators within the Guild, and what are to be their powers and relation to the other members when they have been chosen?

The question of "leadership," "discipline," "authority" in their relation to the democratic principle is, of course, as old as the earliest discussions of democracy itself. The difference between democracy and autocracy is not that the latter recognises leadership and the former does not, but that in democracy the leader stands in an essentially different relation to those whom he leads, and, instead of substituting his will for theirs, aims at carrying out, not their "real will" as interpreted by him,[3] but their actual will as understood by themselves. In short, the democratic leader leads by influence and co-operation and not by the forcible imposition of his will. Leading in this way, he may and should have not less, but far more, "authority" than the autocrat, because he is carrying with him the wills of those whom he leads. A democratic Guild will have leaders, discipline and authority in a fuller and more real sense than these can exist under the industrial autocracy of capitalism.

How, then, will these Guild leaders be chosen? That it will be by the Guild itself goes without saying; for their imposition upon it from without would at once and utterly destroy its democratic character. But this does not mean that every type of leader must be chosen by a mass ballot of the whole Guild.

Let us begin our answer by removing from the discussion the man who is chosen, mainly or exclusively because he possesses a particular technical qualification, for the performance of a function which is essentially technical. He is not really a leader, but a consultant or adviser, and the matter of choosing him is an expert question which does not raise the democratic issue. It is for the leaders in the real sense – the men who, while they may require special expert skill or technical knowledge, are not chosen for these alone, but mainly for personal character or ability – the men whose work is mainly that of directing the work of others, of moving the energies of a group of men towards an accepted end, of expressing the corporate solidarity and co-operative spirit of the group – that we are here concerned to find the right principle of choice. To me it seems clear that, for any function which demands thus essentially the co-operations of wills, the only right principle is that the person who is to perform it should be chosen by those in co-operation with whom it is to be exercised. That is to say, the governing principle in the choice of Guild leaders will be election "from below," by those whom the leaders will have to lead.

This principle, however, is fully compatible with certain necessary safeguards. Whenever a post requires, in addition to personal fitness for leadership, of which those who are to be led are the best judges, definite qualifications of skill or technique, the possession of these qualifications can be made a condition of eligibility for the position. A shipowner to-day can only appoint as captain of his ship a man who holds a master's certificate. The seamen of the future Guild will only be able to choose as their captain a man who is similarly equipped. And such certificates of technical qualification will be issued, as they are in some cases to-day, by bodies predominantly representative of those already qualified, but with safeguards against the adoption by such bodies of an unduly exclusive attitude.

Again, there is no need to lay it down as a rigid principle that the leader must, in every case, be chosen by the actual group of workers whom he is to lead, and that no other worker of the same calling is to play any part in the choice. I believe, indeed, that, in nine cases out of ten at least, the right way is for the actual group that needs a leader to choose him, and that, with the full establishment of industrial democracy, this method would become practically universal; but there is no need to make it a rigid rule, provided that in every case the choice is made by men who are subject to similar leadership within the same calling and over a reasonably small area. Thus, the managers of a number of building jobs in the same district might conceivably be best appointed by the building workers of the district as a whole, rather than by the workers on each particular job; but this is an exception, due to the shifting character of building operations. As a general practice, the men on the job should choose their leaders for the job.

This applies with the greatest force of all in the smallest area over which industrial leadership is normally exercised. It is indispensable to industrial democracy that the foremen, the first grade of industrial supervisors, should be chosen directly by the particular body of men with whom they are to work; for, unless they are so chosen, the spirit of co-operation will not be set flowing at its source, and the whole organisation will be deprived of its democratic impulse. Within the factory, direct election by the individual workers concerned will probably be the best way of choosing nearly all the leaders; but, when units of organisation larger than the factory are reached, I do not suggest that direct election by the whole body of workers is any longer the best or the most democratic course. Election by delegates representing the whole body may often be better and more democratic. This, however, raises the whole question of direct *versus* indirect election, with which I shall have to deal later in connection with a very much wider problem.

This discussion of the methods of choosing leaders under a democratic industrial system may seem to be somewhat dull and detailed; but it is one of the fundamental problems of Guild Socialism. For the most frequent argument urged against industrial democracy is that it is incompatible with workshop discipline and productive efficiency, and recent utterances of the Russian Bolshevik leaders seem to indicate that they have come round, temporarily at least, to this view. Let us admit immediately that the institution suddenly to-day of a complete system of democratic choice of leaders such as I have outlined would be attended by enormous difficulties. The workers have no experience of industrial democracy: they have been accustomed to regard those who hold authority in capitalist industry as their natural enemies; and they could not, in a moment, revise the habits of a lifetime, or become fully imbued, in a day or a year, with the new conception of leadership as a co-operation of wills. The new system will have to make its way gradually, and it will not be perfectly and securely established until it too has become an instinct and a tradition. We have, however, in the long run, no alternative to trying it; for the old idea of leadership by the imposition of will is breaking down with the old industrial system.

We must not, then, in estimating the merits and possibilities of democratic leadership, concentrate our attention too much on the difficulties which would attend its instantaneous introduction: we must try to imagine it as it would be after a period of experience, when the workers were getting used to it, and the purely initial difficulties had been overcome. What, under these conditions, would be the new relation between the leader and those whom he would have to lead?

In a certain sense, he would clearly be less powerful. He could not, in a democratic Guild association, have the uncontrolled power of the "sack," the right to send a man to privation and possibly worse without appeal. For the Guild members would insist that a man threatened with dismissal should be tried by his peers, and every Guildsman would surely have behind him a considerable measure of economic security. Nor would he be able to ignore public opinion in the factory or in the Guild as a whole as a capitalistic manager can ignore it. But to set against these losses – if they were to be so regarded – he would have far more than countervailing gains. He would have a good prospect, if he used ordinary commonsense, of having the public opinion of the factory decisively on his side in his attempt to make things go well and smoothly: he would be able to look for a keen desire on the part of the workers to co-operate with him in producing the best results, and, at the worst, there could be between him and them no such barrier as is presented by the fact that the manager in a factory to-day holds his position as the nominee of a capitalist employer.

I strongly suspect that the managers in such a Guild factory would have no cause to complain of lack of power. If they wanted authority, they would find ample scope for it; but I believe most of them would soon cease to think of their positions mainly in terms of power, and would come to think of them instead mainly in terms of function. Only under the free conditions of democratic industry would the leader find real scope for leadership, and he would find it in a way that would enable him to concentrate all his faculties on the development of his factory as a communal service, instead of being, as now, constantly thwarted and restrained by considerations of shareholders' profit. There is no class of "industrious persons," as the Chartists would have said, to whom the Guild idea ought to have a stronger appeal than to the managers and technicians of industry; for it alone offers them full opportunities to use their ability in co-operation with their fellow-workers and for the service of their fellow-men.

A Guild factory, then, would be a natural centre of self-government, no longer, like the factories of to-day, a mere prison of boredom and useless toil, but a centre of free service and associative enterprise. There would, of course, be dull and unpleasant work still to be done in the world; but even this would be immeasurably lightened if it were done under free conditions and if the right motives were enlisted on its side.[4]

In this factory there would doubtless be workshop committees, meetings, debates, voting, and all the phenomena of democratic organisation; but, though these are essential, they are not so much of the quintessence of the new thing as the co-operative spirit which they exist to safeguard. Given free choice of leaders and free criticism of them when chosen, a good deal of the mere machinery of democracy might remain normally in the background.

But there is one further point on which we must touch in order to make our picture of the leader's position complete. What security of tenure would he have, and how could he be removed if he failed to give satisfaction? The workers who chose their manager need not have an unrestricted right to recall him at any moment. Before he could be deposed, he should have the right to appeal to his peers – his fellow-managers; and, if they held him in the right, but the workers still desired his dismissal, the case should go for judgment to a higher tribunal of the Guild.

But even so I think that after a certain lapse of time the workers under him should have the right to remove him; for a sustained desire to do so would prove incompatibility of temperament, which would unfit him for the co-operative task of democratic leadership in that particular factory. He might go through no fault of his own; but in that case he would be likely soon to find an opening elsewhere.

This factory of ours is, then, to the fullest extent consistent with the character of its service, a self-governing unit, managing its own productive operations, and free to experiment to the heart's content in new methods, to develop new styles and products, and to adapt itself to the peculiarities of a local or individual market. This autonomy of the factory is the safeguard of Guild Socialism against the dead level of mediocrity, the more than adequate substitute for the variety which the competitive motive was once supposed to stimulate, the guarantee of liveliness, and of individual work and workmanship.

With the factory thus largely conducting its own concerns, the duties of the larger Guild organisations would be mainly those of co-ordination, of regulation, and of representing the Guild in its external relations. They would, where it was necessary, co-ordinate the production of various factories, so as to make supply coincide with demand. They would probably act largely as suppliers of raw materials and as marketers of such finished products as were not disposed of directly from the factory. They would lay down general regulations, local or national, governing the methods of organisation and production within the Guild, they would organise research, and they would act on behalf of the Guild in its relations both with other Guilds, and with other forms of organisation, such as consumers' bodies, within the community, or with bodies abroad.

This larger Guild organisation, as we have seen, while it need not conform in all cases to any particular structure, must be based directly on the various factories included in the Guild. That is to say, the district Guild Committee must represent the various factories belonging to the Guild in the district, and probably also in most cases must include representatives of the various classes of workers, by hand or brain, included in the Guild. The national Committee must similarly represent districts and classes of workers, in order that every distinct point of view, whether of a district or of a section, may have the fullest possible chance of being stated and considered by a representative body. To the choice of the district and national officers of the Guild much the same arguments apply as to that of other leaders, save that, as we saw, over the larger areas indirect may often afford a more truly democratic result than direct election.

The essential thing about this larger organisation is that its functions should be kept down to the minimum possible for each industry. For it is in the larger organisation and in the assumption by it of too much centralised power that the danger of a new form of bureaucracy resulting in the ossification of the Guild may be found. A small central and district organisation, keeping within a narrow interpretation of the functions assigned to it, may be an extraordinarily valuable influence in stimulating a sluggish factory; but a large central machine will inevitably at the same time aim at concentrating power in its own hands and tend to reduce the exercise of this power to a matter of routine. If the Guilds are to revive craftsmanship and pleasure in work well done; if they are to produce quality as well as quantity, and to be ever keen to devise new methods and utilise every fresh discovery of science without loss of tradition; if they are to breed free men capable of being good citizens both in industry and in every aspect of communal life; if they are to keep alive the motive of free service – they must at all costs shun centralisation. Fortunately, there is little doubt that they will do so; for men freed from the double centralised autocracy of capitalist trust and capitalist State are not likely to be anxious to make for themselves a new industrial Leviathan. They will rate their freedom high; and highest they will rate that which is nearest to them and most affects their daily life – the freedom of the factory, of the place in which their common service to the community is done.

Notes

1 I have adopted the more correct "Gild" in speaking of the industrial organisation of the Middle Ages, while retaining the more familiar "Guild" to denote the modern theory.

2 It should be understood throughout that, when I speak thus of the "factory," I mean to include under it also the mine, the shipyard, the dock, the station, and every corresponding place which is a natural centre of production or service. Every industry has some more or less close equivalent for the factory.

3 As in Bonapartist pseudo-democracies.

4 Moreover, how much of the world's really dull or unpleasant work could we do away with if we really gave our minds to that instead of to profit-mongering! Machinery would make short work of much; and much we could simply do without.

Chapter 8

Liberty and Equality

R. H. Tawney

A German economist has contrasted the economic robustness of industrial civilization with its psychological delicacy. "Capitalism", he writes, "whilst economically stable, and even gaining in stability, creates … a mentality and a style of life incompatible with its own fundamental conditions."[1] Like other summary designations of complex phenomena, the word "capitalism" is an ambiguous term, which is frequently misused. It gives rise to unmerited indignation and undeserved applause, as when capitalism is attacked for evils that are not its own creation, but a legacy from the pre-capitalist societies from which it emerged, like private rights over minerals and urban land, or commended for achievements which are due, not to any particular form of economic organization, but to the progress of scientific knowledge, like the triumphs made possible by the chemist and electrician. But it possesses, at any rate, two broad connotations, which, though closely connected, are, nevertheless, distinct. It implies, on the one hand, a particular economic method or technique, which distinguishes the cotton-mill or steel-works from the weaver's shop or the village smithy. It implies, on the other hand, a particular system of human relations, resulting in a special type of social organization, which has as its characteristic the separation of labour from ownership and direction, and the employment of the majority of workers as hired wage-earners by the owners of capital or their agents, for the pecuniary gain of the owners of capital. It is thus, at once, both a technical device and a social institution.

The special weakness of capitalism as a social institution is not difficult to state. It is part – some would argue, an inseparable part – of qualities which were in the past its special strength. It consists in the familiar liability of power to pervert the relations between its masters and its subjects. Everyone who encounters authority in his daily life, as on some sides of their lives most men do, is conscious of the need to be satisfied that its title is valid, its use disinterested, and its proceedings, not arbitrary, but governed by settled rules. Everyone who exercises it, on however humble a scale, is aware of the temptation to employ it for personal ends, and to rely, not on reason and persuasion, but on the word of command. The abuse of authority and its correction are the commonplace of history. The former is denounced, when excessive, as oppression or tyranny. The latter is applauded, when successful, as the establishment of freedom.

Liberty and equality have usually in England been considered antithetic; and, since fraternity has rarely been considered at all, the famous trilogy has been easily dismissed as a hybrid abortion. Equality implies the deliberate acceptance of social restraints upon individual expansion. It involves the prevention of sensational extremes of wealth and power by public action for the public good. If liberty means, therefore, that every individual shall be free, according to his opportunities, to indulge without limit his appetite for either, it is clearly incompatible, not only with economic and social, but with civil and political, equality, which also prevent the strong exploiting to the full the advantages of their strength, and, indeed, with any habit of life save that of the Cyclops. But freedom for the pike is death for the minnows. It is possible that equality is to be contrasted, not with liberty, but only with a particular interpretation of it.

The test of a principle is that it can be generalized, so that the advantages of applying it are not particular, but universal. Since it is impossible for every individual, as for every nation, simultaneously to be stronger than his neighbours, it is a truism that liberty, as distinct from the liberties of special persons and classes, can exist only in so far as it is limited by rules, which secure that freedom for some is not slavery for others. The spiritual energy of human beings, in all the wealth of their infinite diversities, is the end to which external arrangements, whether political or economic, are merely means. Hence institutions which guarantee to men the opportunity of becoming the best of which they are capable are the supreme political good, and liberty is rightly preferred to equality, when the two are in conflict. The question is whether, in the conditions of modern society, they conflict or not. It is whether the defined and limited freedom, which alone can be generally enjoyed, is most likely to be attained by a community which encourages violent inequalities, or by one which represses them.

Inequality of power is not necessarily inimical to liberty. On the contrary, it is the condition of it. Liberty implies the ability to act, not merely to resist. Neither society as a whole, nor any group within it, can carry out its will except through organs; and, in order that such organs may function with effect, they must be sufficiently differentiated to perform their varying tasks, of which direction is one and execution another. But, while inequality of power is the condition of liberty, since it is the condition of any effective action, it is also a menace to it, for power which is sufficient to use is sufficient to abuse. Hence, in the political sphere, where the danger is familiar, all civilized communities have established safeguards, by which the advantages of differentiation of function, with the varying degrees of power which it involves, may be preserved, and the risk that power may be tyrannical, or perverted to private ends, averted or diminished. They have endeavoured, for example, as in England, to protect civil liberty by requiring that, with certain exceptions, the officers of the State shall be subject to the ordinary tribunals, and political liberty by insisting that those who take decisions on matters affecting the public shall be responsible to an assembly chosen by it. The precautions may be criticized as inadequate, but the need for precautions is not to-day disputed. It is recognized that political power must rest ultimately on consent, and that its exercise must be limited by rules of law.

The dangers arising from inequalities of economic power have been less commonly recognized. They exist, however, whether recognized or not. For the excess or abuse of power, and its divorce from responsibility, which results in oppression, are not confined to the relations which arise between men as members of a state. They are not a malady which is peculiar to political systems, as was typhus to slums, and from which other departments of life can be regarded as immune. They are a disease, not of political organization, but of organization. They occur, in the absence of preventive measures, in political associations, because they occur in all forms of association in which large numbers of individuals are massed for collective action. The isolated worker may purchase security against exploitation at the cost of poverty, as the hermit may avoid the corruptions of civilization by forgoing its advantages. But, as soon as he is associated with his fellows in a common undertaking, his duties must be specified and his rights defined; and, in so far as they are not, the undertaking is impeded. The problem of securing a livelihood ceases to be merely economic, and becomes social and political. The struggle with nature continues, but on a different plane. Its efficiency is heightened by co-operation. Its character is complicated by the emergence of the question of the terms on which co-operation shall take place.

In an industrial civilization, when its first phase is over, most economic activity is corporate activity. It is carried on, not by individuals, but by groups, which are endowed by the State with a legal status, and the larger of which, in size, complexity, specialization of functions and unity of control, resemble less the private enterprise of the past than a public department. Since, as far as certain great industries are concerned, employment must be found in the service of these corporations, or not at all, the mass of mankind pass their working lives under the direction of a hierarchy, whose heads define, as they think most profitable, the lines on which the common enterprise is to proceed, and determine, subject to the intervention of the State and voluntary organizations, the economic, and to a considerable, though diminishing, extent the social, environment of their employees. Possessing the reality of power, without the decorative trappings – unless, as in England is often the case, it thinks it worth while to buy them – this business oligarchy is the effective aristocracy of industrial nations, and the aristocracy of tradition and prestige, when such still exists, carries out its wishes and courts its favours. Since, in such conditions, authority over human beings is exercised, not only through political, but through economic, organs, the problem of liberty is necessarily concerned, not only with political, but also with economic, relations.

It is true, of course, that the problems are different. The abuses of economic are less menacing than those of political power, for their range of operations is narrower and they are more easily corrected without a violent upheaval. But to suppose that they are trivial, or that they are automatically prevented by political democracy, is to be deceived by words. Freedom is always, no doubt, a matter of degree; no man enjoys all the requirements of full personal development, and all men possess some of them. It is not only compatible with conditions in which all men are fellow-servants, but would find in such conditions its most perfect expression. What it excludes is a society where only some are servants, while others are masters.

For, whatever else the idea involves, it implies, at least, that no man shall be amenable to an authority which is arbitrary in its proceedings, exorbitant in its demands, or incapable of being called to account when it abuses its office for personal advantage. In so far as his livelihood is at the mercy of an irresponsible superior, whether political or economic, who can compel his reluctant obedience by *force majeure*, whose actions he is unable to modify or resist, save at the cost of grave personal injury to himself and his dependents, and whose favour he must court, even when he despises it, he may possess a profusion of more tangible blessings, from beer to motor-bicycles, but he can hardly be said to be in possession of freedom. In so far as an economic system grades mankind into groups, of which some can wield, if unconsciously, the force of economic duress for their own profit or convenience, whilst others must submit to it, its effect is that freedom itself is similarly graded. Society is divided, in its economic and social, though not necessarily in its political, relations, into classes which are ends, and classes which are instruments. Like property, with which in the past it has been closely connected, liberty becomes the privilege of a class, not the possession of a nation.

Political principles resemble military tactics; they are usually designed for a war which is over. Freedom is commonly interpreted in political terms, because it was in the political arena that the most resounding of its recent victories were won. It is regarded as belonging to human beings as citizens, rather than to citizens as human beings; so that it is possible for a nation, the majority of whose members have as little influence on the decisions that determine their economic destinies as on the motions of the planets, to applaud the idea with self-congratulatory gestures of decorous enthusiasm, as though history were of the past, but not of the present. If the attitude of the ages from which it inherits a belief in liberty had been equally ladylike, there would have been, it is probable, little liberty to applaud. For freedom is always relative to power, and the kind of freedom which at any moment it is most urgent to affirm depends on the nature of the power which is prevalent and established. Since political arrangements may be such as to check excesses of power, while economic arrangements permit or encourage them, a society, or a large part of it, may be both politically free and economically the opposite. It may be protected against arbitrary action by the agents of government, and be without the security against economic oppression which corresponds to civil liberty. It may possess the political institutions of an advanced democracy, and lack the will and ability to control the conduct of those powerful in its economic affairs, which is the economic analogy of political freedom.

The extension of liberty from the political sphere, where its battle, in most parts of western Europe, is now, perhaps, won, to those of economic relations, where it is still to win, is evidently among the most urgent tasks of industrial communities, which are at once irritated and paralysed by the failure to effect it. It is evident also, however, that, in so far as this extension takes place, the traditional antithesis between liberty and equality will no longer be valid. As long as liberty is interpreted as consisting exclusively in security against oppression by the agents of the State, or as a share in its government, it is plausible, perhaps, to dissociate it from equality; for, though experience suggests that, even in this meagre and restricted sense, it is not easily maintained in the presence of extreme disparities of wealth and influence, it is possible for it to be enjoyed, in form at least, by pauper and millionaire. Such disparities, however, though they do not enable one group to become the political master of another, necessarily cause it to exercise a preponderant, and sometimes an overwhelming, influence on the economic life of the rest of the community.

Hence, when liberty is construed realistically, as implying, not merely a minimum of civil and political rights, but securities that the economically weak will not be at the mercy of the economically strong, and that the control of those aspects of economic life by which all are affected will be amenable, in the last resort, to the will of all, a large measure of equality, so far from being inimical to liberty, is essential to it. In conditions which impose co-operative, rather than merely individual, effort, liberty is, in fact, equality in action, in the sense, not that all men perform identical functions or wield the same degree of power, but that all men are equally protected against the abuse of power, and equally entitled to insist that power shall be used, not for personal ends, but for the general advantage. Civil and political liberty obviously imply, not that all men shall be members of parliament, cabinet ministers, or civil servants, but the absence of such civil and political inequalities as enable one class to impose its will on another by legal coercion. It should be not less obvious that economic liberty implies, not that all men shall initiate, plan, direct, manage, or administer, but the absence of such economic inequalities as can be used as a means of economic constraint.

The danger to liberty which is caused by inequality varies with differences of economic organization and public policy. When the mass of the population are independent producers, or when, if they are dependent on great undertakings, the latter are subject to strict public control, it may be absent or remote. It is seen at its height when important departments of economic activity are the province of large organizations, which, if they do not themselves, as sometimes occurs, control the State, are sufficiently powerful to resist control by it. Among the numerous interesting phenomena which impress the foreign observer of American economic life, not the least interesting, perhaps, is the occasional emergence of industrial enterprises which appear to them, and, indeed, to some Americans, to have developed the characteristics, not merely of an economic undertaking, but of a kind of polity. Their rule may be, and doubtless often is, a mild and benevolent paternalism, lavishing rest-rooms, schools, gymnasia, and guarantees for constitutional behaviour on care-free employees, or it may be a harsh and suspicious tyranny. But, whether as amiable as Solon, or as ferocious as Lycurgus, their features are cast in a heroic mould. Their gestures are those of the sovereigns of little commonwealths rather than of mere mundane employers.

American official documents have, on occasion, called attention to the tendency of the bare stem of business to burgeon, in a favourable environment, with almost tropical exuberance, so that it clothes itself with functions that elsewhere are regarded as belonging to political authorities. When, for instance, as the Report of the United States Commission on Industrial Relations informed us was the case, the corporations controlled by six financial groups employ 2,651,684 wage-earners, or 440,000 per group; when some of them own, not merely the plant and equipment of industry, but the homes of the workers, the streets through which they pass to work, and the halls in which, if they are allowed to meet, their meetings must be held; when they employ private spies and detectives, private police and, sometimes, it appears, private troops, and engage, when they deem it expedient, in private war; when, while organized themselves, they forbid organization among their employees, and enforce their will by evicting malcontents from their homes, and even, on occasion, by the use of armed force; when they influence the press, educational institutions, and the churches established for the worship of the God who has put down the mighty and exalted the meek – in such conditions business may continue in its modesty, since its object is money, to describe itself as business; but who, on his first introduction to an authority so majestic, would guess that he was confronted with the drab transactions of a prosaic joint-stock company, rather than with the masterful manœuvres of some astute and ambitious *seigneur*, armed with sac and soc, toll and theam, infangentheof and outfangentheof? "The main objection to the large corporation", remarks Mr Justice Brandeis, who, as a judge of the Supreme Court, should know the facts, "is that it makes possible – and in many cases makes inevitable – the exercise of industrial absolutism." Property in capital, thus inflated and emancipated, acquires attributes analogous to those of property in land in a feudal society. It carries with it the disposal, in fact, if not in law, of an authority which is quasi-governmental. Its owners possess what would have been called in the ages of darkness a private jurisdiction, and their relations to their dependents, though contractual in form, resemble rather those of ruler and subject than of equal parties to a commercial venture. The liberty which they defend against the encroachments of trade unionism and the State is most properly to be regarded, not as freedom, but as a franchise.[2]

The conventional assertion that inequality is inseparable from liberty is obviously, in such circumstances, unreal and unconvincing; for the existence of the former is a menace to the latter, and the latter is most likely to be secured by curtailing the former. It is true, of course, that inequalities of economic power, with the consequences they entail, are a matter of degree. It is true that in Europe, where the most portentous of the species have gone the way of the dinosaur and the ichthyosaurus, the behaviour of their descendants, relying, as they must, more on brains and less on force, is respectable and sedate. In England, at any rate, where three generations of trade unionism and state intervention have partially domesticated it, the creature, to do it justice, does not roar intolerably. It is cramped by agreements on this side and legislation on that, while periodically it submits, with soft gnashings of teeth, to a major operation, which insinuates germs of sociability into its primeval roughness. Hence, it is rarely ferocious to-day, unless it is alarmed, and its paroxysms, when they occur, are of moderate duration. Apart from these relapses into the habits of the jungle – apart from the occasions on which a combine holds the public to ransom, or the more exceptional cases in which a body of industrialists, like certain groups of mine-owners in 1927, boycott and blacklist wage-earners whose political or social opinions they disapprove, refuse to negotiate with their accredited representatives, and compel them, under threat of ruin, to subscribe to such organizations as they themselves dictate – it is decorous and bland, with the manners, not of a despot or buccaneer, but of polite society. Provided its premises are conceded, it is all for peace and good will in applying their conclusions. Like the Great Boyg, in *Peer Gynt*, it conquers, but does not fight.

Even in England, however, where the principle of economic autocracy is commonly repudiated, it can hardly be asserted with complete confidence, perhaps, that a discreet and attenuated version of it is as wholly alien to practice as it would be agreeable to suppose. It can hardly be argued that the routine of economic life is so entirely unaffected by inequalities of economic power between property-owners and wage-earners that the general liberty has nothing to fear from them. The pressure of such power is felt by the consumer, when he purchases necessaries which, directly or indirectly, are controlled by a monopoly. It is felt in the workshop, where, within the limits set by industrial legislation and collective agreements, the comfort and amenity of the wage-earners' surroundings, the discipline and tone of factory life, the security of employment and methods of promotion, the recruitment and dismissal of workers, the degree to which successive relays of cheap juvenile labour are employed, the opportunity to secure consideration for grievances, depend ultimately upon the policy pursued by a board of directors, who may have little love, indeed, for their shareholders, but who represent, in the last resort, their financial interests, and who, in so far as they are shareholders themselves, are necessarily judges in their own cause. Its effects are even graver in the sphere of economic strategy, which settles the ground upon which these tactical issues are fought out, and, in practice, indeed, not infrequently determines their decision before they arise. In such matters as the changes in organization most likely to restore prosperity to an embarrassed industry, and, therefore, to secure a tolerable livelihood to the workers engaged in it; methods of averting or meeting a depression; rationalization, the closing of plants and the concentration of production; the sale of a business on which a whole community depends or its amalgamation with a rival – not to mention the critical field of financial policy, with its possibilities, not merely of watered capital and of the squandering in dividends of resources which should be held as reserves, but of a sensational redistribution of wealth and widespread unemployment as a result of decisions taken by bankers – the diplomacy of business, like that of governments before 1914, is still commonly conducted over the heads of those most affected by it. *Quidquid delirant reges, plectuntur Achivi.* The interests of the public, as workers and consumers, may receive consideration when these matters are determined; but it can hardly be argued that the normal organization of economic life offers a reliable guarantee that they necessarily will. It cannot plausibly be asserted that, if they do not, those aggrieved can be certain of immediate redress.

Power over the public is public power; nor does it cease to be public merely because private persons are permitted to buy and sell, own and bequeath it, as they deem most profitable. To retort that its masters are themselves little more than half-conscious instruments, whose decisions register and transmit the impact of forces that they can neither anticipate nor control, though not wholly unveracious, is, nevertheless, superficial. A reference to the laws of gravitation, even if embellished with curves and fortified by tables, is not a good answer to a charge of assault. The question is not whether there are economic movements which elude human control, for obviously there are. It is whether the public possesses adequate guarantees that those which are controllable are controlled in the general interest, not in that of a minority. Like the gods of Homer, who were subject themselves to a fate behind the fates, but were not thereby precluded from interfering at their pleasure in the affairs of men, the potentates of the economic world exercise discretion, not, indeed, as to the situation which they will meet, but as to the manner in which they will meet it. They hold the initiative, have such freedom to manœuvre as circumstances allow, can force an issue or postpone it, and, if open conflict seems inevitable or expedient, can choose, as best suits themselves, the ground where it shall take place.

"Even if socialism were practicable without the destruction of freedom", Lord Lothian writes in an interesting article, "would there be any advantage in converting the whole population into wage or salary earners, directed by the relatively few, also salaried, officials, who by ability, or promotion, or 'pull' could work their way to the top of the political machine or the permanent bureaucracy? ... Is not that community the best, and, in the widest sense of the word, the most healthy, which has the largest proportion of citizens who have the enterprise, and energy, and initiative, to create new things and new methods for themselves, and not merely to wait to carry out the orders of somebody 'higher up'?"[3] In view of the practice of some parts, at least, of the business world, the less said about "pull", perhaps, the better. But how true in substance! And how different the liner looks from the saloon-deck and the stoke-hole! And how striking that the conditions which Lord Lothian deplores as a hypothetical danger should be precisely those which common men deplore as an ever-present fact!

For, in England at any rate, as a glance at the Registrar-General's reports would have sufficed to show him, not only the majority of the population, but the great majority, are to-day "wage or salary earners", who, for quite a long time, have been "directed by the relatively few", and who, if they did not "wait to carry out the orders of somebody higher up", would be sent about their business with surprising promptitude. Unless Lord Lothian proposes to abolish, not only a particular political doctrine, but banks, railways, coal-mines and cotton-mills, the question is not whether orders shall be given, but who shall give them; whether there shall be guarantees that they are given in the general interest; and whether those to whom they are given shall have a reasonable security that, when their welfare is at stake, their views will receive an unbiased consideration.

Freedom, as he rightly insists, is more important than comfort, as the soul than the body. But is a miner, who is not subject to a bureaucracy, or at least, to a bureaucracy of the kind which alarms Lord Lothian, conspicuously more free than a teacher, who is? If a man eats bread made of flour produced to the extent of forty per cent. by two milling combines and meat supplied by an international meat trust, and lives in a house built of materials of which twenty-five per cent. are controlled by a ring, and buys his tobacco from one amalgamation, and his matches from another, while his wife's sewing-thread is provided by a third, which has added eight millionaires to the national roll of honour in the last twenty years, is he free as a consumer? Is he free as a worker, if he is liable to have his piece-rates cut at the discretion of his employer, and, on expressing his annoyance, to be dismissed as an agitator, and to be thrown on the scrap-heap without warning because his employer has decided to shut down a plant or bankers to restrict credit, and to be told, when he points out that the industry on which his livelihood depends is being injured by mismanagement, that his job is to work, and that the management in question will do his thinking for him? And if, in such circumstances, he is but partially free as a consumer and a worker, is not his freedom as a citizen itself also partial, rather than, as Lord Lothian would desire, unqualified and complete?

Lord Lothian, it may be suspected, is misled as to liberty, because he has omitted to consider the bearing upon it of another phenomenon, the phenomenon of inequality. The truth is that, when the economic scales are so unevenly weighted, to interpret liberty as a political principle, which belongs to one world, the world of politics and government, while equality belongs – if, indeed, it belongs anywhere – to another world, the world of economic affairs, is to do violence to realities. Governments, it is true, exercise powers of a great and special kind, and freedom requires that they should be held strictly to account. But the administration of things is not easily distinguished, under modern conditions of mass organization, from the control of persons, and both are in the hands, to some not inconsiderable degree, of the minority who move the levers of the economic mechanism. The truth of the matter is put by Professor Pollard in his admirable study, *The Evolution of Parliament.* "There is only one solution", he writes, "of the problem of liberty, and it lies in equality. … Men vary in physical strength; but so far as their social rela-tions go that inequality has been abolished. … Yet there must have been a period in social evolution when this refusal to permit the strong man to do what he liked with his own physical strength seemed, at least to the strong, an outrageous interfer-ence with personal liberty. … There is, in fact, no more reason why a man should be allowed to use his wealth or his brain than his physical strength as he likes. … The liberty of the weak depends upon the restraint of the strong, that of the poor upon the restraint of the rich, and that of the simpler-minded upon the restraint of the sharper. Every man should have this liberty and no more, to do unto others as he would that they should do to him; upon that common foundation rest liberty, equality, and morality."[4]

It is natural that lawyers, who think in the categories of an earlier age, should utter admonitions against the danger to individual liberty from the encroachments of the executive, nor need it be denied that there are aspects of life to which their warnings are relevant. What makes power oppressive, however, is not the title by which those who wield it happen to be called, but the manner in which in fact it is wielded. If individual liberty means the security of individuals against arbitrary action, then what threatens the liberty of the majority of the population is, not so much public interference, as the insufficiency of it, and the ability, as a consequence, of private interference to take its own course with them. In an industrial civilization the great Leviathan is not the State, which, if a ferocious atavist in time of war, relapses, once its spurs are off, into a docile, and not unfriendly, drudge. It is the sleek, serviceable, but still not wholly domesticated, monster, which sprawls heavily over colliery villages and factory towns, or murmurs, from some unpretentious lair in a business office, the soft ominous prophecies which later it will fulfil. "When he raiseth himself up, the mighty" – and how much more mere Cabinets! – "are afraid. Darts are to him as stubble." Indeed, since he owns five-sixths of the press, he is a principal purveyor of darts himself.

Notes

1   J. Schumpeter, "The Instability of Capitalism," in *Econ. JL.*, Sept. 1928, pp. 385–6.
2   For evidence on these points see USA, *Final Report of Commission on Industrial Relations*, 1916; *Report of the Steel Strike of 1919* and *Public Opinion and the Steel Strike* (Reports of the Commission of Inquiry, Interchurch World Movement), New York, 1920 and 1921; H. C. Butler, *Industrial Relations in the United States* (I.L.O., Studies and Reports, Series A, no. 27), 1927. The quotation from Mr Justice Brandeis occurs in the *Final Report on Industrial Relations*, p. 63.
3   *Manchester Guardian*, Jan. 8, 1930.
4   A. F. Pollard, *The Evolution of Parliament*, 1920, pp. 183–4.

Chapter 9

The Political Economy of Freedom

Michael Oakeshott

The work of the late Professor Henry C. Simons of the University of Chicago will be well known to students of economics, and they will not need their attention called to this collection of some of his more important essays.[1] To others, however, it may be supposed that his name will be unknown. But, in spite of the fact that he is neither a brilliant nor a popular writer, he has something for the general reader; and though much of what he says has the USA for its immediate background, he has something in particular for the English reader. And I propose in this review to recommend him as a writer who should not be neglected by anyone interested in the way things are going. As an economist, Simons was concerned particularly with problems of banking, currency and monetary policy, but (like his teacher and colleague at Chicago, Professor F. H. Knight,[2] who has built up so distinguished a school of economic studies at that university) he was well aware that in every discussion of a special problem and in every proposal of economic policy there lies an often undisclosed preference for a society integrated in one way rather than another. And in order to make his preferences in this matter secure against superstition, he went to some trouble to bring them out into the open and to put them in order. They do not amount to anything so elaborate as a political philosophy, indeed he claims for them only the title of 'a political *credo*'; there is nothing pretentious in this attempt to hold 'economics' and 'politics' together. And it is successful mainly because it is not merely one project among others but represents the permanent habit of his mind. It is true there are a couple of essays in this volume directed expressly to the investigation of political ends and means, but the bulk of them is concerned with special economic problems and he never fails to show how his proposed solution is related to the wider context of the type of society he believes to be desirable. To those anxious to find out where they stand in these matters he offers not only a lucid, if fragmentary, account of his own preferences, but also a profound insight into the compatibility or incompatibility of different economic expedients with different forms of social integration.

Needless to say, Simons does not pretend to invent a political *credo* for himself: he is without the vanity of those who refuse to be convinced of their own honesty of purpose until they have made a desert of their consciousness before beginning to cultivate it for themselves. His pride is in belonging to a tradition. He speaks of himself as 'an old-fashioned liberal', and he allies himself with a line of predecessors which includes Adam Smith, Bentham, Mill, Sidgwick as well as de Tocqueville, Burckhardt and Acton. This strikes one as being a trifle uncritical; the historical nuance is missed. But it is nothing to worry about. Simons was a generous-minded man where the work of others was concerned, accepting gratefully what was offered and providing the critical subtleties for himself. If he was a liberal, at least he suffered from neither of the current afflictions of liberalism – ignorance of who its true friends are, and the nervy conscience which extends a senile and indiscriminate welcome to everyone who claims to be on the side of 'progress'. We need not, however, disturb ourselves unduly about the label he tied on to his *credo*. He calls himself a liberal and a democrat, but he sets no great store by the names, and is concerned to resolve the ambiguity which has now unfortunately overtaken them. It is to be expected, then, that much of what Simons has to say will seem at once familiar and unpardonably out-moded. It will seem familiar, not because it has been unduly chewed over in recent years, but because the leaders of fashion, the intellectual dandies of the Fabian Society, preserved it in their hastily composed syllabus of errors. And it will seem outmoded because of the disapproval of these eccentric arbiters. The great merit of this book, however, is the opportunity it gives to 'this sophisticated generation', which knows all the answers but is sadly lacking in education, to consider for itself what it has been told to reject as mere superstition.

Simons finds in its 'emphasis on liberty' the 'distinctive feature' of the tradition with which he allies himself; he believes in liberty. And this at once will raise a presumption against him. For to be a genuine libertarian in politics is to belong to a human type now sadly out of fashion. Other loves have bewitched us; and to confess to a passion for liberty – not as something worth while in certain circumstances but as the *unum necessarium* – is to admit to a disreputable naïvety, excusable only where it masks a desire to rule. Liberty has become the emblem of frivolous or of disingenuous politics. But the damage which libertarian politics have suffered from open and from hidden enemies is not irreparable; after all, their cunning is only circuitous folly and will find them out. It is self-appointed friends who have often shown themselves more dangerous. We must be clear, they say, about what we mean by 'freedom'. First, let us define it; and when we know what it is, it will be time enough to seek it out, to love it and to die for it. What is a free society? And with this question (proposed abstractly) the door opens upon a night of endless quibble, lit only by the stars of sophistry. Like men born in prison, we are urged to dream of something we have never enjoyed (freedom from want) and to make that dream the foundation of our politics. We are instructed to distinguish between 'positive' and 'negative' freedom, between the 'old' and the 'new' freedom, between 'social', 'political', 'civil', 'economic' and 'personal' freedom; we are told that freedom is the 'recognition of necessity'; and we are taught that all that matters is 'inner freedom' and that this is to be identified with equality and with power: there is no end to the abuse we have suffered. But a generation which has stood so long on that doorstep, waiting for the dawn, that 'le silence éternel de ces espaces infinis' has begun to unnerve it, should now be ready to listen to a more homely message. And anyone who has the courage to tell it to come in and shut the door may perhaps be given a hearing. This at least is what I understand Simons to be saying to us. The freedom which he is to inquire into is neither an abstraction nor a dream. He is a libertarian, not because he begins with an abstract definition of liberty, but because he has actually enjoyed a way of living (and seen others enjoy it) which those who have enjoyed it are accustomed (on account of certain precise characteristics) to call a free way of living, and because he has found it to be good. The purpose of the inquiry is not to define a word, but to detect the secret of what we enjoy, to recognize what is hostile to it, and to discern where and how it may be enjoyed more fully. And from this inquiry will spring, not only a closer under-standing of what we actually enjoy, but also a reliable criterion for judging the proposed abstract freedoms which we are urged to pursue. For a proposed freedom which manifestly could not be achieved by means of the kind of arrangements which secure to us the freedom we now enjoy will reveal itself as an illusion. Moreover, we must refuse to be jockeyed into writing 'freedom', in deference to the susceptibilities of, say, a Russian or a Turk who has never enjoyed the experience (and who, consequently, can think only in abstractions), because any other use of the English word would be misleading and eccentric. *Freedom, in* English, is a word whose political connotation springs as directly from our political experience as the connotations of $\dot{\epsilon}\lambda\epsilon\upsilon\vartheta\epsilon\varrho\acute{\iota}\alpha$, *libertas* and *liberté* spring respectively from quite dif-ferent experiences.

What, then, are the characteristics of our society in respect of which we consider ourselves to enjoy freedom and in default of which we would not be free in our sense of the word? But first, it must be observed that the freedom we enjoy is not composed of a number of independent characteristics of our society which in aggregate make up our liberty. Liberties, it is true, may be distinguished, and some may be more general or more settled and mature than others, but the freedom which the English libertarian knows and values lies in a coherence of mutually sup-porting liberties, each of which amplifies the whole and none of which stands alone. It springs neither from the separation of church and state, nor from the rule of law, nor from private property, nor from parliamentary government, nor from the writ of *habeas corpus*, nor from the independence of the judiciary, nor from any one of the thousand other devices and arrangements characteristic of our society, but from what each signifies and represents, namely, the absence from our society of over-whelming concentrations of power. This is the most general condition of our freedom, so general that all other conditions may be seen to be comprised within it. It appears, first, in a diffusion of authority between past, present and future. Our society is ruled by none of these exclusively. And we should consider a society governed wholly by its past, or its present, or its future to suffer under a despotism of superstition which forbids freedom. The politics of our society are a conversation in which past, present and future each has a voice; and though one or other of them may on occasion properly prevail, none permanently dominates, and on this account we are free. Further, with us power is dispersed among all the multitude of interests and organizations of interest which comprise our society. We do not fear or seek to suppress diversity of interest, but we consider our freedom to be imperfect so long as the dispersal of power among them is incomplete, and to be threatened if any one interest or combination of interests, even though it may be the interest of a majority, acquires extraordinary power. Similarly, the conduct of government in our society involves a sharing of power, not only between the recognized organs of government, but also between the Administration and the Opposition. In short, we consider ourselves to be free because no one in our society is allowed unlimited power – no leader, faction, party or 'class', no majority, no government, church, corporation, trade or professional association or trade union. The secret of its freedom is that it is composed of a multitude of organizations in the constitution of the best of which is reproduced that diffusion of power which is characteristic of the whole.

Moreover, we are not unaware that the balance of such a society is always precarious. 'The history of institutions,' says Acton, 'is often a history of deception and illusions.' Arrangements which in their beginnings promoted a dispersion of power often, in the course of time, themselves become over-mighty or even absolute while still claiming the recognition and loyalty which belonged to them in respect of their first character. To further liberty we need to be clear-sighted enough to recognize such a change, and energetic enough to set on foot the remedy while the evil is still small. And what more than anything else contributes to this clear-sightedness is relief from the distraction of a rigid doctrine which fixes upon an institution a falsely permanent character, and then (when the illusion is at last recognized) calls for a revolution. The best institutions, of course, are those whose constitution is both firm and self-critical, enjoying their character as the repository of a beneficial fragment of power but refusing the inevitable invitation to absolutism. And though these are few, it is perhaps permissible to number among them the hitherto existing parties of English politics.

It might be thought (by those who have not enjoyed the experience of living in such a society, and who can therefore think of it only in the abstract) that a society of this sort could be saved from disintegration only by the existence at its head of some overwhelming power capable of holding all other powers in check. But that is not our experience. Strength we think to be a virtue in government, but we do not find our defence against disintegration either in arbitrary or in very great power. Indeed, we are inclined to see in both these the symptoms of an already advanced decay. For overwhelming power would be required only by a government which had against it a combination so extensive of the powers vested in such a variety of different individuals and interests as to convict the government of a self-interest so gross as to disqualify it for the exercise of its proper function. Normally, to perform its office (which is to prevent coercion) our government requires to wield only a power greater than that which is concentrated in any one other centre of power on any particular occasion. Consequently it is difficult to excite in us the belief that a government not possessed of overwhelming power is on that account a weak government. And we consider that our freedom depends as much upon the moderation of the power exercised by government as upon the proper and courageous use of that power when necessity arises.

But further, our experience has disclosed to us a method of government remarkably economical in the use of power and consequently peculiarly fitted to preserve freedom: it is called the rule of law. If the activity of our government were the continuous or sporadic interruption of the life and arrangements of our society with arbitrary corrective measures, we should consider ourselves no longer free, even though the measures were directed against concentrations of power universally recognized to be dangerous. For not only would government of this kind require extraordinary power (each of its acts being an *ad hoc* intervention), but also, in spite of this concentration of governmental power, the society would be without that known and settled protective structure which is so important a condition of freedom. But government by rule of law (that is, by means of the enforcement by prescribed methods of settled rules binding alike on governors and governed), while losing nothing in strength, is itself the emblem of that diffusion of power which it exists to promote, and is therefore peculiarly appropriate to a free society. It is the method of government most economical in the use of power; it involves a partnership between past and present and between governors and governed which leaves no room for arbitrariness; it encourages a tradition of resistance to the growth of dangerous concentrations of power which is far more effective than any promiscuous onslaught however crushing; it controls effectively, but without breaking the grand affirmative flow of things; and it gives a practical definition of the kind of limited but necessary service a society may expect from its government, restraining us from vain and dangerous expectations. Particular laws, we know, may fail to protect the freedom enjoyed in our society, and may even be destructive of some of our freedom; but we know also that the rule of law is the greatest single condition of our freedom, removing from us that great fear which has overshadowed so many communities, the fear of the power of our own government.

Of the many species of liberty which compose the freedom we enjoy, each amplifying and making more secure the whole, we have long recognized the importance of two: the freedom of association, and the freedom enjoyed in the right to own private property. A third species of liberty is often set beside these two: freedom of speech. Beyond question this is a great and elementary form of freedom; it may even be regarded as the key-stone of the arch of our liberty. But a key-stone is not itself the arch, and the current exaggeration of the importance of this form of liberty is in danger of concealing from us the loss of other liberties no less important. The major part of mankind has nothing to say; the lives of most men do not revolve round a felt necessity to speak. And it may be supposed that this extraordinary emphasis upon freedom of speech is the work of the small vocal section of our society and, in part, represents a legitimate self-interest. Nor is it an interest incapable of abuse; when it is extended to the indiscriminate right to take and publish photographs, to picket and enter private houses and cajole or blackmail defenceless people to display their emptiness in foolish utterances, and to publish innuendos in respect of those who refuse to speak, it begins to reveal itself as a menace to freedom. For most men, to be deprived of the right of voluntary association or of private property would be a far greater and more deeply felt loss of liberty than to be deprived of the right to speak freely. And it is important that this should be said just now in England because, under the influence of misguided journalists and cunning tyrants, we are too ready to believe that so long as our freedom to speak is not impaired we have lost nothing of importance – which is not so. However secure may be a man's right to speak his thoughts, he may find what is to him a much more important freedom curtailed when his house is sold over his head by a public authority, or when he is deprived of the enjoyment of his leasehold because his landlord has sold out to a development company, or when his membership of a trade union is compulsory and debars him from an employment he would otherwise take.

The freedom of association enjoyed in our society has created a vast multitude of associations so that the integration of our society may be said to be largely by means of voluntary associations; and on this account we consider our freedom extended and made more secure. They represent a diffusion of power appropriate to our notion of freedom. The right of voluntary association means the right to take the initiative in forming new associations, and the right to join or not to join or to quit associations already in existence: the right of voluntary association is also a right of voluntary dissociation. And it means also the duty of not forming or joining any association designed to deprive, or in effect depriving, others of the exercise of any of their rights, particularly that of voluntary association. This duty is not to be thought of as a limitation of the right; the right, like all rights, is without any limits except those provided by the system of rights to which it belongs and those inherent in its own character: this duty is merely the negative definition of the right. And when we consider the full nature of the right, it is clear that its exercise can be hostile to what we know as our freedom only when it leads to that which in fact denies its own character – a 'compulsory-voluntary' association. A 'compulsory-voluntary' association is a conspiracy to abolish our right of association; it is a concentration of power actually or potentially destructive of what we call freedom.

It will be agreed that, from one point of view, property is a form of power, and an institution of property is a particular way of organizing the exercise of this form of power in a society. From this point of view distinctions between different kinds of property scarcely appear; certainly all categorical distinctions are absent. Personal and real property, chattels, property in a man's own physical and mental capacities and property in the so-called means of production, are all, in different degrees, forms of power, and incidentally spring from the same sources, investment, inheritance and luck. In every society an institution of property is unavoidable. The ideally simplest kind of institution is that in which all proprietary right is vested in one person who thereby becomes despot and monopolist, his subjects being slaves. But, besides being the least complex, this institution is, to our way of thinking, the most hostile to freedom. We have, perhaps, been less successful, from the point of view of freedom, in our institution of property than in some of our other arrangements, but there is no doubt about the general character of the institution of property most friendly to freedom: it will be one which allows the widest distribution, and which discourages most effectively great and dangerous concentrations of this power. Nor is there any doubt about what this entails. It entails a right of private property – that is, an institution of property which allows to every adult member of the society an equal right to enjoy the ownership of his personal capacities and of anything else obtained by the methods of acquisition recognized in the society. This right, like every other right, is self-limiting: for example, it proscribes slavery, not arbitrarily, but because the right to own another man could never be a right enjoyed equally by every member of a society. But in so far as a society imposes external limits, arbitrarily excluding certain things from private ownership, only a modified right of private property may be said to prevail, which provides for less than the maximum diffusion of the power that springs from ownership. For what may not be owned by any individual must nevertheless be owned, and it will be owned, directly or indirectly, by the government, adding to governmental power and constituting a potential threat to freedom. Now, it may happen that a society determines to with-draw from the possibility of private ownership certain things not inherently excluded by the right of private property itself, and there may be good reason for taking this course. But it should be observed that whatever benefits may flow from such an arrangement, the increase of liberty as we understand it is not among them. The institution of property most favourable to liberty is, unquestionably, a right to private property least qualified by arbitrary limits and exclusions, for it is by this means only that the maximum diffusion of the power that springs, from ownership may be achieved. This is not mere abstract speculation; it is the experience of our society, in which the greatest threats to freedom have come from the acquisition of extraordinary proprietary rights by the government, by great business and indus-trial corporations and by trade unions, all of which are to be regarded as arbitrary limitations of the right of private property. An institution of property based upon private property is not, of course, either simple or primitive; it is the most complex of all institutions of property and it can be maintained only by constant vigilance, occasional reform and the refusal to tinker. And it is instructive to observe how closely many of the private property rights which we all regard as inseparable from freedom are bound up with other private property rights which it is now the custom erroneously to consider hostile to freedom. That a man is not free unless he enjoys a proprietary right over his personal capacities and his labour is believed by every-one who uses freedom in the English sense. And yet no such right exists unless there are many potential employers of his labour. The freedom which separates a man from slavery is nothing but a freedom to choose and to move among autonomous, independent organizations, firms, purchasers of labour, and this implies private property in resources other than personal capacity. Wherever a means of produc-tion falls under the control of a single power, slavery in some measure follows.

With property we have already begun to consider the economic organization of society. An institution of property is, in part, a device for organizing the productive and distributive activity of the society. For the libertarian of our tradition the main question will be how to regulate the enterprise of making a living in such a way that it does not destroy the freedom he prizes. He will, of course, recognize in our institution of private property a means of organizing this enterprise wholly friendly to liberty. All monopolies, or near monopolies, he knows as impediments to that liberty, and the greatest single institution which stands between us and monopoly is private property. Concerning monopolies he will have no illusions; he will not consider them optimistically, hoping that they will not abuse their power. He will know that no individual, no group, association or union can be entrusted with much power, and that it is mere foolishness to complain when absolute power is abused. It exists to be abused. And consequently he will put his faith only in arrangements which discourage its existence. In other words, he will recognize that the only way of organizing the enterprise of getting a living so that it does not curtail the freedom he loves is by the establishment and maintenance of effective competition. He will know that effective competition is not something that springs up of its own accord, that both it and any alternative to it are creatures of law; but since he has observed the creation (often inadvertently) by law of monopolies and other impediments to freedom, he will not think it beyond the capacity of his society to build upon its already substantial tradition of creating and maintaining effective competition by law. But he will recognize that any confusion between the task of making competition effective and the task (to be performed by effective competition itself) of organizing the enterprise of getting a living and satisfying wants will at once be fatal to liberty as he knows it. For to replace by political control the integration of activity which competition (the market) provides is at once to create a monopoly and to destroy the diffusion of power inseparable from freedom. No doubt the libertarian, in this matter, will have to listen to the complaint that he has neglected to consider the efficiency with which his economic system produces the goods; how shall we reconcile the conflicting claims of freedom and efficiency? But he will have his answer ready. The only efficiency to be considered is the most economical way of supplying the things men desire to purchase. The formal circumstances in which this may be at its maximum is where enterprise is effectively competitive, for here the entrepreneur is merely the intermediary between consumers of goods and sellers of services. And below this ideal arrangement, the relevant comparison is not between the level of efficiency attainable in an improved (but not perfected) competitive economy and the efficiency of a perfectly planned economy, but between an improved competitive economy and the sort of planned economy (with all its wastefulness, frustration and corruption) which is the only practical alternative. Everything, in short, that is inimical to freedom – monopoly, near monopoly and all great concentrations of power – at the same time impedes the only efficiency worth considering.

This outline of the political faith of a libertarian in the English tradition will be thought to lack something important unless there is added to it at least a suggestion of the end or purpose which informs such a society. It belongs, however, to some other tradition to think of this purpose as the achievement of a premeditated utopia, as an abstract ideal (such as happiness or prosperity), or as a preordained and inevitable end. The purpose of this society (if indeed it may be said to have one) is not something put upon it from the outside, nor can it be stated in abstract terms without gross abridgment. We are not concerned with a society which sprang up yesterday, but with one which possesses already a defined character and traditions of activity. And in these circumstances social achievement is to perceive the next step dictated or suggested by the character of the society in contact with changing conditions and to take it in such a manner that the society is not disrupted and that the prerogatives of future generations are not grossly impaired. In place of a pre-conceived purpose, then, such a society will find its guide in a principle of *continuity* (which is a diffusion of power between past, present and future) and in a principle of *consensus* (which is a diffusion of power between the different legitimate interests of the present). We call ourselves free because our pursuit of current desires does not deprive us of a sympathy for what went before; like the wise man, we remain reconciled with our past. In the obstinate refusal to budge, in the pure pragmatism of a plebiscitary democracy, in the abridgment of tradition which consists in merely doing what was done 'last time', and in the preference for the short-cut in place of the long way round that educates at every step, we recognize, alike, the marks of slavery. We consider ourselves free because, taking a view neither short nor long, we are unwilling to sacrifice either the present to a remote and incalculable future, or the immediate and foreseeable future to a transitory present. And we find freedom once more in a preference for slow, small changes which have behind them a voluntary consensus of opinion, in our ability to resist disintegration without suppressing opposition, and in our perception that it is more important for a society to move together than for it to move either fast or far. We do not pretend that our decisions are infallible; indeed, since there is no external or absolute test of perfec-tion, infallibility has no meaning. We find what we need in a principle of change and a principle of identity, and we are suspicious of those who offer us more; those who call upon us to make great sacrifices and those who want to impose upon us an heroic character.

Now, though none of these characteristics is fully present in our society at this time, none is wholly absent. We have experienced enough of it over a sufficiently long period of time to know what it means, and from that experience has sprung our notion of freedom. We call ourselves free because our arrangements approxi-mate to this general condition. And the enterprise of the libertarian in politics will be to cultivate what has already been sown, and to avoid the fruitless pursuit of proposed freedoms which could not be secured by the only known method of achieving freedom. Policy will not be the imagination of some new sort of society, or the transformation of an existing society so as to make it correspond with an abstract ideal; it will be the perception of what needs doing now in order to realize more fully the intimations of our existing society. The right conduct of policy, then, involves a profound knowledge of the character of the society, which is to be cultivated, a clear perception of its present condition, and the precise formulation of a programme of legislative reform.

The present condition of our society is exceedingly complex; but, from the point of view of the libertarian, three main elements may be distinguished. There is, first, a widespread and deplorable ignorance of the nature of the libertarian tradition itself, a confusion of mind in respect of the kind of society we have inherited and the nature of its strength and weakness. With eyes focused upon distant horizons and minds clouded with foreign clap-trap, the impatient and sophisticated generation now in the saddle has dissolved its partnership with its past and is careful of everything except its liberty. Secondly, owing to the negligence of past generations, there is an accumulated mass of maladjustment, of undispersed concentrations of power, which the libertarian will wish to correct because it threatens liberty, and which others also may wish to correct for less cogent reasons. Thirdly, there is the contemporary mess, sprung from the attempts of men ignorant of the nature of their society to correct its maladjustments by means of expedients which, because they are not inspired by a love of liberty, are a threat to freedom both in failure and in success.

The two great, mutually exclusive, contemporary opponents of libertarian society as we know it are collectivism and syndicalism. Both recommend the integration of society by means of the erection and maintenance of monopolies; neither finds any virtue in the diffusion of power. But they must be considered mutually exclusive opponents of a free society because the monopoly favoured by syndicalism would make both a collective and a society of free men impossible.

Collectivism in the modern world has several synonyms; it stands for a managed society, and its other titles are communism, national socialism, socialism, economic democracy and central planning. But we will continue to call it collectivism, this being its least emotive name. And we will assume that the problem of imposing a collectivist organization upon a society which enjoys a high degree of freedom has been successfully solved – that is, we will assume that the necessary contemporary *consensus* has been achieved. This is not a tremendous assumption, because (paradoxically enough) collectivism appears most readily to us as a remedy for elements in our society which are agreed to be impediments to freedom. What the libertarian is concerned to investigate is the compatibility of collectivist organization with freedom as he knows it. To be brief, collectivism and freedom are real alternatives – if we choose one we cannot have the other. And collectivism can be imposed upon a society educated in a love of freedom with an appearance of not destroying *continuity*, only if men forget their love of liberty. This, of course, is not a new idea, it is how the matter appeared to observers, such as de Tocqueville, Burckhardt and Acton, when the character of modern collectivism was in process of being revealed.

Neglecting the more scandalous charges which may be brought against collectivism in action, let us consider only the defects (from the point of view of liberty) inherent in the system. The opposition of collectivism to freedom appears first in the collectivist rejection of the whole notion of the diffusion of power and of a society organized by means of a multitude of genuinely voluntary associations. The cure proposed for monopoly is to create more numerous and more extensive monopolies and to control them by force. The organization to be imposed upon society springs from the minds of those who compose the government. It is a comprehensive organization; loose ends, uncontrolled activities must be regarded as the product of incompetence because they unavoidably impair the structure of the whole. And great power is required for the over-all control of this organization – power sufficient not merely to break up a single over-mighty concentration of power when it makes its appearance, but to control continuously enormous concentrations of power which the collectivist has created. The government of a collectivist society can tolerate only a very limited opposition to its plans; indeed, that hard-won distinction, which is one of the elements of our liberty, between opposition and treason is rejected: what is not obedience is sabotage. Having discouraged all other means of social and industrial integration, a collectivist government must enforce its imposed order or allow the society to relapse into chaos. Or, following a tradition of economy in the use of power, it will be obliged to buy off political opposition by favouring groups able to demand favours as the price of peace. All this is, clearly, an impediment to freedom; but there is more to follow. In addition to the rule of law, and often in place of it, collectivism depends for its working upon a lavish use of discretionary authority. The organization it imposes upon society is without any inner momentum; it must be kept going by promiscuous, day-to-day interventions – controls of prices, licences to pursue activities, permissions to make and to cultivate, to buy and to sell, the perpetual readjustment of rations, and the distribution of privileges and exemptions – by the exercise, in short, of the kind of power most subject to misuse and corruption. The diffusion of power inherent in the rule of law leaves government with insufficient power to operate a collectivist society. It will be observed, further, that collectivism involves the abolition of that division of labour between competitive and political controls which belongs to our freedom. Competition may, of course, survive anomalously and vestigially, in spite of policy; but, in principle, enterprise is tolerated only if it is not competitive, that is, if it takes the form of syndicates which serve as instruments of the central authorities, or smaller businesses which a system of quotas and price controls has deprived of all elements of risk or genuine enterprise. Competition as a form of organization is first devitalized and then destroyed, and the integrating office it performs in our society is incorporated in the functions of government, thus adding to its power and involving it in every conflict of interest that may arise in the society. And with the disappearance of competition goes what we have seen to be one of the essential elements of our liberty. But of all the acquisitions of governmental power inherent in collectivism, that which comes from its monopoly of foreign trade is, perhaps, the most dangerous to liberty; for freedom of external trade is one of the most precious and most effective safeguards a community may have against excessive power. And just as the abolition of competition at home draws the government into (and thus magnifies) every conflict, so collectivist trading abroad involves the government in competitive commercial transactions and increases the occasions and the severity of international disharmony. Collectivism, then, is the mobilization of a society for unitary action. In the contemporary world it appears as a remedy for the imperfect freedom which springs from imperfect competition, but it is a remedy designed to kill. Nor is this surprising, for the real spring of collectivism is not a love of liberty, but war. The anticipation of war is the great incentive, and the conduct of war is the great collectivizing process. And large-scale collectivism is, moreover, inherently warlike; the condition of things in which it is appropriate in the end makes its appearance. It offers a double occasion for the loss of liberty – in the collectivist organization itself and in the purpose to which that organization is directed. For though collectivism may recommend itself as a means to 'welfare', the only 'welfare' it is capable of pursuing – a centralized, national 'welfare' – is hostile to freedom at home and results in organized rivalry abroad.

Collectivism is indifferent to all elements of our freedom and the enemy of some. But the real antithesis of a free manner of living, as we know it, is syndicalism. Indeed, syndicalism is not only destructive of freedom; it is destructive, also, of any kind of orderly existence. It rejects both the concentration of overwhelming power in the government (by means of which a collectivist society is always being rescued from the chaos it encourages), and it rejects the wide dispersion of power which is the basis of freedom. Syndicalism is a contrivance by means of which society is disposed for a perpetual civil war in which the parties are the organized self-interest of functional minorities and a weak central government, and for which the community as a whole pays the bill in monopoly prices and disorder. The great concentrations of power in a syndicalist society are the sellers of labour organized in functional monopoly associations. All monopolies are prejudicial to freedom, but there is good reason for supposing that labour monopolies are more dangerous than any others, and that a society in the grip of such monopolies would enjoy less freedom than any other sort of society. In the first place, labour monopolies have shown themselves more capable than enterprise monopolies of attaining really great power, economic, political and even military. Their appetite for power is insatiable and, producing nothing, they encounter none of the productional diseconomies of undue size. Once grown large, they are exceedingly difficult to dissipate and impossible to control. Appearing to spring from the lawful exercise of the right of voluntary association (though as monopolistic associations they are really a denial of that right), they win legal immunities and they enjoy popular support however scandalous their activity. Enterprise monopolies, on the other hand (not less to be deplored by the libertarian), are less dangerous because they are less powerful. They are precariously held together, they are unpopular and they are highly sensitive to legal control. Taken separately, there is no question which of the two kinds of monopoly is the more subversive of freedom. But in addition to its greater power, the labour monopoly is dangerous because it demands enterprise monopoly as its complement. There is a disastrous identity of interest between the two kinds of monopoly; each tends to foster and to strengthen the other, fighting together to maximize joint extractions from the public while also fighting each other over the division of the spoils. Indeed, the conflict of capital and labour (the struggle over the division of earnings) is merely a sham fight (often costing the public more than the participants), concealing the substantial conflict between the producer (enterprise and labour, both organized monopolistically) and the consumer. Syndicalism, then, has some claim to be considered the pre-eminent adversary of freedom, but it is not less the enemy of collectivism. A collectivist government faced with numerous functional minorities each organized monopolistically with power to disrupt the whole plan of production unless its demands are met and each (when not making large demands) keeping the civil war going by means of promiscuous little hindrances to the orderly conduct of business, would be the easy victim of blackmail. And if the collectivist government derived its political strength from highly syndicalist labour organizations, its desperate position would be that of a victim of blackmail in a society which had not made the activity an offence. Of all forms of society, a collectivist society is least able to deal with the disruptive potentialities of syndicalism.

Where collectivism and syndicalism have imposed themselves upon societies which enjoy a libertarian tradition they appear as mutually exclusive tendencies (sometimes anomalously in alliance with one another) threatening achieved freedom. But to the libertarian who still has faith in his tradition, the chief danger lies, not in the possibility that either will establish itself exclusively, but in their joint success in hindering a genuinely libertarian attack upon the accumulated maladjustments in our society and upon our real problems. That attack is certainly long overdue, and the delay must not be attributed entirely to the popularity of these pseudo-remedies. Libertarian society has not been entirely idle in the past fifty years; liberty has been extended by the correction of many small abuses. But the general drift of reform in this country has too often been inspired by vaguely collectivist motives. Liberty has been lost inadvertently through the lack of a clearly formulated libertarian policy of reform.

However, Simons now comes forward with such a policy. He is not the first to do so, but no friend of freedom will fail to benefit by reflecting upon what he has to say. Nobody could be less complacent about the present state of liberty than Simons; and his proposals are not only libertarian, they are in many respects (as he points out) more radical than the projects of the collectivists. A planner who aims at change by means of promiscuous intervention and the use of discretionary anthority, while destroying liberty, does less for reform than a libertarian who would extend and consolidate the rule of law. Simons calls his policy a 'positive programme for *Laissez Faire*', mainly because it aims at making competition effective wherever effective competition is not demonstrably impossible, at re-establishing a diffusion of power now deeply compromised by monopolies of all sorts, and at preserving that division of labour between competitive and political controls which is the secret of our liberty. But, both in England and in America, the policy he proposed in 1934 would now in part be a programme of *laissez faire* in the historical sense – a programme of removing specific restrictions upon competition which have established themselves not by default but by the activity of collectivists. Nevertheless, his proposals have, of course, nothing whatever to do with that imaginary condition of wholly unfettered competition which is confused with *laissez faire* and ridiculed by collectivists when they have nothing better to say. As every schoolboy used to know, if effective competition is to exist it can do so only by virtue of a legal system which promotes it, and that monopoly has established itself only because the legal system has not prevented it. To know that unregulated competition is a chimera, to know that to regulate competition is not the same thing as to interfere with the operation of competitive controls, and to know the difference between these two activities, is the beginning of the political economy of freedom.

The libertarian, then, finds the general tendency towards a policy of collectivism a hindrance; but the unavoidable (and exceedingly uneconomical) collectivism which sprang up in libertarian societies engaged in a war of survival is recognized as an evil not without compensation. The believer in collectivism naturally looks upon war as an opportunity not to be missed, and the demobilization of society is no part of his programme. But to those who believe in liberty and yet remain hesitant about demobilization, Simons addresses some wise words: 'If wars are frequent, victories will probably go to those who remain mobilized … [But] if there are vital, creative forces to be released by demobilization – by return to a free society – the nation may thereby gain enough strength to compensate handsomely for the risks involved.' Every man, whom war took away from his chosen vocation, returned to it with pent-up energies ready to be released; and what is true of an individual may here be true also of an economy. Demobilization offered an opportunity for the springing up of a revitalized and more effectively competitive economy (an opportunity of which the collectivists deprived us), which would have made us more able to withstand future wars. There is a potential gain, if it can be harvested, for a society with a libertarian tradition, in the successive shocks of mobilization and demobilization. And just as a civilian will fight better (for he has something to fight for) if in the intervals of peace he is permitted to be a civilian (and not kept bumming around in an industrial army), so an economy which is, in peace, allowed to stretch itself and flex its limbs will be found, when it is mobilized for war, to possess superior stamina to one kept permanently mobilized.

The main principles of the policy are simple, and we have already noticed them. First, private monopoly in all its forms is to be suppressed. This means the establishment and maintenance (by means of the reform of the law which gives shape to the world of business and industry) of effective competition wherever effective competition is not demonstrably impossible: a genuine 'socialization' of enterprise in place of the spoof 'socialization' of the collectivist. The monopolies and the monopolistic practices to be destroyed are monopolies of labour. Restraint of trade must be treated as a major crime. In respect of enterprise, the absurd powers of corporations must be reduced. 'There is simply no excuse,' says Simons, 'except with a narrow and specialized class of enterprise, for allowing corporations to hold stock in other corporations – and no reasonable excuse (the utilities apart) for hundred-million-dollar corporations, no matter what form their property may take. Even if the much advertised economies of gigantic financial combinations were real, sound policy would wisely sacrifice these economies to preservation of more economic freedom and equality.' The corporation is a socially useful device for organizing ownership and control in operating companies of size sufficient to obtain the real economies of large-scale production under unified management;

but the corporation law which has allowed this device to work for the impediment of freedom is long overdue for reform. In respect of labour, the problem of reducing the existing or threatened monopolies and monopoly practices is more difficult. The best one may hope, perhaps, is that labour monopolies, if not fostered and supported by the law, will cease to grow and even decline in power. And if we deal intelligently with other, easier problems, it is to be expected that this problem will become less intractable by progress in other directions.

Secondly, undertakings in which competition cannot be made to work as the agency of control must be transferred to public operation. Now the difference between this policy and that of the collectivist should be observed. There is, in the first place, a difference of emphasis. The collectivists would, in the end, take over every undertaking the 'nationalization' of which does not offer insuperable technical difficulties; the libertarian would create a government-controlled monopoly only when monopoly of some sort is unavoidable. The collectivist favours monopolies as an opportunity for the extension of political control; the libertarian would break up all destructible monopolies. And the ground of this emphasis is clear. To the libertarian all monopolies are expensive and productive of servility. While the collectivist welcomes and sees his opportunity in a society in which (owing to growth of population and changes in the technique of production) enterprise tends to become gigantic even when the law does not encourage undue size, the libertarian sees in this tendency a threat to freedom which must be warded off (and can be warded off) by the appropriate legal reforms. And from this difference of emphasis springs all the other differences: the disinclination to create monopolies where there are none (in education, for example), the disposition to reduce and to simplify all monopolies taken over so that they may contribute as little as possible to the power of government, the strongest legal discouragement to the appearance of syndicalist tendencies within these monopolies, and the recognition that the effect of all such proposals upon the power of government is as important as their effect upon 'society'. In short, the political economy of freedom rests upon the clear acknowledgment that what is being considered is not 'economics' (not the maximization of wealth, not productivity or the standard of life), but *politics*, that is, the custody of a manner of living; that these arrangements have to be paid for, are a charge upon our productive capacity; and that they are worth paying for so long as the price is not a diminution of what we have learned to recognize as liberty.

The third object of this economic policy is a stable currency, maintained by the application of fixed and known rules and not by day-to-day administrative tricks. And that this belongs to the political economy of freedom needs no argument: inflation is the mother of servitude.

Politics is not the science of setting up a permanently impregnable society, it is the art of knowing where to go next in the exploration of an already existing traditional kind of society. And in a society, such as ours, which has not yet lost the understanding of government as the prevention of coercion, as the power which holds in check the overmighty subject, as the protector of minorities against the power of majorities, it may well be thought that the task to which this generation is called is not the much advertised 'reconstruction of society' but to provide against the new tyrannies which an immense growth in population in a wantonly productivist society are beginning to impose; and to provide against them in such a manner that the cure is not worse than the disease.

Notes

1   *Economic Policy for a Free Society*. University of Chicago Press and Cambridge University Press, 1948, 21s. net.
2   F. H. Knight, *Ethics of Competition* (1935), and *Freedom and Reform* (1947).

Chapter 10

The Pursuit of the Ideal

Isaiah Berlin

I

There are, in my view, two factors that, above all others, have shaped human history in the twentieth century. One is the development of the natural sciences and technology, certainly the greatest success story of our time – to this, great and mounting attention has been paid from all quarters. The other, without doubt, consists in the great ideological storms that have altered the lives of virtually all mankind: the Russian Revolution and its aftermath – totalitarian tyrannies of both right and left and the explosions of nationalism, racism and, in places, religious bigotry which, interestingly enough, not one among the most perceptive social thinkers of the nineteenth century had ever predicted.

When our descendants, in two or three centuries' time (if mankind survives until then), come to look at our age, it is these two phenomena that will, I think, be held to be the outstanding characteristics of our century – the most demanding of explanation and analysis. But it is as well to realise that these great movements began with ideas in people's heads: ideas about what relations between men have been, are, might be and should be; and to realise how they came to be transformed in the name of a vision of some supreme goal in the minds of the leaders, above all of the prophets with armies at their backs. Such ideas are the substance of ethics. Ethical thought consists of the systematic examination of the relations of human beings to each other, the conceptions, interests and ideals from which human ways of treating one another spring, and the systems of value on which such ends of life are based. These beliefs about how life should be lived, what men and women should be and do, are objects of moral enquiry; and when applied to groups and nations, and, indeed, mankind as a whole, are called political philosophy, which is but ethics applied to society.

If we are to hope to understand the often violent world in which we live (and unless we try to understand it, we cannot expect to be able to act rationally in it and on it), we cannot confine our attention to the great impersonal forces, natural and man-made, which act upon us. The goals and motives that guide human action must be looked at in the light of all that we know and understand; their roots and growth, their essence, and above all their validity, must be critically examined with every intellectual resource that we have. This urgent need, apart from the intrinsic value of the discovery of truth about human relationships, makes ethics a field of primary importance. Only barbarians are not curious about where they come from, how they came to be where they are, where they appear to be going, whether they wish to go there, and if so, why, and if not, why not.

The study of the variety of ideas about the views of life that embody such values and such ends is something that I have spent forty years of my long life in trying to make clear to myself. I should like to say something about how I came to become absorbed by this topic, and particularly about a turning-point which altered my thoughts about the heart of it. This will, to some degree, inevitably turn out to be somewhat autobiographical – for this I offer my apologies, but I do not know how else to give an account of it.

II

When I was young I read *War and Peace* by Tolstoy, much too early. The real impact on me of this great novel came only later, together with that of other Russian writers, both novelists and social thinkers, of the mid-nineteenth century. These writers did much to shape my outlook. It seemed to me, and still does, that the purpose of these writers was not principally to give realistic accounts of the lives and relationships to one another of individuals or social groups or classes, not psychological or social analysis for its own sake – although, of course, the best of them achieved precisely this, incomparably. Their approach seemed to me essentially moral: they were concerned most deeply with what was responsible for injustice, oppression, falsity in human relations, imprisonment whether by stone walls or conformism – unprotesting submission to man-made yokes – moral blindness, egoism, cruelty, humiliation, servility, poverty, helplessness, bitter indignation, despair on the part of so many. In short, they were concerned with the nature of these experiences and their roots in the human condition: the condition of Russia in the first place, but, by implication, of all mankind. And conversely they wished to know what would bring about the opposite of this, a reign of truth, love, honesty, justice, security, personal relations based on the possibility of human dignity, decency, independence, freedom, spiritual fulfilment.

Some, like Tolstoy, found this in the outlook of simple people, unspoiled by civilisation; like Rousseau, he wished to believe that the moral universe of peasants was not unlike that of children, not distorted by the conventions and institutions of civilisation, which sprang from human vices – greed, egoism, spiritual blindness; that the world could be saved if only men saw the truth that lay at their feet; if they but looked, it was to be found in the Christian gospels, the Sermon on the Mount.

Others among these Russians put their faith in scientific rationalism, or in social and political revolution founded on a true theory of historical change. Others again looked for answers in the teachings of the Orthodox theology, or in liberal Western democracy, or in a return to ancient Slav values, obscured by the reforms of Peter the Great and his successors.

What was common to all these outlooks was the belief that solutions to the central problems existed, that one could discover them, and, with sufficient selfless effort, realise them on earth. They all believed that the essence of human beings was to be able to choose how to live: societies could be transformed in the light of true ideals believed in with enough fervour and dedication. If, like Tolstoy, they sometimes thought that man was not truly free but determined by factors outside his control, they knew well enough, as he did, that if freedom was an illusion it was one without which one could not live or think. None of this was part of my school curriculum, which consisted of Greek and Latin authors, but it remained with me.

When I became a student at the University of Oxford, I began to read the works of the great philosophers, and found that the major figures, especially in the field of ethical and political thought, believed this too. Socrates thought that if certainty could be established in our knowledge of the external world by rational methods (had not Anaxagoras arrived at the truth that the moon was many times larger than the Peloponnese, however small it looked in the sky?) the same methods would surely yield equal certainty in the field of human behaviour – how to live, what to be. This could be achieved by rational argument. Plato thought that an élite of sages who arrived at such certainty should be given the power of governing others intellectually less well endowed, in obedience to patterns dictated by the correct solutions to personal and social problems. The Stoics thought that the attainment of these solutions was in the power of any man who set himself to live according to reason. Jews, Christians, Muslims (I knew too little about Buddhism) believed that the true answers had been revealed by God to his chosen prophets and saints, and accepted the interpretation of these revealed truths by qualified teachers and the traditions to which they belonged.

The rationalists of the seventeenth century thought that the answers could be found by a species of metaphysical insight, a special application of the light of reason with which all men were endowed. The empiricists of the eighteenth century, impressed by the vast new realms of knowledge opened by the natural sciences based on mathematical techniques, which had driven out so much error, superstition, dogmatic nonsense, asked themselves, like Socrates, why the same methods should not succeed in establishing similar irrefutable laws in the realm of human affairs. With the new methods discovered by natural science, order could be introduced into the social sphere as well – uniformities could be observed, hypotheses formulated and tested by experiment; laws could be based on them, and then laws in specific regions of experience could be seen to be entailed by wider laws; and these in turn to be entailed by still wider laws, and so on upwards, until a great harmonious system, connected by unbreakable logical links and capable of being formulated in precise – that is, mathematical – terms, could be established.

The rational reorganisation of society would put an end to spiritual and intellectual confusion, the reign of prejudice and superstition, blind obedience to unexamined dogmas, and the stupidities and cruelties of the oppressive regimes which such intellectual darkness bred and promoted. All that was wanted was the identification of the principal human needs and discovery of the means of satisfying them. This would create the happy, free, just, virtuous, harmonious world which Condorcet so movingly predicted in his prison cell in 1794. This view lay at the basis of all progressive thought in the nineteenth century, and was at the heart of much of the critical empiricism which I imbibed in Oxford as a student.

III

At some point I realised that what all these views had in common was a Platonic ideal: in the first place that, as in the sciences, all genuine questions must have one true answer and one only, all the rest being necessarily errors; in the second place that there must be a dependable path towards the discovery of these truths; in the third place that the true answers, when found, must necessarily be compatible with one another and form a single whole, for one truth cannot be incompatible with another – that we knew a priori. This kind of omniscience was the solution of the cosmic jigsaw puzzle. In the case of morals, we could then conceive what the perfect life must be, founded as it would be on a correct understanding of the rules that governed the universe.

True, we might never get to this condition of perfect knowledge – we may be too feeble-witted, or too weak or corrupt or sinful, to achieve this. The obstacles, both intellectual and those of external nature, may be too many. Moreover, opinions, as I say, had widely differed about the right path to pursue – some found it in Churches, some in laboratories; some believed in intuition, others in experiment, or in mystical visions, or in mathematical calculation. But even if we could not ourselves reach these true answers, or indeed, the final system that interweaves them all, the answers must exist – else the questions were not real. The answers must be known to someone: perhaps Adam in Paradise knew; perhaps we shall only reach them at the end of days; if men cannot know them, perhaps the angels know; and if not the angels, then God knows. The timeless truths must in principle be knowable.

Some nineteenth-century thinkers – Hegel, Marx – thought it was not quite so simple. There were no timeless truths. There was historical development, continuous change; human horizons altered with each new step in the evolutionary ladder; history was a drama with many acts; it was moved by conflicts of forces, sometimes called dialectical, in the realms of both ideas and reality – conflicts which took the form of wars, revolutions, violent upheavals of nations, classes, cultures, movements. Yet after inevitable setbacks, failures, relapses, returns to barbarism, Condorcet's dream would come true. The drama would have a happy ending – man's reason had achieved triumphs in the past, it could not be held back for ever.

Men would no longer be victims of nature or of their own largely irrational socie-ties: reason would triumph; universal harmonious co-operation, true history, would at last begin.

For if this was not so, do the ideas of progress, of history, have any meaning? Is there not a movement, however tortuous, from ignorance to knowledge, from mythical thought and childish fantasies to perception of reality face to face, to knowledge of true goals, true values as well as truths of fact? Can history be a mere purposeless succession of events, caused by a mixture of material factors and the play of random selection, a tale full of sound and fury signifying nothing? This was unthinkable. The day would dawn when men and women would take their lives in their own hands and not be self-seeking beings or the playthings of blind forces that they did not understand. It was, at the very least, not impossible to conceive what such an earthly paradise could be; and if it was conceivable we could, at any rate, try to march towards it. That has been at the centre of ethical thought from the Greeks to the Christian visionaries of the Middle Ages, from the Renaissance to progressive thought in the last century; and, indeed, is believed by many to this day.

IV

At a certain stage in my reading, I naturally met with the principal works of Machiavelli. They made a deep and lasting impression upon me, and shook my earlier faith. I derived from them not the most obvious teachings – on how to acquire and retain political power, or by what force or guile rulers must act if they are to regenerate their societies, or protect themselves and their States from enemies within or without, or what the principal qualities of rulers on the one hand, and of citizens on the other, must be, if their States are to flourish – but something else. Machiavelli was not a historicist: he thought it possible to restore something like the Roman Republic or Rome of the early Principate. He believed that to do this one needed a ruling class of brave, resourceful, intelligent, gifted men who knew how to seize opportunities and use them, and citizens who were adequately pro-tected, patriotic, proud of their State, epitomes of manly, pagan virtues. That is how Rome rose to power and conquered the world, and it is the absence of this kind of wisdom and vitality and courage in adversity, of the qualities of both lions and foxes, that in the end brought it down. Decadent States were conquered by vigorous invaders who retained these virtues.

But Machiavelli also sets side by side with this the notion of Christian virtues – humility, acceptance of suffering, unworldliness, the hope of salvation in an afterlife – and he remarks that if, as he plainly himself favours, a State of a Roman type is to be established, these qualities will not promote it: those who live by the precepts of Christian morality are bound to be trampled on by the ruthless pursuit of power on the part of men who alone can recreate and dominate the republic which he wants to see. He does not condemn Christian virtues. He merely points out that the two moralities are incompatible, and he does not recognise an overarching criterion whereby we are enabled to decide the right life for men. The combination of *virtù* and Christian values is for him an impossibility. He simply leaves you to choose – he knows which he himself prefers.

The idea that this planted in my mind was the realisation, which came as something of a shock, that not all the supreme values pursued by mankind now and in the past were necessarily compatible with one another. It undermined my earlier assumption, based on the *philosophia perennis*, that there could be no conflict between true ends, true answers to the central problems of life.

Then I came across Giambattista Vico's *Scienza nuova*. Scarcely anyone in Oxford had then heard of Vico, but there was one philosopher, Robin Collingwood, who had translated Croce's book on Vico, and he urged me to read it. This opened my eyes to something new. Vico seemed to be concerned with the succession of human cultures – every society had, for him, its own vision of reality, of the world in which it lived, and of itself and of its relations to its own past, to nature, to what it strove for. This vision of a society is conveyed by everything that its members do and think and feel – expressed and embodied in the kinds of words, the forms of language that they use, the images, the metaphors, the forms of worship, the institutions that they generate, which embody and convey their image of reality and of their place in it; by which they live. These visions differ with each successive social whole – each has its own gifts, values, modes of creation, incommensurable with one another: each must be understood in its own terms – understood, not necessarily evaluated.

The Homeric Greeks, the master class, Vico tells us, were cruel, barbarous, mean, oppressive to the weak; but they created the *Iliad* and the *Odyssey*, something we cannot do in our more enlightened day. Their great creative masterpieces belong to them, and once the vision of the world changes, the possibility of that type of creation disappears also. We, for our part, have our sciences, our thinkers, our poets, but there is no ladder of ascent from the ancients to the moderns. If this is so, it must be absurd to say that Racine is a better poet than Sophocles, that Bach is a rudimentary Beethoven, that, let us say, the Impressionist painters are the peak which the painters of Florence aspired to but did not reach. The values of these cultures are different, and they are not necessarily compatible with one another. Voltaire, who thought that the values and ideals of the enlightened exceptions in a sea of darkness – of classical Athens, of Florence of the Renaissance, of France in the *grand siècle* and of his own time – were almost identical, was mistaken.[1] Machiavelli's Rome did not, in fact, exist. For Vico there is a plurality of civilisations (repetitive cycles of them, but that is unimportant), each with its own unique pattern. Machiavelli conveyed the idea of two incompatible outlooks; and here were societies the cultures of which were shaped by values, not means to ends but ultimate ends, ends in themselves, which differed, not in all respects – for they were all human – but in some profound, irreconcilable ways, not combinable in any final synthesis.

After this I naturally turned to the German eighteenth-century thinker Johann Gottfried Herder. Vico thought of a succession of civilisations, Herder went further and compared national cultures in many lands and periods, and held that every society had what he called its own centre of gravity, which differed from that of others. If, as he wished, we are to understand Scandinavian sagas or the poetry of the Bible, we must not apply to them the aesthetic criteria of the critics of eighteenth-century Paris. The ways in which men live, think, feel, speak to one another, the clothes they wear, the songs they sing, the gods they worship, the food they eat, the assumptions, customs, habits which are intrinsic to them – it is these that create communities, each of which has its own 'lifestyle'. Communities may resemble each other in many respects, but the Greeks differ from Lutheran Germans, the Chinese differ from both; what they strive after and what they fear or worship are scarcely ever similar.

This view has been called cultural or moral relativism – this is what that great scholar, my friend Arnaldo Momigliano, whom I greatly admired, supposed both about Vico and about Herder. He was mistaken. It is not relativism. Members of one culture can, by the force of imaginative insight, understand (what Vico called *entrare*) the values, the ideals, the forms of life of another culture or society, even those remote in time or space. They may find these values unacceptable, but if they open their minds sufficiently they can grasp how one might be a full human being, with whom one could communicate, and at the same time live in the light of values widely different from one's own, but which nevertheless one can see to be values, ends of life, by the realisation of which men could be fulfilled.

'I prefer coffee, you prefer champagne. We have different tastes. There is no more to be said.' That is relativism. But Herder's view, and Vico's, is not that: it is what I should describe as pluralism – that is, the conception that there are many different ends that men may seek and still be fully rational, fully men, capable of understanding each other and sympathising and deriving light from each other, as we derive it from reading Plato or the novels of medieval Japan – worlds, outlooks, very remote from our own. Of course, if we did not have any values in common with these distant figures, each civilisation would be enclosed in its own impenetrable bubble, and we could not understand them at all; this is what Spengler's typology amounts to. Intercommunication between cultures in time and space is possible only because what makes men human is common to them, and acts as a bridge between them. But our values are ours, and theirs are theirs. We are free to criticise the values of other cultures, to condemn them, but we cannot pretend not to understand them at all, or to regard them simply as subjective, the products of creatures in different circumstances with different tastes from our own, which do not speak to us at all.

There is a world of objective values. By this I mean those ends that men pursue for their own sakes, to which other things are means. I am not blind to what the Greeks valued – their values may not be mine, but I can grasp what it would be like to live by their light, I can admire and respect them, and even imagine myself as pursuing them, although I do not – and do not wish to, and perhaps could not if I wished. Forms of life differ. Ends, moral principles, are many. But not infinitely many: they must be within the human horizon. If they are not, then they are outside the human sphere. If I find men who worship trees, not because they are symbols of fertility or because they are divine, with a mysterious life and powers of their own, or because this grove is sacred to Athena – but only because they are made of wood; and if when I ask them why they worship wood they say 'Because it is wood' and give no other answer; then I do not know what they mean. If they are human, they are not beings with whom I can communicate – there is a real barrier. They are not human for me. I cannot even call their values subjective if I cannot conceive what it would be like to pursue such a life.

What is clear is that values can clash – that is why civilisations are incompatible. They can be incompatible between cultures, or groups in the same culture, or between you and me. You believe in always telling the truth, no matter what: I do not, because I believe that it can sometimes be too painful and too destructive. We can discuss each other's point of view, we can try to reach common ground, but in the end what you pursue may not be reconcilable with the ends to which I find that I have dedicated my life. Values may easily clash within the breast of a single individual; and it does not follow that, if they do, some must be true and others false. Justice, rigorous justice, is for some people an absolute value, but it is not compatible with what may be no less ultimate values for them – mercy, compassion – as arises in concrete cases.

Both liberty and equality are among the primary goals pursued by human beings through many centuries; but total liberty for wolves is death to the lambs, total liberty of the powerful, the gifted, is not compatible with the rights to a decent existence of the weak and the less gifted. An artist, in order to create a masterpiece, may lead a life which plunges his family into misery and squalor to which he is indifferent. We may condemn him and declare that the masterpiece should be sacrificed to human needs, or we may take his side – but both attitudes embody values which for some men or women are ultimate, and which are intelligible to us all if we have any sympathy or imagination or understanding of human beings. Equality may demand the restraint of the liberty of those who wish to dominate; liberty – without some modicum of which there is no choice and therefore no possibility of remaining human as we understand the word – may have to be curtailed in order to make room for social welfare, to feed the hungry, to clothe the naked, to shelter the homeless, to leave room for the liberty of others, to allow justice or fairness to be exercised.

Antigone is faced with a dilemma to which Sophocles implied one solution, Sartre offers the opposite, while Hegel proposes 'sublimation' on to some higher level – poor comfort to those who are agonised by dilemmas of this kind. Spontaneity, a marvellous human quality, is not compatible with capacity for organised planning, for the nice calculation of what and how much and where – on which the welfare of society may largely depend. We are all aware of the agonising alternatives in the recent past. Should a man resist a monstrous tyranny at all costs, at the expense of the lives of his parents or his children? Should children be tortured to extract information about dangerous traitors or criminals?

These collisions of values are of the essence of what they are and what we are. If we are told that these contradictions will be solved in some perfect world in which all good things can be harmonised in principle, then we must answer, to those who say this, that the meanings they attach to the names which for us denote the conflicting values are not ours. We must say that the world in which what we see as incompatible values are not in conflict is a world altogether beyond our ken; that principles which are harmonised in this other world are not the principles with which, in our daily lives, we are acquainted; if they are transformed, it is into conceptions not known to us on earth. But it is on earth that we live, and it is here that we must believe and act.

The notion of the perfect whole, the ultimate solution, in which all good things coexist, seems to me to be not merely unattainable – that is a truism – but conceptually incoherent; I do not know what is meant by a harmony of this kind. Some among the Great Goods cannot live together. That is a conceptual truth. We are doomed to choose, and every choice may entail an irreparable loss. Happy are those who live under a discipline which they accept without question, who freely obey the orders of leaders, spiritual or temporal, whose word is fully accepted as unbreakable law; or those who have, by their own methods, arrived at clear and unshakeable convictions about what to do and what to be that brook no possible doubt. I can only say that those who rest on such comfortable beds of dogma are victims of forms of self-induced myopia, blinkers that may make for contentment, but not for understanding of what it is to be human.

V

So much for the theoretical objection, a fatal one, it seems to me, to the notion of the perfect State as the proper goal of our endeavours. But there is in addition a more practical socio-psychological obstacle to this, an obstacle that may be put to those whose simple faith, by which humanity has been nourished for so long, is resistant to philosophical arguments of any kind. It is true that some problems can be solved, some ills cured, in both the individual and social life. We can save men from hunger or misery or injustice, we can rescue men from slavery or imprisonment, and do good – all men have a basic sense of good and evil, no matter what cultures they belong to; but any study of society shows that every solution creates a new situation which breeds its own new needs and problems, new demands. The children have obtained what their parents and grandparents longed for – greater freedom, greater material welfare, a juster society; but the old ills are forgotten, and the children face new problems, brought about by the very solutions of the old ones, and these, even if they can in turn be solved, generate new situations, and with them new requirements – and so on, for ever – and unpredictably.

We cannot legislate for the unknown consequences of consequences of consequences. Marxists tell us that once the fight is won and true history has begun, the new problems that may arise will generate their own solutions, which can be peacefully realised by the united powers of harmonious, classless society. This seems to me a piece of metaphysical optimism for which there is no evidence in historical experience. In a society in which the same goals are universally accepted, problems can be only of means, all soluble by technological methods. That is a society in which the inner life of man, the moral and spiritual and aesthetic imagination, no longer speaks at all. Is it for this that men and women should be destroyed or societies enslaved? Utopias have their value – nothing so wonderfully expands the imaginative horizons of human potentialities – but as guides to conduct they can prove literally fatal. Heraclitus was right, things cannot stand still.

So I conclude that the very notion of a final solution is not only impracticable but, if I am right, and some values cannot but clash, incoherent also. The possibility of a final solution – even if we forget the terrible sense that these words acquired in Hitler's day – turns out to be an illusion; and a very dangerous one. For if one really believes that such a solution is possible, then surely no cost would be too high to obtain it: to make mankind just and happy and creative and harmonious for ever – what could be too high a price to pay for that? To make such an omelette, there is surely no limit to the number of eggs that should be broken – that was the faith of Lenin, of Trotsky, of Mao, for all I know of Pol Pot. Since I know the only true path to the ultimate solution of the problem of society, I know which way to drive the human caravan; and since you are ignorant of what I know, you cannot be allowed to have liberty of choice even within the narrowest limits, if the goal is to be reached. You declare that a given policy will make you happier, or freer, or give you room to breathe; but I know that you are mistaken, I know what you need, what all men need; and if there is resistance based on ignorance or malevolence, then it must be broken and hundreds of thousands may have to perish to make millions happy for all time. What choice have we, who have the knowledge, but to be willing to sacrifice them all?

Some armed prophets seek to save mankind, and some only their own race because of its superior attributes, but whichever the motive, the millions slaughtered in wars or revolutions – gas chambers, gulag, genocide, all the monstrosities for which our century will be remembered – are the price men must pay for the felicity of future generations. If your desire to save mankind is serious, you must harden your heart, and not reckon the cost.

The answer to this was given more than a century ago by the Russian radical Alexander Herzen. In his essay *From the Other Shore*, which is in effect an obituary notice of the revolutions of 1848, he said that a new form of human sacrifice had arisen in his time – of living human beings on the altars of abstractions – nation, Church, party, class, progress, the forces of history – these have all been invoked in his day and in ours: if these demand the slaughter of living human beings, they must be satisfied. These are his words:

> If progress is the goal, for whom are we working? Who is this Moloch who, as the toilers approach him, instead of rewarding them, draws back; and as a consolation to the exhausted and doomed multitudes, shouting 'morituri te salutant', can only give the … mocking answer that after their death all will be beautiful on earth. Do you truly wish to condemn the human beings alive today to the sad role … of wretched

galley-slaves who, up to their knees in mud, drag a barge ... with ... 'progress in the future' upon its flag? ... a goal which is infinitely remote is no goal, only ... a deception; a goal must be closer – at the very least the labourer's wage, or pleasure in work performed.[2]

The one thing that we may be sure of is the reality of the sacrifice, the dying and the dead. But the ideal for the sake of which they die remains unrealised. The eggs are broken, and the habit of breaking them grows, but the omelette remains invisible. Sacrifices for short-term goals, coercion, if men's plight is desperate enough and truly requires such measures, may be justified. But holocausts for the sake of distant goals, that is a cruel mockery of all that men hold dear, now and at all times.

VI

If the old perennial belief in the possibility of realising ultimate harmony is a fallacy, and the position of the thinkers I have appealed to – Machiavelli, Vico, Herder, Herzen – are valid, then, if we allow that Great Goods can collide, that some of them cannot live together, even though others can – in short, that one cannot have everything, in principle as well as in practice – and if human creativity may depend upon a variety of mutually exclusive choices: then, as Chernyshevsky and Lenin once asked, 'What is to be done?' How do we choose between possibilities? What and how much must we sacrifice to what? There is, it seems to me, no clear reply. But the collisions, even if they cannot be avoided, can be softened. Claims can be balanced, compromises can be reached: in concrete situations not every claim is of equal force – so much liberty and so much equality; so much for sharp moral condemnation, and so much for understanding a given human situation; so much for the full force of the law, and so much for the prerogative of mercy; for feeding the hungry, clothing the naked, healing the sick, sheltering the homeless. Priorities, never final and absolute, must be established.

The first public obligation is to avoid extremes of suffering. Revolutions, wars, assassinations, extreme measures may in desperate situations be required. But history teaches us that their consequences are seldom what is anticipated; there is no guarantee, not even, at times, a high enough probability, that such acts will lead to improvement. We may take the risk of drastic action, in personal life or in public policy, but we must always be aware, never forget, that we may be mistaken, that certainty about the effect of such measures invariably leads to avoidable suffering of the innocent. So we must engage in what are called trade-offs – rules, values, principles must yield to each other in varying degrees in specific situations. Utilitarian solutions are sometimes wrong, but, I suspect, more often beneficent. The best that can be done, as a general rule, is to maintain a precarious equilibrium that will prevent the occurrence of desperate situations, of intolerable choices – that is the first requirement for a decent society; one that we can always strive for, in the light of the limited range of our knowledge, and even of our imperfect understanding of individuals and societies. A certain humility in these matters is very necessary.

This may seem a very flat answer, not the kind of thing that the idealistic young would wish, if need be, to fight and suffer for, in the cause of a new and nobler society. And, of course, we must not dramatise the incompatibility of values – there is a great deal of broad agreement among people in different societies over long stretches of time about what is right and wrong, good and evil. Of course traditions, outlooks, attitudes may legitimately differ; general principles may cut across too much human need. The concrete situation is almost everything. There is no escape: we must decide as we decide; moral risk cannot, at times, be avoided. All we can ask for is that none of the relevant factors be ignored, that the purposes we seek to realise should be seen as elements in a total form of life, which can be enhanced or damaged by decisions.

But, in the end, it is not a matter of purely subjective judgement: it is dictated by the forms of life of the society to which one belongs, a society among other societies, with values held in common, whether or not they are in conflict, by the majority of mankind throughout recorded history. There are, if not universal values, at any rate a minimum without which societies could scarcely survive. Few today would wish to defend slavery or ritual murder or Nazi gas chambers or the torture of human beings for the sake of pleasure or profit or even political good – or the duty of children to denounce their parents, which the French and Russian revolutions demanded, or mindless killing. There is no justification for compromise on this. But on the other hand, the search for perfection does seem to me a recipe for bloodshed, no better even if it is demanded by the sincerest of idealists, the purest of heart. No more rigorous moralist than Immanuel Kant has ever lived, but even he said, in a moment of illumination, 'Out of the crooked timber of humanity no straight thing was ever made.'[3] To force people into the neat uniforms demanded by dogmatically believed-in schemes is almost always the road to inhumanity. We can only do what we can: but that we must do, against difficulties.

Of course social or political collisions will take place; the mere conflict of positive values alone makes this unavoidable. Yet they can, I believe, be minimised by promoting and preserving an uneasy equilibrium, which is constantly threatened and in constant need of repair – that alone, I repeat, is the precondition for decent societies and morally acceptable behaviour, otherwise we are bound to lose our way. A little dull as a solution, you will say? Not the stuff of which calls to heroic action by inspired leaders are made? Yet if there is some truth in this view, perhaps that is sufficient. An eminent American philosopher of our day once said, 'There is no a priori reason for supposing that the truth, when it is discovered, will necessarily prove interesting.' It may be enough if it is truth, or even an approximation to it; consequently I do not feel apologetic for advancing this. Truth, said Tolstoy, 'has been, is and will be beautiful'.[4] I do not know if this is so in the realm of ethics, but it seems to me near enough to what most of us wish to believe not to be too lightly set aside.

Notes

1   Voltaire's conception of enlightenment as being identical in essentials wherever it is attained seems to lead to the inescapable conclusion that, in his view, Byron would have been happy at table with Confucius, and Sophocles would have felt completely at ease in quattrocento Florence, and Seneca in the *salon* of Madame du Deffand or at the court of Frederick the Great.

2   A. I. Gertsen, *Sobranie sochinenii v tridtsati tomakh* (Moscow, 1954–66), vol. 6, p. 34.

3   *Kant's gesammelte Schriften* (Berlin, 1900–), vol. 8, p. 23, line 22.

4   *Sevastopol in May*, chapter 16.

Chapter 11

Are There Any Natural Rights?[1]

H. L. A. Hart

I shall advance the thesis that if there are any moral rights at all, it follows that there is at least one natural right, the equal right of all men to be free. By saying that there is this right, I mean that in the absence of certain special conditions which are consistent with the right being an equal right, any adult human being capable of choice (1) has the right to forbearance on the part of all others from the use of coercion or restraint against him save to hinder coercion or restraint and (2) is at liberty to do (i.e., is under no obligation to abstain from) any action which is not one coercing or restraining or designed to injure other persons.[2]

I have two reasons for describing the equal right of all men to be free as a *natural* right; both of them were always emphasized by the classical theorists of natural rights. (1) This right is one which all men have if they are capable of choice; they have it *qua* men and not only if they are members of some society or stand in some special relation to each other. (2) This right is not created or conferred by men's voluntary action; other moral rights are.[3] Of course, it is quite obvious that my thesis is not as ambitious as the traditional theories of natural rights; for although on my view all men are *equally* entitled to be free in the sense explained, no man has an absolute or unconditional right to do or not to do any particular thing or to be treated in any particular way; coercion or restraint of any action may be justified in special conditions consistently with the general principle. So my argument will not show that men have any right (save the equal right of all to be free) which is "absolute," "indefeasible," or "imprescriptible." This may for many reduce the importance of my contention, but I think that the principle that all men have an equal right to be free, meager as it may seem, is probably all that the political philosophers of the liberal tradition need have claimed to support any program of action even if they have claimed more. But my contention that there is this one natural right may appear unsatisfying in another respect; it is only the conditional assertion that *if* there are any moral rights then there must be this one natural right. Perhaps few would now deny, as some have, that there are moral rights; for the point of that denial was usually to object to some philosophical claim as to the "ontological status" of rights, and this objection is now expressed not as a denial that there are any moral rights but as a denial of some assumed logical similarity between sentences used to assert the existence of rights and other kinds of sentences. But it is still important to remember that there may be codes of conduct quite properly termed moral codes (though we can of course say they are "imperfect") which do not employ the notion of *a* right, and there is nothing contradictory or otherwise absurd in a code or morality consisting wholly of prescriptions or in a code which prescribed only what should be done for the realization of happiness or some ideal of personal perfection.[4] Human actions in such systems would be evaluated or criticised as compliances with prescriptions or as *good* or *bad, right* or *wrong, wise* or *foolish, fitting* or *unfitting*, but no one in such a system would have, exercise, or claim rights, or violate or infringe them. So those who lived by such systems could not of course be committed to the recognition of the equal right of all to be free; nor, I think (and this is one respect in which the notion of a right differs from other moral notions), could any parallel argument be constructed to show that, from the bare fact that actions were recognized as ones which ought or ought not to be done, as right, wrong, good or bad, it followed that some specific kind of conduct fell under these categories.

I

(A)

Lawyers have for their own purposes carried the dissection of the notion of a legal right some distance, and some of their results[5] are of value in the elucidation of statements of the form "X has a right to …" outside legal contexts. There is of course no simple identification to be made between moral and legal rights, but there is an intimate connection between the two, and this itself is one feature which distinguishes a moral right from other fundamental moral concepts. It is not merely that as a matter of fact men speak of their moral rights mainly when advocating their incorporation in a legal system, but that the concept of a right belongs to that branch of morality which is specifically concerned to determine when one person's freedom may be limited by another's[6] and so to determine what actions may appropriately be made the subject of coercive legal rules. The words *"droit," "diritto,"* and *"Recht,"* used by continental jurists, have no simple English translation and seem to English jurists to hover uncertainly between law and morals, but they do in fact mark off an area of morality (the morality of law) which has special characteristics. It is occupied by the concepts of justice, fairness, rights, and obligation (if this last is not used as it is by many moral philosophers as an obscuring general label to cover every action that morally we ought to do or forbear from doing). The most important common characteristic of this group of moral concepts is that there is no incongruity, but a special congruity in the use of force or the threat of force to secure that what is just or fair or someone's right to have done shall in fact be done; for it is in just these circumstances that coercion of another human being is legitimate. Kant, in the *Rechtslehre*, discusses the obligations which arise in this branch of morality under the title of *officia juris*, "which do not require that respect for duty shall be of itself the determining principle of the will," and contrasts them with *officia virtutis*, which have no moral worth unless done for the sake of the moral principle. His point is, I think, that we must distinguish from the rest of morality those principles regulating the proper distribution of human freedom which alone make it morally legitimate for one human being to determine by his choice how another should act; and a certain specific moral value is secured (to be distinguished from moral virtue in which the good will is manifested) if human relationships are conducted in accordance with these principles even though coercion has to be used to secure this, for only if these principles are regarded will freedom be distributed among human beings as it should be. And it is I think a very important feature of a moral right that the possessor of it is conceived as having a moral justification for limiting the freedom of another and that he has this justification not because the action he is entitled to require of another has some moral quality but simply because in the circumstances a certain distribution of human freedom will be maintained if he by his choice is allowed to determine how that other shall act.

(B)

I can best exhibit this feature of a moral right by reconsidering the question whether moral rights and "duties"[7] are correlative. The contention that they are means, presumably, that every statement of the form "X has a right to …" entails and is entailed by "Y has a duty (not) to …" and at this stage we must not assume that the values of the name-variables "X" and "Y" must be different persons. Now there is certainly one sense of "a right" (which I have already mentioned) such that it does not follow from X's having a right that X or someone else has any duty. Jurists have isolated rights in this sense and have referred to them as "liberties" just to distinguish them from rights in the centrally important sense of "right" which has "duty" as a correlative. The former sense of "right" is needed to describe those areas of social life where competition is at least morally unobjectionable. Two people walking along both see a ten-dollar bill in the road twenty yards away, and there is no clue as to the owner. Neither of the two are under a "duty" to allow the other to pick it up; each has in this sense a right to pick it up. Of course there may be many things which each has a "duty" not to do in the course of the race to the spot – neither may kill or wound the other – and corresponding to these "duties" there are rights to forbearances. The moral propriety of all economic competition implies this minimum sense of "a right" in which to say that "X has a right to" means merely that X is under no "duty" not to. Hobbes saw that the expression "a right" could have this sense but he was wrong if he thought that there is no sense in which it does follow from X's having a right that Y has a duty or at any rate an obligation.

(C)

More important for our purpose is the question whether for all moral "duties" there are correlative moral rights, because those who have given an affirmative answer to this question have usually assumed without adequate scrutiny that to have a right is simply to be capable of benefiting by the performance of a "duty"; whereas in fact this is not a sufficient condition (and probably not a necessary condition) of having a right. Thus animals and babies who stand to benefit by our performance of our "duty" not to ill-treat them are said *therefore* to have rights to proper treatment. The full consequence of this reasoning is not usually followed out; most have shrunk from saying that we have rights against ourselves because we stand to benefit from our performance of our "duty" to keep ourselves alive or develop our talents. But the moral situation which arises from a promise (where the legal-sounding terminology of rights and obligations is most appropriate) illustrates most clearly that the notion of having a right and that of benefiting by the performance of a "duty" are not identical. X promises Y in return for some favor that he will look after Y's aged mother in his absence. Rights arise out of this transaction, but it is surely Y to whom the promise has been made and not his mother who *has* or *possesses* these rights. Certainly Y's mother is a person concerning whom X has an obligation and a person who will benefit by its performance, but the person *to whom* he has an obligation to look after her is Y. This is something *due to* or *owed to* Y, so it is Y, not his mother, whose right X will disregard and to whom X will have done *wrong* if he fails to keep his promise, though the mother may be physically injured. And it is Y who has a moral *claim* upon X, is *entitled* to have his mother looked after, and who can *waive* the claim and *release* Y from the obligation. Y is, in other words, morally in a position to determine by his choice how X shall act and in this way to limit X's freedom of choice; and it is this fact, not the fact that he stands to benefit, that makes it appropriate to say that he has *a right*. Of course often the person to whom a promise has been made will be the only person who stands to benefit by its performance, but this does not justify the identification of "having a right" with "benefiting by the performance of a duty." It is important for the whole logic of rights that, while the person who stands to benefit by the performance of a duty is discovered by considering what will happen if the duty is not performed, the person who has a right (to whom performance is *owed* or *due*) is discovered by examining the transaction or antecedent situation or relations of the parties out of which the "duty" arises. These considerations should incline us not to extend to animals and babies whom it is wrong to ill-treat the notion of a right to proper treatment, for the moral situation can be simply and adequately described here by saying that it is wrong or that we ought not to ill-treat them or, in the philosopher's generalized sense of "duty," that we have a duty not to ill-treat them.[8] If common usage sanctions talk of the rights of animals or babies it makes an idle use of the expression "a right," which will confuse the situation with other different moral situations where the expression "a right" has a specific force and cannot be replaced by the other moral expressions which I have mentioned. Perhaps some clarity on this matter is to be gained by considering the force of the preposition "to" in the expression "having a duty to Y" or "being under an obligation to Y" (where "Y" is the name of a person); for it is significantly different from the meaning of "to" in "doing something to Y" or "doing harm to Y," where it indicates the person affected by some action. In the first pair of expressions, "to" obviously does not have this force, but indicates the person to whom the person morally bound is bound. This is an intelligible development of the figure of a bond (*vinculum juris: obligare*); the precise figure is not that of two persons bound by a chain, but of *one* person bound, the other end of the chain lying in the hands of another to use if he chooses.[9] So it appears absurd to speak of having duties or owing obligations to ourselves – of course we may have "duties" not to do harm to ourselves, but what could be meant (once the distinction between these different meanings of "to" has been grasped) by insisting that we have duties or obligations *to* ourselves not to do harm to ourselves?

(D)

The essential connection between the notion of a right and the justified limitation of one person's freedom by another may be thrown into relief if we consider codes of behavior which do not purport to confer rights but only to prescribe what shall be done. Most natural law thinkers down to Hooker conceived of natural law in this way: there were natural duties compliance with which would certainly benefit man – things to be done to achieve man's natural end – but not natural rights. And there are of course many types of codes of behavior which only prescribe what is to be done, e.g., those regulating certain ceremonies. It would be absurd to regard these codes as conferring rights, but illuminating to contrast them with rules of games, which often create rights, though not, of course, moral rights. But even a code which is plainly a moral code need not establish rights; the Decalogue is perhaps the most important example. Of course, quite apart from heavenly rewards human beings stand to benefit by general obedience to the Ten Commandments: disobedience is wrong and will certainly harm individuals. But it would be a surprising interpretation of them that treated them as conferring rights. In such an interpretation obedience to the Ten Commandments would have to be conceived as due to or owed to individuals, not merely to God, and disobedience not merely as wrong but as *a wrong to* (as well as harm to) individuals. The Commandments would cease to read like penal statutes designed only to rule out certain types of behavior and would have to be thought of as rules placed at the disposal of individuals and regulating the extent to which *they* may demand certain behavior from others. Rights are typically conceived of as *possessed* or *owned by* or *belonging to* individuals, and these expressions reflect the conception of moral rules as not only prescribing conduct but as forming a kind of moral property of individuals to which they are as individuals entitled; only when rules are conceived in this way can we speak of *rights* and *wrongs* as well as right and wrong actions.[10]

II

So far I have sought to establish that to have a right entails having a moral justification for limiting the freedom of another person and for determining how he should act; it is now important to see that the moral justification must be of a special kind if it is to constitute a right, and this will emerge most clearly from an examination of the circumstances in which rights are asserted with the typical expression "I have a right to …" It is I think the case that this form of words is used in two main types of situations: (A) when the claimant has some special justification for interference with another's freedom which other persons do not have ("*I* have a right to be paid what you promised for my services"); (B) when the claimant is concerned to resist or object to some interference by another person as having no justification ("*I* have a right to say what I think").

(A) Special Rights

When rights arise out of special transactions between individuals or out of some special relationship in which they stand to each other, both the persons who have the right and those who have the corresponding obligation are limited to the parties to the special transaction or relationship. I call such rights special rights to distinguish them from those moral rights which are thought of as rights against (i.e., as imposing obligations upon)[11] everyone, such as those that are asserted when some unjustified interference is made or threatened as in (B) above.

(i) The most obvious cases of special rights are those that arise from promises. By promising to do or not to do something, we voluntarily incur obligations and create or confer rights on those to whom we promise; we alter the existing moral independence of the parties' freedom of choice in relation to some action and create a new moral relationship between them, so that it becomes morally legitimate for the person to whom the promise is given to determine how the promisor shall act. The promisee has a temporary authority or sovereignty in relation to some specific matter over the other's will which we express by saying that the promisor is under an obligation *to* the promisee to do what he has promised. To some philosophers the notion that moral phenomena – rights and duties or obligations – can be brought into existence by the voluntary action of individuals has appeared utterly mysterious; but this I think has been so because they have not clearly seen how special the moral notions of a right and an obligation are, nor how peculiarly they are connected with the distribution of freedom of choice; it would indeed be mysterious if we could make actions morally good or bad by voluntary choice. The simplest case of promising illustrates two points characteristic of all special rights: (1) the right and obligation arise not because the promised action has itself any particular moral quality, but just because of the voluntary transaction between the parties; (2) the identity of the parties concerned is vital – only *this*

person (the promisee) has the moral justification for determining how the promisor shall act. It is *his* right; only in relation to him is the promisor's freedom of choice diminished, so that if he chooses to release the promisor no one else can complain.

(ii) But a promise is not the only kind of transaction whereby rights are conferred. They may be *accorded* by a person consenting or authorizing another to interfere in matters which but for this consent or authorization he would be free to determine for himself. If I consent to your taking precautions for my health or happiness or authorize you to look after my interests, then you have a right which others have not, and I cannot complain of your interference if it is within the sphere of your authority. This is what is meant by a person surrendering his rights to another; and again the typical characteristics of a right are present in this situation: the person authorized has the right to interfere not because of its intrinsic character but because *these* persons have stood in *this* relationship. No one else (not similarly authorized) has any *right*[12] to interfere in theory even if the person authorized does not exercise his right.

(iii) Special rights are not only those created by the deliberate choice of the party on whom the obligation falls, as they are when they are accorded or spring from promises, and not all obligations to other persons are deliberately incurred, though I think it is true of all special rights that they arise from previous voluntary actions. A third very important source of special rights and obligations which we recognize in many spheres of life is what may be termed mutuality of restrictions, and I think political obligation is intelligible only if we see what precisely this is and how it differs from the other right-creating transactions (consent, promising) to which philosophers have assimilated it. In its bare schematic outline it is this: when a number of persons conduct any joint enterprise according to rules and thus restrict their liberty, those who have submitted to these restrictions when required have a right to a similar submission from those who have benefited by their submission. The rules may provide that officials should have authority to enforce obedience and make further rules, and this will create a structure of legal rights and duties, but the moral obligation to obey the rules in such circumstances is *due to* the co-operating members of the society, and they have the correlative moral right to obedience. In social situations of this sort (of which political society is the most complex example) the obligation to obey the rules is something distinct from whatever other moral reasons there may be for obedience in terms of good consequences (e.g., the prevention of suffering); the obligation is due to the co-operating members of the society as such and not because they are human beings on whom it would be wrong to inflict suffering. The utilitarian explanation of political obligation fails to take account of this feature of the situation both in its simple version that the obligation exists because and only if the direct consequences of a particular act of disobedience are worse than obedience, and also in its more sophisticated version that the obligation exists even when this is not so, if disobedience increases the probability that

the law in question or other laws will be disobeyed on other occasions when the direct consequences of obedience are better than those of disobedience.

Of course to say that there is such a moral obligation upon those who have benefited by the submission of other members of society to restrictive rules to obey these rules in their turn does not entail either that this is the only kind of moral reason for obedience or that there can be no cases where disobedience will be morally justified. There is no contradiction or other impropriety in saying "I have an obligation to do X, someone has a right to ask me to, but I now see I ought not to do it." It will in painful situations sometimes be the lesser of two moral evils to disregard what really are people's rights and not perform our obligations to them. This seems to me particularly obvious from the case of promises: I may promise to do something and thereby incur an obligation just because that is one way in which obligations (to be distinguished from other forms of moral reasons for acting) are created; reflection may show that it would in the circumstances be wrong to keep this promise because of the suffering it might cause, and we can express this by saying "*I ought not* to do it though *I have an obligation to him* to do it" just because the italicized expressions are not synonyms but come from different dimensions of morality. The attempt to explain this situation by saying that our real obligation here is to avoid the suffering and that there is only a prima facie obligation to keep the promise seems to me to confuse two quite different kinds of moral reason, and in practice such a terminology obscures the precise character of what is at stake when "for some greater good" we infringe people's rights or do not perform our obligations to them.

The social-contract theorists rightly fastened on the fact that the obligation to obey the law is not merely a special case of benevolence (direct or indirect), but something which arises between members of a particular political society out of their mutual relationship. Their mistake was to identify *this* right-creating situation of mutual restrictions with the paradigm case of promising; there are of course important similarities, and these are just the points which all special rights have in common, viz., that they arise out of special relationships between human beings and not out of the character of the action to be done or its effects.

(iv) There remains a type of situation which may be thought of as creating rights and obligations: where the parties have a special natural relationship, as in the case of parent and child. The parent's moral right to obedience from his child would I suppose now be thought to terminate when the child reaches the age "of discretion," but the case is worth mentioning because some political philosophies have had recourse to analogies with this case as an explanation of political obligation, and also because even this case has some of the features we have distinguished in special rights, viz., the right arises out of the special relationship of the parties (though it is in this case a natural relationship) and not out of the character of the actions to the performance of which there is a right.

(v) To be distinguished from special rights, of course, are special liberties, where, exceptionally, one person is *exempted* from obligations to which most are subject

but does not thereby acquire a *right* to which there is a correlative obligation. If you catch me reading your brother's diary, you say, "You have no right to read it." I say, "I have a right to read it – your brother said I might unless he told me not to, and he has not told me not to." Here I have been specially *licensed* by your brother who had a right to require me not to read his diary, so I am exempted from the moral obligation not to read it, but your brother is under no obligation to let me go on reading it. Cases where *rights,* not liberties, are accorded to manage or interfere with another person's affairs are those where the license is not revocable at will by the person according the right.

(B) General Rights

In contrast with special rights, which constitute a justification peculiar to the holder of the right for interfering with another's freedom, are general rights, which are asserted defensively, when some unjustified interference is anticipated or threatened, in order to point out that the interference is unjustified. "I have the right to say what I think."[13] "I have the right to worship as I please." Such rights share two important characteristics with special rights. (1) To have them is to have a moral justification for determining how another shall act, viz., that he shall not interfere.[14] (2) The moral justification does not arise from the character of the particular action to the performance of which the claimant has a right; what justifies the claim is simply – there being no special relation between him and those who are threatening to interfere to justify that interference – that this is a particular exemplification of the equal right to be free. But there are of course striking differences between such defensive general rights and special rights. (1) General rights do not arise out of any special relationship or transaction between men. (2) They are not rights which are peculiar to those who have them but are rights which all men capable of choice have in the absence of those special conditions which give rise to special rights. (3) General rights have as correlatives obligations not to interfere to which everyone else is subject and not merely the parties to some special relationship or transaction, though of course they will often be asserted when some particular persons threaten to interfere as a moral objection to that interference. To assert a general right is to claim in relation to some particular action the equal right of all men to be free in the absence of any of those special conditions which constitute a special right to limit another's freedom; to assert a special right is to assert in relation to some particular action a right constituted by such special conditions to limit another's freedom. The assertion of general rights directly invokes the principle that all men equally have the right to be free; the assertion of a special right (as I attempt to show in Section III) invokes it indirectly.

III

It is, I hope, clear that unless it is recognized that interference with another's freedom requires a moral justification the notion of a right could have no place in morals; for to assert a right is to assert that there is such a justification. The characteristic function in moral discourse of those sentences in which the meaning of the expression "a right" is to be found – "I have a right to …," "You have no right to …," "What right have you to …?" – is to bring to bear on interferences with another's freedom, or on claims to interfere, a type of moral evaluation or criticism specially appropriate to interference with freedom and characteristically different from the moral criticism of actions made with the use of expressions like "right," "wrong," "good," and "bad." And this is only one of many different types of moral ground for saying "You ought …" or "You ought not …" The use of the expression "What right have you to …?" shows this more clearly, perhaps, than the others; for we use it, just at the point where interference is actual or threatened, to call for the moral *title* of the person addressed to interfere; and we do this often without any suggestion at all that what he proposes to do is otherwise wrong and sometimes with the implication that the same interference on the part of another person would be unobjectionable.

But though our use in moral discourse of "a right" does presuppose the recognition that interference with another's freedom requires a moral justification, this would not itself suffice to establish, except in a sense easily trivialized, that in the recognition of moral rights there is implied the recognition that all men have a right to equal freedom; for unless there is some restriction inherent in the meaning of "a right" on the type of moral justification for interference which can constitute a right, the principle could be made wholly vacuous. It would, for example, be possible to adopt the principle and then assert that some characteristic or behavior of some human beings (that they are improvident, or atheists, or Jews, or Negroes) constitutes a moral justification for interfering with their freedom; *any* differences between men could, so far as my argument has yet gone, be treated as a moral justification for interference and so constitute a right, so that the equal right of all men to be free would be compatible with gross inequality. It may well be that the expression "moral" itself imports some restriction on what can constitute a moral justification for interference which would avoid this consequence, but I cannot myself yet show that this is so. It is, on the other hand, clear to me that the moral justification for interference which is to constitute a *right* to interfere (as distinct from merely making it morally good or desirable to interfere) is restricted to certain special conditions and that this is inherent in the meaning of "a right" (unless this is used so loosely that it could be replaced by the other moral expressions mentioned). Claims to interfere with another's freedom based on the general character of the activities interfered with (e.g., the folly or cruelty of "native" practices) or the general character of the parties ("We are Germans; they are Jews") even when well founded are not matters of moral right or obligation. Submission in such cases even where proper is not *due to* or *owed to* the individuals who interfere; it would be equally proper whoever of the same class of persons interfered. Hence other elements in our moral vocabulary suffice to describe this case, and it is confusing here to talk of rights. We saw in Section II that the types of justification for interference involved in special rights was independent of the character of the action to the performance of which there was a right but depended upon certain previous transactions and relations between individuals (such as promises, consent, authorization, submission to mutual restrictions). Two questions here suggest themselves: (1) On what intelligible principle could these bare forms of promising, consenting, submission to mutual restrictions, be either necessary or sufficient, irrespective of their content, to justify interference with another's freedom? (2) What characteristics have these types of transaction or relationship in common? The answer to both these questions is I think this: If we justify interference on such grounds as we give when we claim a moral right, we are in fact indirectly invoking as our justification the principle that all men have an equal right to be free. For we are in fact saying in the case of promises and consents or authorizations that this claim to interfere with another's freedom is justified because he has, in exercise of his equal right to be free, freely chosen to create this claim; and in the case of mutual restrictions we are in fact saying that this claim to interfere with another's freedom is justified because it is fair; and it is fair because only so will there be an equal distribution of restrictions and so of freedom among this group of men. So in the case of special rights as well as of general rights recognition of them implies the recognition of the equal right of all men to be free.

Notes

1   I was first stimulated to think along these lines by Mr Stuart Hampshire, and I have reached by different routes a conclusion similar to his.

2   Further explanation of the perplexing terminology of freedom is, I fear, necessary. *Coercion* includes, besides preventing a person from doing what he chooses, making his choice less eligible by threats; *restraint* includes any action designed to make the exercise of choice impossible and so includes killing or enslaving a person. But neither coercion nor restraint includes *competition*. In terms of the distinction between "having a right to" and "being at liberty to," used above and further discussed in Section I, B, all men may have, consistently with the obligation to forbear from coercion, the *liberty* to satisfy if they can such at least of their desires as are not designed to coerce or injure others, even though in fact, owing to scarcity, one man's satisfaction causes another's frustration. In conditions of extreme scarcity this distinction between competition and coercion will not be worth drawing; natural rights are only of importance "where peace is possible" (Locke). Further, freedom (the absence of coercion) can be *valueless* to those victims of unrestricted competition too poor to make use of it; so it will be pedantic to point out to them that though starving they are free. This is the truth exaggerated by the Marxists whose *identification* of poverty with lack of freedom confuses two different evils.

3   Save those general rights (cf. Section II, B) which are particular exemplifications of the right of all men to be free.

4   Is the notion of *a* right found in either Plato or Aristotle? There seems to be no Greek word for it as distinct from "right" or "just" ($\delta\iota\kappa\alpha\acute{\iota}o\nu$), though expressions like $\tau\grave{\alpha}\,\grave{\epsilon}\mu\grave{\alpha}\,\delta\iota\kappa\alpha\acute{\iota}\alpha$ are I believe fourth-century legal idioms. The natural expressions in Plato are $\tau\grave{o}\,\grave{\epsilon}\alpha\upsilon\tau o\upsilon\,(\breve{\epsilon}\chi\epsilon\iota\nu)$ or $\tau\grave{\alpha}\,\tau\iota\nu\grave{\iota}\,\grave{o}\phi\epsilon\iota\lambda\acute{o}\mu\epsilon\nu\alpha$, but these seem confined to property or debts. There is no place for a moral right unless the moral value of individual freedom is recognized.

5   As W. D. Lamont has seen: cf. his *Principles of Moral Judgment* (Oxford, 1946); for the jurists, cf. Hohfeld's *Fundamental Legal Conceptions* (New Haven, 1923).

6   Here and subsequently I use "interfere with another's freedom," "limit another's freedom," "determine how another shall act," to mean either the use of coercion or demanding that a person shall do or not do some action. The connection between these two types of "interference" is too complex for

discussion here; I think it is enough for present purposes to point out that having a justification for demanding that a person shall or shall not do some action is a necessary though not a sufficient condition for justifying coercion.

7   I write "duties" here because one factor obscuring the nature of a right is the philosophical use of "duty" and "obligation" for all cases where there are moral reasons for saying an action ought to be done or not done. In fact "duty," "obligation," "right," and "good" come from different segments of morality, concern different types of conduct, and make different types of moral criticism or evaluation. Most important are the points (1) that obligations may be voluntarily incurred or created, (2) that they are *owed to* special persons (who have rights), (3) that they do not arise out of the character of the actions which are obligatory but out of the relationship of the parties. Language roughly though not consistently confines the use of "having an obligation" to such cases.

8   The use here of the generalized "duty" is apt to prejudice the question whether animals and babies have rights.

9   Cf. A. H. Campbell, *The Structure of Stair's Institutes* (Glasgow, 1954), p. 31.

10   Continental jurists distinguish between "*subjektives*" and "*objektives Recht*," which corresponds very well to the distinction between *a* right, which an individual has, and what it is right to do.

11   Cf. Section (B) below.

12   Though it may be *better* (the lesser of two evils) that he should.

13   In speech the difference between general and special rights is often marked by stressing the pronoun where a special right is claimed or where the special right is denied. "You have no right to stop him reading that book" refers to the reader's general right. "*You* have no right to stop him reading that book" denies that the person addressed has a special right to interfere though others may have.

14   Strictly, in the assertion of a general right both the *right* to forbearance from coercion and the *liberty* to do the specified action are asserted, the first in the face of actual or threatened coercion, the second as an objection to an actual or anticipated demand that the action should not be done. The first has as its correlative an obligation upon everyone to forbear from coercion; the second the absence in any one of a justification for such a demand. Here, in Hohfeld's words, the correlative is not an obligation but a "no-right."

Chapter 12

The Public Interest

Brian Barry

I

A Tribunal of Enquiry claims that the public interest requires journalists to disclose their sources of information; the Restrictive Practices Court invalidates an agreement among certain manufacturers as contrary to the Restrictive Practices Act and therefore contrary to the public interest; the National Incomes Commission says that a proposed rise for the workers in an industry would be against the public interest. These examples could be multiplied endlessly. Each day's newspaper brings fresh ones. In arguments about concrete issues (as opposed to general rhetoric in favour of political parties or entire societies) "the public interest" is more popular than "justice", "fairness", "equality", or "freedom".

Why is this? Roughly, there are two possible answers. One is that "the public interest" points to a fairly clearly definable range of considerations in support of a policy and if it is a very popular concept at the moment all this shows is that (for better or worse) these considerations are highly valued by many people at the moment. This is my own view. The other answer is that politicians and civil servants find it a handy smoke-screen to cover their decisions, which are actually designed to conciliate the most effectively deployed interest.

These sceptics often buttress their arguments by pointing out that most theoretical writing about "the public interest" is vague and confused. This theme is copiously illustrated by Frank J. Sorauf in his article "The Public Interest Reconsidered", *Journal of Politics*, XIX (Nov. 1957) and by Glendon Schubert in his book *The Public Interest: Critique of a Concept*. But it is a familiar idea that people who are perfectly well able to *use a* concept may nevertheless talk rubbish *about* it, so even if many of the writings about the concept are confused it does not follow that the concept itself is. A more cogent line of argument is to construct a definition of "the public interest" and then show that, so defined, nothing (or not much) satisfies it. From this, it can be deduced that most uses of the phrase in political discussion must be either fraudulent or vacuous. Like Sorauf and Schubert, the best known expositors of the view are Americans – one may mention A. F. Bentley's *The Process of Government* and D. B. Truman's *The Governmental Process*. But the most succinct and recent treatment is to be found in Chapters Three and Four of *The Nature of Politics* by J. D. B. Miller, and it is to a criticism of these chapters that I now turn.

II

Miller defines "interest" as follows: "we can say that an interest exists when we see some body of persons showing a *common concern* about particular matters" (p. 39). On the basis of this he later puts forward two propositions. First, one is not "justified in going beyond people's own inclinations in order to tell them that their true interest lies somewhere else" (p. 41). It "seems absurd" to suppose that an interest can exist if those whose interest it is are not aware of it (p. 40). And secondly, a "common concern … must be present if we are to say that a general interest exists". "A common concern will sometimes be found in the society at large, and sometimes not. More often it will not be there" (p. 54).

Apart from the last point, which is a statement of fact and one I shall not query here, these propositions follow analytically from the original definition of "interest", though Miller does not see this clearly. Everything hinges on that slippery word "concern" which plays such a crucial part in the definition. One can be concerned *at* (a state of affairs) or concerned *about* (an issue) or concerned *with* (an organization or activity) or, finally, concerned *by* (an action, policy, rule, *etc.*) The noun, as in "so-and-so's concerns" can correspond to any of the first three constructions, and it seems plain enough that in these three kinds of use nobody can be concerned without knowing it. In the fourth use, where "concerned by" is roughly equivalent to "affected by", this is not so: someone might well be affected by an economic policy of which he had never heard. But the noun "concern" does not have a sense corresponding to this, nor does Miller stretch it to cover it. Naturally, if "interest" is understood in terms of actual striving, no sense can be given to the idea of someone's having an interest but not pursuing it. Similarly, if "interest" is defined as "concern" it hardly needs several pages of huffing and puffing against rival conceptions (pp. 52–4) to establish that "common or general interest" must be equivalent to "common or general concern".

Since, then, Miller's conclusions follow analytically from his definition of "interest", with the addition of a factual premise which I am not here disputing, I must, if I am to reject his conclusions, reject his definition. Miller can, of course, define "interest" any way he likes; but if he chooses a completely idiosyncratic definition he can hardly claim to have proved much if it turns out that most of the things that people have traditionally said about interests then become false or meaningless. He clearly believes himself to be taking part in a debate with previous writers and it is because of this that he is open to criticism.

Let us start from the other end. Let us begin by considering the things we normally want to say about interests, the distinctions which we normally want to draw by using the concept, and then see whether it is not possible to construct a definition of "interest" which will make sense of these ordinary speech habits.

The first part of Miller's definition, which makes interests *shared* concerns, conflicts with our normal wish to draw a distinction between someone's private or personal interests on the one hand and the interests which he shares with various groups of people on the other hand. Simply to rule out the former by fiat as Miller does seems to have nothing to recommend it. It might perhaps be argued in defence of the limitation that only interests shared among a number of people are politically important, but it can surely be validly replied that this is neither a necessary nor a sufficient condition.

The second part of the definition equates a man's interests with his concerns. This conflicts with a great many things we ordinarily want to say about interests. We want to say that people can mistake their interests, and that while some conflicts are conflicts of interests, others (*e.g.*, "conflicts of principle") are not. We distinguish between "disinterested" concern and "interested" concern in a particular matter; we find it convenient to distinguish "interest groups" (*e.g.*, The National Farmers' Union) from "cause" or "promotional" groups (*e.g.*, The Abortion Law Reform Association). "They co-operate because they have a common interest" is ordinarily taken as a genuine explanation, rather than a pseudo-explanation of the "*vis dormitiva*" type, as it would be if co-operation were identified with (or regarded as a direct manifestation of) a common interest. We allow that one can recognize something as being in one's interest without pursuing it. Finally, we do not regard it as a contradiction in terms to say, "I realize that so-and-so would be in my interests but nevertheless I am against it." These points are all inconsistent with Miller's definition, and in addition the last of them is inconsistent with any attempt such as that of S. I. Benn to define a man's interests as "something he thought he could *reasonably* ask for" ("'Interests' in Politics", *Proceedings of the Aristotelian Society*, 1960, p. 127).

Can a definition be found which will make sense of all these uses of "interest"? I suggest this: a policy, law or institution is in someone's interest if it increases his opportunities to get what he wants – whatever that may be. Notice that this is a definition of "*in* so-and-so's interests". Other uses of "interest" all seem to me either irrelevant or reducible to sentences with this construction. Thus, the only unforced sense that one can give to "What are your interests?", which Benn imagines being put seriously to a farmer, is that it is an enquiry into his favourite intellectual preoccupations or perhaps into his leisure activities – applications of "interest" whose irrelevance Benn himself affirms. Otherwise, it has no normal application, though a "plain man" with an analytical turn of mind (such as John Locke) might reply:

"Civil interest I call life, liberty, health and indolency of body; and the possession of outward things, such as money, lands, houses, furniture and the like" (*Letter Concerning Toleration*).

This might be regarded as a specification of the kinds of ways in which a policy, law or institution must impinge on someone before it can be said to be "in his interests". Unpacked into more logically transparent (if more long-winded) terms it might read: "A policy, law or institution may be said to be in someone's interests if it satisfies the following conditions …"

The main point about my proposed definition, however, is that it is always a *policy* that is said to be "in so-and-so's interest" – not the actual manner in which he is impinged upon. (From now on I shall use "policy" to cover "policy, law or institution".) There are straightforward criteria specifying the way in which someone has to be affected by a policy before that policy can be truly described as being "in his interests"; but whether or not a given policy will bring about such results may quite often be an open question.

It is this feature of "interest" which explains how people can "mistake their interests" – item number one on the list of "things we want to say about interests". The stock argument against this possibility is that if you assert it you must commit yourself to the view that "some people know what's good for other people better than they do themselves". But this can now be seen to rest on a gross equivocation. The presumably illiberal, and therefore damaging, view to be saddled with would be the view that policies which impinge on people in ways which they dislike may nevertheless be said to be "in their interests". But this is not entailed by the statement that people may "mistake their interests". All that one has to believe is that they may think a policy will impinge upon them in a way which will increase their opportunities to get what they want when in fact it will do the opposite. Whether his opportunities are increased or narrowed by being unemployed is something each man may judge for himself; but it is surely only sensible to recognize that most people's opinions about the most effective economic policies for securing given ends are likely to be worthless. In his Fireside Chat on June 28, 1934, President Roosevelt said:

> "The simplest way for each of you to judge recovery lies in the plain facts of your own individual situation. Are you better off than you were last year? Are your debts less burdensome? Is your bank account more secure? Are your working conditions better? Is your faith in your own individual future more firmly grounded?"

It is quite consistent to say that people can "judge recovery for themselves" without respecting their opinions about the efficacy of deficit financing.

The other "things we normally want to say" also fit the proposed definition. People may want policies other than those calculated to increase their opportunities – hence the possibility of "disinterested action" and "promotional groups". Similarly, a man may definitely not want a policy which will increase his opportunities (perhaps because he thinks that the policy is unfair and that others should get the increase instead). Hence the possibility of someone's not wanting something that he acknowledges would be in his interests. Finally, nothing is more common than for someone to agree that a policy would increase his opportunities if adopted, and to want it to be adopted, but at the same time to say that the addition of his own efforts to the campaign to secure its adoption would have such a small probability of making the decisive difference between success and failure for the campaign that it is simply not worth making the effort; and of course if everyone is in the habit of reasoning like this a policy which is in the interests of a great many people, but not greatly in the interests of any of them, may well fail to receive any organized support at all.

No doubt there is room for amplification of my definition of what it is for a policy to be in someone's interest. In particular the phrase "opportunities to get what he wants" needs closer analysis, and account should be taken of the expression "so-and-so's *best* interests" which tends to be used where it is thought that the person in question would make such an unwise use of increased opportunities that he would be better off without them (*e.g.*, a heavy drinker winning a first dividend on the football pools). However, I doubt whether refinements in the definition of "interest" would alter the correctness or incorrectness of what I have to say about "the public interest", so I turn now to that expression.

III

If "interest" is defined in such a way that "this policy is in *A*'s interest" is equivalent to "*A* is trying to get this policy adopted" it is decisive evidence against there being in any but a few cases a "public interest" that there is conflict over the adoption of nearly all policies in a state. But on the definition of "interest" I have proposed this would no longer be so. A policy might be truly describable as "in the public interest" even though some people opposed it. This could come about in a way already mentioned: those who oppose the policy might have "mistaken their interests". In other words, they may think the policy in question is not in their interests when it really is. Most opposition in the USA to unbalanced budgets can be explained in this way, for example. Disagreements about defence and disarmament policy are also largely disagreements about the most effective means to fairly obvious common goals such as national survival and (if possible) independence.

There are two other possibilities. One is that the group opposing the measure is doing so in order to further a different measure which is outside the range of relevant comparisons. The other possibility is that the opposing group have a special interest in the matter which counteracts their interest as members of the public. I do not expect these two descriptions to be clear; I shall devote the remainder of the paper to trying to make them so, taking up the former in this section and IV, and the latter in V.

Comparison enters into any evaluation in terms of interests. To say that a policy would be in someone's interests is implicitly to compare it with some other policy – often simply the continuance of the *status quo*. So if you say that a number of people have a common interest in something you must have in mind some alternative to it which you believe would be worse for all of them. The selection of alternatives for comparison thus assumes a position of crucial importance. Any policy can be made "preferable" by arbitrarily contrasting it with one sufficiently unpleasant.

Unemployment and stagnation look rosy compared with nuclear war; common interests in the most unlikely proposals can be manufactured by putting forward as the alternative a simultaneous attack by our so-called "independent deterrent" on Russia and the USA. All this need do is remind one that one thing may be "in somebody's interest" *compared with something else* but still undesirable compared with other possibilities. The problem remains: is there (in most matters) any one course of action which is better for everyone than any other? Fairly obviously, the answer is: No. Any ordinary proposal would be less in my interest than a poll tax of a pound a head, the proceeds to be given to me. And this can be repeated for everybody else, taking each person one at a time. This, however, seems as thin a reason for denying the possibility of common interests as the parallel manoeuvre in reverse was for asserting their ubiquity. In both cases the comparison is really irrelevant. But what are the criteria for relevance? The simplest answer (which will later have to have complications added) is that the only proposals to be taken into account when estimating "common interests" should be proposals which treat everyone affected in exactly the same way. Take the traditional example of a law prohibiting assault (including murder). If no limitation is imposed upon the range of alternatives it is easy to show that there is no "common interest" among all the members of a society in having such a law directed equally at everyone. For one could always propose that instead the society should be divided into two classes, the members of the first class being allowed to assault the members of the second class with impunity but not *vice versa*, as with Spartans and Helots; or each member of the first group might be put in this position only *vis-à-vis* particular members of the second group. (Examples of this can be drawn from slave-holding, patriarchal, or racially discriminatory systems such as the *ante-bellum* South, ancient Rome and Nazi Germany respectively.) It could perhaps be argued that the "beneficiaries" under such an unequal system become brutalized and are therefore in some sense "worse off" than they would be under a regime of equality. But the whole point of "interest" – and its great claim in the eyes of liberals – is that the concept is indifferent to moral character and looks only at opportunities.

Yet even the most sceptical writers often admit that a law prohibiting assault by anyone against anyone is a genuine example of something which is "in the public interest" or "in everyone's interest". This becomes perfectly true when the alternatives are restricted to those which affect all equally, for then the most obvious possibilities are (a) that nobody should assault anybody else and (b) that anybody should be allowed to assault anybody else. And of these two it is hardly necessary to call on the authority of Hobbes to establish that, given the natural equality of strength and vulnerability which prevents anyone from having reasonable hopes of gaining from the latter set-up, the former is "in everyone's interest".

IV

A convenient way of examining some of the ramifications of this theory is to work over some of the things Rousseau says in the *Social Contract* about the "General

Will". Judging from critiques in which Rousseau figures as a charlatan whose philosophical emptiness is disguised by his superficial rhetoric, it is hard to see why we should waste time reading him, except perhaps on account of his supposedly malign influence on Robespierre. I doubt the fairness of this estimate, and I am also inclined to deprecate the tendency (often though not always combined with the other) to look on Rousseau through Hegelian spectacles. We need to dismantle the implausible psychological and metaphysical theories (*e.g.*, "compulsory rational freedom" and "group mind") which have been foisted on Rousseau by taking certain phrases and sentences (*e.g.*, "forced to be free" and "moral person") out of context. As a small contribution to this process of demythologising Rousseau I want to suggest here that what he says about "the general will" forms a coherent and ingenious unity if it is understood as a treatment of the theme of common interests.

Rousseau's starting point, which he frequently makes use of, is that any group will have a will that is general in relation to its constituent members, but particular with respect to groups in which it in turn is included. Translating this into talk about interests it means that any policy which is equally favourable to all the members of a given group will be less favourable to member *A* than the policy most favourable to *A*, less favourable to member *B* than the policy most favourable to *B*, and so on; but it will be more favourable to each of the members of the group than any policy which has to be equally beneficial to an even larger number of people. Suppose, for example, that a fixed sum – say a million pounds – is available for wage increases in a certain industry. If each kind of employee had a separate trade union one might expect as many incompatible claims as there were unions, each seeking to appropriate most of the increase for its own members. If for example there were a hundred unions with a thousand members apiece each employee might have a thousand pounds (a thousandth of the total) claimed on his behalf, and the total claims would add up to a hundred million pounds. At the other extreme if there were only one union, there would be no point in its putting in a claim totalling more than a million pounds (we assume for convenience that the union accepts the unalterability of this amount) and if it made an equal claim on behalf of each of its members this would come to only ten pounds a head. Intermediate numbers of unions would produce intermediate results.

Rousseau's distinction between the "will of all" and the "general will" now fits in neatly. The "will of all" is simply shorthand for "the policy most in *A*'s interests, taking *A* in isolation; the policy most in *B*'s interests, taking *B* in isolation; and so on." (These will of course normally be different policies for *A*, *B* and the rest.) The "general will" is *a single* policy which is equally in the interests of all the members of the group. It will usually be different from any of the policies mentioned before, and less beneficial to anyone than the policy most beneficial to himself alone.

We can throw light on some of the other things Rousseau says in the one-page chapter II.iii. of the *Social Contract* by returning to the trade union example. Suppose now that the leaders of the hundred trade unions are told that the money will be forthcoming only if a majority of them can reach agreement on a way of dividing it up. A possible method would be for each leader to write down his preferred solution on a slip of paper, and for these to be compared, the process continuing until a requisite number of papers have the same proposal written on them. If each started by writing down his maximum demand there would be as many proposals as leaders – the total result would be the "will of all". This is obviously a dead end, and if no discussion is allowed among the leaders, there is a good chance that they would all propose, as a second best, an equal division of the money. (There is some experimental evidence for this, presented in Chapter 3 of Thomas Schelling's *The Strategy of Conflict*.) Such a solution would be in accordance with the "general will" and represents a sort of highest common factor of agreement. As Rousseau puts it, it arises when the pluses and minuses of the conflicting first choices are cancelled out.

If instead of these arrangements communication is allowed, and even more if the groups are fewer and some leaders control large block votes, it becomes less likely that an equal solution will be everyone's second choice. It will be possible for some leaders to agree together to support a proposal which is less favourable to any of their members than each leader's first choice was to his own members, but still more favourable than any solution equally beneficial to all the participants. Thus, as Rousseau says, a "less general will" prevails.

In Il.iii. Rousseau suggests that this should be prevented by not allowing groups to form or, if they do form, by seeing that they are many and small. In the less optimistic mood of IV.i., when he returns to the question, he places less faith in mechanical methods and more in widespread civic virtue. He now says that the real answer is for everyone to ask himself "the right question", *i.e.*, "What measure will benefit me in common with everyone else, rather than me at the expense of every-one else?" (I have never seen attention drawn to the fact that this famous doctrine is something of an afterthought whose first and only occurrence in the *Social Contract* is towards the end.) However, this is a difference only about the most effective means of getting a majority to vote for what is in the common interest of all. The essential point remains the same: that only where all are equally affected by the policy adopted can an equitable solution be expected.

> "The undertakings which bind us to the social body are obligatory only because they are mutual; and their nature is such that in fulfilling them we cannot work for others without working for ourselves. ... What makes the will general is less the number of voters than the common interest uniting them; for, under this system, each necessarily submits to the conditions he imposes on others: and this admirable agree-ment between interest and justice gives to the common deliberations an equitable character which at once vanishes when any particular question is discussed, in the absence of a common interest to unite and identify the ruling of the judge with that of the party."
>
> (II.iv., Cole's translation.)

Provided this condition is met, nobody will deliberately vote for a burdensome law because it will be burdensome to him too: this is why no *specific* limitations on "the general will" are needed. Disagreements can then be due only to conflicts of opinion – not to conflicts of interest. Among the various policies which would affect everyone in the same way, each person has to decide which would benefit himself most – and, since everyone else is similarly circumstanced, he is automatically deciding at the same time which would benefit everyone else most. Thus, to go back to our example of a law prohibiting assault: disagreement will arise, if at all, because some think they (in common with everyone else) would make a net gain of opportunities from the absence of any law against assault, while others think the opposite. This is, in principle, a dispute with a right and a wrong answer; and everyone benefits from the right answer's being reached rather than the wrong one. Rousseau claims that a majority is more likely to be right than any given voter, so that someone in the minority will in fact gain from the majority's decision carrying the day. This has often been regarded as sophistical or paradoxical, but it is quite reasonable once one allows Rousseau his definition of the situation as one in which everyone is co-operating to find a mutually beneficial answer, for so long as everyone is taken as having an equal, better than even chance of giving the right answer, the majority view will (in the long run) be right more often than that of any given voter. (Of course, the same thing applies in reverse: if each one has on average a *less* than even chance of being right, the majority will be *wrong* more often than any given voter.) The formula for this was discovered by Condorcet and has been presented by Duncan Black on page 164 of his *Theory of Committees and Elections*. To illustrate its power, here is an example: if we have a voting body of a thousand, each member of which is right on average fifty-one per cent of the time, what is the probability in any particular instance that a fifty-one per cent majority has the right answer? The answer, rather surprisingly perhaps, is: better than two to one (69%). Moreover, if the required majority is kept at fifty-one per cent and the number of voters raised to ten thousand, or if the number of voters stays at one thousand and the required majority is raised to sixty per cent, the probability that the majority (5,100 to 4,900 in the first case or 600 to 400 in the second) has the right answer rises virtually to unity (99.97%). None of this, of course, shows that "Rousseau was right" but it does suggest that he was no simpleton.

To sum up, Rousseau calls for the citizen's deliberations to comprise two elements: (a) the decision to forgo (either as unattainable or as immoral) policies which would be in one's own personal interest alone, or in the common interest of a group smaller than the whole, and (b) the attempt to calculate which, of the various lines of policy that would affect oneself equally with all others, is best for him (and, since others are like him, for others). This kind of two-step deliberation is obviously reminiscent of the method recommended in Mr Hare's *Freedom and Reason*, with the crucial difference that whereas Mr Hare will settle for a willingness to be affected by the policy in certain hypothetical circumstances, Rousseau insists that my being affected by the policy must actually be in prospect. There is no need to construct a special planet to test my good faith – my bluff is called every time. By the same token, the theory I have attributed to Rousseau requires far more stringent conditions to be met before something can be said to be in the common interest of all than the vague requirement of "equal consideration" put forward by Benn and Peters in their *Social Principles and the Democratic State*.

V

Even if Rousseau can be shown to be consistent it does not follow that the doctrine of the *Social Contract* has wide application. Rousseau himself sets out a number of requirements that have to be met before it applies at all: political virtue (reinforced by a civil religion), smallness of state, and rough economic equality among the citizens. And even then, as he points out plainly, it is only a few questions which allow solutions that touch all in the same way. If only some are affected by a matter the "general will" cannot operate. It is no longer a case of each man legislating for himself *along with others*, but merely one of some men legislating *for* others. It is fairly obvious that Rousseau's requirements are not met in a great modern nation state – a conclusion that would not have worried him. But since I am trying to show that "the public interest" is applicable in just such a state it does have to worry me. It is here that I must introduce my remaining explanation of the way in which something can be "in the public interest" while still arousing opposition from some.

Think again of the examples with which I began this paper. The thing that is claimed to be "in the public interest" is not *prima facie* in the interests of the journalist whose sources may dry up, the workers whose rise is condemned or the businessmen whose restrictive practices are outlawed. But do first appearances mislead? After all, the journalist along with the rest gains from national security, and workers or industrialists gain along with the rest from lower prices. To avoid a flat contradiction we need more refined tools; and they exist in ordinary speech. Instead of simply saying that some measure is "in his interests" a man will often specify some rôle or capacity in which it is favourable to him: "as a parent", "as a businessman", "as a house owner" and so on. One of the capacities in which everyone finds himself is that of "a member of the public". Some issues allow a policy to be produced which will affect everyone in his capacity as a "member of the public" and nobody in any other capacity. This is the pure "Rousseau" situation. Then there are other issues which lack this simplicity but still do not raise any problems because those who are affected in a capacity other than that of "member of the public" are either affected in that capacity in the same direction as they are in their other capacity of "member of the public" or at least are not affected so strongly in the contrary direction as to tip the overall balance of their interest (what I shall call their "net interest") that way. Although this is not quite what I have called the "Rousseau" situation, the "Rousseau" formula still works. Indeed, Rousseau sometimes seems explicitly to accept this kind of situation as satisfactory, as when he says (III.xv.) that in a well-ordered state "the aggregate of the common happiness furnishes a greater proportion of that of each individual".

Finally, we have the familiar case where for some people a special interest outweighs their share in the public interest. The journalist may think, for example, that compulsory disclosure of sources would indeed be in the public interest but at the same time conclude that his own special interest as a journalist in getting information from people who want to stay anonymous is more important to him than the marginal gain in security that is at stake. In such cases as this Rousseau's formula will not work, for although everyone still has a common interest in the adoption of a certain policy *qua* "member of the public", some have a net interest in opposing it.

To adopt the policy which is "in the public interest" in such a case is still different from deliberately passing over an available policy which would treat everyone equally, for in the present case there *is* no such policy available. Even so, it involves favouring some at the expense of others, which makes it reasonable to ask whether it is justifiable to recommend it. Various lines of justification are possible. Bentham seems to have assumed that in most matters there was a public interest on one side (*e.g.*, in cheap and speedy legal procedures) and on the other side the "sinister" interest of those who stood to gain on balance from abuses (*e.g.*, "Judge & Co.") and to have believed (what is surely not unreasonable) that a utilitarian calculation would generally give the verdict to the policy favouring "the public". On a different tack, it might be argued that it is inequitable for anyone to benefit from "special privileges" at the expense of the rest of the community. But unfortunately neither of these is as clear as it looks because a hidden process of evaluation has already gone on to decide at what point an interest becomes "sinister" and how well placed someone must be to be "privileged". The cheapest and speediest dispensation of law could be obtained by conscripting the legal profession and making them work twelve hours a day for subsistence rations; but this would no doubt be ruled out by a utilitarian as imposing "hardship" and by the believer in distributive justice as not giving a "just reward" for the work done. Thus, by the time one has fixed the level of rewards beyond which one is going to say that "privilege" and "sinister interest" lie it is virtually analytic that one has defined a "good" solution (whether the criteria be utilitarian or those of distributive justice).

It is clearer to say that in these "non-Rousseauan" situations the public interest has to be balanced against the special interests involved and cannot therefore be followed exclusively. But "the public interest" remains of prime importance *in politics*, even when it runs against the net interest of some, because interests which are shared by few can be promoted by them whereas interests shared by many have to be furthered by the state if they are to be furthered at all. Only the state has the universality and the coercive power necessary to prevent people from doing what they want to do when it harms the public and to raise money to provide benefits for the public which cannot, or cannot conveniently, be sold on the market: and these are the two main ways in which "the public interest" is promoted. This line of thought brings us into touch with the long tradition that finds in the advancement of the interests common to all one of the main tasks of the state. The peculiarity of the last two centuries or so has lain in the widespread view that the other traditional candidates – the promotion of True Religion or the enforcement of the Laws of Nature and God – should be eliminated. This naturally increases the relative importance of "the public interest".

A contributory factor to this tendency is the still continuing process of social and economic change which one writer has dubbed the "organizational revolution". These developments have in many ways made for a more humane society than the smaller-scale, more loosely articulated, nineteenth-century pattern of organization could provide. But they have had the incidental result of making obsolete a good deal of our inherited conceptual equipment. Among the victims of this technological unemployment are "public opinion" and "the will of the people". On most of the bills, statutory instruments and questions of administrative policy which come before Parliament there is little corresponding to the nineteenth-century construct of "public opinion": the bulk of the electorate holding well-informed, principled, serious views. Even when an issue is sufficiently defined and publicized for there to be a widespread body of "opinion" about it these opinions are likely to be based on such a small proportion of the relevant data that any government which conceived its job as one of automatically implementing the majority opinion would be inviting disaster.

This does not entail that voting with universal suffrage is not a better way of choosing political leaders than any alternative; but if "public opinion" is a horse that won't run this means that "public interest" has to run all the harder to make up, since as we have seen it has the advantage of operating where those affected by the policy in question have not even heard of it and would not understand it if they did. Consider for example the arrangements which enable the staffs of organizations whose members are affected by impending or existing legislation to consult with their opposite numbers in government departments about its drafting and administration. This system of "functional representation", which now has almost constitutional status, would not get far if each side tried to argue from the *opinions* of its clients (the organization members and "the public" respectively) on the matter; but their *interests* do provide a basis for discussion, a basis which leaves room for the uncomfortable fact that in a large organization (whether it be a trade union, a limited company or a state) information and expertise are just as likely to be concentrated in a few hands as is the formal power to make decisions.

VI

At the beginning of this paper I suggested that the popularity of "the public interest" as a political justification could be attributed either to its vacuity or to its being used to adduce in support of policies definite considerations of a kind which are as a matter of fact valued highly by many people. If my analysis of "the public interest" is correct, it may be expected to flourish in a society where the state is expected to produce affluence and maintain civil liberties but not virtue or religious conformity, a society which has no distinction between different grades of citizen, and a society with large complex organizations exhibiting a high degree of rank and file apathy. I do not think it is necessary to look any further for an explanation of the concept's present popularity.

Chapter 13

What's Wrong with Prostitution?

Carole Pateman

In modern patriarchy a variety of means are available through which men can uphold the terms of the sexual contract. The marriage contract is still fundamental to patriarchal right, but marriage is now only one of the socially acceptable ways for men to have access to women's bodies. Casual sexual liaisons and 'living together' no longer carry the social sanctions of twenty or thirty years ago, and, in addition to private arrangements, there is a huge, multimillion dollar trade in women's bodies. Prostitution is an integral part of patriarchal capitalism. Wives are no longer put up for public auction (although in Australia, the United States and Britain they can be bought by mail-order from the Philippines), but men can buy sexual access to women's bodies in the capitalist market. Patriarchal right is explicitly embodied in 'freedom of contract'.

Prostitutes are readily available at all levels of the market for any man who can afford one and they are frequently provided as part of business, political and diplomatic transactions. Yet the public character of prostitution is less obvious than it might be. Like other forms of capitalist enterprise, prostitution is seen as private enterprise, and the contract between client and prostitute is seen as a private arrangement between a buyer and a seller. Moreover, prostitution is shrouded in secrecy despite the scale of the industry. In Birmingham, a British city of about one million people, some 800 women work either as street prostitutes, or from their homes or hotels, from 'saunas', 'massage parlours', or 'escort agencies'. Nearly 14,000 men each week buy their services, i.e., about 17 men for each prostitute.[1] A similar level of demand has been recorded in the United States, and the total number of customers each week across the country has been conservatively estimated at 1,500,000 men.[2] One estimate is that $40 million per day is spent on prostitution in the United States.[3] The secrecy exists in part because, where the act of prostitution is not itself illegal, associated activities such as soliciting often are. The criminal character of much of the business of prostitution is not, however, the only reason for secrecy. Not all men wish it generally to be known that they buy this commodity. To be discovered consorting with prostitutes can, for example, still be the downfall of politicians. The empirical evidence also indicates three-quarters of the clients of prostitutes are married men. Certainly, the prostitutes in Birmingham find that trade slackens during holiday periods when men are away from the city with their wives and children.[4]

The sexual subjection of wives has never lacked defenders, but until very recently an unqualified defence of prostitution has been hard to find. Prostitution was seen, for example, as a necessary evil that protected young women from rape and shielded marriage and the family from the ravages of men's sexual appetites; or as an unfortunate outcome of poverty and the economic constraints facing women who had to support themselves; or prostitution was seen as no worse, and as more honest, than 'legal prostitution', as Mary Wollstonecraft called marriage in 1790.[5] As prostitutes, women openly trade their bodies and, like workers (but unlike a wife), are paid in return. So, for Emma Goldman, 'it is merely a question of degree whether [a woman] sells herself to one man, in or out of marriage, or to many men'.[6] Simone de Beauvoir sees the wife as 'hired for life by one man; the prostitute has several clients who pay her by the piece. The one is protected by one male against all the others; the other is defended by all against the exclusive tyranny of each'.[7] Cicely Hamilton noted in 1909 that although women were prevented from bargaining freely in the only trade, marriage, legitimately open to them, they could exercise this freedom in their illegitimate trade; 'the prostitute class ... has pushed to its logical conclusion the principle that woman exists by virtue of a wage paid her in return for the possession of her person'.[8]

A radical change has now taken place in arguments about prostitution. Prostitution is unequivocally defended by contractarians. The terms of the defence again illustrate the ease with which some feminist arguments occupy the contractarian terrain. Many recent feminist discussions have argued that prostitution is merely a job of work and the prostitute is a worker, like any other wage labourer. Prostitutes should, therefore, have trade union rights, and feminists often put forward proposals for workers' control of the industry. To argue in this fashion is not necessarily to defend prostitution – one can argue for trade union rights while calling for the abolition of capitalist wage labour – but, in the absence of argument to the contrary, the implicit suggestion in many feminist discussions is that, if the prostitute is merely one worker among others, the appropriate conclusion must be that there is nothing wrong with prostitution. At the very least, the argument implies that there is nothing wrong with prostitution that is not also wrong with other forms of work.

This conclusion depends on the same assumptions as the contractarian defence of prostitution. Contractarians argue that a prostitute contracts out a certain form of labour power for a given period in exchange for money. There is a free exchange between prostitute and customer, and the prostitution contract is exactly like – or is one example of – the employment contract. From the standpoint of contract, the prostitute is an owner of property in her person who contracts out part of that property in the market. A prostitute does not sell herself, as is commonly alleged, or even sell her sexual parts, but contracts out use of *sexual services*. There is no difference between a prostitute and any other worker or seller of services. The prostitute, like other 'individuals', stands in an external relation to the property in her person. Contract theory thus appears to offer a convincing reply to well-known criticisms of and objections to prostitution. For example, for contractarians, the objection that the prostitute is harmed or degraded by her trade misunderstands the nature of what is traded. The body and the self of the prostitute are not offered in the market; she can contract out use of her services without detriment to herself. Feminists who argue that the prostitute epitomizes women's subjection to men, can now also be told that such a view is a reflection of outmoded attitudes to sex, fostered by men's propaganda and the old world of women's subordination.[9] Contractarians even proclaim that 'people have a human right to engage in commercial sex'.[10]

Defenders of prostitution admit that some reforms are necessary in the industry as it exists at present in order for a properly free market in sexual services to operate. Nevertheless, they insist that 'sound prostitution' is possible (the phrase is Lars Ericcson's).[11] The idea of sound prostitution illustrates the dramatic shift that has taken place in arguments over prostitution. The new, contractarian defence is a universal argument. Prostitution is defended as a trade fit for anyone to enter. Freedom of contract and equality of opportunity require that the prostitution contract should be open to everyone and that any individual should be able to buy or sell services in the market. Anyone who needs a sexual service should have access to the market, whether male or female, young or old, black or white, ugly or beautiful, deformed or handicapped. Prostitution will then come into its own as a form of therapy – 'the role of a prostitute as a kind of therapist is a natural one'[12] – or as a form of social work or nursing (taking care 'of the intimate hygiene of disabled patients').[13] No one will be left out because of inappropriate attitudes to sex. The female hunchback as well as the male hunchback will be able to find a seller of services.[14]

A universal defence of prostitution entails that a prostitute can be of either sex. Women should have the same opportunity as men to buy sexual services in the market. 'The prostitute' is conventionally pictured as a woman, and, in fact, the majority of prostitutes are women. However, for contractarians, this is a merely contingent fact about prostitution; if sound prostitution were established, status, or the sexually ascriptive determination of the two parties (the man as a buyer and the woman as a seller of services), will give way to contract, to a relation between two 'individuals'. A moment's contemplation of the story of the sexual contract suggests that there is a major difficulty in any attempt to universalize prostitution. Reports occasionally appear that, in large cities like Sydney, a few male heterosexual prostitutes operate (the older figure of the gigolo belongs in a very different context), but they are still rare. Male homosexual prostitutes, on the other hand, are not uncommon, and, from the standpoint of contract, they are no different from female prostitutes. The story of the sexual contract reveals that there is good reason why 'the prostitute' is a female figure.

The story is about heterosexual relations – but it also tells of the creation of a fraternity and their contractual relations. Relations between members of the fraternity lie outside the scope of my present discussion, but, as Marilyn Frye has noted, 'there is a sort of "incest taboo" built into standard masculinity'.[15] The taboo is necessary; within the bonds of fraternity there is always a temptation to make the relation more than that of fellowship. But if members of the brotherhood extended their contracts, if they contracted for sexual use of bodies among themselves, the competition could shake the foundations of the original contract. From the standpoint of contract, the prohibition against this particular exercise of the law of male sex-right is purely arbitrary, and the fervour with which it is maintained by men themselves is incomprehensible. The story of the original creation of modern patriarchy helps lessen the incomprehension.

Contractarians who defend an ostensibly sexually neutral, universal, sound prostitution have not, as far as I am aware, taken the logic of their arguments to its conclusion. The final defeat of status and the victory of contract should lead to the elimination of marriage in favour of the economical arrangement of universal prostitution, in which all individuals enter into brief contracts of sexual use when required. The only legitimate restriction upon these contracts is the willingness of another party voluntarily to make services available; the sex of the party is irrelevant. Nor does age provide a determinate limitation, but at least one contractarian draws back from consistent anti-paternalism at this point.[16]

Any discussion of prostitution is replete with difficulties. Although contractarians now deny any political significance to the fact that (most) prostitutes are women, one major difficulty is that, in other discussions, prostitution is invariably seen as a problem about the prostitute, as a problem about *women*. The perception of prostitution as a problem about women is so deep-seated that any criticism of prostitution is likely to provoke the accusation that contemporary contractarians bring against feminists, that criticism of prostitution shows contempt for prostitutes. To argue that there is something wrong with prostitution does not necessarily imply any adverse judgement on the women who engage in the work. When socialists criticize capitalism and the employment contract they do not do so because they are contemptuous of workers, but because they are the workers' champions. Nevertheless, appeals to the idea of false consciousness, popular a few years ago, suggested that the problem about capitalism was a problem about workers. To reduce the question of capitalism to deficiencies in workers' consciousness diverts attention from the capitalist, the other participant in the employment contract. Similarly, the patriarchal assumption that prostitution is a problem about women ensures that the other participant in the prostitution contract escapes scrutiny. Once the story of the sexual contract has been told, prostitution can be seen as a problem about *men*. The problem of prostitution then becomes encapsulated in the question why men demand that women's bodies are sold as commodities in the capitalist market. The story of the sexual contract also supplies the answer; prostitution is part of the exercise of the law of male sex-right, one of the ways in which men are ensured access to women's bodies.

Feminist criticism of prostitution is now sometimes rejected on the grounds that prostitutes exploit or cheat their male clients; men are presented as the injured parties, not women. To be sure, prostitutes are often able to obtain control over the transaction with their customers by various stratagems and tricks of the trade. However, just as arguments about marriage that appeal to the example of benevolent husbands fail to distinguish between the relation of one particular husband and wife and the structure of the institution of marriage, so particular instances of the prostitution contract, in which a prostitute exploits a male customer, should be distinguished from prostitution as a social institution. Within the structure of the institution of prostitution, 'prostitutes' are subject to 'clients', just as 'wives' are subordinate to 'husbands' within the structure of marriage.

There is a huge literature on the subject of prostitution, including many official reports, and a good deal of attention has been devoted to the psychology and psychopathology of the prostitute. In 1969 a pamphlet widely read by probation officers in Britain talked of the 'proof that prostitution is a primitive and regressive manifestation'; and a Home Office report in 1974 stated that the 'way of life of a prostitute is so remarkably a rejection of the normal ways of society as to bear comparison with that of the drug addict'.[17] Much attention is also devoted to the reasons why women become prostitutes. The evidence suggests that there is nothing at all mysterious about why women enter the trade. *In extremis*, women can sell their bodies for food, like the poor unemployed young girl in nineteenth-century England who was asked the question (by the author of *My Secret Life*), 'what do you let men fuck you for? Sausage-rolls?' She replied that she would comply for 'meat-pies and pastry too'.[18] More generally, prostitution enables women to make more money than they can earn at most other jobs open to women in patriarchal capitalism. In the 1870s and 1880s, the women campaigning against the Contagious Diseases Acts in the Ladies National Association in Britain argued that prostitution was the best-paid industry for poor women. In 1980, empirical investigation showed that British prostitutes earned much more than most women workers, and were in the middle- to high-wage band compared to male workers.[19] The American film *Working Girls* illustrates the attraction of prostitution for young, middle-class women with college degrees who want to make relatively large sums of money in a hurry. Prostitutes also refer to the degree of independence and flexibility that the work allows, and to the relative ease with which prostitution can be combined with housework and care of children. Drug addiction is now also an important reason why women become prostitutes.

The reasons why women become prostitutes are fairly straightforward, but what counts as prostitution is less obvious. Most discussions take for granted that the meaning of 'prostitution' is self-evident; 'we seem to know pretty well what we mean by this term'.[20] To draw the line between amateurs and women engaged in the profession in our society is not always easy, but very different activities in widely differing cultures and historical periods are also lumped together. One of the most persistent claims is that prostitution (like patriarchy) is a universal feature of human social life, a claim summed up in the cliché, 'the oldest profession'. The cliché is used to refer to a wide range of cultural phenomena, from ancient times to the present, all of which are called 'prostitution'. So, for example, one contractarian defender of prostitution argues that 'commercial prostitution in the modern sense' developed from ancient temple prostitution.[21] The same social meaning is attributed to such disparate activities as, say, temple prostitution in ancient Babylonia, the sale of their bodies by destitute women for food for themselves and their children, 'white slavery', the provision of field brothels for troops, the proffering of women to white explorers, *maisons d'abattages* or *malaya* prostitution in Nairobi.[22] That all these social practices have the same significance as the prostitution contract of patriarchal capitalism is not immediately self-evident. Indeed, recent studies by feminist historians show that prostitution in the contemporary sense – the form of prostitution that makes possible the contractarian defence of 'sound' prostitution – is a distinct cultural and historical phenomenon, which developed in Britain, the United States and Australia around the end of the nineteenth and beginning of the twentieth century.[23]

There is nothing universal about prostitutes as a discrete group of wage labourers who specialize in a particular line of work, or about prostitution as a specialized occupation or profession within the patriarchal capitalist division of labour. Until the latter part of the nineteenth century in all three countries, prostitutes were part of the casual labouring poor. Women in this class drifted in and out of prostitution as they drifted in and out of other forms of work. Prostitutes were not seen as a special class of women, nor were they isolated from other workers or working-class communities; there was no specialized 'profession' of prostitution. In Britain, for example, prostitution in the contemporary sense emerged from developments precipitated by the Contagious Diseases Acts (1864, 1866, 1869). Under the Acts, women in military towns could be identified as 'common prostitutes' by plain-clothes policemen, compulsorily subjected to gynaecological examination for venereal disease and, if infected, confined to a lock hospital. An enormous political campaign, in which women were very prominent, was waged for repeal of the Acts.

Rejecting the suggestion that public hygiene required regular inspection of soldiers and sailors, as well as women, for venereal disease, the Report of a Royal Commission into the Acts stated that 'there is no comparison to be made between prostitutes and the men who consort with them. With the one sex the offence is committed as a matter of gain; with the other it is an irregular indulgence of a natural impulse'.[24] Feminist campaigners such as Josephine Butler recognized that much more was at issue than the 'double standard' of sexual morality, the only morality compatible with the sexual contract. She argued that all women were implicated in the Acts, and they should not accept that safety and private respectability for most women depended on a 'slave class' of publicly available prostitutes. Butler wrote later to her sister that 'even if we lack the sympathy which makes us feel that the chains which bind our enslaved sisters are pressing on us also, we cannot escape the fact that we are one womanhood, *solidaire*, and that so long as they are bound, we cannot be wholly and truly free'.[25] For feminists who fought against the Acts, prostitution represented in the starkest form the sexual domination of women by men.

However, feminist questions were submerged in the social purity movement that developed in Britain in the 1880s and helped secure the passage of the Criminal

Law Amendment Act in 1885 that gave the police greater summary jurisdiction over poor women. By the time that the Contagious Diseases Acts were repealed in 1886 the character of prostitution was already changing and the trade was being 'professionalized'. Women listed as common prostitutes under the Acts found it hard to have their names removed from the register, or, subsequently, to find other employment. The women had often rented rooms in boarding-house brothels, run by women with families to support who also took in other lodgers in addition to the prostitutes. The 1885 Act gave police powers to close the brothels, which were shut down systematically between 1890 and 1914, and powers against soliciting. The prostitutes turned to pimps for protection. Prostitution shifted from being female-controlled to male-controlled and, as Judith Walkowitz remarks, 'there now existed third parties with a strong interest in prolonging women's stay on the streets'.[26]

In New South Wales, Australia, the elimination of free-lance prostitution took a different path. Unlike many other British colonies, New South Wales did not enact legislation against contagious diseases, nor follow the 1885 Act. Legislation was introduced in 1908 aimed at soliciting, pimping and brothel-keeping and, according to Judith Allen, the aim of policing strategy was the abolition of the most visible aspects of prostitution. The result was that self-employed prostitutes could no longer operate; 'the work of the prostitute became structurally proletarianized'.[27] Prostitutes were forced to turn to organized criminal networks or to pimps employed by the same criminals. A similar consequence ensued from the large campaigns against prostitution in the Progressive Era in the United States. Ruth Rosen summarizes the changes, which included the shift of control of the trade 'from madams and prostitutes themselves to pimps and organized crime syndicates. … The prostitute would rarely work henceforth as a free agent. In addition, she faced increased brutality, not only from the police, but also from her new "employers"'.[28] Once professionalized, prostitution developed into a major industry within patriarchal capitalism, with the same structure as other capitalist industries; prostitutes work in an occupation that is controlled by men. For example, in Birmingham, most prostitutes have ponces (pimps) and the 'saunas' and other such establishments are usually owned or managed by men. Few prostitutes become managers or 'establish some mutually beneficial business enterprise with other women'.[29]

The claim that prostitution is a universal feature of human society relies not only on the cliché of 'the oldest profession' but also on the widely held assumption that prostitution originates in men's natural sexual urge. There is a universal, natural (masculine) impulse that, it is assumed, requires, and will always require, the outlet provided by prostitution. Now that arguments that extra-marital sex is immoral have lost their social force, defenders of prostitution often present prostitution as one example of 'sex without love', as an example of the satisfaction of natural appetites.[30] The argument, however, is a *non sequitur*. Defenders of sex without love and advocates of what once was called free love, always supposed that the relationship was based on mutual sexual attraction between a man and woman and involved mutual physical satisfaction. Free love and prostitution are poles apart. Prostitution is the use of a woman's body by a man for his own satisfaction. There is no desire or satisfaction on the part of the prostitute. Prostitution is not mutual, pleasurable exchange of the use of bodies, but the unilateral use of a woman's body by a man in exchange for money. That the institution of prostitution can be presented as a natural extension of a human impulse, and that 'sex without love' can be equated with the sale of women's bodies in the capitalist market, is possible only because an important question is begged: why do men demand that satisfaction of a natural appetite must take the form of public access to women's bodies in the capitalist market in exchange for money?

In arguments that prostitution is merely one expression of a natural appetite, the comparison is invariably made between prostitution and the provision of food. To claim that 'we all need food, so food should be available to us. ... And since our sexual desires are just as basic, natural, and compelling as our appetite for food, this also holds for them', is neither an argument for prostitution nor for any form of sexual relations.[31] Without a minimum of food (or water, or shelter) people die, but to my knowledge no one has ever died for want of an outlet for their sexual appetites. There is also one fundamental difference between the human need for food and the need for sex. Sustenance is sometimes unavailable but everyone has the means to satisfy sexual appetites to hand. There is no natural necessity to engage in sexual *relations* to assuage sexual pangs. Of course, there may be cultural inhibition against use of this means, but what counts as food is also culturally variable. In no society does the form of food production and consumption, or the form of relations between the sexes, follow directly, without cultural mediation, from the natural fact that all humans feel hunger and sexual impulses. The consequences of sexual inhibitions and prohibitions are likely to be less disastrous than prohibitions on what counts as food.

Another difficulty in discussing prostitution in late twentieth-century patriarchy is that it is also usually assumed to be obvious which activities fall under the heading of 'prostitution'. Prostitution is now part of an international sex industry that includes mass-marketing of pornographic books and films, widespread supply of strip-clubs, peep-shows and the like and marketing of sex-tours for men to poor Third World countries. The general display of women's bodies and sexual parts, either in representation or as live bodies, is central to the sex industry and continually reminds men – and women – that men exercise the law of male sex-right, that they have patriarchal right of access to women's bodies. The story of the original sexual contract helps sort out which of the plethora of activities in the sex industry are appropriately called 'prostitution'. For example, satisfaction of a mere natural appetite does not require a man to have access to a woman's body; what then, is the significance of the fact that 15 to 25 per cent of the customers of the Birmingham prostitutes demand what is known in the trade as 'hand relief'?[32]

The story of the sexual contract suggests that the latter demand is part of the construction of what it means to be a man, part of the contemporary expression of masculine sexuality. The satisfaction of men's natural sexual urges must be achieved through access to a woman, even if her body is not directly used sexually. Whether or not any man is able and willing to find release in other ways, he can exhibit his masculinity by contracting for use of a woman's body. The prostitution contract is another example of an actual 'original' sexual contract. The exemplary display of masculinity is to engage in 'the sex act'. (Hence, sale of men's bodies for homosexual use does not have the same social meaning.) The institution of prostitution ensures that men can buy 'the sex act' and so exercise their patriarchal right. The activities that, above all else, can appropriately be called prostitution are 'the sex act', and associated activities such as 'hand relief' and oral sex (fellatio), for which there is now a very large demand.[33] Some of the most prevalent confusions in discussions of prostitution might be avoided if other activities were seen as part of the wider sex industry. The market includes a vigorous demand for 'bondage and discipline' or fantasy slave contracts. The mass commercial replication of the most potent relations and symbols of domination is a testament to the power and genius of contract, which proclaims that a contract of subordination is (sexual) freedom.

Since the 1970s prostitutes have been organizing in the United States, Britain and Australia – and the International Committee for Prostitutes' Rights held the second World Whores' Congress in 1986 – to improve their working conditions, to combat hostility and violence and to press for the decriminalization of prostitution. In short, prostitutes are endeavouring to be acknowledged as workers in an occupation that lacks trade union safeguards and protection. The prostitute is a woman and thus shares with all women in paid employment an uncertain status as a 'worker'. But the prostitute is not quite like other women workers; her status is even more uncertain. Prostitution is seen as different from other forms of women's work and, especially at the lower end of the market, prostitutes are set apart from other women workers (almost everyone can picture 'the prostitute' soliciting in the street, with her typical costume, stance and heart of gold). Contractarian defences of prostitution attribute the lack of acceptance of the prostitute as a worker, or purveyor of services, to the hypocrisy and distorted attitudes surrounding sexual activity. To be sure, hypocrisy is rife and irrational attitudes abound around the question of prostitution, as George Bernard Shaw's *Mrs Warren's Profession* laid bare some time ago. However, reference to hypocrisy hardly seems to capture the emotions with which some men regard prostitutes.

Prostitutes are murdered because they are seen as fonts of pollution and their murderer's names can become household words, like Jack the Ripper. Less dramatically, prostitutes run considerable risk of physical injury every day from their male customers, especially if they work on the streets. Eileen McLeod found that, in Birmingham, 'almost without exception, prostitutes I have had contact with have experienced some form of serious physical violence from their clients'.[34] Prostitutes are not, of course, the only workers who face physical hazards in their work. Little publicity is given to the large numbers of workers killed or injured each year in the workplace through lack of, or inadequate, or unenforced safety precautions, or through genuine accidents. These injuries, though, do not occur because the worker is a *woman*. Contractarians are not alone in denying significance to the fact that prostitutes are women. Apart from some feminist analyses, it is hard to find discussions that acknowledge that prostitution is part of the patriarchal structure of civil society. The Left and Right, as well as some feminists, share the assumption that the prostitute's work is of exactly the same kind as any other paid employment. The prostitute merely works in a different profession and offers a different service (form of labour power) from that of a miner or electrician, secretary or assembler of electronic goods. Not surprisingly, criticism of prostitution is then usually couched in economic terms. For example, the argument that prostitutes are forced by economic necessity to enter the trade has been heard for a very long time. The conditions of entry into the prostitution contract have received as much attention as entry into the employment or marriage contracts, and involuntary entry is often presented as the problem about prostitution. Thus, Alison Jaggar has stated that 'it is the economic coercion underlying prostitution, ... that provides the basic feminist objection to prostitution'.[35]

Another common argument, now made by the religious Right as well as by the Left, is that what is wrong with prostitution is that, once a woman has entered the trade, she is exploited and degraded like many other workers under capitalism. Once again, the question of subordination is ignored. In arguments about economic coercion and exploitation the comparison is often turned round; instead of prostitutes being seen as exploited workers, workers are held to be in the same position as prostitutes. Marxist critics of prostitution take their lead from Marx's statement that 'prostitution is only a *specific* expression of the *general* prostitution of the *laborer*'.[36] Prostitution then represents the economic coercion, exploitation and alienation of wage labour. As one critic has stated, 'prostitution is the incarnation of the degradation of the modern citizen as producer'.[37] The prostitution contract is not merely one example of the employment contract; rather, the employment contract becomes a contract of prostitution. The figure of the prostitute can, therefore, symbolize everything that is wrong with wage labour.

To see prostitutes as epitomizing exploitation under capitalism, and to represent the worker by the figure of the prostitute, is not without irony. 'The worker' is masculine – yet his degradation is symbolized by a female emblem, and patriarchal capitalism is pictured as a system of universal prostitution. The fact that the prostitute seems to be such an obvious symbol of the degradation of wage labour, raises the suspicion that what she sells is not quite the same as the labour power contracted out by other workers. If prostitution is work in exactly the same sense as any other paid employment, then the present status of the prostitute can only be attributed, as contractarians insist, to legal prohibition, hypocrisy and outdated ideas about sex. The story of the sexual contract provides another explanation for the difference between prostitution and other paid employment in which women predominate. The prostitution contract is a contract with a woman and, therefore, cannot be the same as the employment contract, a contract between men. Even though the prostitution contract is sealed in the capitalist market, it still differs in some significant respects from the employment contract. For example, a worker always enters into an employment contract with a capitalist. If a prostitute were merely another worker the prostitution contract, too, would always involve a capitalist; yet very frequently the man who enters into the contract is a worker.

Supposing, the objection might be raised, that the prostitute works in a 'massage parlour'. She will then be a paid employee and have entered into an employment contract. True; but the prostitution contract is not an employment contract. The prostitution contract is entered into with the male customer, not with an employer. The prostitute may or may not be a paid employee (worker); some prostitutes are 'more adequately described as small-scale private entrepreneurs'.[38] The difference is, however, irrelevant to the question of how prostitution is to be characterized; is it free work and a free exchange, or exploitation, or a specific kind of subordination? Whether the prostitute is a worker or petty entrepreneur she must be seen as contracting out labour power or services if the prostitution contract is also to be seen as an employment contract. From the standpoint of contract, the employment contract is infinitely elastic, stretching from the lifetime of the civil slave to the brief period of the prostitution contract in a brothel for troops or immigrant workers. No matter whether the prostitute is an exploited or free worker or a petty entrepreneur, labour power or services are assumed to be contracted out. As Ericcson asserts, a prostitute must necessarily sell 'not her body or vagina, but sexual *services*. If she actually did sell herself she would no longer be a prostitute but a sexual slave'.[39]

More accurately, she would resemble a slave in something of the same fashion that a worker, a wage slave, resembles a slave. Labour power is a political fiction. The capitalist does not and cannot contract to use the proletarian's services or labour power. The employment contract gives the employer right of command over the use of the worker's labour, that is to say, over the self, person and body of the worker during the period set down in the employment contract. Similarly, the services of the prostitute cannot be provided unless she is present; property in the person, unlike material property, cannot be separated from its owner. The 'john', the 'punter', the man who contracts to use the services of the prostitute, like the employer, gains command over the use of her person and body for the duration of the prostitution contract – but at this point the comparison between the wage slave and the prostitute, the employment contract and the prostitution contract, breaks down.

The capitalist has no intrinsic interest in the body and self of the worker, or, at least, not the same kind of interest as the man who enters into the prostitution contract. The employer is primarily interested in the commodities produced by the worker; that is to say, in profits. The peculiar character of the relation between the owner of labour power and his property means that the employer must organize (embodied) workers, and compel or induce them to labour, in order to produce commodities with his machinery and other means of production. But the employer can and often does replace the worker with machines or, in the 1980s, robots and other computerized machines. Indeed, employers prefer machines to workers because machines are like absolutely faithful slaves; they cannot be insubordinate, resist the employer's commands or combine together in trades unions or revolutionary associations. On the other hand, if the employer replaces all his workers by machines, he becomes merely a proprietor. The employer has an interest in workers as selves in that, without them, he ceases to be a master and loses the enjoyment of command over subordinates.

In contrast to employers, the men who enter into the prostitution contract have only one interest; the prostitute and her body. A market exists for substitutes for women's bodies in the form of inflatable dolls, but, unlike the machines that replace the worker, the dolls are advertised as 'lifelike'. The dolls are a literal substitute for women, not a functional substitute like the machine installed instead of the worker. Even a plastic substitute for a woman can give a man the sensation of being a patriarchal master. In prostitution, the body of the woman, and sexual access to that body, is the subject of the contract. To have bodies for sale in the market, as bodies, looks very like slavery. To symbolize wage slavery by the figure of the prostitute rather than that of the masculine worker is thus not entirely inappropriate. But prostitution differs from wage slavery. No form of labour power can be separated from the body, but only though the prostitution contract does the buyer obtain unilateral right of direct sexual use of a woman's body.

A contractarian might respond at this point that far too much weight is being placed on the body. Even if reference is made to the body rather than (as it should be) to services, moral freedom can be retained when use of the body, or part of the body, is being contracted out. The self or person is not identical to the body, so that the self is not injured if property in the body is used. David Richards has taken issue with Kant, and with Marxists and feminists whom he assumes are following Kant, on this question. Kant condemned prostitution as a *pactum turpe*; to contract out a bodily part for sexual use is to turn oneself into property, a *res*, because of the 'inseparable unity of the members of a Person'. [40] Kant writes that man cannot dispose of himself as he wills:

> He is not his own property; to say that he is would be self-contradictory; for in so far as he is a person he is a Subject in whom the ownership of things can be vested, and if he were his own property, he would be a thing over which he could have ownership … it is impossible to be a person and a thing, the proprietor and the property. [41]

Richards argues that Kant's condemnation of prostitution is inconsistent with his general view of autonomy. I shall not attempt to ascertain whether it is more inconsistent than his view of wage labour or, in particular, the marriage contract, since Richards fails to mention that Kant upholds patriarchal right and so has to deny that women are persons and, hence, autonomous. Kant's inconsistency is that he wants to confine fulfillment of the terms of the sexual contract to conjugal relations; women's bodies may be used as property by men as husbands, but women must not sell this commodity in the market and be paid for sexual use. Richards claims that to argue against prostitution is arbitrarily to limit sexual freedom. The embodiment of the self places no constraints on an individual's moral autonomy. Richards' argument is based on a version of the disembodied, rational entities who inhabit (one aspect of) Kant's contract theory and Rawls' original position. Autonomy is merely 'persons' self-critical capacities to assess their present wants and lives. …

Autonomy occurs in a certain body, occasioning a person self-critically to take into account that body and its capacities in deciding on the form of his or her life'.[42] In short, freedom is the unconstrained capacity of an owner (rational entity), externally related to property in its person (body), to judge how to contract out that property.

Human beings certainly possess the capacity for critical self-reflection – and that capacity can be understood as if it encompassed nothing more than individual rational calculation of how property can be used to the maximum advantage. If a complex, multifaceted capacity could not be reduced to this bleak, culturally and historically specific achievement, patriarchal civil society could not have developed. Richards' 'autonomy' was summed up more economically in Richard Lovelace's lines:

> Stone walls do not a prison make,
> Nor iron bars a cage.

Nor is this very partial and socially tangential (though in some circumstances, heroic) notion of moral – or spiritual – freedom at issue in prostitution or other forms of civil subordination. Civil subordination is a *political* problem not a matter of morality, although moral issues are involved. To try to answer the question of what is wrong with prostitution is to engage in argument about political right in the form of patriarchal right, or the law of male sex-right. Subordinates of all kinds exercise their capacity for critical self-reflection every day – that is why masters are thwarted, frustrated and, sometimes, overthrown. But unless masters are overthrown, unless subordinates engage in political action, no amount of critical reflection will end their subjection and bring them freedom.

To grant that human embodiment is of more than merely contingent or incidental significance for freedom and subordination, may not seem sufficient to distinguish the profession of prostitution from some other forms of work, or sufficient to establish that there is something wrong with prostitution that is not also wrong with wage labour. A prostitute's body is for sale in the market, but there are also other professions in which bodies are up for sale and in which employers have an intrinsic interest in their workers' bodies. For example, now that sport is part of patriarchal capitalism, the bodies of professional sportsmen and sportswomen are also available to be contracted out. Orlando Patterson discusses the case of baseball in the United States where, until 1975, players could be bought and sold like any material property at the will and for the profit of the owners of their teams. Patterson emphasizes that the baseball players were not and are not slaves, they are juridically free citizens, and they now have some voice in their disposition – but their bodies are still bought and sold. Patterson comments that employers do not now demand that workers

> stand naked on an auction block being prodded and inspected by the employers and
> their physicians. But when an employer requires a medical certificate from a worker
> or professional athlete before hiring him, he is not only soliciting the same kind of

information as a slavemaster inspecting his latest cargo of bodies, he is betraying the inherent absurdity of the distinction between 'raw bodies' and the services produced by such bodies.[43]

Hoverver, there is a difference in the uses to which bodies are put when they are sold. Owners of baseball teams have command over the use of their players' bodies, but the bodies are not directly used sexually by those who have contracted for them.

There is an integral relationship between the body and self. The body and the self are not identical, but selves are inseparable from bodies. The idea of property in the person has the merit of drawing attention to the importance of the body in social relations. Civil mastery, like the mastery of the slave-owner, is not exercised over mere biological entities that can be used like material (animal) property, nor exercised over purely rational entities. Masters are not interested in the disembodied fiction of labour power or services. They contract for the use of human embodied selves. Precisely because subordinates are embodied selves they can perform the required labour, be subject to discipline, give the recognition and offer the faithful service that makes a man a master. Human bodies and selves are also sexually differentiated, the self is a masculine or feminine self. One illustration of the integral connection between the body and the self is the widespread use of vulgar terms for women's sexual organs to refer to women themselves, or the use of a slang term for the penis to make disparaging reference to men.

Masculinity and femininity are sexual identities; the self is not completely subsumed in its sexuality, but identity is inseparable from the sexual construction of the self. In modern patriarchy, sale of women's bodies in the capitalist market involves sale of a self in a different manner, and in a more profound sense, than sale of the body of a male baseball player or sale of command over the use of the labour (body) of a wage slave. The story of the sexual contract reveals that the patriarchal construction of the difference between masculinity and femininity is the political difference between freedom and subjection, and that sexual mastery is the major means through which men affirm their manhood. When a man enters into the prostitution contract he is not interested in sexually indifferent, disembodied services; he contracts to buy sexual use of a *woman* for a given period. Why else are men willing to enter the market and pay for 'hand relief'? Of course, men can also affirm their masculinity in other ways, but, in relations between the sexes, unequivocal affirmation is obtained by engaging in 'the sex act'. Womanhood, too, is confirmed in sexual activity, and when a prostitute contracts out use of her body she is thus selling *herself* in a very real sense. Women's selves are involved in prostitution in a different manner from the involvement of the self in other occupations. Workers of all kinds may be more or less 'bound up in their work', but the integral connection between sexuality and sense of the self means that, for self-protection, a prostitute must distance herself from her sexual use.

Women engaged in the trade have developed a variety of distancing strategies, or a professional approach, in dealing with their clients. Such distancing creates a problem for men, a problem that can be seen as another variant on the contradiction of mastery and slavery. The prostitution contract enables men to constitute themselves as civil masters for a time, and, like other masters, they wish to obtain acknowledgment of their status. Eileen McLeod talked to clients as well as prostitutes in Birmingham and, noting that her findings are in keeping with similar investigations in Britain and the United States, she states that 'nearly all the men I interviewed complained about the emotional coldness and mercenary approach of many prostitutes they had had contact with'.[44] A master requires a service, but he also requires that the service is delivered by a person, a self, not merely a piece of (disembodied) property. John Stuart Mill remarked of the subordination of wives that, 'their masters require something more from them than actual service. Men do not want solely the obedience of women, they want their sentiments. All men, except the most brutish, desire to have, not a forced slave but a willing one, not a slave merely, but a favourite'.[45]

An employer or a husband can more easily obtain faithful service and acknowledgment of his mastery than a man who enters into the prostitution contract. The civil slave contract and employment and marriage contracts create long-term relationships of subordination. The prostitution contract is of short duration and the client is not concerned with daily problems of the extraction of labour power. The prostitution contract is, one might say, a contract of specific performance, rather than open-ended like the employment contract and, in some of its aspects, the marriage contract. There are also other differences between the employment and prostitution contracts. For example, the prostitute is always at a singular disadvantage in the 'exchange'. The client makes direct use of the prostitute's body and there are no 'objective' criteria through which to judge whether the service has been satisfactorily performed. Trades unions bargain over pay and conditions for workers, and the products of their labours are 'quality controlled'. Prostitutes, in contrast, can always be refused payment by men who claim (and who can gainsay their subjective assessment?) that their demands have not been met.[46]

The character of the employment contract also provides scope for mastery to be recognized in numerous subtle ways as well as in an open, direct fashion. The worker is masculine, and men must mutually acknowledge their civil equality and fraternity (or the social contract cannot be upheld) at the same time as they create relations of subordination. The brief duration of the prostitution contract gives less room for subtlety; but, then, perhaps it is not so necessary. There need be no such ambiguities in relations between men and women, least of all when a man has bought a woman's body for his use as if it were like any other commodity. In such a context, 'the sex act' itself provides acknowledgment of patriarchal right. When women's bodies are on sale as commodities in the capitalist market, the terms of the original contract cannot be forgotten; the law of male sex-right is publicly affirmed, and men gain public acknowledgment as women's sexual masters – that is what is wrong with prostitution.

Another difference between the prostitution contract and the other contracts with which I am concerned is also worth noting. I have argued that contracts about property in persons take the form of an exchange of obedience for protection.

A civil slave and wives (in principle) receive lifelong protection, the family wage includes protection and the organizational complexities of extracting labour power for use in capitalist production have led to provision of protection over and above the wage. But where is the protection in the prostitution contract? The pimp stands outside the contract between client and prostitute, just as the state stands outside, but regulates and enforces, the marriage and employment contracts. The short-term prostitution contract cannot include the protection available in long-term relations. In this respect, the prostitution contract mirrors the contractarian ideal. The individual as owner will never commit himself far into the future; to do so is to give himself up as hostage to the self-interest of other individuals. The individual will make simultaneous exchanges, an impossible exchange if use is to be made of property in persons. The exchange of money for use of a woman's body comes as close as is feasible in actual contracts to a simultaneous exchange. For Marx, prostitution was a metaphor for wage labour. The more appropriate analogy is also more amusing. The contractarian idea of universal sale of property (services), is a vision of unimpeded mutual use or universal prostitution.

The feminist argument that prostitutes are workers in exactly the same sense as other wage labourers, and the contractarian defence of prostitution, both depend on the assumption that women are 'individuals', with full ownership of the property in their persons. Women are still prohibited from contracting out their property in their sexual parts in some legal jurisdictions in the three countries with which I am concerned. Nevertheless, while I was completing this chapter, a judge in New Jersey, in the leading case of Baby M, ruled that women could contract out another piece of property, their wombs, and that they must be held to this contract. This contract of so-called surrogate motherhood is new, and it provides a dramatic example of the contradictions surrounding women and contract. The surrogacy contract also indicates that a further transformation of modern patriarchy may be underway. Father-right is reappearing in a new, contractual form.

My argument, as I have emphasized, is not about women as mothers, but the significantly named 'surrogate' motherhood has little to do with motherhood as generally understood. The political implications of the surrogacy contract can only be appreciated when surrogacy is seen as another provision in the sexual contract, as a new form of access to and use of women's bodies by men. A 'surrogate' mother contracts to be artificially inseminated with the sperm of a man (usually the sperm belongs to a husband whose wife is infertile), to bear a child, and to relinquish the child to the genetic father. In exchange for use of her services the 'surrogate' receives monetary payment; the market rate at present appears to be US$10,000.

Artificial insemination is far from new – the first human pregnancy was achieved by this means in 1799 – but 'surrogate' motherhood is frequently and confusingly discussed together with a range of developments, such as *in vitro* fertilization, which have resulted from new technologies.[47] (*In vitro* fertilization is now sold on the capitalist market; in the United States the market is estimated at $30–40 million per year, even though the success rate of the technology is very low). New technology also makes other forms of 'surrogacy' possible. For instance, the ovum and sperm of a married couple may be joined and grown *in vitro,* and the embryo then inserted into the uterus of a 'surrogate'. In this case, the baby is the genetic offspring of husband and wife and such a surrogacy contract differs significantly from a contract involving artificial insemination. I shall concentrate on the latter to draw out a point about paternity and patriarchy, but technological developments and *in vitro* surrogacy also raise some general, profoundly important issues about contract and use of women's bodies.

In mid-1987, there is no legal consensus about the legitimacy or status of surrogacy contracts. In the United States, the judgement in the case of Baby M – which arose from a dispute over a contract when the 'surrogate' mother refused to relinquish the baby – unequivocally confirmed the binding legal status of such contracts (the case is currently under appeal to the New Jersey Supreme Court). Long before this, however, surrogacy agencies had been set up and press reports state that some 600 contracts have been made, at least one woman having entered and fulfilled two contracts. The agencies are profitable; one is reported to have made $600,000 gross in 1986. In Australia, only Victoria has legislated on the question and has prohibited commercial surrogacy and denied legal enforcement to informal arrangements. In Britain, the 1985 Surrogacy Arrangements Act has effectively prohibited commercial surrogacy contracts. For third parties to benefit from a surrogacy contract is a criminal offence, and to pay a 'surrogate' mother or for her to receive payment may be an offence under the Adoption Act. Non-commercial surrogacy arrangements are not illegal.[48]

At this point, the old argument about prostitution and legal prostitution (marriage) immediately presents itself. Is not a contract in which money is exchanged for services more honest about the position of the woman involved than marriage or informal surrogacy? The Report of the Waller Committee which led to the Victorian legislation (and which considered 'surrogate' motherhood in the context of *in vitro* fertilization) recommended that neither commercial nor non-commercial surrogacy should form part of *in vitro* programmes.[49] But is a *gift* of the 'surrogate's' services more acceptable than an exchange of her services for money? The British legislation clearly implies that this is the case. To see surrogacy as a gift relation is, however, to beg the question of to whom it is that the service is rendered. Is surrogacy an example of one woman donating a service to another woman, or is it an example of a woman being inseminated with the sperm of a man to bear his child in exchange for money? Prostitution is often defended as a type of social work or therapy, and, similarly, 'surrogate' motherhood is defended as a service offered in the market from compassion for the plight of infertile women. To ask questions about the surrogacy contract is not to deny that women who enter the surrogacy contract may feel compassion for infertile women, nor to deny that women can be made miserable by infertility (although in current debates it is frequently forgotten, or even implicitly ruled out, that infertile women, and their husbands, can come to terms with the condition and lead satisfying lives). As in so many discussions of prostitution, the argument from compassion assumes that any problem about 'surrogate' motherhood is a problem about women, and about the supply of a service.

The character of men's participation in the surrogacy contract and the character of the demand for this service is treated as unproblematic.

In the controversy over 'surrogate' motherhood, the comparison with prostitution is often made. As the eminent historian, Lawrence Stone, commented about the case of Baby M, 'contracts should be fulfilled. This is a rather bizarre contract, I agree. You're renting out your body. But one expects a prostitute to fulfill a contract'.[50] Most of the arguments used to defend or condemn prostitution have reappeared in the controversy over 'surrogate' motherhood. Obviously, surrogacy contracts raise questions about the conditions of entry into the contract and economic coercion. The sexual division of labour in patriarchal capitalism and the 'feminization of poverty' ensure that a surrogacy contract will appear financially attractive to working-class women, although the payment is very meagre for the time involved and nature of the service. Class questions are also clearly raised. In the Baby M case, for instance, the 'surrogate' mother dropped out of high school and was married aged sixteen to a man who is now a sanitation worker earning $28,000 per year. The income of the man who entered into the contract, together with that of his wife, both professionals with doctoral degrees, is about $91,500 per year.[51] However, emphasis on class inequality and economic coercion to enter the contract, draws attention away from the question of what exactly is being contracted for and how the surrogacy contract resembles or differs from other contracts about property in the person.

In Victoria, 'surrogate' motherhood was rejected on the grounds that 'arrangements where fees are paid are, in reality, agreements for the purchase of a child, and should not be countenanced … The buying and selling of children has been condemned and proscribed for generations. It should not be allowed to reappear'.[52] Adoption is strictly regulated to avoid poor women – or, at least, poor white women – being offered incentives to sell their babies. The problem with this line of argument is not that common sense is a poor guide here, but that references to baby-selling completely fail to meet the defence of surrogacy contracts derived from contract theory. From the standpoint of contract, talk of baby-selling reveals that surrogacy is misunderstood in exactly the same way that prostitution is misunderstood. A prostitute does not sell her body, she sells sexual services. In the surrogacy contract there is no question of a baby being sold, merely a service.

The qualifier 'surrogate' indicates that the point of the contract is to render motherhood irrelevant and to deny that the 'surrogate' is a mother. A woman who enters a surrogacy contract is not being paid for (bearing) a child; to make a contract of that kind *would* be tantamount to baby-selling. The 'surrogate' mother is receiving payment in return for entering into a contract which enables a man to make use of her services. In this case the contract is for use of the property a woman owns in her uterus.

From the standpoint of contract, the fact that provision of a service involves motherhood is purely incidental. The womb has no special status as property. A woman could just as well contract out use of a different piece of property in her person. Furthermore, the fact that disposition of a baby is at issue is of no special significance. Contracts for the use of other forms of service, notably that provided through the employment contract, also result in property over which one party alone has jurisdiction. The worker has no claim to the commodities produced through use of his labour; they belong to the capitalist. In a similar fashion, the baby that is produced through use of a 'surrogate' mother's services is the property of the man who contracts to use the service. The judge in the case of Baby M made this point very clearly. In his decision he stated that:

> the money to be paid to the surrogate is not being paid for the surrender of the child to the father. ... The biological father pays the surrogate for her willingness to be impregnated and carry his child to term. At birth, the father does not purchase the child. It is his own biologically genetically related child. He cannot purchase what is already his.[53]

Appeal is often made in discussions of 'surrogate' motherhood to two biblical precedents in the book of *Genesis*. In the first story, Sarai, unable to have a child, says to her husband Abram, 'I pray thee, go in unto my maid; it may be that I obtain children by her'. Then Sarai 'took Hagar her maid the Egyptian, ... and gave her to her husband Abram to be his wife'. In the second story, Rachel, another infertile wife, gives Jacob 'Bilhah her handmaid to wife: and Jacob went in unto her'.[54] In the biblical stories, the 'surrogate' mother is a maid, a servant, a subordinate – and she is the *wife's* servant. The stories will thus seem to reinforce an objection that will be made to my characterization of 'surrogate' motherhood as a contract in which the services of the 'surrogate' mother are used by a man. On the contrary, the objection will be pressed, the biblical stories show that the surrogacy contract has been misrepresented; the service is used by women. The contract is made by a husband and a wife for use of the 'surrogate's' services. The man's infertile wife, not the man himself, is the true user of the service. She is the mother for whom the 'surrogate's' services are contracted. A woman enters a surrogacy contract with another woman (although male sperm is needed for insemination).

Ironies never cease in the matter of women and contract. After the long history of exclusion of women from contract, the surrogacy contract is presented as a woman's contract; women are now seen as the parties to the contract. The question of men's demand for the service is thus obscured, together with the character of the 'exchange' that takes place. The question of who exactly uses the services of a 'surrogate' mother is confused by the strong social pressures in Britain, Australia and the United States to restrict surrogacy contracts (and access to the new reproductive technologies) to married couples. But there is no need at all for a wife to be involved. The comparison with prostitution is revealing here (though not quite in the way that is always intended). From the standpoint of contract, the demand for use of prostitutes is sexually indifferent, and so is the demand for 'surrogate' motherhood; men can contract for the use of a 'surrogate' without the mediation of another woman. All that is taking place is that one individual is contracting to use another's property. A wife is superfluous to the contract (though, socially, her presence legitimizes the transaction). A wife may be a formal party to the surrogacy contract but the substance of her position is quite different from that of her husband. A wife contributes no property to the contract; she merely awaits its outcome.

The exchange in the surrogacy contract is between part of the property of a man, namely his sperm or seed, and part of the property of the 'surrogate', her uterus. A surrogacy contract differs from a prostitution contract in that a man does not make direct sexual use of a woman's body; rather, his use is indirect via artificial insemination. The man's seed, to use Locke's language, is mixed with the woman's uterus, and, if she performs her service faithfully, he can claim the property thereby produced as his own. Locke's language brings out the way in which contract is now taking a new turn. Contract transformed classic into modern patriarchy, but, with the invention of the surrogacy contract, one aspect of classic patriarchy has returned. If a woman's uterus is nothing more than a piece of property to which she is externally related, she is analogous to Sir Robert Filmer's empty vessel. But now the empty vessel can be contracted out for use by a man who fills it with his seed and, in another example of masculine creativity, thereby creates a new piece of property. Perhaps the man who enters into the surrogacy contract might be compared to the employer who, in contract doctrine, is the creative principle who transforms labour power into commodities. But he can now also do much more; in a spectacular twist of the patriarchal screw, the surrogacy contract enables a man to present his wife with the ultimate gift – a child.

Labour power is a political fiction, but the service performed by the 'surrogate' mother is a greater fiction. The worker contracts out right of command over the use of his body, and the prostitute contracts out right of direct sexual use of her body. The selves of the worker and the prostitute are, in their different ways, both put out for hire. The self of the 'surrogate' mother is at stake in a more profound sense still. The 'surrogate' mother contracts out right over the unique physiological, emotional and creative capacity of her body, that is to say, of herself as a woman. For nine months she has the most intimate possible relation with another developing being; the being is part of herself. The baby, once born, is a separate being, but the mother's relation to her infant is qualitatively different from that of workers to the other products that ensue from contracts about the property in their persons. The example of a smoothly completed surrogacy contract and an unconcerned 'surrogate' mother, like examples of husbands who have renounced patriarchal right or prostitutes who exploit clients, reveals little about the *institution* of marriage, prostitution, or 'surrogate' motherhood. The surrogacy contract is another medium through which patriarchal subordination is secured. In one respect, a surrogacy contract is rather like an employment contract. The employer obtains right of command over the use of the bodies of workers in order, unilaterally, to have power over the process through which his commodities are produced. There is no reason why a surrogacy contract should not enable a man to ensure that the service for which he has contracted is faithfully performed by restricting the use to which the 'surrogate' may put her body until the service is fulfilled.

That women are willing to be parties to contracts that constitute other women as patriarchal subordinates is not surprising. Women are still treated as less than women if we do not have children. Contract doctrine entails that there are no limits to the uses that may legitimately be made of property in persons, providing only that access to use is established through contract. Why, then, in a period when contract holds sway, should childless women not take advantage of this new contract? Using the services of a 'surrogate' mother to provide an infertile married couple with a child is often compared to adoption, previously their only legitimate recourse if they were not prepared to accept their condition, but there is a crucial difference between the two practices. An adopting couple are not, except in rare circumstances, genetically related to the child. But the child of the 'surrogate' is also the child of the husband. The wife is more accurately called the surrogate mother, just as, in cases of adoption, the couple are surrogate mother and father. The wife will, of course, like adopting parents, bring up the child 'as if it were her own' but, irrespective of the happiness of the marriage and how well the child flourishes and *is* their own, in the last analysis, the child is the father's.

The story of the original contract tells of the political defeat of the father and how his sons, the brothers, establish a specifically modern non-paternal form of patriarchy. The emergence of 'surrogate' motherhood suggests that contract is helping to bring about another transformation. Men are now beginning to exert patriarchal right as paternal right again, but in new forms. The logic of contract as exhibited in 'surrogate' motherhood shows very starkly how extension of the standing of 'individual' to women can reinforce and transform patriarchy as well as challenge patriarchal institutions. To extend to women the masculine conception of the individual as owner, and the conception of freedom as the capacity to do what you will with your own, is to sweep away any intrinsic relation between the female owner, her body and reproductive capacities. She stands to her property in exactly the same external relation as the male owner stands to his labour power or sperm; there is nothing distinctive about womanhood.

From the standpoint of contract, not only is sexual difference irrelevant to sexual relations, but sexual difference becomes irrelevant to physical reproduction. The former status of 'mother' and 'father' is thus rendered inoperative by contract and must be replaced by the (ostensibly sex-neutral) 'parent'. At least in the case of the surrogacy contract, the term 'parent' is far from sexually indifferent. The shade of Sir Robert Filmer hangs over 'surrogate' motherhood. In classic patriarchalism, the father is *the* parent. When the property of the 'surrogate' mother, her empty vessel, is filled with the seed of the man who has contracted with her, he, too, becomes the parent, the creative force that brings new life (property) into the world. Men have denied significance to women's unique bodily capacity, have appropriated it and transmuted it into masculine political genesis. The story of the social contract is the greatest story of men giving political birth, but, with the surrogacy contract, modern patriarchy has taken a new turn. Thanks to the power of the creative political medium of contract, men can appropriate physical genesis too. The creative force of the male seed turns the empty property contracted out by an 'individual' into new human life. Patriarchy in its literal meaning has returned in a new guise.

Until the present, womanhood has been seen as inseparable from, even subsumed in, maternity. For at least three centuries, feminists have spent enormous efforts endeavouring to show that women, like men, have a range of capacities that could be exercised in addition to their unique capacity to create physical life. Now motherhood has been separated from womanhood – and the separation expands patriarchal right. Here is another variant of the contradiction of slavery. A woman can be a 'surrogate' mother only because her womanhood is deemed irrelevant and she is declared an 'individual' performing a service. At the same time, she can be a 'surrogate' mother only because she is a *woman.* Similarly, the relevant property of the man in the surrogacy contract can only be that of a *man*; it is the property that can make him a father. Appropriately, sperm is the only example of property in the person that is not a political fiction. Unlike labour power, sexual parts, the uterus, or any other property that is contracted out for use by another, sperm *can* be separated from the body. Indeed, sperm can be used in artificial insemination, and the sperm of men deemed genetically superior can be stored away until a suitable woman is located, only because it can be separated from the person.

Until the surrogacy contract was invented, this peculiarity of the male seed rendered genetic paternity inherently problematic; paternity always hinged on a woman's testimony. Maternity, however, was always certain and, according to Hobbes, in the natural condition the mother was the lord, with political right over her child; a man had to contract with a mother to obtain mastery as a father. Thanks to the power of contract, genetic paternity can now be made secure and brought together with masculine political creativity. Through contract, men can at last be certain of paternity. A momentous change has thus occurred in (one aspect of) the meaning of 'fatherhood' and the power of fatherhood – or patriarchy in the traditional sense.

It is far too soon to say exactly how important 'surrogate' motherhood will be in the future development of patriarchal domination. In 1979, when (with Teresa Brennan) I published my first examination of social contract theory from a feminist perspective, the term was unknown to us. There are other straws in the wind that point in the same direction as 'surrogate' motherhood – for instance, men have taken legal action as fathers in Britain, Australia and the United States to try to prevent women obtaining abortions and to keep women's bodies artificially alive in order to sustain a foetus. Fathers are also fighting for custody of children. In recent years, in a reversal of the practice in the mid-nineteenth century, the mother has usually been awarded custody of any children if a marriage breaks down. Indeed, the practice of awarding custody to mothers led Christine Delphy to argue that divorce is merely an extension of marriage in which men, once again, are exempted from responsibility for children. Now that feminists have succeeded in winning some much-needed legal reforms, and now that, in many matters, women and men are being placed on the same civil footing, mothers can no longer assume that they will attain custody. Nor can unmarried mothers be sure that the father will not be awarded access to and rights over the child. Some winds, though, blow in a different direction. For example, artificial insemination enables women to become mothers without sexual relations with men.

The contractual subjection of women is full of contradictions, paradoxes and ironies. Perhaps the greatest irony of all is yet to come. Contract is conventionally believed to have defeated the old patriarchal order, but, in eliminating the final remnants of the old world of status, contract may yet usher in a new form of paternal right.

Notes

1   E. McLeod, *Women Working: Prostitution Now* (London and Canberra, Croom Helm, 1982), pp. 12–13; table 1.1.

2   Figure cited in M. A. Jennings, 'The Victim as Criminal: A Consideration of California's Prostitution Law', *California Law Review*, 64, 5 (1976), p. 1251.

3   Cited in *San Francisco Examiner* (3 February 1985).

4   McLeod, *Women Working*, p. 43.

5   M. Wollstonecraft, 'A Vindication of the Rights of Men' in *A Mary Wollstonecraft Reader*, ed. B. H. Solomon and P. S. Berggren (New York, New American Library, 1983), p. 247. She also uses the phrase in *A Vindication of the Rights of Woman* (New York, W. W. Norton and Co., 1975 [1792]), p. 148. According to her biographer Clair Tomalin, Wollstonecraft was the first to use the phrase 'legal prostitution' to refer to marriage.

6   E. Goldman, 'The Traffic in Women', in *Anarchism and Other Essays* (New York, Dover Publications, 1969), p. 179.

7   S. de Beauvoir, *The Second Sex*, tr. H. M. Parshley (New York, Vintage Books, 1974), p. 619.

8   C. Hamilton, *Marriage as a Trade* (London, The Women's Press, 1981), p. 37.

9   They are so instructed by J. Radcliffe Richards, *The Sceptical Feminist: A Philosophical Enquiry* (Harmondsworth, Penguin Books, 1980), p. 246.

10   D. A. J. Richards, *Sex, Drugs, Death, and the Law: An Essay on Human Rights and Decriminalization* (Totowa, NJ, Rowman and Littlefield, 1982), p. 121.

11   The term is used by L. Ericcson, 'Charges Against Prostitution: An Attempt at a Philosophical Assessment', *Ethics*, 90 (1980), pp. 335–66.

12   D. A. J. Richards, *Sex, Drugs, Death, and the Law*, p. 115; also p. 108.

13   Ericcson, 'Charges Against Prostitution', p. 342.

14   The example comes from M. McIntosh, 'Who Needs Prostitutes? The Ideology of Male Sexual Needs', in *Women, Sexuality and Social Control*, ed. C. Smart and B. Smart (London, Routledge and Kegan Paul, 1978), p. 54.

15   M. Frye, *The Politics of Reality: Essays in Feminist Theory* (Trumansburg, NY, The Crossing Press, 1983), p. 143. Where men are confined together and prevented from obtaining access to women (as in prison) the 'taboo' is not observed; masculinity is then exhibited by using other men, usually young men, as if they were women.

16   Ericcson, 'Charges Against Prostitution', p. 363, argues (unconvincingly) that 'paternalism' does not conflict with his contractual defence of sound adult prostitution and that prostitution by minors should be prevented. He poses the problem as one of the causes (the supply) of child prostitutes, but fails to mention the problem of the *demand*. Why do men demand to have sexual relations with (sometimes very young) children? Why do resorts like Pagsanjan in the Philippines exist to cater for this demand? This question falls outside my concerns here, but a recent survey of investigations of 'incest' (father-daughter is the most common form) notes that in conjugal relations, 'many men are accustomed to the experience of sex with a weaker and unwilling partner': W. Breines and L. Gordon, 'The New Scholarship on Family Violence', *Signs*, 8, 3 (1983), p. 527.

17   Cited E. McLeod, 'Man-Made Laws for Men? The Street Prostitutes' Campaign Against Control', in *Controlling Women: The Normal and the Deviant*, ed. B. Hutter and G. Williams (London, Croom Helm, 1981), p. 63.

18   Cited in E. M. Sigsworth and T. J. Wyke, 'A Study of Victorian Prostitution and Venereal Disease', in *Suffer and Be Still: Women in the Victorian Age*, ed. M. Vicinus (Bloomington, Indiana University Press, 1972), p. 181. Contemporary prostitutes may still receive food from 'regulars' if, for example, he is a baker, see McLeod, *Women Working*, p. 6.

19   McLeod, *Women Working*, pp. 17, 20; tables 1.2(a), 1.2(b), 1.3.

20   Ericcson, 'Charges Against Prostitution', p. 348.

21   D. A. J. Richards, *Sex, Drugs, Death, and the Law*, p. 88. For a different view of temple prostitution, see G. Lerner, *The Creation of Patriarchy* (New York, Oxford, Oxford University Press, 1986), chapter 6.

22   On *maisons d'abbatages* see K. Barry, *Female Sexual Slavery* (Englewood Cliffs, Prentice Hall, 1979), pp. 3–4; 80–3. The *malaya* form flourished in Nairobi before the Second World War, and is discussed by L. White, 'Prostitution, Identity and Class Consciousness in Nairobi during World War II', *Signs*, II, 2 (1986), pp. 255–73. Working men in Nairobi could not support their wives if they left their farms to come to the city to join their husbands, and the colonial administration did not supply sufficient accommodation for labourers. The men visited *malaya* prostitutes who 'provided bed space – cleaning, cooking, bath water, companionship, hot meals, cold meals, and tea, and … men who spent the night … received breakfast' (p. 256). How should these services be categorized; as an enlarged prostitution contract or a truncated marriage contract?

23   On Britain, see J. R. Walkowitz, *Prostitution and Victorian Society: Women, Class and the State* (Cambridge, Cambridge University Press, 1980); on the United State, see R. Rosen, *The Lost Sisterhood: Prostitution in America, 1900–1918* (Baltimore and London, The Johns Hopkins University Press, 1982); on New South Wales, see J. Allen, 'The Making of a Prostitute Proletariat in Early Twentieth-Century New South Wales', in *So Much Hard Work: Women and Prostitution in Australian History*, ed. K. Daniels (Sydney, Fontana Books, 1984).

24   Cited in M. Trustram, 'Distasteful and Derogatory? Examining Victorian Soldiers for Venereal Disease', in *The Sexual Dynamics of History*, ed. The London Feminist History Group (London, Pluto Press, 1983), pp. 62–3. At present AIDS is provoking a similar response; for example a Bill has been presented to the Nevada legislature to allow murder charges to be brought against prostitutes who have the disease and continued to work. No mention is made of their male customers in the report that I read in *Washington Post* (24 April 1987).

25   J. E. Butler, *An Autobiographical Memoir*, 3rd edn (London, J. W. Arrowsmith, 1928), p. 215.

26   Walkowitz, *Prostitution and Victorian Society*, p. 212.

27   Allen, 'The Making of a Prostitute Proletariat', p. 213.

28   Rosen, *Lost Sisterhood*, p. xii. Rosen (p. 172) also notes new hazards facing American prostitutes today, such as being used by the CIA to extract information or in experiments with drugs.

29   McLeod, *Women Working*, p. 51.

30   For this use of the phrase, see, e.g., J. R. Richards, *The Sceptical Feminist*, p. 244.

31   Ericcson, 'Charges Against Prostitution', p. 341. Compare D. A. J. Richards, *Sex, Drugs, Death, and the Law*, p. 49.

32   McLeod, *Women Working*, p. 69. The men give a variety of reasons, all of which beg the question of the capitalist virtue of self-help.

33   In the 1930s in the United States, only 10 per cent of customers demanded oral sex; by the 1960s nearly 90 per cent did so, either instead of or in addition to intercourse (figures cited by R. Rosen, *The Lost Sisterhood*), p. 97. Could it be conjectured that men's current widespread demand to buy women's bodies to penetrate their mouths is connected to the revitalization of the feminist movement and women's demand to speak?

34   McLeod, *Women Working*, p. 53.

35   A. Jaggar, 'Prostitution', in *The Philosophy of Sex: Contemporary Readings*, ed. A. Soble (Totowa, NJ, Rowman and Littlefield, 1980), p. 360.

36   K. Marx, *Economic and Philosophic Manuscripts of 1844*, ed. D. J. Struik (New York, International Publishers, 1964), p. 133, footnote.

37   J. H. Reiman, 'Prostitution, Addiction and the Ideology of Liberalism', *Contemporary Crises*, 3 (1979), p. 66.

38   Ericcson, 'Charges Against Prostitution', p. 351.

39   Ibid., p. 341.

40   I. Kant, *The Philosophy of Law*, tr. W. Hastie (Edinburgh, T. and T. Clark, 1887), third section, §26, p. 112; cf. I. Kant, *Lectures on Ethics*, tr. L. Infield (New York, Harper and Row, 1963), p. 166.

41   Kant, *Lectures on Ethics*, p. 165.

42   D. A. J. Richards, *Sex, Drugs, Death, and the Law*. p. 109.

43   O. Patterson, *Slavery and Social Death: A Comparative Study* (Cambridge, MA and London, Harvard University Press, 1982), p. 25.

44   McLeod, *Women Working*, p. 84.

45   J. S. Mill, 'The Subjection of Women', in *Essays on Sex Equalily*, ed. A. S. Rossi (Chicago and London, University of Chicago Press, 1970), p. 141.

46   I owe thanks to Mary Douglas for drawing my attention to this point.

47   See V. Stolcke, 'Old Values, New Technologies: Who Is the Father?', paper presented to the Kolloquium am Wissenschaftskolleg zu Berlin, March 1987, p. 6. (My thanks to Verena Stolcke for sending me a copy of the paper.)

48   Information from D. Brahams, 'The Hasty British Ban on Commercial Surrogacy', *Hastings Center Report*, February 1987, pp. 16–19. (Lionel Gossman kindly supplied me with a copy of this paper.)

49   The Committee to Consider the Social, Ethical and Legal Issues Arising from In Vitro Fertilization, *Report on the Disposition of Embryos Produced by In Vitro Fertilization* (Victoria, August 1984), §4.17. (I am grateful to Rebecca Albury for sending me a copy of the relevant part of the *Report*.)

50   *The New York Times* (5 April 1987).

51   Information from *The New York Times* (12 January 1987).

52   Committee to Consider In Vitro Fertilization, *Report on the Disposition of Embryos*, §4.6; §4.11.

53   Cited in excerpts from the decision by Judge Harvey R. Sorkow, printed in *The New York Times* (1 April 1987).

54   *Genesis* 16:2, 3; *Genesis* 30:4.

Chapter 14

Dealing with Difference: A Politics of Ideas or a Politics of Presence?

Anne Phillips

In the post-communist world of the 1980s and 1990s, liberalism and liberal demo-cracy have achieved an impressive ascendancy, and can more plausibly present themselves as the only legitimate bases for equality, justice or democracy. Critics, of course, remain, but the grounds of complaint have shifted considerably. For many years, the central arguments against liberalism fell into three broad categories: that the liberal emphasis on individual freedoms and rights reflected a self-protec-tive and competitive egotism that refused any wider community; that the liberal focus on 'merely' political equalities ignored or even encouraged gross inequalities in social and economic life; and that the liberal consolidation of representative democracy reduced the importance of more active citizen participation. None of these complaints has disappeared, but each has been reformulated in terms of diversity and difference. Feminist theorists, in particular, have identified liberalism with an abstract individualism that ignores its own gendered content, and many have criticized the homogenizing ideals of equality that require us to be or become the same.[1] Accusations of gender-blindness and race- or ethnicity-blindness have added weight to older complaints that liberalism is blind to class. At a moment when most political theorists have situated themselves more firmly in the liberal tradition, liberalism is extensively criticized for erasing diversity and difference.

From the standpoint of that much maligned visitor from Mars (whose technical brilliance in negotiating the journey always combines with an astonishing ignorance of political ideas) it might well appear that liberals never thought about difference. Left at such a level of generality, the accusation is distinctly odd, for notions of diversity and difference have been central to liberalism from its inception and to liberal democracy throughout its formation. What gave the original impetus to liberalism was the perception that neither nature nor tradition guaranteed political order, and that the very equality of what we now see as male subjects increased the potential diversity and conflict. Hence the search for a contractual basis for political authority that would bind these different individuals into a coherent whole; hence the concern with rights and autonomies that would allow them to pursue part of their lives under their own steam. In these and subsequent developments, difference remained politically significant and theoretically important: a driving force, indeed, in the separation between public and private affairs.

The defining characteristics of liberal democracy, as Robert Dahl among others has clarified,[2] are also grounded in the heterogeneity of the societies that gave it birth. It was the diversity of the citizenry, as much as its absolute size, that made the earlier (more consensual) practices of Athenian democracy so inappropriate to the modern world. Lacking any half-credible basis for seeing citizens as united in their goals, theorists of liberal democracy took issue with the homogenizing presumptions of a common good or common purpose, and made diversity a central organizing theme. John Stuart Mill's famous vacillations over democracy derived from a double sense of democracy as both impetus and threat to diversity: something that breaks the hold of any single notion of the good life, but can also encourage a deadening conformity. In more straightforwardly confident vein, Georg Kateb has presented constitutional and representative democracy as that system *par excellence* that encourages and disseminates diversity. The procedures of electoral competition do not merely chasten and circumscribe the powers of government. By promoting a more sceptical attitude towards the basis on which competing claims are resolved, they also cultivate "a general tolerance of, and even affection for diversity: diversity in itself, and diversity as the source of regulated contest and competition."[3]

Difference is not something we have only just noticed. What we can more usefully say is that difference has been perceived in an overly cerebral fashion as differences in opinions and beliefs, and that the resulting emphasis on what I will call a politics of ideas has proved inadequate to the problems of political exclusion. The diversity most liberals have in mind is a diversity of beliefs, opinions, preferences and goals, all of which may stem from the variety of experience, but are considered as in principle detachable from this. Even the notion of interests, which seems most thoroughly grounded in differential material conditions, lends itself to at least semi-detachment. The preference for higher taxes on those with higher incomes may be stronger among those with little money, especially if they believe the proceeds will finance public provision of educational or health services that would be otherwise beyond their reach. But support for higher taxation and better public provision is not restricted to those who most directly benefit: political preferences are influenced by material circumstances without being reducible to these. The interests of pensioners or the long-term unemployed can then be championed by those who are neither retired nor out of work; the interests of geographical localities can be represented by people who no longer live in the area; the interests of mothers with young children can be represented by childless men.

One consequence for democracy is that what is to be represented then takes priority over who does the representation. Issues of political presence are largely discounted, for when difference is considered in terms of intellectual diversity, it does not much matter who represents the range of ideas. One person may easily stand in for another; there is no additional requirement for the representatives to "mirror" the characteristics of the person or people represented. What concerns us in the choice of representative is a congruity of political beliefs and ideals, combined perhaps with a superior ability to articulate and register opinions. The quality of the democracy is guaranteed by the extension of suffrage to all adults, each of whom contributes his or her vote to the opinions that gain public weight. Stripped of any pre-democratic authority, the role of the politician is to carry a message. The messages will vary, but it hardly matters if the messengers are the same. (Those who believe that men have a monopoly on the political skills of articulating policies and ideas will not be surprised that most messengers are men.)

The notion of representation as primarily a matter of ideas has not, of course, gone unchallenged. In 1789, a group of Frenchwomen laid claim to a place in the Estates General in the following terms:

> Just as a nobleman cannot represent a plebeian and the latter cannot represent a nobleman, so a man, no matter how honest he may be, cannot represent a woman. Between the representatives and the represented there must be an absolute identity of interests.[4]

Shared experience here takes precedence over shared ideas; more precisely, no amount of thought or sympathy, no matter how careful or honest, can jump the barriers of experience. This assertion came, however, at a very particular point in the development of democracy, when the challenge to privilege momentarily centered around questioning which 'estates' were entitled to representation. Subsequent notions of citizenship seemed to make this an anachronism, the last gasp of a feudal tradition. Hard fought extensions of suffrage combined with the evolution of political parties as the basic medium of representation to encourage an alternative notion of politics as a battleground for contested ideas.

The socialist tradition is of interest here, not only because it threw up a politics of pressing for the "representation of labour" (which seems to echo the earlier idea of representing different estates) but because it has been persistently troubled by tensions between a politics of ideas and an alternative politics of presence. Those involved in socialist parties often argued fiercely over the relationship between intellectuals and the 'authentically' working class, some feeling that a socialist politics should privilege the voices and presence of workers, others that class identities should signify less than adherence to socialist ideas. In *What Is To Be Done*, Lenin offered one classic refutation of the politics of presence. Stressing the multiplicity of arenas within which the power of capital was exerted, he argued the limits of an experience confined to any one of these, and the overriding importance of strategic links between one set of struggles and another. This privileged the all-seeing intellectual (who might in principle originate from any class position or faction), the political activist who could look beyond each specific struggle or campaign to its wider connections and ramifications, and fit the various pieces of the jigsaw together. When socialist feminists challenged such views in the 1970s, one of the things they pointed out was that they denied legitimacy to women's self-understandings; another was that they presumed an objectivity on the part of these activists that raised them to a God-like level. As Sheila Rowbotham remarked in her critique of Leninist conceptions of the vanguard party, "(t)he Party is presented as soaring above all sectional concerns without providing any guarantees that this soaring will not be in fact an expression of the particular preoccupations of the group or groups with power within it."[5] Part of what was at issue in the development of an autonomous women's movement was the arrogance of those who thought that ideas could be separated from presence.

In Hanna Pitkin's influential discussion of representation, she criticizes the mirror view as beginning and ending with who is present, setting to one side the far more important question of what the representatives actually do. "Think of the legislature as a pictorial representation or a representative sample of the nation," she argues, "and you will almost inevitably concentrate on its composition rather than its activities."[6] But looking back at her discussion from a distance of twenty-five years, what is notable is how she elides the mapping of ideas with the mapping of people, not really distinguishing between a representative sample that captures the range of ideas, the range of interests, or the range of socially significant groups. Her emphasis throughout is on the distinction between being and doing, and her arguments are as much directed against versions of proportional representation that would more adequately reflect the multiplicity of parties and opinion as against later preoccupations with representing excluded or marginalized groups. Questions of power and inequality do not figure largely in Pitkin's account. Such questions have become central to democratic debate today.

It is no part of my intention to disparage politics as a battleground for ideas. Much of the radicalizing impetus to democracy has centered around initiatives to make ideas more rather than less important, as in efforts to bind representatives more closely to the opinions they profess to hold, or in measures to reduce the backstage manipulations of pressure groups that disrupt the higher politics of ideas. But when the politics of ideas is taken in isolation from the politics of presence, it does not deal adequately with the experiences of those social groups who by virtue of their race or ethnicity or religion or gender have felt themselves excluded from the democratic process. Political exclusion is increasingly – I believe rightly – viewed in terms that can only be met by political presence, and much of this development has depended on a more complex understanding of the relationship between ideas and experience. The separation between who and what is to be represented, and the subordination of one to the other, relies on an understanding of ideas and interests as relatively unproblematic. It is as if the field of politics is already clearly demarcated, containing with it various clusters of preferences or ideas or concerns that exist independently of any process of formation. This is in stark contrast with the preoccupations that ran through the early years of the contemporary women's movement, when women talked of the difficulties in finding a voice, the way that dominant definitions of politics blocked out alternatives, or hegemonic culture controlled what could or could not be said. The emphasis then shifted from an objectively defined set of interests (that just needed more vigorous pursuit) to a more exploratory notion of possibilities so far silenced and ideas one had to struggle to express. In this later understanding of the processes that generate needs and concerns and ideas, it is harder to sustain the primacy of ideas over political presence. If it is simply a question of representing a given range of ideas and interests, it may not much matter who does the work of representation. But if the range of ideas has been curtailed by orthodoxies that rendered alternatives invisible, there will be no satisfactory solution short of changing the people who represent and develop the ideas.

The renewed concern over the relationship between ideas and experience also figures in recent arguments over the limits of tolerance in dealing with difference. The classically liberal treatment of difference allows for private spaces within which people can get on with their own chosen affairs and a public realm ordered around a set of minimum shared presumptions. But the relegation of difference to a private world of private variation has been experienced as an injunction to keep peculiarities a secret, and the shared presumptions that control the public world have proved less than even-handed in their treatment of different groups. The separation of church from state has long been considered the solution to the problems of religious difference, but it achieves this by requiring all religions to adopt a similarly self-denying ordinance that will limit the relevance of religious precepts to practices in the private sphere. This resolution is more amenable to some religions than to others; in particular, it is more acceptable to the heavily secularized forms of Christianity that became the norm in contemporary Europe. In similar vein, we might say that the relegation of homosexuality to a private affair between consenting adults helps reduce more overt forms of discrimination, but it achieves this at the expense of any more public disruption of a heterosexual norm. Private deviation is permitted, but not equal public worth.

Part of the dissatisfaction with liberalism's treatment of difference is the feeling that toleration is a poor substitute for recognition.[7] We only tolerate what we do not like or approve of (otherwise there is no need for toleration[8]), and yet where difference is bound up with identity, this is hard for the tolerated to accept. You can put up with people thinking you a harmless freak for your membership in the flat earth society. You may even revel in people thinking you a dangerous lunatic for your belief in communist revolution. It is not so easy to live with mere tolerance of your perverted sexuality or your denial of femininity or your irrationally fundamentalist religion. Tolerance is perceived as non-egalitarian, resting in some way on a distinction between majority norms and minority deviance, and incorporating some implied preference for a particular way of life.[9] It is perhaps one of the tributes to democracy that people do not find tolerance satisfactory for long, and that the imperatives of democratic equality seem to press on further towards the recognition of equal worth. One reflection of this pressure has been the emerging school of thought that looks to 'democratic' rather than 'liberal' ways of dealing with diversity:[10] instead of treating difference as something that can flourish in the private domain, it turns to public manifestations in which differences can be confronted and (hopefully) resolved. Here, too, presence becomes crucial, for any public domain marked by the systematic absence of significant groups cannot even approach this resolution.

Once raised, the issues of presence are unlikely to go away: these are questions that must be addressed if democracies are to deliver on political equality. My concern in the rest of this paper is with what happens next, and in particular, with the tensions that arise between ideas and political presence. In the caricatures of those most resistant to a politics of presence, it is frequently misrepresented as a kind of 'group-think': something that is necessarily separatist, necessarily corrosive of any wider community, and falsely presuming not only that one has to be a member of a particular group in order to understand or represent that group's interests, but that all members of the group in question will think along similar lines.[11] The caricature misses its mark. Faced, for example, with that 1789 claim that "between the representatives and the represented there must be an absolute identity of interests," most contemporary theorists will shy away from the implications of an essential female subject, or an authentic black subject, that can be represented by any one of its kind. Far more dominant today is the notion of multiple identities or multiple "subject positions," each of which is subject to political transformation and change. An attention to difference does not entail an essentialist understanding of identity; nor does it demand any wholesale rejection of the politics of competing ideas. But then the very sophistication of contemporary theories of identity can paralyze development; the very distance people have travelled from the caricatures of their position can remove them from democracy as it currently exists. In both the theoretical and the movement-centered literature which I now go on to discuss, issues of difference have been construed within a robustly democratic future that bears little relationship to contemporary political life. One of the challenges of democracy is how to combine the insights from such discussion with prescriptions that can be made relevant to representative democracy as practiced today.

Democracy as Public Contestation

Much of the contemporary literature on democracy and difference operates with notions of a more active and vigorous democracy that depends crucially on public debate. Rejecting both the false harmony that stamps out difference, and the equally false essentialism that defines people through some single, authentic identity, many theorists look to a democracy which maximises citizen participation, and requires us to engage and contest with one another. In a recent essay on feminism and democracy, Susan Mendus suggests that difference is the rationale for democracy, and that "whereas traditional democratic theory tends to construe difference as an obstacle to the attainment of a truly democratic state, feminist theory should alert us to the possibility that difference is rather what necessitates the pursuit of democracy."[12] In his work on multiculturalism, Charles Taylor calls for a politics of democratic empowerment as the way of dealing with demands for equal recognition without

thereby entrenching people in fragmented identities.[13] In his discussion of the republican revival, Cass Sunstein argues for a deliberative democracy to which all citizens
will have equal access, and where all perspectives can be equally addressed.[14]

All such arguments assume equality of access (without necessarily exploring the
conditions that would deliver this result), and all differentiate themselves from
merely majoritarian decision-making by anticipating some process of transformation and change. Where the classically liberal resolution of difference relies on a
combination of private spaces and majority norms (these in turn established by
majority vote), the democratic resolution of difference expects us to engage more
directly with each other. We bring our differences to the public stage; we revise
them through public debate. Major disagreements then surface between those who
anticipate a full 'resolution' in some newly achieved public consensus, and those
who see differences as contingent but never as 'difference' going away. The first
position looks more utopian than the second, but both operate at a level of generality that barely touches on democracy as practiced today.

Consider William Connolly's arguments in *Identity/Difference*,[15] which are particularly interesting in that they both say what should happen and why it almost
certainly won't. Here, a 'robust' politics of democratic engagement is presented as
something that neither evades nor confirms difference: a politics that enables people
to disturb settled conventions and expose settled identities. All identities are formed
through difference – you know who you are through your difference from some
other – and all identities are simultaneously threatened by the difference(s) of the
other. There is always a danger that identities will be dogmatized into some naturalistic or unchanging essence, and always a danger that difference will generate
destructive resentments and fears. What keeps these at bay is a politics of mutual
challenge and disruption in which we are constantly reminded of the contingent
nature of our identities. This politics depends in turn on the successful permeation
of a "culture of genealogy" which helps us to see our identities as ambiguous and
contestable and contested. Democracy then appears as an exciting engagement with
difference: the challenge of 'the other'; the disruption of certainties; the recognition
of ambiguities within one's self as well as one's differences with others.

All this is tremendously refreshing, and in no way relies on a future transcend-
ence of difference. But just at the point where he has achieved the philosophical
resolution, Connolly backs off from claiming any immediate relevance for today.
The confidence that enables people to dispense with settled identities or to accept
the contingencies of fate may not be available to those suffering from economic
inequality and political exclusion. Indeed, in an environment characterized by
systematic inequality, the appeals to a robust democracy in which no-one shelters
behind accusations of the other could "too readily be received as yet another attack
on those already excluded from democratic politics."[16]

> One compelling attraction of democracy is that it enables anyone to enage in funda-
> mental riddles of existence through participation in a public politics that periodically
> disturbs and denaturalizes elements governing the cultural unconscious. But these

same characteristics can intensify the reactive demand to redogmatize conventional identities if a large minority of the society is already suffering under severe burden of material deprivation and effective exclusion from the good life offered to a majority.[17]

Robust democracy then becomes possible only when economic inequalities are substantially reduced. My problem with this is not that it begs the question of how we might achieve such a precondition (we all have difficulties answering this), but that so much of what currently drives a politics of identity and difference is precisely the sense of deprivation and exclusion that Connolly sees as making such a politics so dangerous. Again, this is a point Connolly himself makes, noting that against the background of US neo-conservatism, any politics of identity and difference tends to fuel "the energies of ressentiment and the dogmatization of identity."[18] The philosophical resolution of democracy and difference remains largely that.[19]

Democracy Inside Social Movements

The second context in which these discussions take place is as interventions into specific movements that have formed around the politics of race, gender, sexuality and ethnicity. All these movements have involved a critique of the phony essentialisms that disguised systematic difference and inequality; nearly all of them, however, have also generated their own essentialisms that at some point or other claimed a unified female or lesbian or black or some other experience. Thus feminists took issue with the gender amnesia that transformed man "into a paradigm of humankind as such"[20] but, in the further explorations of sexual difference, they often insisted on a primary distinction between men and women that obscured further differences between women. Lesbian feminists took issue with the hegemonic controls of a heterosexual norm but, in the search for an affirming identity, they often constructed 'the' authentic lesbian who would not tolerate differences of sexual practice or political attitudes within the lesbian community.[21] Anti-racists took issue with the mythologies of nation that had rendered black people invisible but, in the subsequent racial dualism that focused so exclusively on differences between 'black' and 'white', they tended to obscure the cultural and religious pluralism that characterizes the many non-white minorities.[22]

The problems of essentialism have, as a consequence, figured largely in the internal politics and debates of these movements. Much contemporary attention is focused on the conditions that can articulate group difference without thereby 'disciplining' group members into a single authentic identity; in the process, many have suggested limits to the very notion of 'a' group. As Shane Phelan puts it in her discussion of lesbian feminism in the United States: "Politics that ignores our identities, that makes them 'private', is useless; but nonnegotiable identities will enslave us whether they are imposed from within or without."[23] Speaking from the British context, Stuart Hall has suggested that we should pay more attention to the ways in which black experience is a diaspora experience, one in which the constructions of history and politics and culture are therefore fundamental, and not to be captured through notions of an essential black subject.[24] He talks here of "the end of innocence," "the recognition of the extraordinary diversity of subject positions, social experiences and cultural identities which compose the category 'black',"[25] and the impossibility of grounding the black subject or black experience in the essentialisms of nature or any other such guarantee.

These arguments cut across the balder distinction between ideas and presence, for what is being identified are differences in experiences and identities within what has hitherto been seen as an all-embracing category or group. It is not simply that 'black' people or women or lesbians will disagree among themselves as to the appropriate policies and ideas and goals (they will vote for different parties, for example), but that their very senses of what it means to be black or female or lesbian will necessarily vary. In the context of the political movements with which these arguments engage, there seem to be two important implications. One is that the diversity of "subject positions" should be reflected within the organizational structures that define who does or doesn't get into the conversation. There should be no privileging of some voices as more authentic than others, and no coercive imposition of a supposedly unified point of view. The other implication, however, is that there is no way of knowing in advance whether this diversity has been successfully acknowledged. Any prior setting of the boundaries risks restoring some version of the authentic subject, for even if the boundaries are significantly pluralized, they still define in advance what are the appropriate or relevant differences. Thus Stuart Hall argues that it is no longer possible to represent 'the black subject' without reference to class, gender, sexuality, ethnicity. But if this were taken as a series of guidelines about the different characteristics that must be covered within the membership of some campaigning organization, that would hardly be doing justice to his critique.

This is a problem that in some way or another besets every radical initiative, whether it is a matter of deciding whom to invite to address a meeting, who is to join an editorial board, or which groups are to participate in a campaign. We have become sufficiently attuned to the politics of presence to distrust the notion that anyone can "stand in" for anyone else, and sufficiently alert to the coercive powers of homogeneity to want to reflect diversity. But the critiques of essentialism deprive us of any simple mechanism for achieving the appropriate balance, and remind us that diversity is too great to be captured in any categorial list.

In the context of political movements, this is not such a serious difficulty. At their best, such movements already enjoy the kind of robust democracy that is proposed as an ideal for the polity as a whole: allowing for, indeed incapable of containing, the kind of contestation and mutual challenge that acknowledges difference and simultaneously disrupts it. The vehemence of debate indicates both a recurrent tendency towards essentialism and a continuous challenge to this: people are tough enough to resist prior classification and far too argumentative to accept someone else's definition of their selves. It is also worth noting that the fluidity of this politics lends itself more easily to a kind of learning through trial and error, for none of the consequences that people may derive from their current understandings of identity or difference is likely to be set in stone. The larger difficulties arise where we seek out more compromised intervention into democracies that are still pretty feeble.

Political Prescriptions for the Polity as a Whole

When we turn to the political prescriptions that might flow from a new understanding of democracy and difference, we are not dealing in far-off utopias: There is a range of policies already proposed or implemented; and change is neither distant nor unlikely. The problem, rather, is that because such prescriptions operate in a half-way house of remedial reform, they are less able to resolve the contradictory pressures between the politics of ideas and the politics of presence. The kinds of mechanisms I have in mind include the quota systems adopted by a number of European political parties to achieve gender parity in elected assemblies, the redrawing of boundaries around black-majority constituencies to raise the number of black politicians elected in the United States, and the longer established power-sharing practices of those European consociational democracies that have distributed executive power and economic resources between different religious and linguistic groups. In each of these instances, the initiatives operate within the framework of an existing (not very robust) democracy. Tensions that might more readily resolve themselves in a future ferment of activity and deliberation become more acute in what everyone knows is a compromised situation.

All the more immediate proposals for reform insist on deliberate intervention as necessary to break the link between social structures of inequality or exclusion and the political reflection of these in levels of participation and influence. All of them also agree in looking to specifically *political* mechanisms – rather than, or sometimes as well as, longer term social transformation. They take issue therefore with the complacencies of a free market in politics, which sees political equality as sufficiently guaranteed by the procedures of one person one vote; they also challenge the more standard radical alternative, which has focused attention on prior economic or social change. Whatever their differences on other issues, the traditions of revolutionary Marxism and welfare state social reform have tended to agree on a broadly materialist analysis of the problems of political equality, seeing equal political access as something that depends on more fundamental changes in social, economic, and sometimes educational, conditions. The current interest in achieving equal or proportionate presence reverses this, focusing instead on institutional mechanisms – its critics would say 'political fixes' – that can achieve more immediate change.

The roots of this reversal lie partly in frustration with what has proved an unbelievably slow process of structural transformation (*first* eliminate the sexual division of labor ... the racial ordering of income and education and employment ... the class patterning that decides children's futures – is it any wonder we search for short cuts?) But political frustration is not new, and people do not normally change direction just because things take so long. The additional impetus comes from the kind of arguments already outlined, which suggest that the range of political ideas and preferences is seriously constrained by the characteristics of the people who convey them. In a more traditional base-superstructure model, we were advised to concentrate first on generating the social conditions for equal citizenship, then to enjoy the political equalization that flows from this. Such an approach, however, treats policy choices as more straightforward than they are, and fails to observe the way that strategies devised for equality reflect the limits of those currently in power.[26] Where policy initiatives are worked out *for* rather than *with* a politically excluded constituency, they rarely engage all relevant concerns. Again, it is only if we consider the field of politics as already clearly demarcated, with all possible options already in play, that we can put much confidence in such an approach.

I do not discount the criticism that regards institutional mechanisms for achieving equal or proportionate presence as a species of diversionary 'political fixing', but we should not be required to choose between these and other urgent tasks of social and economic transformation. When political exclusion is such a marked feature of contemporary democratic life, it seems inappropriate to rely on distant prospects of a more robustly participatory democracy and/or structural changes in social and economic conditions. The very distance of such prospects puts a premium on political prescriptions that can be made relevant to representative democracy as currently practiced, and most of these will involve some form of affirmative action that can guarantee more equal representation in existing decision-making assemblies. Any specifically political mechanism, however, risks imposing a rigid definition of the identities that have to be included or the interests so far left out. The more complex understanding of multiple identities that change both over time and according to context is a potential casualty here, as is the continuing importance we would all want to attach to political disagreement and debate.

If we consider, for example, the mechanisms that might be appropriate in contemporary Britain to redress racial exclusions, one immediate problem is the diversity of non-white experience, and the major disagreements that have surfaced between taking race or ethnicity or religion as the basis of social identity and political exclusion. When we take race as the central indicator, this encourages a dualism of 'black' or 'white', a division of the universe which is often said to be closer to the political perceptions of Afro-Caribbeans than to the self-definitions of the significantly more numerous Asians. Tariq Modood, indeed, has argued that "the concept of Black is harmful to Asians and is a form of political identity that most Asians do not accept as their primary public identity."[27] But if we take ethnicity or religion instead, these are felt to be too closely associated with a politics of multiculturalism that has looked to the greater dissemination of knowledge about ethnic and religious minorities as the way of breaking down racial stereotypes, and has been thought insufficiently vigorous in its challenges to racism *per se*. Alternative ways of defining group identities or redressing group exclusions have become loaded with political significance, with an attention to cultural diversity being variously perceived as something that depoliticizes the anti-racist struggle or is a crucial corrective to the simplicities of racial dualism.[28]

What, in this context, is an appropriate mechanism for dealing with political exclusion? Can Asians be represented by Afro-Caribbeans, Hindus by Muslims, black women by black men? Or do these groups have nothing more in common than their joint experience of being excluded from power? In their recent book on *Racialized Boundaries*, Floya Anthias and Nira Yuval-Davies conclude that "the form of political representation which has grown out of identity politics and equal opportunities and which has attempted to represent social difference more genuinely, has created an impossible mission for itself,"[29] and that what is a positive diversity of overlapping identities becomes dangerously constrained in efforts towards proportional representation. But does this mean that nothing can be done: that given the risks, on the one hand, of an imposed and misleading uniformity, and the absurdities, on the other, of an endless search for sufficiently pluralized categories, we have to abandon the quest for specifically political mechanisms? Caucuses and quotas are the most obvious political mechanisms for dealing with political exclusion, yet both of these depend on a prior categorization of the basis on which people have been excluded. Neither seems adequate to the complexity of political identities.

The politics that has developed in the United States around the strategy of black-majority, single-member constituencies might seem more straightforward, for it seems clear enough that it is race rather than ethnicity that has been at issue in the political exclusion of African-Americans, and racial bloc voting is plausibly described as "the single most salient feature of contemporary political life."[30] But even so, a political resolution that privileges race as the prime consideration can make it more difficult for people to articulate what are complex and multiple identities: obscure tensions, for example, around gender and class, can block out major disagreements over policy preferences and political ideas. The implication that black representatives are representative merely by virtue of being black is inevitably problematic, even where 'blackness' is a less contested category.

Those who consider the problems of political equality as adequately dealt with by provision for the equal right to vote will be happy to rest their case there, but criticism of the strategy of black electoral success has not been confined to these quarters. Equally powerful criticism comes from those who regard proportionate presence as a necessary but insufficient condition, and are concerned that the focus on numbers alone can reduce political accountability, limit prospects for multiracial coalition, and undermine the urgency of policy debate.[31] There is, in other words, a strong sense of the tensions that can develop between a politics of presence and a politics of ideas. But instead of resolving this by opting for the second over the first, critics have looked to alternative patterns of representation that can make it possible to combine the two. Some of the most innovative work in this area comes from those pressing for a return to the more competitive politics of multi-member constituencies but based on forms of proportional representation and cumulative voting that would maintain the scope for electing representatives from minority groups.[32] It is felt, in other words, that mechanisms *can* be devised which continue the gains in black political presence without forcing an either/or choice between the politics of presence and the politics of ideas.

European initiatives on gender parity can also be seen as successfully negotiating the competing demands of ideas and presence – and here we enter the realm of policies already in position rather than proposals in contested debate. The favored strategy involves pressuring existing political parties to introduce a more balanced ticket of both women and men in their candidates for winnable seats, thus maintaining accountability through party policies and programs while changing the gender composition of elected assemblies. Often enough, the mechanism has been a straightforward quota, which has contributed to a remarkable increase in the numbers of women elected in the Nordic countries. Critics of such strategies usually rest their case on the paucity of "experienced" women, the potential loss of "good" men to politics, and the risk that the overall caliber of politicians (not too high in my opinion) will fall. They do not dwell particularly on the essentialist presumptions of 'a' women's perspective, or the dangerous potential for women pressing only narrowly sectional concerns. There are just too many women for them to be considered as a unified or sectional group, and they are spread across every class or ethnic or religious dimension and every conceivable political persuasion. When it is applied to women, the politics of presence does not seriously disrupt the politics of competing ideas; it is relatively easy to pursue both of these together.

Outside the more established democracies of Europe and the United States, the arguments often start from the opposite direction, a feeling that *who* is to be represented has so far taken precedence over *what*, and that what is missing is the higher politics of ideas. One might think, for example, of the abuse of kinship networks and ethnic solidarities by political elites in post-colonial Africa, many of whom evacuated the terrain of contested policies and ideals to cultivate a power base around exclusionary identities. When the colonial powers retreated from Africa, they left behind societies in which the state had become the main avenue for economic and social advancement, and where the politics of patronage was almost doomed to flourish. In this context, people lived under what seemed an absence of politics, with the contrast between a civilian or military regime seeming of far less consequence than whether you had access to any of the rulers. As ethnic connections emerged as one of the main routes of access, ethnic rivalries became literally deadly, even when the ethnicities in question were relatively recent creations.[33] It is against this background that African radicals and writers have so eloquently called for a politics based on vision and ideals.[34]

Through all these examples, the biggest mistake is to set up ideas as the opposite of political presence: to treat ideas as totally separate from the people who carry them; or worry exclusively about the people without giving a thought to their policies and ideas. It should be said, however, that this is not such a frequent mistake as the caricatures suggest, and that those exploring equal or proportionate presence rarely regard it as a substitute for the politics of competing ideas. If anything, the most acute criticisms of the politics of presence have come from those most committed to challenging political exclusions, and the debate has long shifted beyond its either/or axis. What is, perhaps, emerging is that the more satisfactory ways of redressing group exclusion are those which are the less group-specific. This seems to be the case in relation to gender quotas, if only because the category of 'woman' is so inclusive of other kinds of difference and division that it leaves open the necessary space for a multiplicity of political identities. It also seems to be the case in the proposals that have developed around the implementation of the Voting Rights Act in the United States, which have moved away from the more tightly drawn voting districts that provide a 'safe seat' for minority representatives towards a larger geographical constituency that can no longer pretend to contain only one voice.

Such developments acknowledge the danger in preemptive classifications of people's political identities, and are well aware that essentialist definitions of the groups that have been excluded can work to reduce political accountability and debate. They nonetheless take issue with the more traditional treatment of diversity and difference as simply a matter of contested ideas. The overly cerebral understanding of difference has not engaged sufficiently with the problems of political presence, for it has encouraged an unacceptable level of complacency over the homogeneity of political elites. We can no longer pretend that the full range of ideas and preferences and alternatives has been adequately represented when those charged with the job of representation are all white or all male or all middle class; or that democracies complete their task of political equality when they establish a free market in political ideas. One would not want to take up permanent residence in the half-way house of remedial reform, but mechanisms should be – and can be – devised that address the problems of group exclusion without fixing the boundaries or character of each group.

Notes

1 I summarize and discuss many of these arguments in *Engendering Democracy* (Pennsylvania: University of Pennsylvania State Press, 1991). See also Jane Flax, "Beyond equality: gender, justice and difference," in G. Bock and S. James, eds, *Beyond Equality and Difference* (London: Routledge, 1992).

2 Robert A. Dahl, *Democracy and Its Critics* (New Haven: Yale University Press, 1989).

3 George Kateb, "The Moral Distinctiveness of Representative Democracy," *Ethics* 91:3 (1981): 361.

4 Cited by Silvia Vegetti Finzi, "Female identity between sexuality and maternity," in Bock and James, eds, *Beyond Equality and Difference*, 128.

5 Sheila Rowbotham, "The women's movement and organising for socialism," in S. Rowbotham, L. Segal and H. Wainwright, *Beyond the Fragments: Feminism and the making of socialism* (London: Newcastle Socialist Centre and Islington Community Press, 1979), 61.

6 Hanna F. Pitkin, *The Concept of Representation* (Berkeley: University of California Press, 1967), 226.

7 See Shane Phelan's discussion of the way that lesbian feminists in the United States came to reject liberalism. *Identity Politics: Lesbian Feminism and the Limits of Community* (Philadelphia: Temple University Press, 1989).

8 See Susan Mendus, *Toleration and the Limits of Liberalism* (London: Macmillan, 1989).

9 I do not know if this is intrinsic to tolerance, but I suspect it is. If we could imagine a world in which difference was genuinely detached from power – in which there really were multiple differences

and none carried more weight than any other – than I am not sure we would be talking of the need for toleration. See also Kirstie McClure, "Difference, Diversity and The Limits of Toleration," *Political Theory* 18:3 (1990).

10   I owe this formulation to Peter Jones's paper "Groups, Beliefs and Identities," presented at the European Consortium for Political Research, Leiden, April 1993.

11   All these points can be found in Cynthia V. Ward, "The Limits of 'Liberal Republicanism,': Why Group-Based Remedies And Republican Citizenship Don't Mix," *Columbia Law Review* 91:3 (1991). In querying the notion that *only* the members of particular disadvantaged groups can understand or represent their interests, she might usefully turn this question round to ask whether such understanding or representation is possible without the presence of *any* members of the disadvantaged groups.

12   Susan Mendus, "Losing the Faith: Feminism and Democracy" in John Dunn, ed., *Democracy: The Unfinished Journey 508BC to AD1993* (Oxford: Oxford University Press, 1992), 216.

13   Charles Taylor, *The Ethics of Authenticity* (Cambridge, Mass.: Harvard University Press, 1992); Charles Taylor and Amy Gutmann, *Multiculturalism and The Politics of Recognition* (Cambridge, Mass: Harvard University Press, 1992).

14   Cass Sunstein, "Beyond the Republican Revival," *Yale Law Journal* 97:8 (1988).

15   William Connolly, *Identity/Difference: Democratic Negotiations of Political Paradox* (Ithaca: Cornell University Press, 1991).

16   Connolly, 197.

17   Connolly, 211.

18   Connolly, 213.

19   In a review of Connolly's book, Iris Young describes his prescriptions as "therapies." *Political Theory* 20:3 (1992): 514.

20   Adriana Cavarero, "Equality and sexual difference: amnesia in political thought," in Bock and James, eds, *Beyond Equality and Difference*, 36.

21   Phelan *Identity Politics*. Phelan notes in particular the rows that broke out over sado-masochism, and whether this was an "acceptable" part of lesbian identity.

22   See the essays in Tariq Modood, *Not Easy Being British: colour, culture and citizenship* (Stoke on Trent: Runnymede Trust and Trentham Books, 1992). The largest non-white group in Britain is Asians of Indian origin, many of whom have felt the racial dualism of anti-racist politics rendered them invisible.

23   Phelan, *Identity Politics*, 170.

24   Stuart Hall, "New Ethnicities," in J. Donald and A. Rattansi, eds, *'Race', Culture and Difference* (London: Sage and Open University Press, 1992).

25   Hall, 254.

26   Obvious examples include the post-war preoccupation with full employment as a condition for equal citizenship, where full employment was either unthinkingly equated with full employment for men, or else extended formally to include women without any serious consideration of the structural changes that would then become necessary to re-order the relationship between paid and unpaid work. Will Kymlicka provides a different example in his discussion of the Trudeau reforms which set out to promote more equal citizenship in Canada, but equated full and equal participation for the native Indian population with a color-blind constitution that would dismantle the system of segregated reserves. Though widely applauded by the country's media and even opposition parties, the proposals had to be withdrawn in the face of almost unanimous opposition from the Indians themselves. Kymlicka, *Liberalism, Community and Culture* (Oxford: Clarendon Press, 1989).

27   Modood, *Not Easy Being British*, 29.

28   For an excellent overview of these debates, and an attempt to push beyond them, see the essays in Donald and Rattansi, eds, *'Race', Culture and Difference*.

29   Floya Anthias and Nira Yuval-Davies, *Racialized Boundaries: Race, Nation, Gender, Colour and Class and the Anti-Racist Struggle* (London: Routledge, 1992), 192.

30   S. Issacharoff, "Polarized Voting and the Political Process: the Transformation of Voting Rights Jurisprudence," *Michigan Law Review* 90:7 (1992): 1855.

31   Bernard Grofman and Chandler Davidson, eds, *Controversies in Minority Voting: The Voting Rights Act in Perspective* (Washington DC: The Brookings Institution, 1992) provides a comprehensive range of the arguments that have developed around minority representation.

32   Lani Guinier, "The Triumph of Tokenism: The Voting Rights Act and The Theory of Black Electoral Success," *Michigan Law Review* 89:5 (1991); "No Two Seats: The Elusive Quest for Political Equality," *Virginia Law Review* 77:8 (1991). 1 discuss this material at greater length in "Political Inclusion and Political Presence. Or, Why Does It Matter Who Our Representatives Are?" (Paper presented at the Joint Sessions of the European Consortium on Political Research, Leiden, 2–7 April, 1993).

33   Think here of the Nigerian civil war and the attempted secession of Biafra. The Ibo people who provided the ethnic basis for Biafra only came into substantial existence as a unified 'people' through this war.

34   See especially Chinua Achebe's novels and essays, especially *The Anthills of The Savannah* and *The Trouble With Nigeria.*

Chapter 15

In Defence of Nationality

David Miller

My story begins on the river bank of Kenneth Grahame's imagination.

> 'And beyond the Wild Wood again?' [asked the Mole]: 'Where it's all blue and dim, and one sees what may be hills or perhaps they mayn't, and something like the smoke of towns, or is it only cloud drift?'
>
> 'Beyond the Wild Wood comes the Wide World,' [said the Rat]. 'And that's something that doesn't matter, either to you or me. I've never been there, and I'm never going, nor you either, if you've got any sense at all. Don't ever refer to it again, please.'[1]

The Rat, so very sound in his opinions about most things, boats especially, seems in this moment to reveal exactly what so many people find distasteful about national loyalties and identities. He displays no overt hostility to foreign lands and their ways. But the combination of wilful ignorance about places beyond the Wild Wood, and complete indifference to what is going on there, seems particularly provoking. Aggressive nationalism of the 'my country right or wrong' variety is something we might at least argue with. But the narrowing of horizons, the contraction of the universe of experience to the river bank itself, seems to amount to the triumph of sentiment over reasoned argument.

Philosophers, especially, will have great difficulty in coming to grips with the kind of national attachments for which I am using the Rat's riverbankism as an emblem. Philosophers are committed to forms of reasoning, to concepts and arguments, that are universal in form. 'What's so special about this river bank?' a philosophical Mole might have asked in reply. 'Why is this river bank a better place than other river banks beyond the Wood?' To which the Rat could only have said. 'This is *my* place; I like it here; I have no need to ask such questions.'

The Rat, clearly, is no philosopher. Yet in contemplating his frame of mind we might be led to recall the words of one who was:

> ... there are in *England*, in particular, many honest gentlemen, who being always employ'd in their domestic affairs, or amusing themselves in common recreations, have carried their thoughts little beyond those objects, which are every day expos'd to their senses. And indeed, of such as these I pretend not to make philosophers ... They do well to keep themselves in their present situation; and instead of refining them into philosophers, I wish we cou'd communicate to our founders of systems, a share of this gross earthy mixture, as an ingredient, which they commonly stand much in need of, and which wou'd serve to temper those fiery particles, of which they are composed.[2]

Plainly the Rat is well supplied with gross earthy mixture, literally and metaphorically, and the question is whether any philosophical system can make use of what he has to offer. The sort that can is the Humean sort. By this I mean a philosophy which, rather than dismissing ordinary beliefs and sentiments out of hand unless they can be shown to have a rational foundation, leaves them in place until strong arguments are produced for rejecting them. The Rat's beliefs cannot be deduced from some universally accepted premise; but that is no reason for rejecting them unless the arguments for doing so seem better founded than the beliefs themselves. In moral and political philosophy, in particular, we build upon existing sentiments and judgements, correcting them only when they are inconsistent or plainly flawed in some other way. We don't aspire to some universal and rational foundation such as Kant tried to provide with the categorical imperative.

It is from this sort of stance (which I shall not try to justify) that it makes sense to mount a philosophical defence of nationality. There can be no question of trying to give rationally compelling reasons for people to have national attachments and allegiances. What we can do is to start from the premise that people generally do exhibit such attachments and allegiances, and then try to build a political philosophy which incorporates them. In particular we can do two things: we can examine the critical arguments directed against nationality – arguments trying to undermine the validity of national loyalties – and show that they are flawed; and we can try to assuage the tension between the ethical particularism implied by such commitments and ethical universalism, by showing why it may be advantageous, from a universal point of view, that people have national loyalties.[3]

Philosophers may protest that it is a caricature of their position to suggest that the only reasons for belief or action that they will permit to count are those that derive from an entirely impersonal and universal stand-point. It is common now to distinguish between agent-neutral and agent-relative reasons and to give each some weight in practical reasoning.[4] But what motivates this concession is mainly a concern for individuals' private goals and for their integrity: people must be given the moral space, as it were, to pursue their own projects, to honour their commitments, to live up to their personal ideals. National allegiances, and the obligations that spring from them, are harder to fit into this picture, because they appear to represent, not a different segment of moral life, but a competing way of understanding the concepts and principles that make up the impartial or agent-neutral stand-point (consider, for example, the different conceptions of distributive justice that emerge depending on whether you begin from a national or a universal starting-point). That is why such loyalties appear to pose a head-on challenge to a view of morality that is dominant in our culture, as Alasdair MacIntyre has argued.[5]

It is a curious paradox of our time that while nationalism is politically on the advance, its would-be defenders (in the West at least) find themselves on the defensive. I have just given one reason for this: the view that national allegiances cannot withstand critical scrutiny, so a rational person cannot be a nationalist. There is also a more mundane reason: nationality is widely felt to be a backward-looking, reactionary notion; it is felt to stand in the way of progress. In the European context, for instance, we are invited to look forward to a 'Europe of the regions' in which Catalonia, Brittany, Bavaria, Scotland and the rest co-exist harmoniously under a common administrative umbrella, free from the national rivalries which have plunged us into two world wars. Progress means the overcoming of nationality. In the Oxford branch of the Body Shop (and doubtless in the branches in Paris, Tokyo, and elsewhere) you can buy a lapel badge that quotes H. G. Wells: 'Our true nationality is mankind.' H. G. Wells and the Body Shop in tandem epitomise the modern idea of progress, whose disciples were described by George Orwell in such a wonderfully acid way: 'all that dreary tribe of high-minded women and sandal-wearers and bearded fruit-juice drinkers who come flocking towards the smell of "progress" like bluebottles to a dead cat'.[6] If you are one of these bluebottles, and most of us are to some degree, then you will think that ordinary national loyalties amount to reactionary nostalgia and queue up to sport the H. G. Wells slogan.

So the would-be nationalist has two challenges to meet: the philosophical challenge and the progressive challenge. And now it is time to spell out more precisely the notion of nationality that I want to defend.[7] Nationality as I shall understand it comprises three interconnected propositions. The first concerns personal identity, and claims that it may properly be part of someone's identity that they belong to this or that national grouping; in other words that if a person is invited to specify those elements that are essential to his identity, that make him the person that he is, it is in order to refer to nationality. A person who in answer to the question 'Who are you?' says 'I am Swedish' or 'I am Italian' (and doubtless much more besides) is not saying something that is irrelevant or bizarre in the same way as, say, someone who claims without good evidence that he is the illegitimate grandchild of Tsar Nicholas II. Note that the claim is a permissive one: national identity may, but need not, be a constitutive part of personal identity.

The second proposition is ethical, and claims that nations are ethical communities. They are contour lines in the ethical landscape. The duties we owe to our fellow-nationals are different from, and more extensive than, the duties we owe to human beings as such. This is not to say that we owe *no* duties to humans as such; nor is it to deny that there may be other, perhaps smaller and more intense, communities to whose members we owe duties that are more stringent still than those we owe to Britons, Swedes, etc at large. But it is to claim that a proper account of ethics should give weight to national boundaries, and that in particular there is no objection in principle to institutional schemes that are designed to deliver benefits exclusively to those who fall within the same boundaries as ourselves.

The third proposition is political, and states that people who form a national community in a particular territory have a good claim to political self-determination; there ought to be put in place an institutional structure that enables them to decide collectively matters that concern primarily their own community. Notice that I have phrased this cautiously, and have not asserted that the institution must be that of a sovereign state. Historically the sovereign state has been the main vehicle through which claims to national self-determination have been realised, and this is not just an accident. Nevertheless national self-determination *can* be realised in other ways, and as we shall see there are cases where it must be realised other than through a sovereign state, precisely to meet the equally good claims of other nationalities.

I want to stress that the three propositions I have outlined – about personal identity, about bounded duties and about political self-determination – are linked together in such a way that it is difficult to feel the force of any one of them without acknowledging the others. It is not hard to see how a common identity can support both the idea of the nation as an ethical community and the claim to self-determination, but what is more subtle – and I shall try to bring this out as I go along – is the way in which the political claim can reinforce both the claim about identity and the ethical claim. The fact that the community in question is either actually or potentially self-determining strengthens its claims on us both as a source of identity and as a source of obligation. This interlinking of propositions may at times seem circular; and the fact that the nationalist case cannot be spelt out in neat linear form may confirm philosophical suspicions about it. But I believe that if we are to understand the power of nationality as an idea in the modern world – the appeal of national identity to the modern self – we must try to understand its inner logic.

So let me now begin to look more closely at national identities themselves, and in particular ask what differentiates them from other identities – individual or communal – that people may have. What does it mean to think of oneself as belonging to a national community?

The first point to note, and it has been noted by most of those who have thought seriously about the subject, is that national communities are constituted by belief: a nationality exists when its members believe that it does. It is not a question of a group of people sharing some common attribute such as race or language. These features do not of themselves make nations, and only become important in so far as a particular nationality takes as one of its defining features that its members speak French or have black skins. This becomes clear as soon as one looks at the candidates that have been put forward as objective criteria of nationhood, as Ernest Renan did in his famous lecture on the subject:[8] to every criterion that has been proposed there are clear empirical counter-examples. The conclusion one quickly reaches is that a nation is in Renan's memorable phrase 'a daily plebiscite'; its existence depends on a shared belief that its members belong together, and a shared wish to continue their life in common. So in asserting a national identity, I assume that my beliefs and commitments are mirrored by those who I take to share that identity, and of course I might be wrong about this. In itself this does not distinguish nationality from other kinds of human relationship that depend on reciprocal belief.

The second feature of nationality is that it is an identity that embodies historical continuity. Nations stretch backwards into the past, and indeed in most cases their origins are conveniently lost in the mists of time. In the course of this history various significant events have occurred, and we can identify with the actual people who acted at those moments, reappropriating their deeds as our own. Often these events involve military victories and defeats: we imagine ourselves filling the breach at Harfleur or reading the signal hoisted at Trafalgar. Renan thinks that historical tragedies matter more than historical glories. I am inclined to see in this an under-standable French bias, but the point he connects to it is a good one: 'sorrows have greater value than victories; for they impose duties and demand common effort.'[9] The historic national community is a community of obligation. Because our fore-bears have toiled and spilt their blood to build and defend the nation, we who are born into it inherit an obligation to continue their work, which we discharge partly towards our contemporaries and partly towards our descendants. The historical community stretches forward into the future too. This then means that when we speak of the nation as an ethical community, we have in mind not merely the kind of community that exists between a group of contemporaries who practise mutual aid among themselves and which would dissolve at the point at which that practice ceased; but a community which, because it stretches back and forward across the generations, is not one that the present generation can renounce. Here we begin to see something of the depth of national communities which may not be shared by other more immediate forms of association.

The third distinguishing aspect of national identity is that it is an active identity. Nations are communities that do things together, take decisions, achieve results, and so forth. Of course this cannot be literally so: we rely on proxies who are seen as embodying the national will: statesmen, soldiers, sportsmen, etc. But this means that the link between past and future that I noted a moment ago is not merely a causal link. The nation becomes what it does by the decisions that it takes – some of which we may now regard as thoroughly bad, a cause of national shame. Whether this active identity is a valuable aspect of nationality, or whether as some critics would allege merely a damaging fantasy, it clearly does mark out nations from other kinds of grouping, for instance churches or religious sects whose identity is essen-tially a passive one in so far as the church is seen as responding to the promptings of God. The group's purpose is not to do or decide things, but to interpret as best it can the messages and commands of an external source.

The fourth aspect of a national identity is that it connects a group of people to a particular geographical place, and here again there is a clear contrast with most other group identities that people affirm, such as ethnic or religious identities. These often have sacred sites or places of origin, but it is not an essential part of having the identity that you should permanently occupy that place. If you are a good Muslim you should make a pilgrimage to Mecca at least once, but you need not set up house there. A nation, in contrast, must have a homeland. This may of course be a source of great difficulties, a point I shall return to when considering objections to the idea of nationality, but it also helps to explain why a national community must be (in aspiration if not yet in fact) a political community. We have seen already that nations are groups that act; we see now that their actions must include that of controlling a chunk of the earth's surface. It is this territorial element that makes nations uniquely suited to serve as the basis of states, since a state by definition must exercise its authority over a geographical area.

Finally it is essential to national identity that the people who compose the nation are believed to share certain traits that mark them off from other peoples. It is incompatible with nationality to think of the members of the nation as people who merely happen to have been thrown together in one place and forced to share a common fate, in the way that the occupants of a lifeboat, say, have been accidentally thrown together. National divisions must be natural ones; they must correspond to real differences between peoples. This need not, fortunately, imply racism or the idea that the group is constituted by biological descent. The common traits can be cultural in character: they can consist in shared values, shared tastes or sensibilities. So immigration need not pose problems, provided only that the immigrants take on the essential elements of national character. Indeed it has proved possible in some instances to regard immigration as itself a formative experience, calling forth qualities of resourcefulness and mutual aid that then define the national character – I am thinking of the settler cultures of the New World such as the American and the Australian. As everyone knows, there is nothing more illustrious for an Australian today than to have an ancestor who was carried over in chains by the First Fleet.

When I say that national differences must be natural ones, I mean that the people who compose a nation must believe that there is something distinctive about them-selves that marks them off from other nations, over and above the fact of sharing common institutions. This need not be one specific trait or quality, but a range of characteristics which are generally shared by the members of nation A and serve to differentiate them from outsiders. In popular belief these differences may be exag-gerated. Hume remarked that the vulgar think that everyone who belongs to a nation displays its distinctive traits, whereas 'men of sense' allow for exceptions; nevertheless aggregate differences undoubtedly exist.[10] This is surely correct. It is also worth noting that people may be hard pressed to say explicitly what the national character of their people consists in, and yet have an intuitive sense when con-fronted with foreigners of where the differences lie.[11] National identities can remain unarticulated, and yet still exercise a pervasive influence on people's behaviour.

These five elements together – a community constituted by mutual belief, extended in history, active in character, connected to a particular territory, and thought to be marked off from other communities by its members' distinct traits – serve to distinguish nationality from other collective sources of personal identity. I shall come in a moment to some reasons why such identities may be thought to be particularly valuable, worth protecting and fostering, but first I should empha-sise what has so far merely been implicit, namely the mythical aspects of national identity. Nations almost unavoidably depend on beliefs about themselves that do not stand up well to impartial scrutiny. Renan once again hit the nail on the head when he said that 'to forget and – I will venture to say – to get one's history wrong, are essential factors in the making of a nation'.[12] One main reason for this is that the contingencies of power politics have always played a large part in the formation of national units. States have been created by force, and, over time, their subject peoples have come to think of themselves as co-nationals. But no-one wants to think of himself as roped together to a set of people merely because the territorial ambitions of some dynastic lord in the thirteenth century ran thus far and no further. Nor indeed is this the right way to think about the matter, because the effect of the ruler's conquests may have been, over time, to have produced a people with real cultural unity. But because of the historical dimension of the nation, together with the idea that each nation has its own distinct character, it is uncomfortable to be reminded of the forced nature of one's national genesis. Hence various stories have been concocted about the primeval tribe from which the modern nation sprang. The problem is, of course, particularly acute in the case of states created relatively recently as a result of colonial withdrawal, where it is only too obviously the case that the boundaries that have been drawn reflect the vagaries of imperial competition. It is easy for academic critics to mock the attempts made by the leaders of these states to instil a sense of common nationhood in their people. I myself recall, when teaching in Nigeria in the mid-1970s, reading with some amusement earnest newspaper articles on the question whether the country did or did not need a national ideology – it seeming obvious that a national ideology was not something you could just decide to adopt.

The real question, however, is not whether national identities embody elements of myth, but whether they perform such valuable functions that our attitude, as philosophers, should be one of acquiescence if not positive endorsement. And here I want to argue that nationality answers one of the most pressing needs of the modern world, namely how to maintain solidarity among the populations of states that are large and anonymous, such that their citizens cannot possibly enjoy the kind of community that relies on kinship or face-to-face interaction.[13] That we need such solidarity is something that I intend to take for granted here.[14] I assume that in societies in which economic markets play a central role, there is a strong tendency towards social atomisation, where each person looks out for the interests of herself and her immediate social network. As a result it is potentially difficult to mobilise people to provide collective goods, it is difficult to get them to agree to practices of redistribution from which they are not likely personally to benefit, and so forth. These problems can be avoided only where there exists large-scale solidarity, such that people feel themselves to be members of an overarching community, and to have social duties to act for the common good of that community, to help out other members when they are in need, etc.

Nationality is *de facto* the main source of such solidarity. In view of the broadly Humean approach that I am adopting, where our moral and political philosophy bends to accommodate pre-existing sentiments, this in itself would be enough to commend it. But I should like to say something more positive about nationality before coming to the difficulties. It is precisely because of the mythical or imaginary elements in national identity that it can be reshaped to meet new challenges and new needs. We have seen that the story a nation tells itself about its past is a selective one. Depending on the character of contemporary politics, the story may gradually alter, and with it our understanding of the substance of national identity. This need not take the crude form of rewriting of history as practised in the late Soviet Union and elsewhere (airbrushing pictures of Trotsky out of the Bolshevik central committee and so on). It may instead be a matter of looking at established facts in a new way. Consider, as just one example, the very different interpretation of British imperialism now current from that which prevailed at the time of my father's birth in Edwardian Britain. The tone has changed from one of triumphalism to one of equivocation or even mild apology. And this goes naturally along with a new interpretation of British identity in which it is no longer part of that identity to shoulder the white man's burden and carry enlightenment to the heathen.

From a political stand-point, this imaginary aspect of nationality may be a source of strength. It allows people of different political persuasions to share a political loyalty, defining themselves against a common background whose outlines are not precise, and which therefore lends itself to competing interpretations. It also shows us why nationality is not a conservative idea. A moment's glance at the historical record shows that nationalist ideas have as often been associated with liberal and socialist programmes as with programmes of the right. In their first appearance, they were often associated with liberal demands for representative government put forward in opposition to established ruling elites. Linda Colley's studies of the emergence of British nationalism in the late 18th and early 19th centuries show that nationalist ideas were developed by middle class and popular movements seeking to win a place in the public realm, and resisted by the state and the landowning class that supported it.[15] This picture was repeated in its essentials throughout Europe.[16] It is easy to see why a conservative may resist nationalism.[17] Nationality invokes the activist idea of a people collectively determining its own destiny, and this is anathema to the conservative view of politics as a limited activity best left in the hands of an elite who have been educated to rule. Two of the most swingeing of recent attacks on nationalism have come from acolytes of Michael Oakeshott, Elie Kedourie and Kenneth Minogue.[18] Minogue regards nationalism as essentially a revolutionary theory and 'therefore a direct enemy of conservative politics'. He offers a reductive psychological explanation of its appeal: 'Nationalist theories may thus be understood as distortions of reality which allow men to cope with situations which they might otherwise find unbearable'.[19]

Nationality, then, is associated with no particular social programme: the flexible content of national identity allows parties of different colours to present their programmes as the true continuation of the national tradition and the true reflection of national character.[20] At the same time it binds these parties together and makes space for the idea of loyal opposition, an individual or faction who resist prevailing policy but who can legitimately claim to speak for the same community as the government of the day. But its activist idea of politics as the expression of national will does set it against conservatism of the Oakeshott-Kedourie-Minogue variety.

I have referred to the liberal origins of the idea of nationality, but the first objection that I want to consider amounts essentially to a liberal critique of nationality. This holds that nationality is detrimental to the cultural pluralism that liberals hold dear; it is incompatible with the idea of a society in which different cultural traditions are accorded equal respect, and whose vitality springs from competition and exchange between these traditions. The classic statement of this critique can be found in Lord Acton's essay on 'Nationality' in which he argues in favour of a multi-national state in which no one nation holds a dominant place.[21] Such a state, he claims, provides the best guarantee of liberties, 'the fullest security for the preservation of local customs' and the best incentive to intellectual progress.

This argument derives from the assumption that national identities are exclusive in their nature; that where a state embodies a single nationality, the culture that makes up that nationality must drive out everything else. There is no reason to hold this assumption. Nationality is not of its nature an all-embracing identity. It need not extend to all the cultural attributes that a person might display. So one can avow a national identity and also have attachments to several more specific cultural groups: to ethnic groups, religious groups, work-based associations and so on and so forth. A line can be drawn between the beliefs and qualities that make up nationality, and those that fall outside its scope. The place where the line is drawn will be specific to a particular nationality at a particular time, and it will be a subject for debate whether its present position is appropriate or not. For instance one may argue in a liberal direction that a person's religion, say, should be irrelevant to their membership of this nation, or argue in a nationalist direction that language is not irrelevant, that each member should at least be fluent in the national tongue. The Acton argument supposes that no such line can be drawn. It supposes, contrary to all evidence, that one cannot have a pluralist society in which many ethnic, religious etc groups co-exist but with an overarching national identity in common.

Indeed one can turn Acton's argument around, as J. S. Mill did by anticipation in his chapter on Nationality in *Representative Government*. Unless the several groups that compose a society have the mutual sympathy and trust that stems from a common nationality, it will be virtually impossible to have free institutions. There will, for instance, be no common interest in stemming the excesses of government; politics becomes a zero-sum game in which each group can hope to gain by the exploitation of the others.

This was Mill's argument, and there is plenty of subsequent evidence to back it up. But I want now to consider a more subtle variation on the theme that nationality and liberalism are at odds. This concedes that national identity and group identity can be kept separate, but points to the fact that national identities are always in practice biased in favour of the dominant cultural group, the group that historically has dominated the politics of the state. The state may be liberal in the sense that it does not suppress minority groups, but it does not accord equal respect and equal treatment to cultural minorities. Practical examples of this would include what is prescribed in the curricula in state-run schools, the content of what is broadcast through the national media, and so forth. The national identity includes elements drawn from the dominant culture, this is reproduced politically through the state, and minority groups are put at a disadvantage both in various practical respects and in the less tangible sense that their cultures are devalued by public neglect.

Concrete versions of this critique will be familiar to most readers. I want to reply to it first by conceding that it is descriptively true in many historical cases – national identities have very often been formed by taking over elements from the group culture that happens to be dominant in a particular state – but then adding that it is not integral to national identities that they should be loaded in this way. I have stressed the malleability of nationality already, and one thing we may be doing in the course of redefining what it means to be British, French, etc is to purge these identities of elements that necessarily entail the exclusion of minority groups. Here there is one particular aspect of nationality that needs underlining. Although in standard cases a national identity is something one is born into – and I have argued that this factor of historical continuity is a source of strength – there is no reason why others should not acquire it by adoption. In this respect it contrasts with ethnic identities which generally speaking can only be acquired by birth. Although a priori a nation might define itself tightly by descent, in practice nations extend member-ship more or less freely to those who are resident and show willingness to exhibit those traits that make up national character. So although this does impose certain constraints on them, minority groups, particularly those migrating to the society in question, have the option of acquiring a new identity alongside their existing ones. Nationality, precisely because it aims to be an *inclusive* identity, can incorpo-rate sub-groups in this way without demanding that they forsake everything they already hold dear.

Indeed one can take this further and say that what best meets the needs of minor-ity groups is a clear and distinct national identity which stands over and above the specific cultural traits of all the groups in the society in question. The argument here has been well put by Tariq Modood, who has particularly in mind the position of Muslims in British society. He writes:

> As a matter of fact the greatest psychological and political need for clarity about a common framework and national symbols comes from the minorities. For clarity about what makes us willingly bound into a single country relieves the pressure on minorities, especially new minorities whose presence within the country is not fully accepted, to have to conform in all areas of social life, or in arbitrarily chosen areas, in order to rebut the charge of disloyalty. It is the absence of comprehensively respected national symbols in Britain, comparable to the constitution and the flag in America, that allows politicians unsympathetic to minorities to demand that they demonstrate loyalty by doing x or y or z, like supporting the national cricket team in Norman Tebbit's famous example.[22]

To make my position clear here, I do not suppose that the superimposition of national identity on group identity that I am arguing for can be wholly painless on either side. While national identities are thinned down to make them more accept-able to minority groups, these groups themselves must abandon values and ways of behaving that are in stark conflict with those of the community as a whole. National identity cannot be wholly symbolic; it must embody substantive norms. This will be readily apparent if a formal constitution occupies a central place in such an identity, as I believe it should. Forms of belief and behaviour inconsistent with those laid down in the constitution will be ruled out. So, as I have argued elsewhere,[23] one cannot aspire to unlimited tolerance in this area. But the view I am defending does appear consistent with the kind of politically sensitive liberalism exhibited by J. S. Mill.

This, I hope, sufficiently addresses the liberal objection to nationality. Now I want to come to a second objection which might be termed the Balkan objection. This claims that the principle of nationality cannot in practice be realised, but meanwhile the belief that it can leads to endless political instability and bloodshed. This is because would-be nationalities are so entangled with one another that there is no way of drawing state boundaries that can possibly satisfy all claims. Minority group B secedes from state A in search of national self-determination, but this only pro-vokes group C *within* B to attempt secession in its turn and so on *ad infinitum*. I call this the Balkan objection because of a view one frequently hears expressed nowadays that so long as the peoples of that region were governed from afar by the Austro-Hungarian and Turkish empires, different ethnic groups lived and worked happily side-by-side, but once those empires were weakened and the idea of national self-determination was let loose, impossible conflicts were generated.[24] Recent events in Yugoslavia seem to confirm the view, and any day now I expect to hear President Tito's reputation being salvaged on the same terms as that of Emperor Franz Joseph.

The principle of nationality as formulated earlier holds that people who form a national community in a particular territory have a good claim to political self-determination. This principle should not be confused with a certain liberal view of the state which makes individual consent a necessary and sufficient condition of a state's authority. If each person must consent to the existence of the state, it follows that the borders of states should be drawn wherever people want them to be drawn. The practical implication is that any sub-community in any state has the right to secede from that state provided that it is in turn willing to allow any sub-sub-community the equivalent right and so on indefinitely.[25] This view confronts the Balkan problem in its most acute form: where populations are intermingled, con-sistent application of the consent principle points directly towards an anarchic outcome in which no stable frontiers can be established.

The principle of nationality is quite different from this. Central to the idea of nationality is not individual *will*, but individual *identity*, even though some formu-lations confuse these two – Renan's idea of the nation as 'a daily plebiscite' which I cited earlier is *in this respect* misleading. When we encounter a group or com-munity dissatisfied with current political arrangements the question to ask is not 'Does this group now want to secede from the existing state?' but 'Does the group have a collective identity which is or has become incompatible with the national identity of the majority in the state?' There are broadly three answers that might be given to this question. First it may turn out that the dissatisfied group is an ethnic group which feels that materially speaking it is not getting a fair deal from the existing set-up and/or that its group identity is not being properly respected in national life. Black Americans would exemplify this: what is needed in such cases is domestic political reform, perhaps of a quite radical and painful kind, not dreams of secession. Second, the group may have a national identity, but one that is not radically incompatible with the identity of the majority community, there being common elements as well as elements of difference. The dissenting group thinks of itself as sharing a common historical identity with the majority, but also as having its own distinct national character which is currently not recognised.[26] This may (I say this with some trepidation) represent the position of the Scots and Welsh in Britain, or the Bretons in France, and the appropriate outcome is again not outright secession (which violates the shared identity) but a constitutional arrangement which gives the sub-community rights of self-determination in those areas of decision which are especially central to its own sense of nationhood.

Finally there are cases where the state as presently constituted contains two or more nations with radically incompatible identities. The reason for this might be that one community takes as constitutive of its identity some feature such as language or race not shared with the others, or that its historical self-understanding includes military conquest of the territory now occupied by the second community, or some other such factor. In these cases there is no realistic possibility of formulating a shared identity, and the minority group has a prima case for secession. But to make the case a conclusive one, further conditions must be met.[27] First, there has to be some way of redrawing the borders such that two viable states are created and this in itself may pose insoluble problems. Second, the territory claimed by the seceding community should not contain minorities whose own identity is radically incompatible with the new majority's, so that rather than creating a genuine nation-state, the secession would simply reproduce a multi-national arrangement on a smaller scale. Third, some consideration must be given to small groups who may be left behind in the rump state; it may be that the effect of secession is to destroy a political balance and leave these groups in a very weak position. It is, for instance, a strong argument against the secession of Quebec from the Canadian federation that it would effectively destroy the double-sided identity that Canada has laboured to achieve, and leave French-speaking communities in other provinces isolated and politically helpless.

What I am trying to stress is that the principle of nationality does not generate an unlimited right of secession. What it says is that national self-determination is a good thing, and that states and their constitutions should be arranged so that each nation is as far as possible able to secure its common future. Since homogeneous nation-states are not everywhere feasible, often this will require second-best solutions, where each nationality gets partial self-determination, not full rights of sovereignty. Equally, there may be cases where communities are intertwined in such a way that no form of national self-determination is realistically possible, and the best that can be hoped for is a modus vivendi between the communities, perhaps with a constitutional settlement guaranteed by external powers.

That, somewhat elliptically, is my answer to the Balkan objection. The final objection I want to consider arises from the second aspect of the idea of nationality, the claim that nations are ethical communities. It runs as follows. You say that nations are ethically significant, that the duties we owe to fellow-members are greater in scope than those we owe to outsiders. You ground this in a shared sense of identity which is based not upon concrete practices but upon sentimental ties, on historical understandings which you have conceded to be imaginary in part. But how can duties of justice, especially, depend in this way on our feelings about others? Does this not make justice an entirely subjective idea, and abandon its role as a critical notion which serves to correct both our beliefs and our behaviour?

Observe to begin with that our sense of national identity serves to mark out the universe of persons to whom special duties are owed; it may do this without at the same time determining the content of those duties. In particular my recognition of X as a co-national to whom I have obligations may depend upon a sense of nationality with sentimental content, but it does not follow that my duties to X depend on my feelings about X as a person. An analogy with the family makes this clear. A family does not exist as such unless its members have certain feelings towards one another, yet obligations within the family are not governed by sentiment. I may feel more sympathy for one child than another, yet in allocating the family's resources I ought to consider their needs impartially.

It appears nonetheless that obligations in this account are being derived from the existence of a certain kind of community, while in the national case the community is sentiment-based. It would follow that if nation A embodies a strong sense of fellow-feeling whereas nation B embodies a relatively weak sense, then obligations within A are more extensive than those within B, and this seems paradoxical. What this overlooks, however, is the role played by political culture within national identity. It is not merely that I feel bound to a group of people defined in national terms; I feel bound to them as sharing in a certain way of life, expressed in the public culture. The content of my obligations stems immediately from that culture. Various interpretations of the public culture are possible, but some of these will be closer to getting it right than others, and this also shows to what extent debates about social justice are resolvable. It follows that what social justice consists in will vary from place to place, but not directly in line with sentiments or feelings. A Swede will acknowledge more extensive obligations to provide welfare for fellow-Swedes than an American will for fellow-Americans; but this is because the public culture of Sweden, defining in part what it means to be Swedish, is solidaristic, whereas the public culture of the US is individualistic. It is not part of the story that Swedes must have more sympathetic feelings for other individual Swedes than Americans do for other Americans.

This may still sound an uncomfortably relativistic view to some. What I have argued is that nationalists are not committed to the kind of crude subjectivism which says that your communal obligations are whatever you feel them to be. Membership of a national community involves identifying with a public culture that is external to each of us taken individually; and although we may argue with one another about how the culture should be understood, and what practical obligations stem from it, this is still a question to which better or worse answers can be given.

Philosophers may find it restricting that they have to conduct their arguments about justice with reference to national identities at all. My claim is that unless they do they will lose contact entirely with the beliefs of the people they seek to address; they must try to incorporate some of Hume's gross earthy mixture, the unreflective beliefs of everyday life. Nonetheless there is a tension here. We should return to Kenneth Grahame's Rat who on his first appearance seems to stand for unlimited acquiescence in the everyday world of the river bank. As the story draws towards its conclusion, however, a more troubled Rat emerges. Disturbed first by the departure of the swallows to Southern climes, he then encounters a seafaring Rat who regales him with tales of the colourful and vibrant world beyond the river bank. The Rat is mesmerised. His eyes, normally 'clear and dark and brown' turn to 'a streaked and shifting grey'. He is about to set out for the South with stick and satchel in hand, and has to be physically restrained by the Mole, who gradually leads his thoughts back to the everyday world, and finally leaves him writing poetry as a kind of sublimation of his wandering instincts.

The Rat's earlier refusal to contemplate the Wide World, it emerges, was a wilful repression of a part of himself that it was dangerous to acknowledge. Something of the same dilemma confronts the philosophical nationalist. He feels the pull of national loyalties, and he senses that without these loyalties we would be cast adrift in a region of great moral uncertainty. Yet he is also alive to the limitations and absurdities of his and other national identities. He recognises that we owe something to other human beings merely as such, and so he strains towards a more rationally defensible foundation for ethics and politics. There is no solution here but to strive for some kind of equilibrium between the everyday and the philosophical, between common belief and rational belief, between the river bank and the Wide World. But, as the cases of both the Rat and of David Hume in their different ways demonstrate, this is far easier said than done.

Notes

1   K. Grahame, *The Wind in the Willows* (London, Methuen, 1926), pp. 16–17.

2   D. Hume, *A Treatise of Human Nature*, ed. L. A. Selby-Bigge, 3rd edn revised P. H. Nidditch (Oxford, Clarendon Press, 1978), p. 272.

3   I have attempted the second especially in 'The Ethical Significance of Nationality', *Ethics*, 98(1987–8), 647–62. I am mainly concerned with the first in the present paper.

4   See for instance T. Nagel, *Equality and Partiality* (New York and Oxford, Oxford University Press, 1991) whose organising idea is the contrast between personal and impersonal ethical standpoints.

5   A. Macintyre, 'Is Patriotism a Virtue?' (Lawrence, University of Kansas, Department of Philosophy, 1984).

6   G. Orwell, *The Road to Wigan Pier* (Harmondsworth, Penguin, 1962), p. 160.

7   I speak of 'nationality' rather than 'nationalism' because the latter term usually carries with it unwelcome assumptions about what nations are entitled to do to advance their interests; however there is no alternative to 'nationalist' as an adjective. An alternative approach would be to follow Neil MacCormick in distinguishing different conceptions of nationalism; like MacCormick's, the conception I want to defend includes the condition that in supporting my nation's interests, I should respect others' national identities (and the claims that follow from them) as well. See N. MacCormick, 'Nation and Nationalism' in *Legal Right and Social Democracy* (Oxford, Clarendon Press, 1982) and N. MacCormick, 'Is Nationalism Philosophically Credible?' in W. Twining (ed.), *Issues of Self-Determination* (Aberdeen, Aberdeen University Press, 1991).

8   E. Renan, 'What is a Nation?' in A. Zimmern (ed.), *Modern Political Doctrines* (London, Oxford University Press, 1939).

9   *Ibid.*, p. 203.

10   D. Hume, 'Of National Characters' in *Essays Moral, Political, and Literary*, ed. E. Miller (Indianapolis, Liberty Classics, 1985), pp. 197–8.

11   'It is only when you meet someone of a different culture from yourself that you begin to realise what your own beliefs really are.' (Orwell, *Wigan Pier*, p. 145).

12   Renan, 'What is a Nation?', p. 190.

13   I should make it clear that this consideration could not be put forward as a reason for having or adopting a national identity. A national identity depends upon a prereflective sense that one belongs within a certain historic group, and it would be absurd to propose to the subjects of state X that because things would go better for them if they adopted a shared national identity, they should therefore conjure one up. The argument points to benefits that national allegiances bring with them as by-products. Others who have defended nationality in this way include B. Barry, 'Self-Government Revisited' in D. Miller and L. Siedentop (eds), *The Nature of Political Theory* (Oxford, Clarendon Press, 1983), reprinted in B. Barry, *Democracy, Power and Justice* (Oxford, Clarendon Press, 1989); and Nagel, *Equality and Partiality*, ch. 15.

14   I have argued this with specific reference to socialism in 'In What Sense Must Socialism Be Communitarian?', *Social Philosophy and Policy*, 6(1988–9), 51–73; but I believe the point holds more generally.

15   See especially L. Colley, 'Whose Nation? Class and National Consciousness in Britain 1750–1830', *Past and Present*, 113 (1986), 97–117.

16   See E. J. Hobsbawm, *Nations and Nationalism since 1780* (Cambridge, Cambridge University Press, 1990).

17   It is also true, however, that conservatives of a different persuasion may embrace national identities as a source of social cohesion and authority; see in particular R. Scruton, 'In Defence of the Nation' in *The Philosopher on Dover Beach* (Manchester, Carcanet, 1990). I hope on another occasion to look more closely at what distinguishes this kind of conservative nationalism from other forms of communitarianism.

18   E. Kedourie, *Nationalism* (London, Hutchinson, 1966); K. Minogue, *Nationalism* (London, Batsford, 1967).

19   Minogue, *Nationalism*, p. 148.

20   There is a fine and suitably controversial example of this in Margaret Thatcher's recent attempt to represent her political views as the logical outcome of British history and national character.

'I always said and believed that the British character is quite different from the characters of people on the Continent – quite different. There is a great sense of fairness and equity in the British people, a great sense of individuality and initiative. They don't like being pushed around. How else did this really rather small people, from the times of Elizabeth on, go out in the larger world and have such an influence upon it? ...

I set out to destroy socialism because I felt it was at odds with the character of the people. We were the first country in the world to roll back the frontiers of socialism, then roll forward the frontiers of freedom. We reclaimed our heritage ...' (M. Thatcher, 'Don't Undo My Work', *Newsweek*, vol. 119, No. 17, April 27 1992, p. 14).

21 Lord Acton, 'Nationality' in *The History of Freedom and other essays*, ed. J. N. Figgis (London, Macmillan, 1907).

22 T. Modood, 'Ethno-Religious Minorities, Secularism and the British State' forthcoming in T. Murphy (ed.), *Religious Freedom in Plural Societies*.

23 D. Miller, 'Socialism and Toleration' in S. Mendus (ed.), *Justifying Toleration* (Cambridge, Cambridge University Press, 1988); *Market, State and Community*, ch. 11.

24 One can find it expressed, for example, in Kedourie, *Nationalism*, chs 6–7.

25 See, for instance, H. Beran, 'A Liberal Theory of Secession', *Political Studies*, 32(1984), 21–31 – though Beran would deny the consequence I wish to infer from this doctrine.

26 If this is allowed, it follows that there can be no simple answer to the question 'How many nations are there in area A?'. Nations are not discrete and easily counted entities like billiard balls. The criteria that I have offered to define them admit of degree, and that is why it is possible to have a smaller nationality nesting within a larger one.

27 The conditions given are intended to be necessary rather than sufficient. I have addressed the issue of justified secession at greater length in 'The Nation-State: a modest defence' forthcoming in C. Brown (ed.), *Political Restructuring in Europe*.

Chapter 16

From Statism to Pluralism

Paul Hirst

The future of socialism is often debated as if socialism had a single past. In the 1980s the radical right have tried to bury socialism. One of their best tactics in doing so has been to identify socialism with the authoritarian states and failing economies of the communist world. Western socialism can then be presented as a lesser version of this greater failure, but sharing essential features of authoritarian collectivism and economic stagnation. Socialism is defined by the right in terms of the triad of collective ownership, state intervention and centralized planning, and it is still defended by some of its supporters in those terms.

The vast majority of socialists, however, recognize the need for a more libertarian political creed compatible with an open society. Some radical revisionists think it necessary to go outside the socialist tradition altogether in order to do so. They embrace the free market and redefine socialism in terms of liberal democratic theory. This is to behave as if there are no *socialist* sources for a libertarian socialism. In fact certain important socialist doctrines have been strongly anti-collectivist and opposed to centralized public ownership. They have also been strongly anti-statist, advocating reliance on the self-governing activities of freely associated individuals. Associational socialism is the most valuable alternative to the undiluted individualism of the free-market right and to the centralist and authoritarian trends in modern society.

1 Associational Socialism

Associational socialism, which flourished between the 1840s and the early 1920s, was a third force in the history of socialism, distinct from both Bolshevism and social democracy. It embraced a variety of movements and ideas, including Proudhon and the mutualist and syndicalist traditions in France; William Morris and the Arts and Crafts movement; and G. D. H. Cole and the Guild Socialists in the UK. Associational socialism often won the battle of ideas, only to lose out to other socialist movements which relied on the more effective means of either electoral or insurrectionary politics. In an era of world wars, big government and highly concentrated industry, associational socialism came to seem an irrelevancy. Its stress on self-government and local autonomy ran counter to a period in which there were strong imperatives to central control. Because it believed in the virtue of voluntary action in civil society, it neglected the forms of political action necessary to create a state sympathetic to such voluntary activity and also failed to compete with other political forces to influence the existing state. The associational socialists were pushed aside by the 1920s. Yet the view of the associational socialist tradition as utopian and unworldly is quite wrong. Associationalism was not inherently impractical, rather it required the right context in which it could become practical politics.

The major wars of this century promoted centralization and bureaucratic control; tendencies inimical to the autonomy of self-governing associations. The wars also gave the political rivals of libertarian socialism the conditions in which to flourish. However, in the 1980s the international environment has changed radically – and perhaps irrevocably – with the end of the second Cold War. The tranformation of east–west politics, the pace of reform in eastern Europe, and the prospect of at least partial demilitarization, all weaken the imperatives for centralized and secretive state security institutions to dominate national politics. A movement that seemed naive in the 1920s can profit from the liberalization of great power politics in the 1980s.

Associational socialism may also benefit from recent economic changes in the west. The imperatives towards the large scale in industrial organization have been perceived to be closely connected with standardized mass production for homogeneous mass markets. However, since the OPEC oil price shock and the consequent world depression of the early 1970s markets have both internationalized and differentiated. The reasons for this are ably explained by Michael Piore and Charles Sabel in *The Second Industrial Divide* (1984). Markets have become more volatile, product ranges have differentiated and firms have now to contend with changing demands for a more varied range of products across a series of national markets with specific characteristics. This undermines the relevance of "economies of scale" and encourages firms to change their production methods to permit more flexible output.

In such an open international economy, in which the major industrial nations trade manufactured goods ever more intensively one with another, there is less scope for purely national regulation. The social democratic strategy of using Keynesian measures to boost national consumer demand and thereby sustaining mass markets has given way to more complex strategies for preserving the local manufacturing base, particularly at the regional level. In such a competitive and rapidly changing industrial environment the scope for a central state-directed industrial policy is much reduced, thus undercutting the traditional socialist advocacy of "planning". The two major forms of active state intervention, Keynesian macroeconomic management and *dirigiste* planning, are thus both weakened as socialist answers to the problems of economic policy.

In this new environment both regional economic regulation and small-to-medium scale firms have grown in importance. But at the same time, other, quite contradictory tendencies have developed and these are most marked in the USA and the UK. If the logic of *industrial* concentration based on economies of scale in production has weakened, the purely *financial* pressures towards concentration of ownership have accelerated. The divorce of financial operations from the direct investment in new industrial plant and processes, conjured up in the phrase "casino capitalism", has led to the concentration of ownership of industry based almost solely on stockmarket opportunities. The acquisition and takeover of firms is often devoid of manufacturing or marketing logic. In this context, top management becomes ever more powerful and yet more remote and unaccountable. The operations of subsidiary firms will thus tend to suffer from such remote control. It can hardly be a matter of chance that it is the UK and the USA that have shown the greatest import penetration and consequent deindustrialization. These countries have participated least in the recent changes towards flexible specialization in production and the regional regulation of manufacturing sectors.

The financially based conglomerate holding companies lack a *raison d'être* in economic necessity; they are not essential for the organization of manufacturing. They are beyond the control of the formal machinery of shareholder representation and are unaccountable to their employees. Industrial concentration without economic rationality turns large-scale firms from a source of economic strength into a very real weakness. It represents a form of pure ownership increasingly divorced from managerial necessity. Traditional socialist remedies such as nationalization do not offer an answer to such concentration, since the component parts of such conglomerate companies make little industrial or administrative sense when gathered together. Decentralization and the promotion of economic self-government offer the best prospect of a form of industrial organization in which the major contributing interests – the providers of capital, management expertise and labour – have an active interest in the continued manufacturing success of the firm.

This need for democratization and decentralization is where associational socialism becomes relevant; because it stresses above all that economic units should be co-operatively owned self-governing associations. The tradition undoubtedly needs to be modernized. It is also true that traditional associational socialism was highly workerist and emphasized manufacturing industry, and it could hardly cope with today's complex division of labour within the enterprise or with the increasing diversity of occupations in the wider society. However, G. D. H. Cole's stress on organizing society on the basis of voluntarily formed self-governing associations was basically correct.

2 Battlefield

The left has been mesmerized by statism. Even moderate democratic socialists have constantly advocated giving more and more tasks to the state. The result, when such advocacy is successful, is to give more power to the state and less to socialists, and this in turn drains socialism of creative energy as a *social* movement and diverts it from constructive enterprise in civil society. We have built socialism (or rather tried to) through the agency of the state and encouraged passivity in the recipients of state services. Yet we wonder why socialism is no longer a mass movement.

The more tasks that are given to the state, the greater is the stake in controlling it and the more the state can take away if control changes hands. We have learnt that lesson through our experience of Mrs Thatcher, but we have hardly adapted to the fact that we need to devolve activities from the state to civil society as far as is possible. Socialists in the west, just as in the east, have seen the need to "capture" the state, to make certain changes in policy "irreversible". Yet such a vision is hardly compatible with a pluralist society, in which there are other groups and social projects than socialism. It rests on the belief that socialists have a natural majority in society and, therefore, a right to a monopoly of effective political power. This belief has been widely held by democratic socialists; it is not a peculiarity of the authoritarian left. This belief is almost inevitable if the state does come to control more and more of the affairs of society. Democracy becomes a battlefield; the only issue, who shall control the levers of power?

As the state has directly provided more services, so the individual has enjoyed less and less liberty in determining *how* they are provided. The recipient of collectiv- ized services administered by officials, the individual is also increasingly likely to work for a large private organization in which she or he has little or no say. The growth of state activity has not checked the growth of big business: often it has actively promoted it. The result is to place much of the affairs of "civil society" into the hands of unaccountable private governments that dwarf many pre-twentieth- century states in size.

If socialists could accept the idea of a state that facilitated the work of democrati- cally run associations in providing work and welfare, then they might have some chance of finding a more secure future for socialism. Democratic socialists seek to encourage co-operation, mutual assistance, fellowship and the greatest measure of equality attainable. They are not necessarily tied to particular social institutions like state ownership or central planning in meeting these objectives. Understood in this wider sense socialism can co-exist with a society of plural organizations and differ- ing objectives. It could build its institutions of co-operative work and mutual assist- ance alongside other active groups of citizens and their projects: religious groups, ethnic communities, lifestyle communities. A socialism committed to a pluralist society and to concentrating on organizing social life through self-governing asso- ciations in civil society would pose less of a threat to others than a statist socialism, and might therefore expect to command more support. In particular it would be more open to Green conceptions of social organizations and to co-existing with Green associations.

A challenge to statist socialism does not mean a return to the Marxist illusions of "smashing" the state. On the contrary, even if as many social activities as possible are devolved to self-governing associations in civil society, there will still be a need for a public power to regulate the actions of these associations and to ensure that they have the resources to carry out their tasks. A pluralist society with diverse social projects needs a public power to ensure order, but that public power need not be a "sovereign state": that is, a state claiming the exclusive control of power, asserting its primacy in every social domain, and imposing itself through a single centralized hierarchy. A pluralist state – as conceived by such English political pluralists as J. N. Figgis, G. D. H. Cole and H. J. Laski – would be based on a quite different principle: that the state exists to protect and serve the self-governing associations. The state's powers would be limited by its function and such a state would recognize the inherently plural nature of all free social organization. Pluralism requires that distinct locally and functionally specific domains of authority should have the autonomy necessary to carry out their tasks. This pluralist conception of the state is essential to a libertarian society, for "decentralization" and "devolution" of power will accomplish little if all they do is to recreate centralized authorities at lower levels.

Traditional state socialists raise two major objections to such a society of self-administering associations. The first is that while self-governing firms may give employees more say within the workplace, the wider economy remains anarchic and at the mercy of the "laws" of the market. This, however, is to treat the market economy as if it were a single self-sufficient system divorced from control by the wider society. There are no "laws" of the market; rather there are specific markets with diverse social conditions and consequences. Markets are embedded in social relations, and it is these relations that play a major role in deciding how markets work. Moreover, there are other ways of organizing an economy than centralized planning. Associational socialists like Cole always stressed the important role of voluntary co-ordination between associations at national industry and local levels. Some of Cole's conceptions of how to accomplish such co-ordination were naive, but this does not diminish his general point. There is much evidence that those national and regional economies that achieve such patterns of co-ordination, that provide for the effective consultations of social interests and that support firms with a surrounding network of social institutions which provide essential services, are the ones that have been most successful under modern conditions of manufacturing competition. West Germany, Italy and Japan offer excellent examples of different patterns of such co-ordination. It is the most unregulated "free-market" economies in the west, the UK and the USA that have done least well.

Centralized state planning is, moreover, no answer to the supposed inherent anarchy of the market. Planning produces its own anarchy, its own distortions of economic behaviour and its own corruptions. This brings us to the second objection. This is the claim that a system which assigns most welfare tasks to voluntary associations must produce inequalities in provision, benefiting some households and localities at the expense of others. Yet this inequality is just the result that centralized bureaucratic welfare systems have managed to accomplish. Nothing, moreover, prevents the state in such an associationalist system from enforcing minimum standards on associations in receipt of public funds or from providing its own welfare safety net.

3 Cats' Homes

In such an associationalist society there would be public funds raised by taxes and there would be capital markets to provide investment resources for firms. Voluntary associations would not finance all social activity through flag days. The state could, for example, collect an "associational tax" as a substantial percentage of total tax revenue, and allow taxpayers to nominate, say, about 25 per cent of their associational tax payments to a limited number of organizations (perhaps five to ten). That would prevent all revenue going to cats' homes and the like. The state would then distribute the bulk of the remainder of the associational tax according to the registered membership of associations and retain a reserve for meeting shortfalls. Such a system would ensure funds would flow towards the more popular associations. Moreover, industrial finance would become a mutually owned sector. Firms would establish credit unions: pension funds, insurance companies, etc., would lend to industrial banks and buy industrial associations' bonds. Self-governing firms would thus have access to external sources of capital and would be subject to the disciplines of borrowing at interest on organized capital markets.

Such a society is administratively and organizationally feasible. It is not a utopia, nor does it – as most utopias do – make unwarranted assumptions about human stamina and motivation. Self-governing associations need not be participatory democracies nor need they be small scale: representative elections and a professional management answerable to a democratic governing body may well be sufficient for most purposes. Many voluntary associations at present are of this nature, and providing they perform their tasks well enough, members are happy to subscribe and do no more than vote for the existing council. A society of self-governing associations leaves people free to choose the extent of their involvement. It does not compel endless hours of voluntary service above the demands of home and work.

But how to create a society of associations? How to tackle the current big corporations? How can one seek the greatest measure of equality possible when top tycoons are paid up to £1 million a year? Clearly, big business would regard the conversion of firms into self-governing associations with horror and would resist it root and branch. But if the public could be persuaded of the virtues of democratically accountable business, top managers would find themselves in the predicament that they are relatively few in number and that even executives in their subsidiary firms might welcome a reform. The 1988 British Social Attitudes survey shows that the British public are anything but enamoured of the motives and performance of top management.

If a reforming government tried to convert existing firms into self-governing associations, what would that involve? First, making management accountable to the relevant interests represented on a supervisory board of a company – let us assume that shareholders, employees and community interests have equal importance and that they should each elect one-third of the board. Secondly, creating a single membership status – *all* permanent employees to have the same rights and conditions of service, from the managing director to the lavatory attendant. Let us assume that inequalities in income will be flattened, to create a ratio of no more than 1:8. Thirdly, instituting a comprehensive system of co-determination, participation and consultation at all levels within the firm.

This is not so radical as it might appear. West German firms have comprehensive industrial democracy and co-determination measures, while many Japanese firms have single employee status, and in the period of most dramatic Japanese growth many companies had very low salary differentials. Nevertheless, it would be very unpopular with top management in Britain.

Measures likely to be unpopular with influential people need to be practical. How could these changes be applied to big conglomerate firms? While many aspects of industrial concentration may be economically unnecessary there are many cases where large-scale organizations are essential. How can these organizations be effectively run by democratic methods? The simple answer to this is that if we believe *states* can be made democratically accountable to their citizens to some significant degree, then companies surely can. But let us accept that the structure and operations of a complex company may be difficult to understand and therefore difficult for representatives to govern. There are then two answers: unscrambling into their component parts those companies where size has little economic logic, and creating different organizational structures for those companies where large-scale operations are necessary.

First, large size can be attained by partnerships of semi-autonomous subunits: firms that share work and contract one with another; firms that subscribe to marketing networks; firms that create collective bodies to represent their common interests or to provide common services such as training. These links can be by interfirm co-operation alone or through linkage with and co-ordination by public bodies. In such cases firms enjoy all the advantages of scale, without the participating units becoming too large or complex to be democratically governable. These relationships are already common in the most successful regions of the western industrial economies, and, far from being pie-in-the-sky, are widely identified as a key source of industrial efficiency, as many contributors argue in my edited collection (with Jonathan Zeitlin), *Reversing Industrial Decline?* (1988).

Secondly, large firms can be stripped down to a "core" of absolutely necessary activities that must be under direct control. Such a core might well be strategic management, R&D, and some crucial manufacturing operations. To get down to this core firms would follow a strategy of "internal privatization": sub-contracting non-core activities to co-operatives, promoting labour/capital partnerships and management-worker buy-outs of peripheral activities. For labour-intensive core activities the firm would contract with a labour co-operative on a fixed term deal. The result would be an economy of modestly sized units, capable of operating in combination on a very large scale. None of them would justify vast differentials of income, since firms would be smaller than the conglomerates of today and their internal hierarchies would be flatter. The overpaid top managers could be bought out as their positions were abolished by reorganization.

How could one prevent such contracting out to labour co-operatives giving rise to iniquities as great as the conditions of gang labour in the Durham mines in the nineteenth century? Surely, management would exploit such changes to dump liabilities upon labour? But two ready answers present themselves: that the state requires compliance with a law regulating contracts with labour co-operatives and that trades unions remain to police and protect workers' interests.

Such a process of turning firms into associations and stripping them down by internal privatization would create an economy based on manageably sized and internally accountable units. It would offer an end to the servile state, in which most people earn their living as employees without either a stake in or a measure of control over their workplace. It would also create a genuine "enterprise society" in which there would be scope for individual initiative and responsibility. Mrs Thatcher's conception of an enterprise culture is one in which choice is offered to individual consumers through the market. But confronted with an economy dominated by big corporations, the individual's choice as employee or consumer is severely limited. This is exacerbated by the Conservatives' ruthless trimming of the countervailing power of the unions in defence of employees, and their indifference to the need to extend further the role of law and regulatory agencies to protect consumers' rights. As J. N. Figgis argued persuasively in *Churches in the Modern State* (1913), it is difficult for individuals to pursue freedom except by freely associating with others. In an enterprise society based on self-governing associations, individuals have both opportunities for choice and the power to make those choices stick. Such a society permits a wide range of competing associations, and therefore choice based on genuine pluralism, and all the advantages of large scale where necessary, without unaccountable hierarchy. Through associations, such a society offers to its citizens unparalleled opportunities for individuation and freedom.

4 What About the Workers?

I have tried to indicate the ways in which the economy of self-governing associations would be possible and defensible against the hostility of management. But what about the unions? Surely, they have as much to fear from the growth of self-government at work? What would be the place of unions in such a scheme? The answer is: stronger certainly than in either state socialism or corporate capitalism, and more constructive than in either of them.

In an economy of self-governing associations the majority of workers would still receive the main part of their income in wages. Therefore, wage determination would remain important and would need to be institutionalized. Wage determination would take place at three levels:

1. National bargaining between the major interests – the state, associations and unions – leading to a fixed-term accord for overall norms.
2. Regional councils in which public bodies, associations and unions operate arbitration machinery to settle disputes about the application of norms to groups of workers in particular firms – at this level unions would also co-operate to ensure the provision of collective services such as training for firms and workers in the region.
3. Unions would ensure the firm's compliance with laws governing labour contracts and ensure that wage norms were democratically arrived at.

There would be a positive right to strike, but the combination of internal self-government in firms, and the unions' participation in comprehensive measures of collective wage determination would be designed to make strikes measures of last resort. The system of self-government in firms would be based on free votes of individual employees rather than through the union branches, thus maintaining the unions' independence and also preventing them from taking control of firms' internal decision-making procedures. Unions would therefore remain voluntary bodies to which individual workers could choose to subscribe. Like every other association they would be required to meet minimum legal standards of democratic self-governance. They would have the power to enforce fair contracts for employees: firms could not create "labour rackets" under the cover of self-government.

In an associational welfare system the unions could greatly extend their role as providers of welfare and other services compared with their position today. Unions would be eligible to get funds under the "write-in" provisions for 25 per cent of the associational tax, to receive funds proportional to membership and to bid for projects from the reserves. Unions would potentially control very large funds to use for the benefit of their members. They would also contribute to training policy through co-determination machinery and control training funds and offer training themselves. The benefits of belonging to a union would be very real for members. Unions would provide benefits as associations in civil society and directly organize welfare. Socialists in combination with the unions would directly carry out policy instead of campaigning for it to be done by the state, and they would be directly responsible to their own membership for the success of that policy. They would have to compete with non-socialist associations like churches in providing welfare.

Unions would not, however, directly organize or own production (such activities would be *ultra vires* under associational law). Thus associationalism would be quite unlike syndicalism. Workers would be free not to join unions and the self-government procedures of firms would be independent of the unions. Workers, therefore, would not be compelled to be part of a rigid corporatist structure, and unions would have to win and keep members to ensure influence. Workers would have the union to protect them if for some reason a firm became riven by factional strife or dominated by a management clique. They would also have unions to ensure that their job rates, skill classifications and training were protected. Unions would have an interest in and would help to maintain labour mobility and, therefore, the liberty of the worker.

Because it can be adapted to large-scale industry and permits a complex division of labour, associationalism is one of the few nineteenth-century social doctrines that remains fully relevant today. It combines liberty with effective management, and decentralization and self-action with professionalism and efficiency. It offers a radically greater range of choice than most other social doctrines: greater consumer choice than state socialism and more real choice for the worker than corporate capitalism. Associationalism also allows diverse groups to choose their own form of social organization: it offers possibilities of self-action to religious and other groups as well as to socialists. Because it avoids the authoritarianism of a socialist society fit only for dogmatic socialists, associationalism may appeal to enough groups in society for them to tolerate it and work along with it. It is the only socialist doctrine of which this can credibly be said, and therefore it is, in the long run, the only practical socialism.

Chapter 17

The Logic of Intercultural Evaluation

Bhikhu Parekh

A multicultural society is likely to include minorities some of whose values and practices differ from and even offend against those of its own. It cannot tolerate them indiscriminately for that involves abdicating moral judgement and compromising its commitment to its own values. However to disallow them is to be guilty of extreme intolerance and to forgo the opportunity to take a critical look at itself. This raises the question as to how a multicultural society should decide what minority practices to tolerate and within what limits. This essay addresses that question.

Before dealing with the question a point of clarification is necessary. One might ask why the fact that a practice is cultural should make any difference to our evaluation of it. It should be allowed or disallowed depending on whether it is desirable or undesirable, and the fact that it is part of a community way of life is irrelevant. There are two important reasons why the cultural embeddedness of a practice should make a difference to our evaluation of it.[1]

First, unlike such self-chosen practices or life-styles as cohabitation and homosexuality, cultural practices are part of a way of life, have a normative authority and are generally regarded as binding by the members of the community concerned. In this respect they are somewhat like the laws of a country. We may disapprove of a law and yet obey it out of respect for the authority enacting it or for the way of life of which it is a part. Cultural practices cannot therefore be judged exclusively in terms of their content. Even when we disapprove of them, we may have a duty to allow them out of respect for the way of life of which they are an integral part. This is why, for example, drug-taking by the Rastafarians or the AmerIndians and by a group of white adolescents are different in nature, and require and generally receive different responses. For white adolescents, taking drugs is a self-chosen action, whereas for the Rastafarians and AmerIndians it is a requirement of their way of life. We may decide to disallow it to both, but our modes of reasoning would be different. Or we may allow it to Rastafarians and

AmerIndians but not to others without incurring the charge of discriminating against the latter.

Secondly, evaluating a practice is a complex activity. Since a practice derives its meaning and legitimacy from a wider way of life and cannot be judged desirable or undesirable in the abstract, we need to locate it in the system of meanings and values of the cultural community concerned, and examine its internal rationality and significance. We might not be persuaded by the defence of a practice and decide to ban it, but we owe it to the community to do so only after giving it an opportunity to explain and justify it.

I

The following are a sample of minority practices that have generated different degrees of public debate in most liberal societies.

(1)   female circumcision;

(2)   polygamy;

(3)   Muslim and Jewish methods of slaughtering animals;

(4)   arranged marriages, practised mainly but not only by Asians. The practice ranges from the largely formal parental approval of their children's choices of spouses to foisting the latter on them;

(5)   marriages within prohibited degrees of relationship; for example, Muslims may marry their first cousins, and Jews their nieces, both of which are viewed with some disfavour in some Western societies;

(6)   the practice, common among some African communities, of scarring children's cheeks or other parts of the body as part of the initiation ceremony;

(7)   the Muslim practice of withdrawing their school-going girls from such activities as sports, athletics and swimming lessons that involve wearing shorts and exposing parts of the body;

(8)   Muslim girls wearing the *hijab* or headscarf in schools. This became *a cause célèbre* in France in 1990, and provoked some controversy in Britain, Germany, Belgium and the Netherlands as well. Although the headscarf is banned in France, it is allowed in almost all other European countries;

(9)   Sikh insistence on wearing their traditional turbans rather than helmets when driving motor cycles or doing dangerous work on building sites, carrying their ceremonial swords or daggers at all times, wearing their turbans when taking oaths in courts or bowing before the speaker in the House of Commons, and refusing to shave off their beards when working in places that involve handling food;

(10)   Muslim demands for time off from work to offer their daily prayers and to visit mosques on Fridays, and for appropriate facilities for prayer within their workplaces;

(11)   refusal by the Roma and the Amish community in the United States to send their children to schools either altogether or after reaching a certain age, on

the grounds that modern education is useless for their children and alienates them from their community;

(12)   requests by the Hindus to be allowed to cremate their deceased on a funeral pyre, to scatter the ashes in rivers and, in rare cases, to drown rather than to cremate the corpses.

In order to decide whether or not to tolerate these and other practices, we need guiding principles. In much of the public discussion the following four are generally invoked.

1.   Some appeal to universal values and think that since they are culturally neutral, they are binding on all and involve no moral coercion. For convenience I shall call this moral universalism.
2.   Some argue that every society has an historically acquired character or identity articulated in a specific body of values. These core, fundamental, basic or foundational values make it the kind of society it is and form the basis of its way of life. It has therefore a right and a duty to disallow practices that offend against them. I shall call this the principle of core values.
3.   Some either deny the existence of core or fundamental values or think that imposing these on minorities violates their cultural integrity and involves an unacceptable degree of moral coercion. In their view society should therefore disallow only those practices that cause harm to others or to society, harm being defined in terms of such things as public hygiene, public order and violation of basic individual rights and interests. I shall call this the no-harm principle.
4.   Finally, some argue that since the universally valid values are not available, the concept of core values is problematic, and harm cannot always be defined in a culturally neutral or interculturally acceptable manner, the only possible and desirable course of action is to engage in an open-minded and morally serious dialogue with the minority spokesmen and to act on the resulting consensus. Such a consensus is not ideal and might involve concessions and compromises. However, it has the compensating advantages of showing respect for minorities, involving them in decisions affecting them, deepening intercommunal understanding, and arriving at a realistic and widely acceptable decision. I shall call this the principle of dialogical consensus.

Although each of these views contains important insights, none is wholly satisfactory. I shall take each in turn. Since I am primarily concerned to point out their inadequacies, I shall ignore their strengths.

Moral universalism is open to several objections. First, it is an extremely ambitious philosophical claim to provide a universally valid body of values, and so far the claim remains unredeemed. It is even doubtful if the claim is coherent, given the vastly different ways in which human beings define their conceptions of the good and organise their personal and collective lives. One might be able to tease out common moral principles such as human dignity and respect for life and liberty, but they are necessarily too thin and abstract to be of any or much use in practical deliberations on substantive issues.

Secondly, even if the principles are shown to be philosophically valid, some might not accept them or, if they do, they might not feel so committed to them as to be motivated by them in their relations with others. It is difficult to see how they can be compelled to accept and live by them, especially when liberty and self-determination must form part of any list of universally valid principles.

Thirdly, even if they are accepted by all concerned, the abstract universal principles need to be interpreted, and here people are likely to disagree. Respect for human life, for example, is a major contender for the status of a universal principle, but people disagree about when human life begins and ends and what respect for it entails. Again, universal moral principles have to be balanced, prioritised and applied to the unique circumstances of specific societies, and that too generates much disagreement. Since such disagreements cannot by definition be resolved by reference to the principles themselves, we are left without any guidance.

The principle of core values offers a more promising line of inquiry but runs into difficulties at a different level.[2] First, the concept of fundamental or core values is too elusive to be of much use. If it refers to values that constitute the foundation of *any* society such that their rejection would spell its disintegration, the list is too long to be of much help. If it refers to values that lie at the basis of a *specific* society such that their rejection would undermine its character and turn it into a very different kind of society, the concept of fundamental values makes more sense. However no society is static, and its very survival requires that it should constantly redefine its identity and modify its values including those that are central to it. Finally, if the term fundamental values refers to values shared by *all* the members of a society, the demand is unrealistic. Is equality of the sexes a value shared by all the members of a liberal society? Racists, sexists and most religious people disagree. It is certainly an important liberal value, but not all the citizens of a liberal society are liberals. Is respect for persons such a value? Racists, fascists and others disagree or agree only because it is so weakly defined as to make no moral demands. As we shall see later, it is doubtful if even monogamy can be considered a core of fundamental value of liberal society.

Secondly, even if we were able to give the concept of fundamental values a coherent meaning, it would always be possible to ask if they are desirable. Inequality is a fundamental value in slave-owning, racist and caste-based societies, but we would not wish to argue that it should therefore be retained let alone enforced. Furthermore, the fundamental values of a society might include respect for minority values, as they do in liberal and most other societies, and then they cannot be used as a non-negotiable moral standard.

Thirdly, values can be interpreted, related and traded off in several different ways. Liberal society cherishes both liberty and equality. However its members deeply disagree about their meanings, limits and relative importance. The appeal to fundamental values therefore does not take us very far. It does of course help us formulate disputed issues in a mutually acceptable manner, but does not help us resolve them.[3]

As for the no-harm principle, it is largely unproblematic when physical harm is involved, but offers little guidance when we move beyond it. It tells us nothing about whether or not to ban such practices as incest, polygamy, arranged marriages, euthanasia, and any of the others listed earlier. They either involve highly complex questions of emotional, moral and other types of harm about which consensus is difficult to obtain, or cannot be adequately conceptualised in the language of harm. Similar difficulties bedevil the ideas of public order and public interest.

As for the principle of dialogical consensus, dialogue is certainly necessary to resolve deep moral and cultural disagreements, and we shall later see how it should proceed. However, it is unlikely to take us far in the abstract and contextless form proposed by its advocates. A political dialogue does not occur in a vacuum. It presupposes a specific society with a specific moral structure, whose members happen to disagree about the desirability of a specific practice. And their dispute is not about whether the practice is desirable 'in general' or 'in principle', but whether it is desirable in their society and fits in with their values and self-understanding. The dialogue cannot therefore avoid starting with and centring on these values. The values specify what aspects of the practice are unacceptable and why, what kinds of reasons can properly be advanced in defence or criticism of it, and so on, and structure the content and parameters of the debate.

In the absence of such a structure and context, the dialogue either does not get off the ground or degenerates into irrelevant and mutually unintelligible assertions that hardly amount to an exchange of reasons let alone arguments. A political dialogue must therefore begin with and centre on the community's values and show why they need to be changed or reinterpreted. In other words there can be no dialogue without a context, and once the context is introduced, the dialogue cannot be free-ranging and open-ended. Furthermore, unlike an academic dialogue, a political dialogue is intended to yield a decision. Since deep disagreements cannot always be resolved, we need ways of reaching a decision, on which again there may be considerable disagreement. It is difficult to see how else a decision can be reached than by minorities accepting, at least temporarily, the society's established decision-making procedure and the values embedded in it. In the absence of such finality, no decision is possible and the point of the dialogue is lost.

II

I suggest that the best way to decide what minority practices to allow or disallow is to appeal to what I shall call the society's *operative public values*. Every society consists of different classes, regions, and social and religious groups, each with its overlapping values and practices. They cannot live together and constitute a more or less cohesive society without sharing at least a minimum body of values and practices in common. The values articulate and are underpinned by the society's broadly shared conception of how its members should live together and conduct their relations. The values are rarely acceptable to all its members, some of whom

avoid their constraints at every available opportunity. However, most of them
accept and seek to live by them, and even those who do not live by them know what
they are and acknowledge their authority at least in public. It is true that the values
often acquire their authority and dominant position through a prolonged process
of indoctrination and coercion, and sometimes they continue to be actively or pas-
sively contested by different groups. Whatever their origins and history, they have
become a part of the society's moral structure and are embodied in its major social,
economic, political and other institutions. Since the society's integrity and smooth
functioning depend on the observance of these values, it ensures that its members
grow up imbibing them. They may personally hold what values they like, but in
their interpersonal relations they are expected to abide by the values the society
cherishes.

The shared life is lived at three levels, and hence the society's public values are
suitably articulated at each of them. First, they are enshrined in its constitution.
The constitution lays down the basic design of the polity including the fundamental
rights and sometimes the obligations of its citizens. Second, the values are also
embodied in laws, which flesh out the constitutionally enshrined values and relate
them to the countless daily activities undertaken by citizens. Although legal and
constitutional values are closely related, they are different in nature. Those embodied in the constitution are general and regulative and largely deal with the government's relations with its citizens, whereas those embodied in laws are specific and
substantive and largely deal with the citizens' relations with one another. Values
embodied in laws are subject to the constraints of constitutional values, but are not
derived from them. For example, the constitution may require that men and women
should be treated equally. That does not by itself entail monogamy, for the equality
of the sexes only implies that men and women should enjoy equal freedom to
choose their marriage partners, not that they should marry only one person. When
the law prescribes monogamy, it both respects and goes beyond the constitutional
value of the equality of the sexes, the former because it enforces the same form of
marriage on both men and women, the latter because it permits only one of several
possible forms of marriage.

The society's common values are also embodied in what I shall call the civic
relations between its members. These relations occupy an intermediate realm
between the structured relations of organised public life and the intimate relations
of personal and private life. Although some aspects of these relations are sometimes
governed by laws, most are not and cannot be. Relations between neighbours,
people queuing for or travelling by public transport, car drivers, fellow-students,
and colleagues belong to this category. They are regulated by a body of civic values
and practices, and constitute a society's civic culture. When the newly arrived North
African immigrants to Israel haggled over the fare with the bus driver or asked him
to stop the bus nearer their homes, they were told that this was not how things were
done in Israel, that is, that the Israeli civic culture was different from the one they
were used to. And when a visiting Pakistani professor in a British university was
told not to ask his students to do his weekly shopping for him, he was in effect told

that such relations in Britain were governed by different civic values from those prevailing in his country.

The constitutional, legal and civic values represent a society's public culture, define its inevitably vague conception of the good life and constitute what I have called its *operative public values*. They are values because the society cherishes and endeavours to live by them, and judges its members' behaviour in terms of them. They are public because they are embodied in its constitutional, legal and civic institutions and practices, regulate the public conduct of its citizens, and represent their collective self-conception. And they are operative because they do not represent utopian and abstract ideals, but are customarily practised and constitute a lived social reality. The operative public values of a society constitute the basic or primary moral structure of its public or shared life. Although they inescapably influence and are influenced by the personal values of its members, the two are distinct in their nature, authority and mode of legitimation.

Unlike the so-called core or fundamental values, the operative public values relate only to the public life of society. They regulate the conduct of public affairs, the relations between the government and the citizens, and the public relations between the latter, and do not prescribe how the individuals should organise their personal lives and the ideals they should follow. The operative public values are not always coherent and sometimes pull in different directions. They are embodied in and cannot be easily disengaged from a body of practices. They are not static, and change in response to changes in the society's circumstances and self-understanding. They are not beyond criticism and are often contested. They are not rigid either and are amenable to different and sometimes opposite interpretations. They are also interlocked in the sense that each limits and partly defines the content of the others, and they cannot be neatly catalogued or summarised. They are of varying degrees of generality, interpenetrate each other and cannot be easily individuated. By and large they form a complex and loosely knit whole from which none of them can be abstracted without distortion. Since they represent values to which a society is collectively and publicly committed, their authority remains unaffected even if some of its members do not personally subscribe to them. Some members of liberal society may not believe in the equality of the sexes or races, but that does not excuse them from adhering to it in their public behaviour.

Since the operative public values represent the society's shared moral structure and are *its* values as distinct from those of a section of it, they provide the only valid moral standpoint from which to evaluate minority practices. When a minority practice offends against the society's operative public values, it merits disapproval. However, that is not a reason to disallow it. Since it forms part of the minority way of life, society owes it to the minority to explore what the practice means to it, what place it occupies in its way of life and why it considers it valuable, before deciding whether or not to disallow it. Furthermore the operative public values of a society are not themselves beyond criticism and change. Since they articulate a specific conception of the good life, and since every conception of the good life is partial, they are likely to discriminate against or bear unduly heavily on those whose historical experiences and conceptions of the good are different. Every society therefore needs periodically to reassess its operative public values, and the fact that a minority practice offends against some of them provides it with a good opportunity to do so.

Rather than dogmatically use the operative public values as a crude and non-negotiable criterion for evaluating minority practices, the society concerned should therefore engage in a dialogue with the minority concerned. The dialogue is necessarily two-dimensional. Since the society disapproves of the minority practice, it needs to give reasons, and that involves showing why it holds certain values and how the minority practice offends against them. For its part the minority needs to show why it values the practice and thinks that the latter deserves to be respected by the wider society. By its very nature the dialogue cannot centre on the merits and demerits of the minority practice alone, for the practice would not have been a subject of dispute if the wider society had not disapproved of it on the basis of its operative public value. The dialogue is therefore bifocal, centring both on the minority practice and the society's operative public values, both on the minority and the wider society's ways of life.

The dialogue need not be and is not generally polarised. The debate on the merits and demerits of a disputed practice is likely to trigger off a debate within the minority community itself. Since the society at large questions the practice and asks the minority community to defend it, some members of that community would wish to take advantage of the occasion to inquire if it is really central to their way of life and whether, on balance, it is worth continuing. It is likely that outsiders too will join in this internal debate, some defending and others criticising the practice. A similar debate is also likely to occur within the society at large.

While some might fiercely defend the relevant operative public values, others might use the occasion to take a critical look at them, asking whether they are really worth preserving or mere historical excrescences surviving out of inertia and reflective of an earlier and now superseded moral consensus or balance of power. It is more than likely that minority spokesmen might themselves wish to participate in the wider social debate and seek to influence it in a specific manner.

The debate about a minority practice then takes place at several levels and has a profoundly transformative effect on all involved. It triggers debates within the minority community, within the wider society, and between the two. And in each case the participants are unlikely to be confined to the communities concerned. Furthermore although the debate begins with a specific practice, it broadens out to cover both the majority and minority ways of life and sometimes opens up a large and unexpected set of issues. It also forces each party to become conscious of its values and reasons for doing so, and contributes to their critical self-knowledge. Although the context of the public debate sometimes encourages each to close ranks and feel unduly defensive about its values, especially when one of them is perceived as a threatening other, the stronger compulsions of the shared life often tend to prevail, encouraging both to explore and stress their common interests and values.

In the debate surrounding a controversial practice, the minority is called upon to defend it. Every practice has two dimensions. First, it is embedded in a way of life and carries a measure of authority. And second, it affects its adherents in a specific way and has social consequences. The defence of a practice is therefore two-dimensional, and reasons advanced in support of it are of two kinds. First, minority spokesmen would wish to maintain that the practice is binding on them because it is an integral part of their way of life, that it is interlocked with other practices and sustains their way of life, and that disallowing would destroy or weaken the latter and cause disorientation and confusion. As we shall see later, this is how such practices as female circumcision and polygyny are defended by many a Muslim. This kind of argument makes an important point, for a practice derives its meaning and authority from its place in a way of life and cannot be judged in isolation. However no way of life is a monolithic whole such that it is shaken to its roots by challenging its every practice. And if an offensive practice were really central to it, the latter itself would become suspect. The critic could therefore rightly demand that a minority spokesman cannot merely appeal to the cultural authority of the practice and should offer a reasonably convincing defence of it.

In order that the defence can convince outsiders, it should be articulated in terms of values they can share. Not that they should themselves subscribe to or live by the values, but rather that they should be able to see the point of them and recognise them as possible values to which people can legitimately subscribe. Defending a practice thus requires that minority spokesmen should view it and their way of life from the standpoint of outsiders, as also that the wider society should be able to suspend its moral certainties and open up itself to the possibility of different but equally legitimate visions of the good life. Minority spokesmen cannot insist on appealing to their values alone, for that would carry no conviction with the outsiders. For their part spokesmen of the wider society cannot insist that only their values should be appealed to, for then many a minority practice would be rejected straight away. If the dialogue is to be both possible and not be biased from the beginning, it should not be conceived in static and positivist terms but seen as a creative and unpredictable encounter in which both parties defend as well as re-examine their moral beliefs and are open to new insights. The dialogue *between* them is meaningful and fruitful only if accompanied and enriched by an internal dialogue *within* each of them.

When challenged to defend an offensive practice, minority spokesmen would need to point to values others either share or can appreciate. They could argue that, contrary to its self-understanding, the wider society does really share them, or that it once cherished them but has now unwisely abandoned, or that it never held them but really ought to, or that although it might not be persuaded of them, they enrich its way of life and that it ought to allow others to live by them. The wider society might either be convinced by the arguments and allow the practice to continue, or it might remain unpersuaded and decide to ban it.

In the latter case the wider society needs to show why it is unconvinced and chooses to insist on its operative public values. The minority spokesmen have put the latter on the public agenda, and society needs to defend them. Its defence is, again, in two stages. Its spokesmen could argue that the disputed values are an integral part of their way of life and hence binding, or that they are bound with its other values and practices and could not be compromised without causing large-scale disorientation and chaos. The minority critic could rejoin that the values are a historical excrescence and not integral to the society's way of life or at least not as central as its spokesmen maintain, or that although they are, they are indefensible, discriminatory or biased against the minorities and in need of revision. If the critic's rejoinder has a point, the wider society needs to offer a reasonably persuasive defence of the values in question along the lines discussed earlier. If it is unable to provide one, it might need to reconsider them.

In the light of our discussion four interrelated considerations structure the debate on a disputed minority practice: (1) its importance to the minority way of life; (2) the minority's ability to offer a persuasive defence of it; (3) the wider society's operative public values or, what comes to the same thing, the importance of the relevant value to its way of life; and (4) the society's ability to offer a persuasive defence of them. The four considerations open up a range of possibilities. If a minority practice is central to its way of life and only differs from but does not offend against any of the operative public values of the wider society, it should be tolerated and even welcomed. If it is not central to the minority way of life or cannot be adequately defended, and if it offends against one or more of the wider society's operative public values, it should be disallowed; indeed the minority community itself should abandon it. If a practice is central to the minority way of life and deeply offends against one or more of the wider society's operative public values, we face a difficult situation. The two parties then need to engage in an open-minded dialogue with a view to exploring where and why they disagree and whether one of them can convince the other.

The dialogue in such cases is never easy, both because the two parties are likely to talk past each other on areas of such deep differences, and because one or both parties are likely to prove intransigent on matters of such great emotional and moral significance to them. If the minority proved intransigent, the wider society would need to be firm with it. If the wider society were to be intransigent and to refuse to engage in an open-minded dialogue, the minority might have to put pressure on it by democratic means. If for some reason the dialogue were to be impossible, it might be advisable to postpone the decision in the hope that the passage of time and the fusion of ideas brought about by formal and informal public discussions will create enough common ground and goodwill to facilitate a judicious and mutually acceptable compromise.

If the matter is urgent or if the impasse persists, the values of the wider society should prevail for at least three important reasons. First, they are woven into its institutions and practices, form part of the lived social reality, and cannot be changed without causing considerable moral and social disorientation. Second, while a society has an obligation to accommodate the minority way of life, it has no obligation to do so at the cost of its own, especially if it is able to make out a reasonably good case for its values and remains genuinely unconvinced by the minority's defence of the disputed practice. Third, when the minority consists of immigrants, they need to appreciate that since they are unfamiliar with the wider society's way of life, its nature and inner workings are likely to elude them, and that they should therefore defer to its judgement in doubtful matters. They also need the wider society's goodwill and support to counter the resentment their presence provokes among some sections of society, and are more likely to secure these if, after making their point, they gracefully accept its decision.

III

Since our discussion so far has been abstract, it would be useful to take a few minority practices, ranging from the least to the most controversial, to show how our analysis applies to them. For convenience I shall take all my examples from Britain.

It is a Hindu practice to scatter the ashes of the dead in rivers, and sometimes to submerge the corpses rather than to cremate them. Both practices, especially the latter, arouse a considerable degree of unease in Britain. However they mean a great deal to the Hindus, and do not offend against any of the operative public values of British society. The only relevant public interest in the matter is that neither practice should put public health at risk. Quite sensibly the Water Act 1989 allows both, provided that the persons concerned obtain a licence. The licence is given if the ashes are disposed of in tidal or estuary waters or in the sea within 12 miles of the coastline. The suitably weighted down corpses can also be disposed of in this manner, and local boatsmen are available for making the necessary arrangements.

Many Hindus also prefer to cremate their dead on a funeral pyre rather than by electric means. This is disallowed in almost all Western societies largely on aesthetic and hygiene grounds. The objections seem to be ill-conceived. Aesthetic considerations are a matter of taste not of morality, and the Hindu practice poses no risk to public hygiene. Since it is difficult to see what operative public values it offends against, the practice should be allowed in closed and officially designated places, as is the case in such countries as India, Nepal, Guyana, Trinidad and the Netherlands.

The Jewish and Muslim method of slaughtering animals has been a subject of continuing debate in Britain. For a variety of religious reasons having to do with the nature of slaughter and the symbolic significance of food, the two communities believe that the animal should be conscious at the moment of death and not be stunned before being slaughtered. Some animal rights activists and even others have argued that although this method of killing is quick and efficient, the animal suffers pain for at least a few seconds and that the practice should be banned. This is not as easy a question as the Hindu practice of scattering the ashes, but there are good reasons to allow the practice. Although it is not integral to the Jewish and Muslim ways of life in the sense that they would collapse if it were to be disallowed, it is religiously sanctioned, means a great deal to the two communities, and is closely tied up with their other beliefs and practices. Spokesmen of the two communities are also able to offer a reasonable defence of it, arguing that pain to the animal is nil or at best minimal and that, if the animals were to be allowed to be killed at all, pain lasting barely a few seconds should not be given greater moral weight than the community's feelings. Furthermore the practice does not violate any of the operative public values of the wider society, and the popular sensibility to animal pain is not, at least as yet, so intense and widespread that the practice causes deep unease in the society at large. If things were to change radically, the practice might need to be reconsidered as was done in Norway which, after much public discussion, banned the practice with the willing consent of its Jewish and Muslim citizens.

The Asian practice of arranged marriages has aroused some unease in Britain and elsewhere. It covers a wide spectrum ranging from almost automatic parental endorsement of spouses freely chosen by their offspring to parental imposition of spouses on them. Some sections of British society would like it banned or at least discouraged, largely on the ground that it violates the values of personal autonomy and individual choice. Their demand is justified against some forms of arranged marriages but not others. Although the practice has no religious or cultural basis, it is an important part of the Asian way of life, plays a role in sustaining it, and means a great deal to Asians. Furthermore they are able to offer a reasonable defence of it. They argue that marriages are likely to be happier and last longer if parents consent to them and feel morally and emotionally committed to their success. Furthermore in the Asian view individuals are an integral part of their family, and their lives belong not just to them but also to their families. It therefore makes sense for parents to have a say in whom their sons and daughters marry and how they lead their lives. Asian spokesmen also point to the fact that many of their youths themselves welcome both the parental advice and the wider network of social support that the arranged marriages provide.

While parental involvement in the choice of marriage partners has something to be said for it at least in the Asian context, parental coercion has none. It denies the youth control over their lives and largely treats them as a means of serving parental interests and ambitions. This is indefensible in any society especially the liberal, both because the latter cherishes and depends for its smooth functioning on uncoerced individual choice and because the young Asians growing up in it greatly value the freedom to make their own decisions on such important matters. There is also much evidence that coerced marriages cause considerable resentment against the parents, are often unhappy and lead to much domestic violence including suicide.

This means that rather than take a homogeneous and undifferentiated view of arranged marriages, we should appreciate and respond differently to their diverse forms. British parliament struck a right balance when it legislated that, although arranged marriages were acceptable, those contracted under duress were not. The law was preceded and followed by a widespread debate within the Asian community, which accepted it as a fair compromise.

IV

The origins of female circumcision are unknown, but in one form or another it seems to have existed for centuries.[4] In ancient Rome metal rings were passed through the labia minora of slaves to prevent procreation; in medieval England women were made to wear metal chastity belts to prevent promiscuity during their husband's absence; evidence from mummified bodies in ancient Egypt suggests both excision and infibulation were performed; in Tsarist Russia as well as in nineteenth-century England, France and America, the practice of clitoridectomy was not uncommon, especially as a 'cure' for epilepsy, hysteria and insanity.

Female circumcision takes three forms. First, circumcision or Sunna ('traditional') circumcision involving the removal of the prepuce and the tip of the clitoris. Second, excision or clitoridectomy involving the removal of clitoris and often also the labia minora. Third, infibulation or pharaonic circumcision. This is the most severe operation, involving excision as well as the removal of the labia minora and the labia majora and the stitching up of the two sides of the female genitals leaving a smooth surface and a small opening to permit urination and the passing of menstrual blood.

Since, strictly speaking, the term female circumcision refers to its last two forms, and since they involve physical mutilation, I shall concentrate on them. In either of these two forms, it is practised in at least 25 countries in Africa, the Middle East, and parts of South East Asia. There are two million female circumcisions a year, and over 80 million women living today have undergone it. It is banned in all Western countries, and this has caused considerable unease among Muslim immigrants. The practice deeply offends against some of the operative public values of liberal society. It inflicts irreversible physical harm, is sexist in nature, violates the integrity of the child, leaves her with deep psychological scars, makes irreversible decisions for her, endangers her life, leads to sexual frustration and removes a source of pleasure. The practice is therefore deeply suspect, and liberal society is right to ban it unless Muslims can offer a strong and convincing defence of it that measures up to its enormity.

Muslim defence proceeds along the two stages mentioned earlier. First, it is required by their religion or culture, and hence binding on them. It is also tied up with their other moral and social beliefs and practices. It guarantees the girl's virginity and saves her from social suspicion, makes it easier for her to find a suitable husband, protects her family against ignominy resulting from her likely indiscretions, and so forth, and plays a crucial role in sustaining their way of life. Secondly, Muslim spokesmen appeal to the values which they think are shared by the rest of the society as well, and argue that the practice regulates the girl's sexuality, facilitates sexual self-discipline and self-control, protects her against obsession with sex during her adolescence, and leads to a psychologically healthy life. In societies where female circumcision is practised, it is also sometimes defended on aesthetic grounds. Female genitals are deemed to be ugly, and circumcision is seen as a way of making them more attractive. Notions of cleanliness and strange myths about the nature and significance of the clitoris are also invoked. Since these are not moral arguments and are rarely advanced at least in public by Muslim spokesmen, I shall ignore them.

The first defence is flimsy for, as we saw earlier, the fact that a practice is sanctioned by a religion or a way of life is *a* reason but never a *conclusive* reason for allowing it. As it happens, it has no religious or cultural sanction. There is no mention of it in the Koran and only a passing and ambiguous reference in the hadiths. It is not common in most Muslim countries, and has provoked strong opposition among some sections of the very communities in which it is common. The practice does, of course, play the kind of social role claimed on its behalf. However, it is open to several objections. As several anthropologists have shown, it neither guarantees virginity as the premarital practice of hymenorrhappy shows, nor protects the girl against social suspicions and indiscretions. It causes deep psychological trauma, renders her incapable of normal sex life and leads to irritability, moodiness, and a constant state of depression and anxiety. It is striking that a substantial percentage of the women involved dread sexual intercourse on their wedding night, and post-marital frigidity too is fairly common. Furthermore such social benefits as are claimed on behalf of the practice do not obtain in urbanised and industrialised society, especially Western society in which the immigrants have decided to settle. Again other societies, which also cherish virginity, manage to achieve it by less harmful means, and blocking the physical possibility of a vice is hardly the way to cultivate the relevant virtue. We can also point to the largely critical views of women who have themselves undergone the practice, and to the indefensible beliefs about female sexuality from which it derives its legitimacy. The practice assumes that only female sexuality needs to be regulated, that only she needs to retain and prove her virginity, and so forth, and contains a deep sexist bias. It is, of course, true that there is a considerable social pressure to conform to it, and that dissenting families sometimes pay a heavy price. However, the answer lies not in continuing the practice but in judiciously reforming the way of life that makes it necessary. Social pressure forms a vicious cycle often forcing each individual to do things he or she would rather not, and can only be removed by legally banning the unacceptable practice.

The second defence fares no better. The practice has grave consequences of the kind described earlier. There is also enough evidence to show that it not only does not eliminate or even reduce obsession with sexuality during adolescence but tends to intensify it. Besides, since normal forms of sexuality are blocked, it is known to take perverse forms. In short we can successfully challenge the Muslim defence of female circumcision by questioning its underlying assumptions, biases, claims and the allegedly beneficial consequences, and rightly ban the practice. For obvious reasons the ban needs to be enforced with compassion and sensitivity, and accompanied by a reformist campaign by the leaders of the communities involved.

We have so far discussed female circumcision in relation to children. What if it were to be demanded by an adult woman in full possession of her senses? This is not a purely hypothetical situation. A 30-year-old Nigerian academic recently told a conference that it was not uncommon among some groups of women in her community to undergo clitoridectomy after the birth of their first child, and that she herself had had it done when she was 26. The reasons cited had to do with the regulation of sexuality, a symbolic break with the past and a constant reminder that they were now primarily mothers rather than wives and that their maternal duties took precedence over personal pleasure.

How should we respond to such a demand? Surely an adult and sane woman should be free to do what she likes with her body. Naturally such a right cannot be absolute. If someone wanted her arms amputated or eyes removed as a form of penance, or out of a sense of guilt, or to avoid doing or being tempted by evil, we would not allow her on such grounds as that it would render her incapable of discharging her normal social obligations, lead her to make excessive demands on society's resources, and that her demand violates our ideas of how human beings should treat their bodies. None of these grounds, except perhaps the last, applies in the case of circumcision.

The woman involved could also argue that Western society allows breast transplants and reconstruction of the nose, lips or the entire face, and that her action falls within this category. Unlike Western women who feel strongly about their facial parts, she feels equally strongly about her genitals, and she cannot see that there is a radical difference between the two. She might go further and argue that, since society allows males to engage in surgical enlargements of their genitals, denying her the right to circumcision is discriminatory and a form of sexism. Indeed, if she is an uncompromising feminist, she might contend that males disapprove of clitoridectomy because they define female sexuality in a specific way, prefer women to offer them or to experience themselves a particular kind of sexual pleasure, and that denying her the right to circumcision amounts to denying her the right freely to define her sexual identity.

While all this suggests that an adult woman should be free to undergo clitoridectomy and even infibulation, other factors point in the opposite direction. Once the practice is permitted, there is a danger, given the history of the communities concerned, that it might be exploited for purposes we disapprove of or extended to younger women and even to children. There is also the danger that other adult women might be put under pressure to engage in it.

Our decision as to whether or not to allow adult female circumcision then needs to be based on a careful weighing up of a number of conflicting factors. We should respect women's choices, but we should also ensure that the offensive practice is not exploited, becomes an occasion for intense social pressure, or is used to perpetuate women's subordination. We have therefore four choices. First, we might allow it to adult women without restriction. Second, we might allow it subject to such clearly specified conditions as that it should be voluntary and followed in response to deeply held beliefs. Third, we might ban it altogether as is the case in Britain under the 1985 Act. And fourth, we might ban it but make exceptions when the demand is genuinely voluntary or is based on deeply held beliefs. The first course of action does not signify society's collective disapproval of it, and is to be ruled out. Since the third shows no respect for women's free choices and cultures, it too should be ruled out. This leaves us with the second and fourth courses of action. In practice they amount to more or less the same thing, but they send out very different messages. The second course of action implies that society sees nothing inherently wrong in the practice and only objects to its misuse; the fourth implies the opposite. Since the practice is objectionable for reasons discussed earlier, the fourth seems to be the best course of action.

I have argued that no practice can be judged in abstraction from the wider way of life or in terms of individual rights alone, and that we should look at its contemporary context, historical background, and the weight and bias of the tradition as well. This becomes strikingly clear if we take the case of *sati*, the Hindu 'practice' of a widow immolating herself on her husband's funeral pyre. The practice is of unknown origin, and in one form or another goes back a long time. Megasthenes, the Greek chronicler, recorded cases of it in India in the fourth century BC, and there have also been records of it during the succeeding periods. During the early years of Muslim invasion there were quite a few cases of *sati*, performed mainly by women of the warrior class in order to avoid being dishonoured by the invaders. The practice reappeared during the early years of British rule, mainly in east India where the colonial rule first consolidated itself and led to considerable moral and social disorientation. There were five deaths per day at the height of the epidemic, and these were almost all confined to higher castes.

The practice of *sati* received an idealised justification in some Hindu religious texts. It was argued that the woman proved the truth or *sat* of her marriage and marriage vows by ending her life with her husband's. This was her way of demonstrating her total identification with and absolute commitment to him. Since the woman was viewed as the 'true' wife, she was considered quasi-divine and a source of considerable spiritual power. Not surprisingly she became part of the folklore and an object of worship. The classical conception was, of course, never realised in practice. Widows often took their lives because of the privations that lay in store for them and the likely coercion of their in-laws.

The practice aroused considerable unease among the Muslim rulers, who nevertheless allowed it to continue provided that it was voluntary as determined by the local officials. During the early days of British rule when it became fairly widespread in some parts of the country, Hindu leaders themselves began to campaign against it and created a climate which made it easier for the British to outlaw it in 1829. Incidents of *sati* however continued to occur, including in post-independence India, but they were relatively rare and aroused no public concern. The scene changed in 1987 when Roop Kanwar, a well-educated Rajput girl of 18 and married for 8 months to a 24-year-old, well-educated young man, mounted her husband's funeral pyre watched by thousands of enthusiastic admirers. Although accounts of the incident vary, the circumstantial evidence suggests that she was drugged. In any case the incident aroused considerable passion all over India, some strongly supporting and others vehemently condemning it. It would seem that a large number of Hindus approved of the woman's action as judged by the size of demonstrations in support of it. Although the practice of *sati* was already banned, the pressure on the government of India to do something was considerable. Within a few months it passed a law outlawing its 'glorification'. Indians remained free to argue in favour of it, but not to idealise and celebrate it in public.

The Indian government's ban on both the practice and the glorification of *sati* aroused strong opposition from influential sections of public opinion including the liberal and progressive. In their view the ban restricted the woman's right to do what she liked with her life, violated her right to live out her deeply held religious beliefs, and interfered with the Hindu way of life. Although these objections cannot be lightly dismissed as was done by the secularists and the feminists, they are deeply flawed. The individual's life is not exclusively his or hers; others including those closely related to him or her as well as the society at large also have a claim on it. Furthermore, like other kinds of freedom, religious freedom can never be absolute, and may be restricted in the public interest. Since the practice of *sati* has only a limited religious sanction, it has the authority of the tradition behind it and puts intense social and religious pressure on a distraught, emotionally unhinged, confused and socially vulnerable woman. This is particularly so because the practice is a source of financial gain; the woman's death removes a claimant to both the dead man's property and to the rest of the family's resources, and enables her in-laws to turn their house into a commercially profitable shrine. The practice also reinforces the woman's inferiority, devalues human life, generates intense fear bordering on psychological terror among newly wedded women and even men, and deprives children of parental love and support.

For these and related reasons, the practice deserves to be banned. This would, of course, cause deep distress to a genuine *sati* who might sincerely believe that it is her duty to die with her husband or that she would go to hell if she did not. However such women are rare, and their religious freedom can be ignored in the wider interest of women as a whole and the society's own moral values. It might be argued that while banning the practice, the law could perhaps make an exception, a kind of 'conscientious exemption', for such women after duly ascertaining that this was their long-held religious belief and that their actions were entirely voluntary, the sort of thing the Muslim rulers had done. Although there is something to be said for such a compromise, it has its dangers. Women might be brainwashed in preparation for the official test, and subjected to acute social pressure. The genuine *sati*'s action might also set precedents for others and strengthen the hold of a largely defunct tradition. In a state given to much corruption, the honesty of government officials cannot be taken for granted either. What is more, the compromise neither challenges the sexist bias of the practice, nor counters the influence of obscurantist religious leaders eager to manipulate the religious sensibilities of illiterate and gullible people. On balance banning the practice altogether is therefore the best course of action. If Hindu society were to ensure full equality to women in all areas of life, if they were able to think independently and decide for themselves between alternative ways of understanding their religious and cultural traditions, and if they could be counted on to act freely, the practice might be allowed to genuine *satis*. None of these preconditions obtains in contemporary India. This is not paternalism, an ideologically loaded term that rules out collective concern for individual well-being, but a way of contextualising rights and liberties and creating proper conditions for their intelligent exercise.

V

The practice of polygamy in its twofold forms of polygyny (more than one wife) and polyandry (more than one husband) is invariably banned in all Western societies. Since polygyny is practised by some Muslims, they feel unjustly treated and have campaigned for the ban to be lifted on two grounds, one positive the other negative. First, the practice is both culturally sanctioned and morally defensible. Second, since Western society's own commitment to monogamy is suspect, the ban is dishonest, hypocritical and even racist.[5]

The Muslim defence of polygyny is fivefold. First, it is permitted by the *Koran*, and an integral part of their way of life.

Secondly, in most societies it is common to divorce a woman if she is infertile or sexually incapacitated, or if the married partners are emotionally or sexually incompatible. Since divorce causes considerable suffering to all involved, it is more humane to allow the husband to take a second wife without having to divorce the first.

Thirdly, all males are tempted to stray from the path of matrimonial fidelity and sometimes strike up extra-marital liaisons with all the deception, insecurity and tensions that these entail. It would help all concerned and would also be more honest if the man were allowed to marry the woman involved rather than break up the existing marriage or lead a life of deceit.

Fourthly, extra-marital liaisons sometimes result in children. The latter carry the stigma of illegitimacy all their lives, and the males involved have no social or even financial obligations to them or to their mother. In such cases it is more sensible not only to allow but to require the man concerned to marry the woman and to accept full responsibility for the consequences of his action.

Fifthly, in some societies the gender ratio is skewed and women outnumber men. This results in compulsory spinsterhood for many women, undesirable pressures on monogamous marriages and even prostitution. In such situations polygyny has much to be said for it. After the Nigerian civil war when the Christian town of Cababar was swarming with unmarried women and widows, the tribal elders decided to allow polygyny to their fellow Christians rather than risk the obvious dangers.

Muslim spokesmen also argue that Western society's ban on polygyny is dishonest and hypocritical. Strictly speaking monogamy implies that sexual intercourse should be confined to marriage, and that one should marry only one person. This is how it has been defined for centuries in most societies including the West. For quite some time Western societies have stopped attaching stigma to pre-marital sex, and define monogamy almost entirely as sexual fidelity to the married partner. In recent decades even this view has been further narrowed, and monogamy is taken to mean no more than that one may *marry* only one person. This is how it is defined by the law, a good barometer of public opinion and an official expression of the society's considered view on the subject. In the Muslim view this implies a number of things.

First, the law and even much of the social opinion are only concerned with marriage, leaving the individual free to cohabit with more than one woman (or man) so long as they do not marry. Since cohabitation is little different from marriage, both the law and social opinion endorse polygamy in practice.

Second, a married man is at liberty to take a mistress (or mistresses) or to enter into a long-term relationship with another woman. Although there are important differences between wife and mistress, they ought not to be exaggerated. The relationship in both cases is long-term and non-casual, free from monetary transactions characteristic of prostitutes and call-girls, involves emotional commitments and mutual obligations, and is not easily terminated. Legally a mistress or a lover is quite different from a wife, but not morally and emotionally. For all practical purposes a man with a mistress or a lover is engaged in polygyny, and neither the law nor the social opinion is much exercised about it.

Third, unlike most past and present societies, the law in liberal society imposes no hardships on either the married man or his mistress. He is at liberty to bequeath his property to her; she is at liberty to take his name; neither is deprived of their civil and other rights, branded as 'devoid of character', or their testimony in the courts of law discounted or given less weight. No doubt, the law does recognise adultery as a ground for divorce but only if the spouse finds it 'intolerable'; it does not automatically dissolve the marriage as in pre-modern Europe and many traditional societies.

Fourth, the law allows easy divorce. Given the prevailing rate of matrimonial breakdowns, on average nearly a third of men (and women) enter into two or three marriages over a lifetime. Muslims ask why this is not considered polygamy. Polygamy means more than one marriage partner irrespective of whether they are simultaneous or consecutive. To restrict it to simultaneous partners is to offer a biased and morally convenient definition of it; and even if one accepted such a view, there is no reason to believe that having consecutive partners is morally superior to having them simultaneously. Muslims also argue that divorce often occurs against the background of a new relationship, so that for a while the two relationships are run in a tandem. This is virtual polygamy, and shows that the dividing line between it and monogamy is difficult to draw.

Finally, in some countries the law recognizes gay and lesbian marriages and allows married partners to adopt or to have children of their own. Muslims argue that this not only removes some of the sanctity of the traditional monogamous marriage but also eliminates the need for it by enabling people to secure such things as stability, respectability, legal status and children that have traditionally been available only through marriage. Liberal society therefore is not entitled to claim that the traditional monogamous marriage is its deeply held value.

In the Muslim view all this shows that liberal society's rhetoric about monogamy does not match its practice, and that it is legally and even morally not as committed to monogamy as it pretends. It not only does little to create the necessary preconditions of monogamy, such as punishing adultery, depriving those involved of their civil rights, and denying their children the right to inherit property, but also does much to weaken and even subvert it. Since liberal society allows cohabitation, it is not serious about *marriage*, and since it acquiesces in extramarital relationships and cohabitation with multiple partners, it is not serious about monogamy either. Muslims argue that since liberal society acquiesces in practical polygamy, that is, in relations that are for all practical purposes polygamous, it is being inconsistent and hypocritical in banning Muslim polygyny. Liberal society allows only one wife, but connives at affairs and illegitimate children. Muslim polygyny allows the maximum of four wives, though only a few marry more than two, and severely punishes adulterous affairs. Each wife knows who the other woman is, and that rules out secrecy and anxiety. There are no illegitimate children either for, if there are any, the man is required to marry the woman concerned. And since polygyny is permitted by Muslim law, it is subject to the latter's strict discipline. Muslims argue that their 'open', 'honest' and socially regulated polygyny is better than, or at least as good as, its secret, deceptive and unregulated Western counterpart.

I have so far sketched the Muslim defence of polygyny and their critique of liberal society's ban on it. Although both make interesting points, neither is convincing.

As we saw, Muslim spokesmen offer a fivefold defence of polygyny. As for the first argument, the Koran does not require but only permits polygyny, and that too is subject to several conditions. It permits polygyny only if the husband is able to treat his wives impartially and with *equal* respect and love, a condition the vast majority of men cannot meet and which, as we shall see, is rendered exceedingly difficult by the very dynamics of the polygamous relationship. Indeed as the Koran itself says: 'You are never able to be fair and just as between women even if you desire' (4: 129). This was one of the reasons given by the Tunisian religious authorities for disallowing it. Furthermore the fact that the Koran permits it is at best *a* reason but not a conclusive reason for allowing it. The Koran rules out a number of things such as interest on the savings, lust, consumption of alcohol, accumulation of wealth, and even the nation state and nationalism. Since most Muslims disregard most of these injunctions, their selective adherence to polygyny is disingenuous.

The next three arguments assume that polygyny is the best way to cope with such evils as divorce, infidelity and illegitimate children. It views polygyny in exclusively instrumental terms and does not appreciate the important moral problems it raises. Furthermore polygyny has several unfortunate consequences, which often far outweigh the evils it seeks to eliminate. It is not, for example, obvious that polygyny is better than divorce, or eliminates or even reduces infidelity, or successfully copes with illegitimate children. As for the fifth argument it makes an important point, but it is only valid in a condition of extremely imbalanced gender ratio, and that is not the case in any society we know.

When Muslims defend polygamy, they only have polygyny in mind, and that violates the principle of the equality of the sexes. The principle is central to the liberal way of life, and that is a good enough reason to insist on it. It is true that liberal society's practice falls far short of it, as its sexism and discriminatory treatment of women amply demonstrate. However this is true of all principles, and does not detract from the fact that liberal societies deeply cherish the principle of equality, are embarrassed by their violations of it, implement it in at least some areas of life and endeavour to do so in others. One can go further and argue that equality is not just a Western or liberal but a rationally defensible moral value that deserves to be universally accepted. Men and women share distinctively human capacities and needs in common, have a broadly equal potential, are capable of choice and self-determination, etc., and are therefore equal in relevant respects and entitled to equal rights. What is no less important, the opposite assertion is extremely difficult to substantiate. No Muslim has been able to make out a defensible case for women's inequality except on the basis of such discredited arguments as that they have poorly developed powers of rational thought, that their physiology renders their judgements unreliable, and that granting them equality would undermine the institution of the family and subvert the social order.[6] Since liberal society can rightly insist on the equality of the sexes, it can ban polygyny on that ground alone without having to justify monogamy. This is its easiest and most effective strategy, and not surprisingly all liberal societies have resorted to it.

Muslims rejoin that they do not accept the principle of the equality of the sexes, and that imposing it on them violates their moral and religious integrity. Liberal spokesmen can make a twofold response. They can argue that they hold the principle dear, that any compromise with it violates *their* moral integrity, and that they feel entitled to ask Muslims to live by it in so far as they have chosen to live in a liberal society. They can go further and argue that they are able to offer a reasonably persuasive defence of the principle, that Muslims have advanced no convincing arguments against it, and that they therefore feel entitled to insist on it. The principle of the equality of the sexes may offend against the Muslim's deeply held beliefs, but no beliefs are incorrigible and self-authenticating. If they are ill-founded or rationally indefensible, and in addition result in patently harmful consequences, they may rightly be disregarded.

The debate on polygamy would become more complex if Muslims conceded the principle of the equality of the sexes and allowed women an equal right with men to marry polygamously. Since polygamy is now permitted to both sexes, it does not violate the principle of equality. Should it be allowed? In order that anti-Muslim prejudice does not influence our judgement, let us assume that some sections of liberal society itself plead for polygamy, not at all an unlikely prospect if the present trends were to continue. Two women (or men) might love one man (or woman) deeply enough to wish to live together, and demand that they be allowed to marry in order to enjoy all the current rights of monogamously married couples, to give legal and social respectability to their relationship, and to legitimise their children in the eyes of the law and public opinion.

If such a demand were to be made, liberal society would have to decide what to do about it.[7] Contrary to the general belief, the decision is not at all easy, for liberal spokesmen cannot say that monogamy is their deeply cherished value which they have a right and even perhaps a duty to uphold, both because for many of them it is more a social practice than a moral value, and more importantly because some of its citizens do not consider it a value as is evident in their plea for the recognition of polygamous marriages. Indeed it might be argued that polygamy does *not* violate any of the operative public values of liberal society and that the law is wrong to ban it. It is a result of uncoerced choices of the parties involved, and liberal society is expected to respect such choices. Liberal society claims to encourage experiments in living, and polygamy is one of them. It claims to be non-paternalist, and should not tell people how to lead their personal lives. It respects diversity of tastes and temperaments, and should respect individual preferences for polygamy. It welcomes healthy competition between different ways of life as a means of discovering the truth about them, and cannot consistently insist on monogamy as the only acceptable way of life. In the light of all this, can a liberal spokesman make out a reasonably strong case for monogamy? Since I cannot undertake such a large inquiry here, a few general remarks should suffice.

In constructing a case for monogamy we should be careful not to confuse it with such related but irrelevant issues as how and why a marriage is entered into. We are not concerned to defend the freely chosen as opposed to the arranged, romantic as different from non-romantic, or love-based as different from convenience-based marriages. In other words our defence of monogamy should be as neutral as possible between its various forms. Again, monogamy is a common practice in many cultures, which defend it in their own different ways. Since liberal society is culturally diverse, we need to defend monogamy in a manner intelligible and hopefully acceptable to different communities especially the Muslims, the main party to the debate. To offer a standard Christian or romantic defence of marriage is relatively easy, but it does not serve the purpose. By contrast an interculturally acceptable defence is difficult but indispensable. I sketch below the outlines of such a defence.

Whatever its form, marriage is a two-dimensional relationship. First, it involves at least two individuals who wish to live together, hopefully but not necessarily for ever. Although their relations with each other are not and need not be closer or morally more important than those with their parents, brothers, friends, and so on, the fact remains that they are qualitatively different from the latter. Marriage involves sexual intimacy, and all that goes with it. Married partners know each other in a way that others do not, they wittingly or unwittingly reveal aspects of themselves to each other that they cannot reveal to others, they are emotionally bonded to each other in a way that they are not to others, and their relationship has an intensity that is unique to it. They share their deepest feelings, make common plans for themselves and their children, and relate to others as a single unit. All this remains true whether their marriage is arranged or self-chosen, romantic or non-romantic, and occurs within a nuclear or a joint family.

Given the nature of their relationship, married partners need to build up at least some degree of mutual trust, commitment and affection, and an instinctive understanding of each other's desires, needs and moods. Even if they have known each other before marriage, their relationship acquires a different character after marriage, and they need to get to know each other at a different level. In the case of an arranged marriage, this task begins after the marriage and is even more demanding. Getting to know another person well enough to live with him or her is a difficult and prolonged process, and requires time, energy, leisure, a relative absence of outside interference and an emotionally relaxed environment. The monogamous relationship provides these conditions better than the polygamous. Not that the latter cannot, but rather that it is unlikely to do so under normal circumstances.

To develop a relationship of trust, commitment and understanding with even one person is taxing enough; to introduce a third person let alone several more is the surest way to kill it. Time, energy, patience, capacity for deep emotional commitment and goodwill are limited, and the more they are shared the less is available for each person. Besides, as we know from the accounts of polygamous marriages in other societies and triangular relationships in our own, they breed jealousy, rivalry, anxiety, insecurity, invidious comparisons and mutual manipulations.[8] In a polygamous marriage, the feeling of being valued, of meaning something special to another person, is also missing. Since each wife (or husband) knows that she (or he) is substitutable and hence dispensable, they lack a sense of their own worth and their relationships remain superficial and insecure.

Marriages involve children, and the latter need ideal conditions in which to grow up into sane and responsible adults. They require a secure, stable and loving environment, constant personal attention, opportunities to build up close relationships with their parents and with each other, and identifiable figures of authority to discipline them and to build up their willpower and capacity for self-determination. Children also need to feel valued and to build up a sense of their own worth, and that requires that they are and know themselves to be unique and irreplaceable in the eyes of specific persons. A monogamously based family is best equipped to create these conditions.

Having made out a case for monogamy along these lines, which obviously needs to be considerably tightened up if it is to be more than a biased pleading for monogamy, we would need to show that, despite liberal society's failure to live up to its demands, its commitment to monogamy is genuine and deep. The argument could proceed along the following lines.

Since the monogamous marriage is highly demanding, it sometimes fails. However it is striking that when it fails, the parties involved do not reject the practice of monogamy, but rather change their partners. Even those who opt for gay or lesbian relationships generally prefer single and steady partners. When people go through more than one marriage, each marriage is self-contained, lived in its own terms, and involves exclusive and total mutual commitment. To have two consecutive wives is therefore qualitatively different from having them simultaneously. Since the nature of the relationship in each case is wholly different, to call the former serial polygamy is as perverse as calling polygamy plural monogamy.

Since monogamy has its own sexual discipline, which some find trying, they seek from time to time to escape its constraints. However such lapses are associated with a sense of guilt or at least unease, and incur at least some measure of social disapproval. This is why such lapses occur secretly, provoke charges of cheating, deception and betrayal, and require an explanation. None of these would happen if monogamy were not a deeply valued practice. Since lapses occur, liberal society has to decide what to do about them. It could either take a harsh view and impose social and legal punishment of the kind familiar in pre-modern and some contemporary Muslim societies, or it could tolerate them with varying degrees of disapproval. Muslims are right to argue that, strictly speaking, the former is the only course of action open to a society deeply committed to monogamy, and that liberal society has become too permissive and indulgent.

However such a punitive approach has its dangers. It has not worked in traditional including Muslim societies where lapses are not at all uncommon. And since they attract severe punishment, they often lead to considerable hypocrisy, social blackmail and witchhunts. Besides, although liberal society values monogamy, it also values freedom of self-exploration, tolerance, learning through one's mistakes, self-fulfilment, and so on, and needs to strike a balance between them. It prefers its members to observe the constraints of monogamy voluntarily rather than under threat of death or loss of basic rights, and encourages married partners to be honest with each other rather than practise sexual fidelity against the background of dishonest feelings and adulterous thoughts. Again, an institution can easily lose its credibility if it becomes excessively rigid and intolerant of deviations. The fact that liberal society connives at deviations does not mean that it does not value the institution. Institutions stabilise social life, lay down the socially necessary moral minimum, affirm society's values, provide a moral compass, impose at least some discipline on human behaviour, and influence motives. This is why we chafe against the discipline of monogamy and yet insist on retaining it. The Muslim critic rightly exposes the lapses and hypocrisy of liberal society, but misreads their nature and rationale.

Our defence of monogamy against the Muslim criticism then is this. Marriage is a kind of relationship that is most likely to flourish when limited to two individuals. All our knowledge of our own and other societies supports this view. Since monogamy is a valuable institution, we want the law to express and reinforce our collective commitment to it and to guard us against the all too frequent temptations to circumvent it. At the same time we recognise that since human beings differ greatly in their temperaments, tastes, needs and capacities to sustain relationships, some might find monogamy unsuitable and we need to find ways of accommodating them. We have a choice. Either we could allow people to choose whatever form of marriage they like and give them all equal protection. Or we could insist on monogamy, but allow people to live the way they like so long as they marry only one person. This safeguards their choices of life-styles, but neither grants their choices equal protection of the law nor regards them all as equally good. The first alternative neither institutionalises our collective commitment to monogamy nor provides people with moral standards. The second does, and hence we prefer it.

How would a Muslim critic respond to the kind of case we have made out for monogamy? As we saw, the case for monogamy is twofold. First, it is necessary to build up a non-manipulative, trustful, affectionate and mutually supportive relationship between married partners. Second, it provides a propitious environment for bringing up children. The Muslim critic might reject one or both of these arguments.

As against the first argument, he could rejoin that it uncritically privileges the Western individualist view of marriage. Marriage is conceptualised differently in different cultures, some of which view it as a familial or communal rather than an individual act. In these cultures married partners are embedded in a wider network of relationships, and their marriage is expected not to replace or disturb but to subserve and fit into these relationships. In addition to being a good wife, the spouse should also be a good daughter-in-law or sister-in-law and help look after the husband's parents, younger brothers and sisters. Unlike the Western romantic view of marriage, the relationship between husband and wife here is not morally and socially privileged or emotionally more intense than other relationships. As such there is nothing special about it, and it does not call for friendship, romance, or exclusive mutual commitment. A romantic marriage may perhaps need to be monogamous, but there is no obvious reason why all marriages must be romantic. A society might view marriage in functional terms, as a way of sustaining the community rather than as a form of personal fulfilment or deep emotional bonding. When such a view of marriage is widely accepted in a society, its members are suitably socialised into accepting the necessary discipline and developing the required mental attitudes. As a result their polygamous relationship is free from the possessiveness, jealousy, etc. that characterise the triangular or quadrangular relationships in the individualist West.

As for the second argument that monogamy provides ideal conditions for the development of children, a Muslim might rejoin that it is unconvincing. Children do need a stable and loving environment, but a polygamous marriage can provide it just as well as and even better than the monogamous. It has more role models, more adults of diverse talents and temperaments to identify with, and more children to play with. Besides, unlike a monogamous marriage children in a polygamous marriage are not so intensely and exclusively identified with one or both of the parents that they are haunted by the fear of rejection or devastated by their death, and develop a greater sense of security, self-confidence and independence.

Although the Muslim rejoinder makes important points, it is unconvincing. There is no necessary connection between monogamy and individualism. Historically, the former preceded the latter by centuries, and there is no reason why monogamous marriage should not be embedded in a communal network. Furthermore, although human beings can be socialised into marrying multiple partners, all the available evidence indicates that the relationship is never easy and nothing like the Muslim idealisation of it, which is in any case based only on polygynous marriages and not tested against the background of the full equality of the sexes. Besides, as societies become industrialised and urbanised, communal networks tend to disintegrate and married couples set up separate units. If they are to make a success of their marriage, they need to build up a relationship of mutual trust, understanding and friendship that we talked about earlier. Again, once traditional communities break up and most human relations come to lack warmth and intimacy, marital relationship acquires unusual importance in the sense that married partners look to each other for a sense of security, intuitive understanding, deep emotional reassurance, a feeling of being specially bonded to someone. As we saw the monogamous relationship is far more likely to provide these than the polygamous.

Since the polygamous marriage is likely to be marked by jealousy, unhealthy competition for affection, insecurity, intrigue and mutual manipulation, it is also unlikely to create an environment conducive to the growth of children. It is true that the child in a polygamous family has more role models and is not intensely identified with one of them. However there are at best no more than one or two more adults than in a monogamous family, which hardly provides the kind of community the Muslim critic imagines. And although the plurality of role models has its advantages, it also has its disadvantages. The opportunity to play off adults against each other, the rivalry among them for the child's affection, the relative lack of a clear structure of authority, and so on mean that he lacks a moral and emotional focus, is subjected to conflicting moral and emotional demands, and is unlikely to develop his powers of self-direction and self-discipline.

Although the principle of the equality of the sexes is formally neutral between monogamy and polygamy, monogamy is more conducive to its realisation. Muslim and for that matter Hindu, Christian and most other cultures contain a deep-seated sexist bias, and have for centuries subjected women to social, economic and other inequalities. If polygamy were to be permitted, men would be more likely to take advantage of it than women, thereby reinforcing and even increasing the inequality between the sexes and further devaluing the status of women. Besides, monogamy has a strong equalising influence. It gives a woman a sense of dignity, self-esteem and security, a relatively inviolable private space of her own, and more or less equal rights over her husband's property and their children. As against this, some Muslim spokesmen and even spokeswomen have argued that polygyny in fact increases the status and power of women because they now have the security and strength of solidarity, can share the domestic responsibility and release each other for a career. There is little evidence to support this view. Since wives can be played off against each other and easily dispensed with, they have neither a sense of security nor enough common interests to build up bonds of solidarity. Polygyny does reduce the demands on each of the wives, but such advantages as this brings are outweighed by the psychological tensions and anxieties mentioned earlier and can in any case be secured in more acceptable ways.

These and similar responses to the Muslim critic ought to go at least some way towards convincing him of the value of monogamy. They involve appeals to certain values, empirical generalisations about the conditions under which they are most likely to be realised and judgements based on them. The values involved in stressing a trustful, affectionate and non-manipulative relationship are fairly general, thin and shared by the Muslims themselves. There may be some disagreements about empirical generalisations, but these can be resolved or at least minimised by appealing to psychological and sociological researches, anthropological accounts of polygamous marriages, and above all the experiences of Muslim societies themselves as described by their own writers. Once the disagreements over values and empirical generalisations are reduced, it ought not to be too difficult to arrive at an agreement. To counter the charge of cultural bias we might point to the fact that many Muslim societies have themselves begun to move away from polygyny. Although only Tunisia has banned it, several others positively discourage it.[9] Since they can be expected to have a deep regard for their religion and culture as well as considerable experience of the social effects of polygyny, their actions further strengthen the case for monogamy.

Liberal society then is right to ban the practice of polygyny. The practice violates the principle of the equality of the sexes, which is not only one of its operative public values but can also be shown to be the most defensible manner of ordering inter-gender relations. So far as polygamy is concerned, the case is not so conclusive. Although one can show that monogamy is socially and morally more defensible than polygamy, the latter is not an unmitigated evil and does not *by itself* violate human dignity, equality, freedom, or any other great moral value.[10] If the current inequality of power, social status and self-esteem between men and women were to end such that women could be depended on to make equally uncoerced choices, if a sizeable section of society were freely to opt for and successfully to cope with the demands of polygamy, and if the latter could be shown not to have the kinds of harmful consequences mentioned earlier, there would be a good case for permitting it. Since these conditions do not obtain today, we are right to disallow it at least at present. This no doubt restricts the choices and liberties of those inclined to polyga-mous relationships, but the restriction is justified in the larger moral interest of the community as a whole.

Notes

1   For a valuable discussion, see Will Kymlicka, *Multicultural Citizenship: A Liberal Theory of Minority Rights* (Oxford: Clarendon Press, 1995).

2   For further discussions, see my 'The Concept of National Identity', *New Community* Vol. 21, No. 2, April 1995; and 'Discourses on National Identity', *Political Studies*, Vol. 42, No. 3, September 1994.

3   For a further discussion see my 'The Cultural Particularity of Liberal Democracy' in David Held (ed.), *Prospects for Democracy* (Cambridge: Polity Press, 1993).

4   See O. Koso-Thomas, *The Circumcision of Women* (London: Zed Books, 1987); and *Harmful Traditional Practices Affecting the Health of Women and Children*, fact sheet no. 23 (United Nations, 1995).

5   See R. Cligent, *Many Wives, More Powers: Authority and Power in Polygamous Families* (Evanston: North Western University Press, 1970); and S. Gbadegesin, 'The Ethics of Polygyny', *Quest: Philosophical Discussions*, Vol. VII, No. 2, 1993.

6   For such absurd assertions, see Jan Goodwin, *Price of Honour: Muslim Women Lift the Veil of Silence on the Islamic World* (London: Werner Books, 1995) pp. 64, 65, 123, 264, 343 and 346.

7   Stephen Toulmin thinks that there is no rational way to discuss whether polygamy should or should not be allowed. The question is 'an unreal one' because polygamy is not an 'alternative' for us. Since monogamy is central to our way of life, to ask if it is better than polygamy is to ask if our way of life is better than the Muslim, an inherently unanswerable question. (*Reason in Ethics*, p. 153). As I argue, polygamy can become an alternative for 'us' and that it can be rationally debated without discussing the relative merits of 'our' and Muslim ways of life.

8   Ibid., pp. 33 and 337. A woman comments: 'He just moved her into our home. One day she wasn't there, the next day she was. After that time I sit in the same room with them and he hardly speaks to me, he has never come into my bed again, and he ignores our children and favours hers. It is difficult to get him even to buy clothes for mine' (p. 33).

9   Although polygyny is permitted in many Muslim countries, it is subjected to various restrictions. In Syria it is disallowed if the husband is unlikely to have the resources to maintain more than one wife, and in Morocco and Iraq if he is unlikely to treat them with equal justice. In Pakistan and Bangladesh it is allowed only with the permission of an arbitration council. In Jordan a woman can stipulate at the time of her marriage that her husband will not take another wife during their marriage.

10   It is worth noting that polygyny is allowed in the Old Testament, and that Jesus of Nazareth attacks adultery and divorce but is silent about polygyny. See J. Cairncross, *After Polygamy Was Made a Sin: The Social History of Christian Polygamy* (London: Routledge, 1974), and Adrian Hastings, *Christian Marriage in Africa* (London: SPCK, 1974). For a good general discussion of polygamy, see Eugene Hillman, *Polygamy Reconsidered* (New York: Maryknoll, Orbis Books, 1975). J. S. Mill, *On Liberty*, ch. 4, argues that polygamy is a 'direct infraction' of the principle of liberty because it subordinates women to men. This is only true of polygyny and does not apply to polygamy. Mill allows Mormon polygyny because Mormonism is a voluntary religion and women join it and accept polygyny out of free will. There is therefore no reason to launch 'a civilizade' against it. The Utah branch of the American Civil Liberties Union petitioned its parent body 'to make legal recognition of polygamy a national cause like gay and lesbian rights'. Its argument was based on 'diversity of life-styles'. Mayor Dan Barlow, who has five wives, remarked that 'in the liberal age with all the alternative life-styles that are condoned, it is a height of folly to censure a man for having more than one family'. A female lawyer, herself one of nine wives, thought that 'it is the ideal way for a woman to have a career and children'. For all this, see *New York Times*, 9 April 1991.

Notes on Contributors

Ernest Barker (1874–1960) studied at Balliol College, Oxford and came under the influence of the Philosophical Idealism of T. H. Green and the 'Greats' tradition of Benjamin Jowett. After a Fellowship at Oxford, he was briefly at the London School of Economics and Political Science. From 1920 to 1927 Barker was Principal of King's College, London and in 1928 he became the first Professor of Political Science at Cambridge University. Barker was the author of numerous books including *Greek Political Theory* (1918), *Reflections on Government* (1942) and *Principles of Social and Political Theory* (1951).

Brian Barry (1936–2009) At the time of his death Brian Barry was Emeritus Professor of Political Science at the London School of Economics and Political Science and Lieber Professor of Political Philosophy Emeritus at Columbia University. Educated at Oxford University, Barry held posts at many universities in Britain and the United States. He was instrumental in shaping the development of political theory in Britain and the United States. He was the author of *Political Argument* (1965), *Sociologists, Economists and Democracy* (1970), *The Liberal Theory of Justice* (1973), *Democracy, Power and Justice* (1989), *Theories of Justice* (1989), *Justice as Impartiality* (1995), *Culture and Equality* (2001) and *Why Social Justice Matters* (2005).

Isaiah Berlin (1909–98) Born in Riga, Berlin moved to Russia where in 1917 he witnessed the Bolshevik revolution. After his family moved to England Berlin was assimilated into English intellectual life at St Paul's School and then Corpus Christi, Oxford. Except for a brief period of war service in the United States, Berlin's life and career remained closely tied to Oxford. He held fellowships at All Soul's and New College and succeeded G. D. H. Cole as Chichele Professor in 1958. His favoured style was the essay and lecture and his impact on students, colleagues and the profession and wider intellectual life of Britain was considerable. His essays are collected in many volumes which have become well-known books such as *Four Essays on Liberty* (1969), *Concepts and Categories* (1980), *Against the Current* (1979), *The Proper Study of Mankind* (1998), *The Crooked Timber of Humanity* (1990) and *Personal Impressions* (1982). Berlin was founding President of Wolfson College and President of the British Academy.

Bernard Bosanquet (1848–1923) was a student at Balliol College where he fell under the influence of T. H. Green's Philosophical Idealism and his example of active citizenship. In 1871 he became a tutor at New College, Oxford. He became financially independent on his father's death and resigned his fellowship, moving to London in 1881 to concentrate on writing, social work and adult education. He was active in the Charity Organisation Society which was committed to private philanthropy. He held a further academic post as Professor of Moral Philosophy at St Andrews University from 1903 to 1908. He was the author of numerous books across a wide range of philosophical topics. His major publications in political philosophy include *The Philosophical Theory of the State* (1899), *The Principle of Individuality and Value* (1912), *The Value and Destiny of the Individual* (1913), *Social and International Ideals* (1917) and *Some Suggestions in Ethics* (1918).

G. D. H Cole (1889–1959) was educated at St Paul's School and Balliol College, Oxford. He was a conscientious objector during the Great War. He met and married Margaret Postgate with whom he co-authored many detective stories. Cole was closely involved in Labour politics and was a member of the Fabian Society Executive. In 1925 Cole became Reader in Economics at University College, Oxford and in 1944 he became the first Chichele Professor of Social and Political Theory. Cole was an extraordinarily prolific author and his books include *Self-Government in Industry* (1917), *Guild Socialism Re-stated* (1920), *A History of the Labour Party from 1914* (1948) and *A History of Socialist Thought* (7 vols, 1959).

J. N. Figgis (1866–1919) was educated at Brighton College and Cambridge University where he studied history under Lord Acton. After a brief period as a lecturer at Birkbeck College, Figgis entered the Community of the Resurrection at Mirfield in 1896 as an Anglican monk. He was the author of many books including *The Divine Right of Kings* (1896), *Studies in Political Thought from Gerson to Grotius* (1907), *Churches in the Modern State* (1914) and *The Political Aspects of St Augustine's City of God* (1921).

H. L. A. Hart (1907–92) was Professor of Jurisprudence at Oxford University (1952–68) and Principal of Brasenose College. After a career at the Chancery Bar, Hart returned to Oxford after the war and became part of an influential group of British philosophers including Berlin, Austin, Ryle and Hampshire. Hart's *The Concept of Law* (1961) resurrected the English tradition of positivism from Hobbes, Bentham and Austin, and transformed the study of legal and political theory. Hart was an important influence on Rawls and Barry. He was the author of many books and articles including *Causation in the Law* with A. M. Honoré (1959),

Law, Liberty and Morality (1963), *Punishment and Responsibility* (1968), *Essays on Bentham* (1982) and *Essays in Jurisprudence and Philosophy* (1982).

Paul Hirst (1946–2003) studied at the University of Leicester and the University of Sussex. In 1969, he moved to Birkbeck College where he was to spend the rest of his career, and where he was to co-found the Department of Politics and Sociology. Following an early enthusiasm for Althusser's work he subsequently became a critic of Althusser and of Marxism, turning instead to the English pluralists. He is the author of many books including *On Law and Ideology* (1979), *Law, Socialism and Democracy* (1986), *Representative Democracy and its Limits* (1990) and *Associative Democracy* (1993).

L. T. Hobhouse (1864–1929) Educated at Oxford University, Hobhouse briefly became a philosophy tutor before moving to a temporary lectureship at the London School of Economics and Political Science from 1896 to 1897. In 1897 he became a journalist for the Manchester *Guardian*. He returned to the LSE in 1904 and in 1907 became the first Professor of Sociology at a British university. He was one of the most influential thinkers among the 'new' liberals and influenced the reforms of the Asquith government. Although he was influenced by the Idealism of T. H. Green, his *Metaphysical Theory of the State* (1918) was an assault on the statism of Bosanquet. Hobhouse's books include *Liberalism* (1911), *Theory of Knowledge* (1896), *Morals in Evolution* (1906), *Development and Purpose* (1913) and *The Elements of Social Justice* (1922).

Paul Kelly is Professor of Political Theory and Head of the Department of Government at the London School of Economics and Political Science where he has taught since 1995. He is the author, editor and co-editor of ten books including *Utilitarianism and Distributive Justice* (1990), *The Social Contract from Hobbes to Rawls* (1994), *Impartiality, Neutrality and Justice* (1998), *British Political Science* (2000), *Multiculturalism Reconsidered* (2002), *Political Thinkers* (2002), *Liberalism* (2004) and *Locke's Second Treatise* (2007). He was joint editor of *Political Studies* and is currently the editor of *Utilitas*.

Harold Laski (1893–1950) Educated at Manchester Grammar School and New College, Oxford, Laski was a Professor at Harvard before succeeding Graham Wallas as Professor of Political Science at the London School of Economics and Political Science in 1926. Laski served on the Executive Committee of the Fabian Society and subsequently the National Executive Committee of the Labour party. An enormously prolific author, his books include *Studies in the Problem of Sovereignty* (1917), *A Grammar of Politics* (1925), *Liberty in the Modern State* (1930) and *The Rise of Liberalism* (1936).

David Miller Educated at Cambridge and Oxford Universities, Miller is Professor of Political Theory at Oxford University and Official Fellow, Nuffield College. Miller's work has covered a broad range of topics in political theory and political philosophy, from anarchism and the political theory of David Hume to social justice and democracy. Much of his recent work has been on the question of national identity, political membership and global responsibility and justice. His is one of the most distinctive and influential voices in British political theory. Miller is the author of many books including *Social Justice* (1976), *Market, State and Community* (1989), *Nationality* (1995), *Principles of Social Justice* (1999) and *National Responsibility and Global Justice* (2007). He is a Fellow of the British Academy.

Michael Oakeshott (1901–90) read History at Gonville and Caius, Cambridge where he studied with the Idealist philosopher J. M. E. McTaggart. He studied at Marburg and Tübingen Universities in the 1920s before becoming a Fellow at Gonville and Caius in 1927. He joined the army in 1939. After war service he returned to Cambridge, but on failing to succeed Sir Ernest Barker to the chair of political science, Oakeshott moved briefly to Nuffield College, Oxford. In 1951 he succeeded Harold Laski at the London School of Economics and Political Science and remained closely associated to that institution for the rest of his life. He influenced generations of students and had a profound impact on the development of the study of politics in Britain, being one of the leaders of the opposition to a naturalistic form of political science. His books include *Experience and its Modes* (1933), *Rationalism in Politics* (1962), *On Human Conduct* (1975) and *On History* (1984).

Bhikhu Parekh is Professor of Political Philosophy at the University of Westminster, a Fellow of the British Academy and Member of the House of Lords. Educated in India and at the London School of Economics and Political Science, Parekh has been a prominent political theorist as well as vice-chair of the former Commission for Racial Equality and subsequently chair of the Committee on the Future of a Multiethnic Britain. He has published on a wide variety of thinkers and issues in political theory, but is most notable as one of the most prominent theorists of multiculturalism and is the author of *The Future of a Multi-Ethnic Britain* (2000), *Rethinking Multiculturalism* (2000) and *A New Politics of Identity* (2008).

Carole Pateman is Professor of Political Science at the University of California, Los Angeles and has been Distinguished Visiting Professor at the School of European Studies, Cardiff University. She has held numerous visiting fellowships in Australia and Europe and was President of the International Political Science Association in 1991–4. Her books include *Participation and Democratic Theory* (1970), *The Problem of Political Obligation* (1985), *The Sexual Contract* (1988) and *The Disorder of Women* (1989). She is the co-editor of *Feminist Interpretations and Political Theory* (1991). Her most recent book is *Contract and Domination*, with Charles Mills (2007). She is a Fellow of the British Academy.

Anne Phillips is Professor of Political and Gender Theory at the London School of Economics and Political Science, where she has taught since 1999. She has been influential in shaping the development of feminist political theory in Europe and America. Her books include *The Enigma of Colonialism* (1989), *Engendering Democracy* (1991), *Democracy and Difference* (1993), *The Politics of Presence: The*

Political Representation of Gender, Ethnicity, and Race (1995), *Which Equalities Matter?* (1999) and *Multiculturalism without Culture* (2007). She co-edited, with John Dryzek and Bonnie Honig, the *Oxford Handbook of Political Theory* (2007). She is a Fellow of the British Academy.

R. H. Tawney (1880–1962) was educated at Rugby School and Balliol College, Oxford. His Christian social moralism and the intellectual climate at Balliol, inspired by Green's Idealism, led Tawney to educational social work at Toynbee Hall in London's East End and subsequently for the Workers' Educational Association. The impact of service during the Great War reinforced his egalitarianism. Tawney became Professor of Economic History at the London School of Economics and Political Science, though he retained a close involvement in Labour party politics. His most influential books include *The Acquisitive Society* (1921), *Religion and the Rise of Capitalism* (1926) and *Equality* (1931).

Sources for Contributions

Chapter 2   Bosanquet, B. (1899) 'Nature of the End of the State and Consequent Limit of State Action', in *The Philosophical Theory of the State*. London: MacMillan, pp. 177–216.

Chapter 3   Hobhouse, L. T. (1964 [1911]) 'The State and the Individual', in *Liberalism*. Oxford: Oxford University Press, pp. 74–87.

Chapter 4   Figgis, J. N. (1913) 'The Great Leviathan', in *Churches in the Modern State*. London: Longmans, Green and Co., pp. 54–93.

Chapter 5   Barker, E. (1919) 'Nationality', *History*, IV (15), pp. 135–45.

Chapter 6   Laski, H. (1919) 'The Pluralistic State', *Philosophical Review*, 28 (6), pp. 562–75.

Chapter 7   Cole, G. D. H. (1921) 'A Guild in Being', in *Guild Socialism Re-stated*. London: Leonard Parsons, pp. 42–62.

Chapter 8   Tawney, R. H. (1931) 'Liberty and Equality', in *Equality*. London: Allen & Unwin, pp. 237–55.

Chapter 9   Oakeshott, M. (1962) 'The Political Economy of Freedom', in *Rationalism in Politics*. London: Methuen, pp. 37–58.

Chapter 10   Berlin, I. (1998) 'The Pursuit of the Ideal', in *The Proper Study of Mankind*. London: Pimlico, pp. 1–16.

Chapter 11   Hart, H. L. A. (1955) 'Are There Any Natural Rights?', *Philosophical Review*, 64, pp. 175–91.

Chapter 12   Barry, B. (1964) 'The Public Interest', *Proceedings of the Aristotelian Society*, 38, pp. 1–18.

Chapter 13   Pateman, C. (1988) 'What's Wrong with Prostitution?', in *The Sexual Contract*. Cambridge: Polity Press, pp. 189–218.

Chapter 14   Phillips, A. (1994) 'Dealing with Difference', *Constellations*, 1, pp. 74–91.

Chapter 15   Miller, D. (1993) 'In Defence of Nationality', *Journal of Applied Philosophy*, 10 (1), pp. 3–16.

Chapter 16   Hirst, P. (1997) 'From Statism to Pluralism', in *From Statism to Pluralism*. London: University College London Press, pp. 60–70.

Chapter 17   Parekh, B. (1999) 'The Logic of Intercultural Evaluation', in J. Horton and S. Mendus (eds), *Toleration, Identity and Difference*. Basingstoke: Macmillan, pp. 163–97.

Index